# the doors

## ARTISTIC VISION

D1502824

Design: David Houghton
Printed by: Staples of Rochester, UK

Published by Castle Communications plc, A29 Barwell Business Park,
Leatherhead Road, Chessington, Surrey KT9 2NY.

Cover photograph: Elliott Landy / Redferns
Photographs: Freddy Tornberg, Jack Rosen, Barry Plummer, Elliott
Landy & Michael Ochs Archives (Redferns), The Doors Collectors
Magazine.

ISBN: 1-86074-139-8

# the doors

## ARTISTIC VISION

Their vision of America and life
portrayed in their six studio albums

by Doug Sundling with Diana Bittner

Art is revolutionary.

Unfortunately, most of what is called "art" nowadays is marketed for consumption, not transformation.

"Authentic art...communicates the general attitudes of both negation and affirmation.
This duality is a necessary condition of art to be genuine.
Negation and affirmation are thus
the two dimensions of one transforming (revolutionary) process –
a process that must relate to and yet transcend the status quo."

*Robert G. Pielke,*
*You Say You Want a Revolution:*
*Rock Music in American Culture (pp. 14, 15)*

# table of contents

# foreword

"It's a great book. Not only is this book an appreciation of The Doors, but it's a book The Doors themselves will appreciate. It's an appreciation for everybody, especially for those who love The Doors. The mystery and inspiration of every Doors song is probed and explored. It's about time a book like this was written and this in depth."

Danny Sugerman

co-author  *No One Here Gets Out Alive*
author      *Wonderland Avenue*

# introduction
# a door opens

This book looks at what The Doors were saying as artists. The detailing of the personal stories about The Doors (or of Jim Morrison) or the speculation on those stories have been only of casual interest to me; what The Doors express through their music has always been more important.

My journey with The Doors began when Jim Morrison's ended. On my 16th birthday my parents gave me, as I had requested, my first Doors' album, *L.A. Woman*. I had thought if I liked two cuts on an album (in this case, the two radio tunes, 'Love Her Madly' and 'Riders On The Storm'), then that album was worth having. When the opening of 'The Changeling' ('See me change!') hit my restless 16-year-old spirit, I was enthralled until the final wave of thunder in 'Riders On The Storm'. Then I played the album again...and again...and again... Three days later, Jim was dead.

I have never viewed Jim Morrison as a demigod, as a twentieth century Dionysus, or The Doors as a greater-than-life entity. From my 16th birthday onward, I have looked to The Doors as fellow artistic spirits who had successfully forged a path to express a creative vision we share. Consequently, I haven't had the problem I see of so many Doors fanatics: as they begin to leave their adolescent view of life, Jimbo falls from the previously held Dionysian throne on Mt. Olympus back to Earth with a thud. When the worshipers grow-up, the god becomes all too human. Having now outlived Morrison, I understand what Jim's – and The Doors' – artistic vision can't portray: the wisdom that comes with having lived into your thirties, into mid-life, into old age. That perspective of life never came to Morrison, for like a fiery and intense burst of brilliance, like so

11

many artistic spirits who choose not to burn the candle at both ends but with a blowtorch in the middle, Jim, though very gifted, paid a dear price for being a jerk.

But on my 16th birthday, I had peered through an opened door inside me, and a journey had begun. I collected all The Doors' recordings and bootlegs I could find and began a decade-long research into all the mainstream and underground literature I could unearth on The Doors. In 1979, life having diverted me onto other paths, I put most of it on the shelf, at the same time that there began a resurgence in The Doors, spurred by three events: the release of Francis Ford Coppola's movie, *Apocalypse Now*, which uses 'The End' to open its imagery of the Vietnam War; the publication of Jerry Hopkins' and Danny Sugerman's *No One Here Gets Out Alive*; and the release of *An American Prayer*, an album on which the three surviving Doors blended their music to some resurrected tapes of Jim reading poetry. In the summer of 1985, needing to write a thesis to fulfill my requirements for a Master's in English, I resurrected those notes from that research and composed a paper entitled, 'The Poetic Imagery and Themes in the Works of James Douglas Morrison', which sounded better on the proposal sheet submitted to the department head than, 'The Poetry of Jim Morrison, lead singer of The Doors'.

While I was teaching at college, in 1987, and corrupting youthful minds with such topics as 'The Poetics of Rock 'n' Roll', a friend introduced me to Diana Maniak (later to marry and become Bittner), thinking Diana's and my interests in The Doors would be mutually beneficial. Diana provided not only an intent audience for the critical renderings of the albums, but also insights on The Doors' sound and imagery I was not perceiving. By the spring of 1990, we had finished this critique of The Doors' six albums.

To read the way we explain the lyrical and musical themes of The Doors' songs isn't to read the way The Doors created. Despite the overwhelming pervasiveness of linear ethics as the organizational pattern for our modern life, the creative process is quite oblivious to such orientation. Artistic spirits don't produce like that. Morrison the artist, a shamanic spirit of sorts, understood symbols and their relationships in the context of our culture, and he could perceive and express them with impressions that have become the hallmark of The Doors' legacy.

A shamanic spirit is attuned to his or her culture beyond rationalized processes. Anthropology attempts to illustrate the shamanic spirit to our Western mind-set, but these well-rendered sketches don't have the vitality of a more encompassing portrait of the esoteric landscape the shaman has. The shamanic spirit understands the metaphors, the symbols, and the matrix of values and beliefs upon which the shaman's culture is built, and the shaman knows how to tap into these without necessarily needing to intellectualize.

That is not to say The Doors didn't intellectualize their songs; they had to on some levels, piecing together the artistic impressions each member grasped at – a lyrical image, an organ interlude, a guitar riff, a drum cadence. And especially with the ordering of songs on the six studio albums was there intellectualizing. (While all four had attended college, two of The Doors, Ray Manzarek and Jim Morrison, had earned college degrees – a rarity among rock musicians.)

The Doors insisted their work was art, and each album they created was a cohesive and integrated composition, as any endearing painting or sculpture is. The vinyl album had a given format – two sides with a beginning and an end to each side; the compact disc has eliminated the need for a transition from one side to another. Thus, artists conscientious of creating within such a format had to recognize: the beginning of side one; a closing statement on side one; either a restating of the theme or some sort of transition to open side two; and the ending on side two.

And The Doors quite consciously structured their albums based on this format. Worthwhile to note is Manzarek's comment, which echoed what the other Doors thought, on the compilation albums released by Elektra: "We never wanted those compilations albums released at all."1

In essence, each album was a concept album. Appreciating the concept album means recognizing the puzzle's pieces and fitting them together to see the picture the artist is painting, consciously and unconsciously. Not all concept albums follow a smooth, chronological order, taking the listener comfortably through a storyline. Organizational patterns have been: traditional modes of moving chronologically through events, such as The Who's *Tommy* and Pink Floyd's *The Wall*; thematic statements which take the listener through a kaleidoscope of images, such as The Beatles' *Sergeant Pepper's Lonely Hearts Club Band* or many of Frank Zappa's albums, notably the early ones with the Mothers of Invention, like *Freak Out*; extended metaphors, such as the Moody Blues' albums, notably *Days of Future Past.*

The concept album usually results from one of two processes: artists consciously write and produce an album within an intended structure – which exemplifies the original notion of a concept album as the term came into use in the 1960s; or, a recording reflects the thoughtful orchestration of songs, written independent of a specific purpose, to reflect an artistic statement – a theme or feeling, if you wish – inherent in all the songs or in the whole created by the collection of the songs. The second process is characterized by the significant contribution of a producer, someone who is independent of the artist and co-ordinates the ordering of songs from the artist's repertoire. It is this latter process that typifies The Doors under the guidance of producer Paul Rothchild.

Our critical rendering of The Doors' songs is in large part intellectualizing – or as some have said, "mental masturbating". A common criticism of "artistic critiques" uses the analogy that dissecting kills the specimen. If one limits oneself to the tools of the laboratory, then one has to kill in some manner what one is studying.

We are no more dissecting The Doors than The Doors were dissecting the L.A. scene. Our critical rendering of The Doors' artistic vision is a variation of The Doors' musical rendering of the Western dream. Just as our critical rendering is a piecing together of many artistic impressions by The Doors, it is also our way of painting a portrait of America and of being human in the twentieth century, a portrait quite similar to the artistic vision The Doors render. We both use one language to help explain the secret alphabet of another. Instead of destroying the secrecy and mystery with the light of exposure, we hope to develop the understanding of why the artistic vision of The Doors remains a viable portrait of modern life. Critical analysis should heighten understanding, and the power and impact, of any artistic vision of life, of what it means to be human.

The intensity and uniqueness of The Doors' artistic vision emerged from the four members functioning as a cohesive creative spirit. Most of the songs started with an idea from Morrison and occasionally from the group's guitarist, Robby Krieger. And then, as keyboardist Ray Manzarek explained in the radio special, *History of Rock 'n' Roll*, the four of them worked like a "communal brain", and the songs then evolved from "all four guys putting their input into the song".2 The other three Doors – Manzarek, Krieger, and drummer John Densmore – meshed their musical expressions to Morrison's poetic imagery and themes. And all four were aware of this. After describing the universal rejection of the group's initial

14

acetate six-song demos (recorded before Krieger joined the group) in his book, *Riders On The Storm*, Densmore wrote: "Incredible, I thought. They just don't understand our vision. They don't get it!"3 Well, a quick listen to the demos would easily convince most people why their vision wasn't understood.

The creative guidance as the main lyricist Morrison provided became quite evident upon his death. The group cut two more albums, but the albums lacked the spirit and impact of the previous works; as Manzarek reflected, the three of them could make music, "but somehow the whole lyrical, vocal thing just wasn't right without Jim".4 In a 1972 interview with *ZigZag* magazine, Krieger stated when Morrison was in the group, "it was like the band with the voice of God up front".5 Morrison's verbal imagery and themes set the tone of the six original studio albums.

The other three Doors simply didn't fill in the music to accompany Jim's lyrics. The Doors' sound – which has been put into the categories of rock, blues, and psychedelic – is unique, a sound that arises from the way all four fit their individual parts together creating the inner structure of their music. In the video, *The Doors: A Tribute To Jim Morrison*, Krieger stated that on stage, instead of performing a show or an act, they tried to do reality: "The music was what we were really feeling." Mike Jahn, in his "unauthorized" 1969 book, *Jim Morrison And The Doors*, wrote that Morrison's words, like the other three Doors' musicianship, "come directly from his own head, not as phrases constructed to provoke a certain reaction, but as creations that are the special friend to his psyche."6 The relationship between the music and the musicians was direct; hence, The Doors' sound cannot be duplicated and has not given rise to any new styles. It was not one shaman with a back-up band; it was four shamanic spirits working as one.

"The poet always knows that just beyond the chaos of the poem is the silence of poetry. Rimbaud was one of the very few poets who consecrated his work by a silence which has done more than any manifestoes and explanations to reveal it and to make it known."

*Wallace Fowlie*
*Rimbaud (A Critical Study) (p. 105)*

15

Each of the four Doors had certain functions in certain situations, felt and predicted unconsciously by individual musical instinct and collectively by the inner dynamics of the group. Outwardly, their technique is not definitive, nor are their songs very advanced in terms of theoretical construction on paper. Most Doors' songs are built on very basic chord progressions and drum lines. Yet, except for the work on the fourth album, the music of The Doors doesn't sound like anything or anybody else. It is rare even to hear the exact sound within a repeated pattern of a song. The moment guided the creative input by each of the four members, and no two moments are ever the same.

So then, what characterizes the music of The Doors? First, the instrumentation. The prominent use of the electric organ was unique, as was the lack of a bass player and use of only one guitarist. As Jim Ladd said in *No One Here Gets Out Alive: The Doors' Story* on his radio special, *The Inner View*, Manzarek's organ and other keyboards provided a "haunting, chanting undertone".[7] The lack of a bass player allowed The Doors' sound to be, as Densmore told Ladd, "more ethereal". A standard practice in the music field is to use different guitar players for different styles; Krieger did it all himself and incredibly well. Having a jazz background, drummer Densmore brought an essential quality of blending to help mold The Doors' sound. Never just a timekeeper, he used his drumming to comment on whatever Morrison said or sang; during their formative period of nightly gigs at Whisky-A-Go-Go, Densmore wrote that he developed a "technique of 'vamping' Jim's wild singing with a kind of shamanistic drumming".[8] Also, The Doors didn't use, except for on one album, extra woodwinds, horns, or percussion, which was a popular practice of the time.

Second, Morrison's voice. His sensual crooning, sarcastic laughter, and screams are all givens. In the radio special, *Rock & Roll Never Forgets: Jim Morrison*, Rothchild said of Morrison's voice: "He was a rock 'n' roll Bing Cosby; the first crooner of the new era." In *Wilderness: The Lost Writings Of Jim Morrison, Volume I*, Jim wrote in a poem that his voice was, at best, a "scream" or a "sick croon" with the "squeaks" and "furies" of a repressed teenager's "nasal whine".[9] Despite a lack of training, Morrison demonstrated a good sense of control and appropriateness of phrasings and feelings to get maximum audience impact. Somehow, his voice always makes you take him seriously, even on the occasional bubble-gum tunes, or "radio songs" as Jim called them.

16

Third, the inner structure of the music. This structure stems mainly from The Doors' somewhat unusual instrumentation. The lack of a bass player meant the lack of the typical Sixties-rock bass line, which was usually a simple outline of a basic chord progression – repetitive, obtrusive, and, most of the time, boring. Some of the better bands like Yes, Led Zeppelin, and The Jimi Hendrix Experience had virtuoso bass players that actually played lines that fit with the other parts instead of being a simple building block on which everything else rested. Normally, on top of the bass line was the guitar part. The guitar line could either be a rhythm part (almost exclusively chords that simultaneously filled in the bass line and supported the upper parts) or a lead part (mainly melody lines and few chords). Sometimes, the piano or organ was used in this supporting capacity if the guitar played a lot of melody. The organ was almost never the main focus like Manzarek's was. When trendy instruments, like flutes and recorders, made their appearances, it was to play an upper part. The vocals almost always carried the melody, which was supposedly the most important line, so the instrumental parts tended to mold into compact layers underneath the singer.

For The Doors – this is the most crucial point of difference – they never, ever played in predictable or well-defined layers or even concentric circles, but in swirls. None of The Doors sticks to a musical role or limits himself to playing one piece of music. The creation of music was a constant process every time The Doors played a song. The most ingenious interplay occurred between Manzarek and Krieger, who managed to produce simple bass lines, complex bass lines, supporting chord parts or melodic lines, and solo lines, as well as original combinations of inner harmonic lines. So adept were they at recognizing and developing the harmonic structure of a song that at times it is difficult to tell who is playing what kind of line at a given moment.

The music swirls because the relationship between all the parts constantly changes. One player throws out a piece of a bass line, and, for a few measures, everybody builds on that. Then, the texture shifts subtly, with someone else picking up the line, and the ensemble falls together in a different configuration. The most impressive thing about the group is not that they didn't use patterns, but that they did with subtle discernment. A lot of the songs have a definable chord structure and lyric/chorus/bridge/coda configuration, but each time a pattern is repeated it is different somehow. Each song seems to unfold and fall into place, instead of plodding along in disjointed or predictable steps. Even without the words, which are themselves an integral factor in the swirling process, the music always sets a mood, playing with the listener's ears, mind, and emotion.

Morrison was the wordsmith, but Densmore, Krieger and Manzarek were poets in the musical sense. This is especially evident in the first three albums, where the artistic vision was still fairly cohesive and defined. The words, music, and drums all fit together, complementing and moving amongst each other in such a way that The Doors presented not only music and ideas, but an undefinable essence that far transcends four guys having a jam session. Because of their artistic vision, the music became a vehicle and not a goal. Having a bigger ideal in mind, albeit an intangible one, these guys could play together and just know by instinct where the music needed to go without getting caught up in details along the way.

Fourth, The Doors' sound. The first three albums, though a little fuzzy on the artistic vision in the third one, are for all purposes musically equivalent. The style is consistently the same and so is the sound. The few lightweight songs (especially on the third album) are legitimized by the way they contribute to the sequence of metaphors developed on the respective albums. Even where that excuse is questionable, The Doors get away with it by pure, brute musical talent. Some of these songs, if nothing else, are just all-out, kick-ass jams. Even when they totally sell out to pop idioms (i.e., the fourth album), these guys are far better than average.

Above all, they were innovative in their sound. They aren't comparable to any of their predecessors or contemporaries, and nobody since has ever sounded like them. For the first three albums, the overall sound is generally psychedelic, but not self-consciously so. Mike Jahn wrote that the group's music had a gentle sound without pretending to hide the "violence beneath that cloud of beauty": a violence "of ideas repressed, of youth suppressed, of tensions waiting to be murdered and hopes aching to be set free".10 The Doors, during this time, were so much a feeling beyond music itself that it is wrong to label them as anything specific.

A comparison of the bootleg recordings from the gigs by The Doors at The Matrix in San Francisco in March of 1967 (before they exploded on the national scene) with the live recordings on the 1983 release, *Alive,*

*She Cried*, gives a good indication of what being thrust into the mass market did to The Doors' sound. The Matrix recordings reflect the kind of intimate nightclub scene where people came to sit back, slowly get stoned, listen to the band tell you how it is, applaud, and then drift home. The pleasant applause and a cordial Morrison at the microphone seem so distant from the soon-to-be raucous, arena-filled concerts. And the sound, which was still contoured to fit the intimacy of the nightclub, would blossom into the amplified renderings that grace the 1983 *Alive, She Cried*.

Pete Johnson, in a May 1967 review of The Doors at the Whisky-A-GoGo for the *Los Angeles Times*, wrote that their consistently spirited music was "too raw for comfort" and the symbolism in their lyrics bordered "on tastelessness", but they had nurtured their own "distinctive style, melting jazz improvisation, a hard rock beat and freewheeling word imager".11

Despite the sell-out to pop idioms in the fourth album, The Doors' sound definitely shifts to a blues tone. The underlying style is still there on the fifth and sixth albums, but the interplay is not quite so ambiguous. The musical outlook mellowed along with the artistic vision, which is why these albums don't really pack the gut-twisting punch that the others did. Not that they aren't as good or as meaningful, but these later albums have to be approached differently. The blues are more mature and versatile human emotions, and the bluesman has a laid-back outlook. Anger and impatience tend to cloud one's true inner feelings, keeping one from facing and accepting all the pain and all the joy of being human. On the fourth album, Morrison begins to make the shift away from the anger and impatience, but the rest of the band don't catch up until the next album. Here, the swirling tempest of sound slows to a blues pace, which actually allows for deeper feeling to emerge. The Doors rely more on the chordal and rhythmic patterns inherent to the blues style, which brings the intensity level down a notch. By sacrificing the inner energy a little, the music becomes less introspective and more relative to life the way all humans experience it. The Doors' essence is still there, perhaps even stronger because the fist-clenching anger is gone.

Life is relationships. Living expresses those relationships which embody patterns – social, physical, mental, spiritual, artistic, and so on. Some of those patterns are quite consciously known, others quite unknown. There are patterns, clearly restated themes musically and lyrically, from which The Doors drew in order to render their artistic vision. The Doors were quite conscious of some of these patterns, while other patterns were reflections of insights and perceptions they themselves were not conscious of, merely being conduits of those perceptions, as are all artistic spirits truly expressing what it means to be human in their time.

In looking at the six albums, we identify many of these patterns and images and then piece them together to form a reflection of The Doors' artistic vision. What we offer to share is not a definitive interpretation of the works of The Doors. There can never be a definitive critique of any work of art, let alone that of The Doors. Any work of art renders a different impression on each beholder. The different impressions evoked by The Doors spread from one end of the emotional and intellectual spectrum to the other, from "it's all sophomoric psychedelic babble of a bozo laureate" to "he's a god"; and for the most part, each are valid renderings of The Doors. What struck me as a reoccurring trait of many reviews on and comments about The Doors was the lack of any support save for the writer's personal reaction. In essence, many of the praises or gripes emanated from subjective reactions by that particular writer, which doesn't make such impressions less valid than others, just less comprehensive of the overall artistic vision.

Art ends and begins stories – stories of what it means to be human, to be alive, to aspire and ascend beyond the mundane of the day-to-day. Every work of art not only tells a story, but also has its own story. A work of art offers a beginning of a story that unfolds within each individual who is willing to ponder that work of art. And each story is different – sometimes minutely, sometimes remarkably – because the life experiences of each individual are unique summations. Moreover, the creation of each work of art usually ends a story.

We have fitted our impressions of this vision together no less unambiguously than the answers The Doors offered in their artistic renderings. With you, we wish to share those impressions along with some of the stories that begot these songs. And so, ladies and gentlemen, The Doors.

Listeners should use discretion – and their own imaginations.

# chapter 1
# breakin' on through:
## the debut album

"Genuine art must speak the language of the people who are engaged in the revolutionary process, whatever form their 'language' may take."

"To communicate successfully, however, a nonconformist language (understood in the widest possible sense) is necessary. ...the established language must be 'spoken', but in unforeseen and subversive ways... Not only has [rock music] not conformed to musical convention, it has communicated a negation of the established reality and an affirmation of the goals of liberation."

> *Robert G. Pielke,*
> *You Say You Want A Revolution:*
> *Rock Music In American Culture (pp. 17, 14)*

"A successful rock group has to combine technical virtuosity with a savage kind of grace."

> *Richard Goldstein,*
> *in Critique,*
> *1969 NET (National Education Television) special*

SIDE 1
Break On Through (To The Other Side)
Soul Kitchen
The Crystal Ship
Twentieth Century Fox
Alabama Song (Whiskey Bar)
Light My Fire

SIDE 2
Back Door Man
I Looked At You
End Of The Night
Take It As It Comes
The End

There was a magical tension in the mid and late 1960s, the times a whirlwind of social, political, and creative forces. Political and social winds kept the vibrant air swirling with tensions, and creative energies, especially of the young, tossed and turned in those winds, sensitive to an uneasiness with the traditional Western way of life. Creative expression, in turn, focused and honed itself upon this growing sense of uneasiness.

The first wave of the post-WW II generation had matured to young adulthood. Under the shadow of the nuclear bomb and fallout from WW II, American society had spent almost two decades rebuilding a sense of security while maintaining its new position as leader of the Free World. The generation that came of age in the Sixties had grown up in an "unreal" world of technological wizardry which was a very "real" everyday world to them.

They questioned traditional paths. As Don J. Hibbard and Carol Kaleialoha noted in their book, *The Role Of Rock*, this generation "revitalized and garbed in mod clothing" the Christian ethic of "love thy neighbour" as an alternative to the Cold War rhetoric of "us vs. them": a brotherhood of love where people treated others as equals, "everyone viewed as a brother or sister involved in the experience of living".1 Moreover, the youth, especially the artists, perceived what Hibbard, Kaleialoha, and others did: "The ludicrousness of an American economic system with no social purpose other than its own self-preservation and expansion."2 Yet this same dissident generation could live off the fat of society and enjoy the fruits of both worlds of technology and of freedom that such affluence begot – and do so without becoming part of the system.

Here within laid the fertile soil for strange times.

The early Sixties had been a turbulent mixture of the charm of Camelot and impending darkness of the nuclear shadow, of the energetic post-WW II generation coming of age and the lingering, entrenched values of moral and political providence shaped by The Great Depression and two world wars. The election of John F. Kennedy as president in 1960 signalled the arrival of youthful energy and idealism, an ushering in of an age of Camelot, but the Americanized version of royalty quickly became a trial of political will with the Bay of Pigs Invasion fiasco and the building of the Berlin Wall in 1961. The Cuban Missile Crisis of October 1962 cast the imminent shadow of Soviet nuclear bombs parked just beyond the tip of Florida and aimed at U.S. land. Rachel Carson's book, *Silent Spring*, a well-documented indictment of the indiscriminate use of pesticides and other chemicals – particularly DDT, signaled that the threat to this age of America Camelot wasn't just coloured red by Soviet communism. In 1963, Americans had to deal with events that shook the post-WW II compliancy: the assassination of civil rights leader Medgar Evers in June, the emergence of Martin Luther King Jr. which was consummated with his "I have a dream..." speech during the Washington D.C. Freedom March for job opportunity and employment equality in August, and the vacant senselessness of John F. Kennedy's assassination in November followed two days later by Jack Ruby's killing of the accused assassin, Lee Harvey Oswald, on live television. The age of JFK's Camelot with all its flaws became the back room reality of political arm twisting of LBJ.

On February 7, 1964, The Beatles arrived at Kennedy Airport in New York City. They appeared on the *Ed Sullivan Show* and began a phenomenally successful tour – and conquest – of America. The court of Camelot shifted to the upbeat and sanguine music of the mop tops. In movie theatres, the American public was entertained by Julie Andrews and Dick Van Dyke in Walt Disney's *Mary Poppins* and by Peter Sellers and George C. Scott in Stanley Kubriek's *Dr. Strangelove, Or: How I Learned To Stop Worrying And Love the*

*Bomb* (whose Cold War and nuclear saber-rattling rhetoric would echo with a frigthening clarity during the Reagan presidency of the 1980s). With the success of the second and third James Bond films, *From Russia With Love* (1963) and *Goldfinger* (1964), the "superhero" – both the character, Agent 007, and the actor, Sean Connery – consummated the transition to the very marketable and commercially successful "superstar". Lyndon Baines Johnson got his landmark Civil Rights Act passed in July, but the Gulf of Tonkin incident in August signalled the beginning of American's longest involvement in a war. North Vietnamese PT boats clashed with a U.S. destroyer and carrier which lead to the initial U.S. bombing of North Vietnam and the subsequent Gulf of Tonkin resolution passed by Congress giving the President authority to use all necessary measures to help any member nation of SEATO (Southeast Asia Treaty Organization). Though he would overwhelmingly defeat conservative Republican Barry Goldwater in November for the office of president, LBJ had laid the foundation for a decade of protest and social division and for his own political demise.

In February 1965, in New York City, rival Black Muslims set the tone for the ensuing decades of violence among Afro-Americans: they gunned down Malcolm X, 39, who had broken from the Black Muslims and founded the Black Nationalist movement. Meanwhile, Martin Luther King Jr. continued to spearhead civil rights marches and demonstrations which led to violent confrontations and deaths of civil rights advocates, both black and white. The dream of a Great Society was coming at a nightmarish pace from out of the shadows of such technological wizardry like the opening of the Harris County Dome Stadium in Houston, Texas, for the April 9th home opener of the Houston baseball team; the arena would soon be renamed the Astrodome. Bob Dylan shattered the haven many had sought in his music when he went "electric" on stage at the Newport Folk Festival in July, and what many consider the epitome of a rock song, The Rolling Stones' 'Satisfaction', crested the airwaves through the summer of 1965. The Mod Look became the garb of the emerging counter-culture – tight bell-bottom jeans and stylized long hair cuts designed by Vidal Sassoon, a London-based hairdresser.

But the impoverished reality in America's own backyard of racial minorities would erupt with riots in many cities, notably several days of riots in August in Watts, a densely populated, mostly black section of Los Angeles. After white Californian state highway patrolmen stopped a 21-year-old black who was driving while drunk, Watts exploded with riots of economic and social frustration that left 34 dead, over a thousand injured, and damage estimated at $200 million which was revised down to $40 million. Despite the efforts and pleas of leaders like Dr. Martin Luther King Jr., some 13,900 National Guardsmen were required to restore order as the smoggy skies of L.A. became gray with the smoke of the buildings burning in Watts.

During 1966 a more aggressive "black power" began organizing. Though the purpose of "black power", a slogan used in a June 1966 civil rights march in Mississippi by Stokely Carmichael, was to promote pride and organization among the Negro community, outspoken blacks began sticking stark images into America's consciousness through the media. Using street-smart rhetoric and resolve which was sharply distinct to Martin Luther King Jr., Bobby Seale and Huey Newton (founders of the Black Panther Party), H. Rap Brown ("Violence is as American as apple pie"), Eldridge Cleaver, and Carmichael cut at the well worn white social fabric that was laggardly easing its resistance to the marches and demonstrations for civil rights. The black community was now quite aware of its inequality, but the promise of The Great Society hadn't relieved it. The U.S. economy was booming, led by unprecedented federal government spending on both domestic programmes and the Vietnam War, and powers-to-be in both government and business were not anxious to use restraint with the overheating economy. "Medicare" went into effect. Anti-war demonstrations began descending on the isolated policy makers in Washington D.C..

Internationally, French President Charles De Gaulle, the general who was France's WW II hero, was undermining NATO's objectives by asserting French autonomy while the Soviets and Chinese continued to escalate the tension over who would lead the communist half of humanity's political world. The "Great Proletarian Cultural Revolution" in China to purge bourgeois ideology, though far more deadly, paralleled similar apprehension to the intellectual and artistic unrest in Western culture. Despite the Cold War tensions, within Russia was the appreciation, if not desire, for the former country's ties with Europe; ironic as it was then, a book was published titled,

*The Soviets In NATO.* The Middle East continued to be a boiling cauldron with military actions justified by previous provocations. Though the world, like the U.S., simmered in polarizing ideologies, life wasn't all that black-and-white.

By the fall season of 1966, almost all the prime-time programming on the three major U.S. television networks (ABC, CBS, NBC) was in colour. Lee J. Cobb's riveting portrait of Willie in the television adaption of Arthur Miller's *Death Of A Salesman* juxtaposed to the twice-a-week campiness of *Batman* led by Adam West (Batman) and Burt Ward (Robin). *Star Trek*, the television series, debuted, while the season's half-hour comedies formed the foundation of syndicated shows for cable two decades later: *Andy Griffith Show*, *Bewitched*, *The Beverly Hillbillies*, *Get Smart*, *Gilligan's Island*, *Green Acres*, *I Dream Of Jeannie*, *The Lucy Show*, and *That Girl*. And from the 1966 fall world of television came The Monkees, whose music would soon rule the sales charts leading up to 1967's Summer of Love. Despite the overwhelming presence of The Monkees, popular music was filled with rock's political and social commentary – which was not beyond The Monkees (i.e. 'Pleasant Valley Sunday'). The swelling ranks of college-aged young people embodied a commixture of naive ideals and reactionary desires for change.

In August of 1966, Charles Whitman barricaded himself in the tower at the University of Texas in Austin and began shooting and killing people until he was shot and killed. Truman Capote's *In Cold Blood*, a non-fiction account of the murder of a farm family in Holcomb, Kansas, using fictional techniques, became a bestseller book, along with Jacqueline Susann's elaborate and seedy harlequin novel, *Valley Of The Dolls*, whose film version would include the young actress Sharon Tate. Ralph Nader's book, *Unsafe At Any Speed*, challenged the automobile industry's apathetic attitude to safety, and the federal government quickly responded with legislation – change could happen, if it were politically expedient. Timothy Leary was proselytizing about LSD, still legally sold, mostly notably at head shops in California: "Turn on, tune in, and drop out." A 55-year-old former film actor, Ronald Reagan, was elected governor of California in the November elections, and Walt Disney died in December of lung cancer. Aptly, the April 8, 1966, cover of *Time* magazine asked, "IS GOD DEAD?" and spurned a slew of responses in other publications around the theme of "the Challenge of God Being Dead". Notable was the April 25 cover of *U.S. News* which proclaimed: "GOD IS NOT 'DEAD'"/Interview With Billy Graham; inside was the magazine's eight-page interview of affirmation with America's leading evangelist.

By the mid-1960s, artistic imagination had begun turning towards social commentary because the social protest of the early Sixties – most conspicuous in the music of Bob Dylan, Joan Baez, Phil Ochs, and others – had made its point: social protest didn't change the problems; it only made others, especially authority, more immutable. The Atlantis of folk-rock, before sinking beneath the onrush of the next wave of the rock era, provided a brief but significant bridge from the Sixties folk music and the commercialization of the rock 'n' roll of the late Fifties to the onrush of what has been called the Golden Age of Rock. The Beatles and Bob Dylan consolidated the artistic potential of rock 'n' roll and then sent it scattering in infinite directions.

> "We live in an age of revolutionary transformation.
> We can seek to shape it or
> we can doom ourselves to irrelevance.
> We can accept the challenge to our creativity or
> we can resign ourselves to ineffectual bitterness.
> We can lose ourselves in passionate and paralyzing controversy
> over technical aspects of individual problems, or
> we can, as I deeply believe we must,
> develop a more creative perspective –
> one which enables us to see
> the inner relationship of great issues and
> the larger framework within which they can be solved."
>
> *New York Governor Nelson A. Rockefeller, "Policy*
> *and the People" Foreign Affairs (January 1968) (p. 231)*

And with the advent of the cassette tape, pioneered and promoted by Philips, this explosion of creativity via music became accessible to anyone – both artist and listener. A portable, inexpensive tape deck could now both record and play music without the need for elaborate and expensive electronic equipment. From the West Coast came hippies, love children, flower power, and a music which was turning people on to more than just the endless summer of the Beach Boys and Jan & Dean.

President Johnson had escalated the war in Vietnam to proportions previously undreamed of while pushing his vision of The Great Society. America's youth were leery of being told not to stray from the path leading to materialistic success, and college-age students were beginning to discover the power of sit-ins and marches. Despite Martin Luther King Jr.'s non-violent tactics, frustrated militant black leaders were mobilizing a stifled black spirit. Detroit was about to erupt into a hot summer of riots and fires.

Lines were being drawn – for the American way of fitting into the system, or for the American spirit of freedom and revolution. Authority vs. Youth. Them vs. Us. Establishment vs. Pop culture. The rhetoric and attitudes of the Cold War were not limited to just the world political stage.

The vision of brotherhood had not yet been shattered by the events of 1968 and 1969, by the reality of the political machinery of America, by Richard Nixon and Watergate, by the assassination of Bobby Kennedy and Martin Luther King Jr., by the killing of students at Kent State and Jackson State Universities, by the disaster at the Rolling Stone free concert at Altamont. There was a magical tension – and in 1965 in Los Angeles, an obscure rock group was formed named The Doors fronted by one Jim Morrison.

The Jekyll and Hyde nature of the times was evident in the works of many rock artists, notably The Doors whose six-year history embodied such a dualistic nature. By 1966, The Doors consisted of John Densmore, 21, drummer; Robby Krieger, 20, guitarist; Ray Manzarek, 27, keyboards; and Jim Morrison, 22, vocals. The period from the summer of 1965 through late 1966 marks the group's often labelled acid fertility period when the group played nightly gigs on the Los Angeles Sunset Strip. Free of commercial demands and constraints, the group worked out their songs during the gigs, filling in with old blues numbers. The bulk of these original compositions eventually provided the material for their first three albums. In late 1966, Elektra Records signed the group to a recording contract, and Paul Rothchild, 30, was assigned as the group's producer. In January

1967, what many critics have labelled "the best debut album in rock 'n' roll", *The Doors*, was released.

At the top of the singles charts were The Monkees' 'I'm A Believer' and the Royal Guardsmen's 'Snoopy vs. The Red Baron'. The Beach Boys' 'Good Vibrations' was on the way out, and The Rolling Stones' 'Ruby Tuesday' was on the way up; The Beatles' were about to release the double single, 'Penny Lane'/'Strawberry Fields Forever'. The Monkees' debut album was number one on the album charts, ahead of the durable selling soundtracks for the 1966 film, *Dr. Zhivago*, and the 1965 film, *The Sound Of Music*. Simon & Garfunkel's *Parsley, Sage, Rosemary And Thyme*, The Rolling Stones' *Got Live If You Want It* and *Aftermath*, and The Beatles' *Revolver* shared slots on the top selling albums along with albums from The Mamas & The Papas, Eric Burdon & The Animals, The Association, Lovin' Spoonful, Donovan, Herman's Hermits, Paul Revere & The Raiders, Lou Rawls, and five albums by Herb Albert & The Tijuana Brass. The Doors would steadily work its way up the chart of top selling albums in America, sitting behind The Beatles' *Sergeant Pepper's Lonely Hearts Club Band*, The Rolling Stones' *Flowers*, and The Monkees' *Headquarters*; eventually The Doors' debut album reached #2 behind *Sgt. Pepper's*, an interesting statement by artists on the culture blossoming from and nurtured by their rock music.

"For both art and life
depend wholly on the laws of optics,
on perspective and illusion;
both, to be blunt,
depend on the necessity of error."

"In opposition to all who would derive the arts from a single vital principle, I wish to keep before me those two artistic deities of the Greeks, Apollo and Dionysos. They represent to me, most vividly and concretely, two radically dissimilar realms of art. Apollo embodies the transcendent genius of the *principium individuationis*; through him alone is it possible to achieve redemption in illusion. The mystical jubilation of

Dionysos, on the other hand, breaks the spell of individuation and opens a path to the maternal womb of being."

"...every artist must appear as 'imitator',
either as the Apollonian dream artist
or the Dionysiac ecstatic artist,
or, finally (as in Greek tragedy, for example)
as dream and ecstatic artist in one."

*Friedrich Nietzsche,*
*The Birth Of Tragedy (pp. 10, 97, 24)*

The Doors found little comfort in either the established system or the emerging Pop culture. The American way clothed itself in arrogant, aggressive attire – a facade of plastic machismo, a costume Morrison felt little comfort in wearing. He perceived fitting-in to the system as a subtle form of murder as he explained to Lizze James: "When others demand that we become the people they want us to be, they force us to destroy the person we are."3 As often portrayed in Doors' songs, the American way of life was too mechanical, too self-enslaving for the soul. Nor did Morrison dress himself in the Pop culture's cloak of brotherly love. As Lester Bangs in *Creem* magazine observed, Morrison saw that "machismo equal bozo in the drag" and that rock stars were just "huge oafus cartoons, more gushers of American snake-oil".4

Reactions to The Doors – especially to Morrison – ranged from Nik Cohn's opinion in his book, *Rock From The Beginning*, that The Doors "are no great band" and a lot of Morrison's lyrics "come across as pure pretentious bullshit"5 to underground newspaper *Los Angeles Free Press* writer Gene Youngblood's view that The Doors "reach for outer limits of inner space" and Morrison and The Doors "are a demonic and beautiful miracle that has risen like a shrieking Phoenix from the burning bush of the new music".6 Somewhere between falls the review from *Disk Review* magazine which labelled The Doors' style as "hard rock with slippery, psychedelic overtones" and defined "Morrison therapy" as: "to become more real, to be a better person, cut your ties to the establishment past, swim in your emotions, suffer symbolic death and rebirth, rebirth as a new man, psychologically cleansed."7

Morrison therapy reveals a poetic perspective Jim rendered to express his view of life, just as other artists do, drawing from the paraphernalia of their times to create images that express these perspectives of the human condition. For rock 'n' roll, drugs and sex – and in the Sixties, violence and the Vietnam War – provided a fountain of imagery for artistic spirits to draw from. Like his contemporaries, Morrison sketched many pictures with imagery of sex, death, drugs, and the unknown to convey this "Morrison therapy" of self-realization and rebirth. As John Densmore wrote in *Riders On The Storm*, Jim's poetry was "erotic, but not pornographic; mystical, but not pretentious".8 Wallace Fowlie, in his comparative study of Jim Morrison and the French poet Morrison so admired, Arthur Rimbaud, wrote that Morrison's poetry "appears as a reflection of great poetry", a reflection that is "obsessive and subtle", and images in Jim's verses "spring up...like reflexes and answers to the subconscious law of chance and free association".9 Shadowed with such bizarre and dark imagery, Morrison's poetic perspective reflects seemingly confusing renderings, leaving the impression of a negative portrait of the world of man. However, Morrison sought to reveal that some basic forces were being suppressed behind the facades of both the Western way of life and the romantic notions of this latest, newly born Pop culture, an offspring of rock 'n' roll.

The Sixties being a time of activism, The Doors as artists wanted people to react. Morrison understood the power of obscurity, and Fred Powledge noted in an insightful article for *Life* that Morrison's lyrics "challenge you to try to interpret".10 Tantalize the mind. Entice it with a short, beautiful or terrifying burst of imagery. Arouse its curiosity. In an interview with Lizze James, Morrison said that the facades we live behind block "perceptions from coming in" and "feelings from coming out" and that he tried to shatter those facades in two ways: "one way is violence, pain", and "the other is eroticism".11 Excite with sexual tension. With drug imagery. With the threat of violence. Of unknown fears within the soul. Of death. Then leave the mind and emotions in a state that they must seek to complete the aroused experience.

Short snatches of poetic imagery and themes from Morrison's poetic vision had a chance to take hold in the fast-paced, temporal-orientated contemporary mind, especially the impressionable minds of either the youth or the media. Poetry built in the traditional sense upon a central theme within a well-defined format couldn't begin to get a foothold in a culture attuned for immediate, sensory impressions. These snatches of poetic images and themes are like fragments that piece together and ultimately form a coherent picture of Morrison's – and, hence, The Doors' – artistic perspective of life, a reflection that isn't always clear and can be described in many different ways.

"The music is stark, brutal."

"Within the inner reaches
of the barely suppressed consciousness,
The Doors scream the cry of a twisted grotesque."

"A girl has disappeared and
you are lying there, naked, cold, alone."

"Lost in a strange forest,
with the last rays of light slipping away
one is at the mercy of his hunters.
The primeval ooze of the earth
is damply sucking at your feet.
Soon you will be absorbed."

"Far away a slight form huddles
against the tree to keep from freezing."

"The music fascinates.
Perhaps in us...a little...Doors, or...doors."

*Ed Jilek, "Records" (his entire review of The Doors)*
*The Paper (underground newspaper), Michigan State*
*University (East Lansing, MI), 9 May 1967 (p. 12)*

32

The picture of life The Doors paint from this artistic perspective may appear to be puzzling and fragmentary, mostly because of Morrison's rich rendering with universal symbols rather than specific ones. And this was evident early. In the October 1968 issue of *Crawdaddy*, Robert Somma criticized the "supremacy of the banal" in The Doors' repetition of the elemental – like sun, moon, earth, fire, water, river, and sea: The Doors "dwell in the universe, probably because it is thus easier to pass from one century to another, to fornicate with the earth, to fuck the archetypes of the mind."[12] However, if an artist's works reflect the times, then The Doors' works, even in their copious universal imagery, echo the fragmentary nature of our society and the yearning for a connection to truths expelled from an artificial environment which has segmented the world into days, hours, minutes, seconds, into disjointed plastic images detached from life. And such fragmentation creates disquieting despair in even the most basic sanctuaries of a house or of love.

With the guidance of producer Paul Rothchild, the three albums drawing from this pool of songs generated during The Doors' formative years each reflect a well-composed portrait of The Doors' artistic imagination, a distinct artistic vision that emerged on each of the six albums. In producing The Doors' work, Rothchild explained to Paul Williams in an interview published in *Crawdaddy* that he focused upon his own perception that Morrison was saying that every trip we take brings a death "of concepts, of bullshit, a death of laughter and soft lies" and that we need to "kill the alien concepts" and return to "the beginning of personal concepts... to your own reality".[13] This theme of searching through death and self-realization weaves together the first album, *The Doors*, which opens with a yearning for revelation in 'Break On Through', progresses through a series of songs which oscillate between pursuing the need both for the sanctuary of love and for the freedom to explore the unknown, and then arrives at a resolution with 'The End'.

"Jim's great talent was to do something that made you respond as who you really were. He made you drop your guard. He provoked you."

*Bill Siddens, Doors' manager, in Westwood One Radio Special, "Rock & Roll Never Forgets: Jim Morrison".*

"Great poets are insurgents.
They are in revolt against
the limitations of reason and logic."

*Wallace Fowlie,*
*Rimbaud (A Critical Study) (pp. 230-31)*

Hank Zevallos: "Why do you write lyrics and what are you trying to do with them?"
Jim Morrison: "Achieve clarity and alter fate. Deepen a strange hue in the clan tartan."

*"Jim Morrison (interview)", Poppin (March 1970; p. 47)*

## SIDE ONE

'Break On Through' opens side one of *The Doors* and provides an overture that etches out The Doors' artistic vision which remains consistent throughout the six albums: The Doors offer no elaborate answers or alternatives; the music and lyrics probe life as something that is to be lived, yet always recognizing that life is mystical, is dualistic, is made of many realities. The song, as Manzarek said on the radio special, *In The Studio*, "is about expansion of consciousness; the other side is freedom".

Inexperienced in the marketing of Top 40 singles, Elektra had released this song in early 1967 as The Doors' debut single, but the poignant and ambiguous lyrics proved too cacophonic for Top 40 ears, the song portraying the need to experience life beyond a one-dimensional, plastic reality. The song hit #126 on the Billboard 'Hot 100' chart for April 8, 1967, and that was it; the number one song that week, for the third consecutive week, the Turtles' 'Happy Together', was followed by The Mamas and The Papas 'Dedicated To The One I Love' and Nancy and Frank Sinatra's 'Somethin' Stupid'. Densmore wrote he was worried the Brazilian-like bossa nova beat he used was "too eccentric for the mass market".14 So the album and the group

34

remained, for a while longer, comfortable commodities for the heady underground.

The opening lines imply life is dualistic and can be violent – that day destroys night and night ruptures day. A light side, a dark side. Waking time, dream time. Things known, things unknown. But the known destroys access to the unknown because waking destroys dream time: the rosy fingers of dawn don't softly push away the canopy of velvet violet; the day destroys the night.

The inability to break through frustrates Morrison who yearns to experience life beyond chasing "pleasures" and digging for "treasures", but he also recalls the times "we cried". Crying suggests pain, and it runs with life's pleasures and lies buried with life's treasures.

Uncomfortable with the pleasures, treasures and crying which surround him, Morrison seems as intense in his need to be free, to break through to "the other side", as in his pursuit to find sanctuary in love. Snatches of temporary sanctuary in a lover's embrace yield to his yearning for freedom which gives way to his desire for sanctuary, a thematic pattern followed by the ensuing songs of the album. And his lover is no less pursuing the same. The recorded chorus, "She gets", omits a final word, high, which was censored from the studio version but which was often explicitly resounded in live recordings.

Morrison found the tranquillity and sanctuary of an "island" in his lover's arms and the serene nature of "country" in her eyes, yet those same arms "chained" and those same eyes "lied". Life is dualistic, and Morrison does not trust what he feels is meaningful. And he is just as uncomfortable with the urban scene, unadorned save to the short, concise rhythm of time to which it is chained – making the scene from "week to week, day to day, hour to hour". The imagery is practically verbatim from John Rechy's 1963 novel, *City Of Night*, the "scene" being but one repeated moment after another.15 The urgency of the music conveys the underlying tension reality imposes upon the lyric's desire to break through to "the other side" or to enjoy the "island" in a lover's arms or "country" in her eyes.

Unable to break through to some sanctuary, Morrison, in the second song, turns to the sanctuary of a "Soul Kitchen". Though, as Densmore adeptly describes in *Riders On The Storm*, the song was a tribute to Olivia's, a small soul food restaurant Morrison frequented

35 .

during his stay on Venice Beach, Morrison doesn't miss the obvious sexual metaphor of warming his head next to her oven as he wooingly urges to let him "sleep" in her "soul kitchen" and "warm" his "mind" near her "gentle stove".

Though "soul kitchen" and "gentle stove" represent images from a traditional source of sanctuary – the home – there is something uneasy about this sanctuary of love. This sanctuary cannot provide asylum from time ("the clock" is saying it's closing time) or from the outside world into which he is turned out to wander. Morrison often portrayed the tension with the man-made world in harsh, alien images of the urban scene, its inhabitants in a state of resigned alienation, of cars crawling by "stuffed with eyes" under the "hollow glow" of the street lights. The dissonant, ominous mixture of images and sounds leaves a disturbing impression of the urban scene, of the shadow cast by Los Angeles's endless summer light.

This world of neon groves and hollow glow of street lights doesn't offer the comfort of a lover's gentle stove in her soul kitchen nor of an island in a lover's arms and country in her eyes. As the organ drops out, Morrison is drawn to fingers that weave "quick minarets" and speak "in secret alphabets", drawn to a new language evoked by exotic minarets which may unlock a way to break on through. Yet Morrison will not surrender to love. He does not close with a lingering sense of satisfaction; he sings of learning "to forget". It has been but a brief moment of sanctuary.

The search for sanctuary wanders from a lover's 'Soul Kitchen' to the 'Crystal Ship' of drugs. Morrison's voice wavers and drifts in a sedate, drug-like tone over the music, as if just a fraction off the beat. Morrison croons that before his lover slips into unconsciousness to the other side, he wants one more kiss, one more "flashing chance at bliss". Kiss equals bliss? But what about the drug trip? Isn't that the ticket to bliss? Morrison didn't need to have The Beatles' 'All You Need Is Love' tell him that love was the answer. The equality of kiss equals bliss is emphasized by the more definitive rhyme of kiss and bliss than the off-rhyme of unconsciousness and bliss. So, why did Morrison forsake the bliss of another kiss for another "chance to fly"?

Living is "filled with pain", and even though his lover can enclose him in her "gentle rain" and love could provide bliss, Morrison wants freedom. It's so easy to fly rather than to cry or to tarry in "streets" that are unnatural fields which "never die". Youthful urgency has yet to understand the "gentle rain" of the rainman in 'L'America' on the sixth album.

The song closes with overexaggeration. Though Morrison's lover offers "bliss" and a "gentle rain", the "crystal ship" offers a "thousand girls" and "thrills" and a "million ways" to kill time, the great inhibitor of trying to break through. And when the ship gets back, Morrison croons he will "drop a line". Perhaps the phrase evokes the image of an anchor line, suggesting settling down, but the undercurrent tone of the song suggests the opposite. Don't expect a commitment, because people will drop another line that they want a kiss or another line of whatever drug they are sailing on.

Yet Morrison understood the danger of drowning if he sailed on such a crystal ship. The crystal ship doesn't guarantee what Grace Slick's White Rabbit could: one pill to make you small, another to make you tall. Nor does the crystal ship take you down to the carefree land of 'Strawberry Fields Forever' or 'Lucy In The Sky With Diamonds'. Nor provide the metaphysical fireworks of Jimi Hendrix's 'Purple Haze'. The crystal ship is crystal – expensive and fragile, very breakable and hardly the type of sanctuary or security one needs in life. Though Morrison's crystal ship sails with the winds of youthful fancy, he is as leery of sailing on the Pop culture's crystal ship of drugs as he is of the established American crystal ship filled with a Martini.

After sailing on a crystal ship, The Doors return to the theme of love in the fourth song, a love song not of compassion, but of cynicism, panned out in the lyrics and in the twangy, countryish guitar sound rendered by Krieger. 'Twentieth Century Fox', regarded by many as one of Morrison's best lyrics, opens with a portrait of a "fashionably lean" and "fashionably late" female who never breaks a date or ranks a scene. She is a 'Twentieth Century Fox' – not a chick, not a lady, but a fox, "a liberated hunter on the prowl", as Richard Goldstein wrote in his edited collection, *The Poetry Of Rock*.16 In his unprecedented book of critical analysis, *The Poetry Of Rock: The Golden Years*, David Pichaske considered the fox a "brilliant image" suggesting "sexual appetite, woman the huntress, the tinsel glamour of Twentieth Century Fox films" – and he noted Morrison's singing suggests a pun between fox and fucks.17

A product of the twentieth century, she won't be found in the nineteenth or eighteenth or seventeenth century. She is too perfect, too mechanical, too twentieth centurish: she has neither "tears" nor "fears" nor "ruined years" nor "clocks". She is too plastic, frozen in time and displaying no emotions, no feelings, no chances of growing as a human being. Though "the queen of cool", she is sterile, a mass produced product. Onto the Twentieth Century Fox Morrison stamps a contemporary female attitude, one no less plastic than many of the images created by her counterparts on the plastic film of movies by the studios of MGM or Paramount or Twentieth Century Fox.

She might have reality "locked up" in a "plastic box", but this fox, as Goldstein wrote in *Poetry of Rock*, is quite "at home amid the plastic shrubbery because she herself is plastic, to the roots".18 And she doesn't "waste time" with "elementary talk", a basic building block of a relationship. There is no way a red, red rose is going to bloom in Morrison's heart for such a girl. Frozen in both time and the images of the times, she is impervious to the concept of giving trust to the growth of a personal relationship.

Morrison, finding scant sanctuary with the Twentieth Century Fox, turns back to another crystal ship, a traditional American drug – whiskey.

The next to last song on side one is a cover of a post-WW I German song written in the 1920s by Bertolt Brecht, 'Alabama Song'. The song, whose lyrics were English, was reworked by Brecht (words) and Kurt Weill (music) into their 1930 operetta called 'Rise And Fall Of The City Of Mahagonny', in their native German. The Doors picked up this song, according to Manzarek, from an album he had of Brecht and Weill songs.19 According to W.H. Auden and Chester Kallman, English translators of 'Mahagonny', the operetta represents what Brecht saw as "two faces of contemporary capitalistic society" that required either "a grinding obedience which produces empty 'pleasure' or an equally oppressive freedom based on the ability to pay" or both.20 Much like The Doors' artistic perspective, Brecht's lyrics paint a picture of how "modern capitalistic society destroys human choice".21 *The East Village Other*, an underground newspaper from New York City, wrote in 1967 that The Doors had discovered 'Mahagonny' and its "echoes of pre-Hitlerite Germany" as a reflection of what was happening in "New York, San Francisco, Louisville": "In every field of art, Germany blew its mind."22

In the operatta, several prostitutes sing of needing to find the next whiskey bar, the next pretty boy, and the next little dollar so they can make it in a world gone berserk in materialistic pursuits. Morrison sings for someone to show him the way "to the next whiskey bar" and "the next little girl". Effectively rendering a bar room bantering tone to the song, The Doors sing of seeking guidance from someone, yet avoiding the pains of life without offering a reason why, "Oh, don't ask why". But life is dualistic, and we know the answer: "Man must have whiskey / Oh, you know why."

Side one closes with a return to love and one of the most intense sexual anthems in rock, 'Light My Fire'. Paul Williams wrote that no one has ever been able to make the music "feel so Dionysian, yet look so Apollonian" as The Doors did in what became the signature song for the group.23 But it was the shortened version of 'Light My Fire' trimmed for Top 40 radio airplay which catapulted The Doors and this debut album out of the underground into the spotlight of mass consumption in the summer of 1967. According to Densmore, a local disc jockey in L.A., Dave Diamond "who spun records from the psychedelic depths of the Diamond Mine", showed Robby and John piles of letters requesting 'Light My Fire' and suggested editing the song down to the then-standard three-minute format for radio.24 Though Robby and John didn't like the idea of shortening the solos, they approached a less-than-excited Rothchild with the idea. John wrote that Paul grudgingly edited the song, but still believed the record didn't have a chance.25 Eventually, on July 29, 1967, the song replaced the Association's 'Windy' as the #1 selling song in America for the next three weeks before being displaced by The Beatles' 'All You Need Is Love' which was displaced by Bobbie Gentry's 'Ode To Billie Joe'.

The heart of the song is driven by instrumental solos, based, according to Densmore and Krieger, on chords similar to John Coltrane's jazz version of 'My Favourite Things'. The rudimentary structure from which Manzarek and Krieger build their interplay between the organ and guitar is quite similar to that between Coltrane's soprano sax and McCoy Tyner's piano on their rendition of Richard Rogers and Oscar Hammerstein II's song. (The song became one of America's best known songs after Julie Andrews sang it in the film version of the musical *The Sound Of Music*.) Ray's weaving, spiralling organ solo dances with John's drumming, while Robby's guitar smoulders beneath as a steady, gentle pulse. Then Robby rolls through a solo, the electric organ quieting to a soothing ebbing in the background with John easing into a steady back beat with an occasional accent. After the foreplay of the two solos, the organ and guitar begin sputtering to a climax, John's drumming providing exclamations before a final lyrical statement. No wonder The Doors felt compromised – the radio version had gutted the song, leaving a skeleton of the song's interwoven, rich musical tapestry. In short, it was a sell-out and a far inferior artistic statement. Nonetheless, the 45 single was released, and, hence forth, The Doors would no longer be an underground commodity for a smouldering consciousness of revolution.

The song reflects the simple imagery of its creator, Robby Krieger. How much higher can we get than love, and the easiest way to love is to light one's fire. The lover's innocent asking for a kiss in the opening of 'Crystal Ship' yields to the passionate urging of his baby to "light my fire". The urgent rhythms of the music are not those of a soothing love song, and the lyric Morrison contributed to the song about wallowing in the mire and only losing as love became a "funeral pyre" leaves the disquieting sense the lover seeks a haven of lust, not of love. The song appeals to the urgent passions of love, not the sanctuary of a trusting relationship. The plastic images of the Pop culture's free love and the established Victorian attitude of sexuality melt under the pulsating rhythms of the song. To experience life's passions may require destroying sanctuaries of existing values which deny those passions.

> "Is there really any point in saying something like,
> 'The instrumental in 'Light My Fire' builds at the end
> into a truly visual orgasm in sound'
> when the reader can at any time
> put the album onto even the crummiest phonograph
> and experience that orgasm himself?"
>
> *Paul Williams, "Rock Is Rock: A Discussion*
> *of a Doors Song", Crawdaddy (May 1967; p. 43)*

## SIDE TWO

Side two opens with one of The Doors' favourite blues numbers, Willie Dixon's 'Back Door Man'. Musically and lyrically a gutsy, earthy tune, this song juxtaposes nicely with the urgency of 'Light My Fire', the plasticity of 'Twentieth Century Fox', the elusive tone of the 'Crystal Ship', and the uneasiness of 'Soul Kitchen'. Morrison's vocals and the other three Doors' instrumentals droll through Dixon's bluesy love song.

In the song Morrison interjects verses he borrowed from Howlin' Wolf's version of Dixon's song: "You men eat your dinner/Or eat your pork and beans/I eat more chicken /Any man ever seen."

The chicken Morrison drools over isn't plastic Twentieth Century Fox's. Morrison isn't the hesitant, unsure lover in 'Soul Kitchen'. Nor is he the lover in 'Crystal Ship' innocently asking for another kiss. Nor the cynical and frustrated, yet harmless lover in 'Twentieth Century Fox'. Nor the passionate lover in 'Light My Fire'. Dixon's blues number allows Morrison to grovel behind the brash mask of audacity, of boasting that he is a back door man whom men don't know, "but the little girls understand". He is the lover who is in and out of back doors, leaving behind moments of sanctuary, of being alive, of breaking through to the other side.

Interestingly, Morrison doesn't include lyrics that Willie Dixon unassumingly slips into his laid-back blues version of the song, lyrics depicting the Back Door Man being shot full of holes, of being accused of first degree murder, of being "in six feet of ground". In short, the risks of being a Back Door Man. Nonetheless, Morrison's youthful 'Back Door Man' celebrating passions of love being gratified with the craftiness of a fox contrasts to the ensuing three songs' portrayal of his uneasiness of seeking sanctuary in relationships and his yearning for freedom.

Ray's swirling organ in the opening of 'I Looked At You' sweeps us into the passion of the moment: two lovers looked and smiled at each other...and now they're on their way. The Twentieth Century Fox and the Twentieth Century Stud don't waste time on elementary talk, and they don't hesitate. The music is a rapid, impulsive tempo, Robby's guitar sounding like a driving bass pushing heatedly onward along with John's driving drum beat. There is no time for a relationship or love to grow. Time is short, life is simple; the pains and sufferings of a loving relationship are unwanted and unnecessary. But something isn't quite right with this type of relationship, for the song closes with the lovers on their way and unable to turn back because "it's too late".

The relationship is impersonal, the last verse suggesting that only walking and talking together is enough to bind them. Even this little superficial bit establishes two people as a couple, by either traditional or contemporary standards. Just "looking" at someone is enough to precipitate relations, especially the superficial, lustful type which Jim both explores and deplores. However, the past tense of the verbs which bind the two lovers – "walked" and "talked" – suggests that there is no real communication or feeling involved, that "it's too late".

The Doors leave the rapid, impulsive rhythms of such a plastic relationship and hit the road, slowing into the drawn out journey to 'End Of The Night'. Morrison opens the song singing about taking the "highway to the end of the night", an image Hopkins and Sugerman wrote Jim borrowed from the novel, *Journey To The End Of The Night*, written by "the French Nazi apologist and adamantine pessimist, Louis-Ferdinand Ce'line".26 Morrison often used the "life is a journey" metaphor, and appropriately so – aren't youth and motion synonymous? Isn't the highway the great American symbol of freedom via motion? The great American pathway upon which to find oneself? Morrison invokes the theme of breaking through to the other side by journeying to the unknown, to the mysterious side of life, by travelling to the "bright midnight", to "realms of bliss". And the musical interlude rendered by the organ and guitar conjures up a sensation of such a surreal landscape.

The images may be those evoked by drugs, but Morrison turns towards the mysterious, not necessarily towards drugs. The journey into the night does not necessarily lead to an end; the journey leads to light and truth, not to death or destruction of life, but to death and destruction of senseless ways of the day, of the known. Though night is considered dark and ominous, Morrison sees it as the bright midnight illuminating life's realms of bliss.

The slow, drawn out tempo of this song's invitation to journey to the other side contrasts sharply with the driving tempo of 'Break On Through'. Released as A/B sides of a 45 single, the two songs reflect life's dualistic nature, fast and slow: people born to "sweet delight" and people born to "the endless night". Both songs invite the same journey into the unknown to find bliss, the bright midnight, the other side.

Manzarek's spinning organ and Krieger's driving bass-like guitar pick up the tempo again with the next song, 'Take It As It Comes'. The song opens with imagery of time which isn't the eloquent, poetic imagery of time found in *Ecclesiastes 3* or the Byrds' 'Turn! Turn! Turn!'. This imagery is short and crisp: a time "to live", "to lie", "to laugh", and "to die". But, as if to be ironic, Morrison sings to this rapid beat to "take it easy", to take life as it comes and not to move too fast so your love will last. Two songs earlier, Morrison was singing about the hurried brevity of love. An apparent contradiction?

On the journey down the highway of modern life, we look at each other and we're on our way – no need for elementary talk. But, if you ride the highway to the end of night and trek to the bright midnight, then you realize there is a time to live and to die. You "take it easy" and you don't move too fast so you can make love last. When you reach the other side, you realize there is a time to walk and to run. If the doors of perception, our senses, are cleansed and you see things as they are – infinite – then why can't you aim yourself at infinity, as Morrison sings for us to aim our "arrows at the sun"?

> "The voyage is one of the most persistent of literary themes... Even if the major modern novels... are static and voyageless, the modern poets... are constantly narrating a voyage in their work... voyages, not literal in a geographical sense, but explorations of the spirit, moments filled with the action of progress and conquest."
>
> *Wallace Fowlie,*
> *Rimbaud (A Critical Study) (p. 47)*

But living doesn't allow absolute freedom, a human condition which leads Morrison to search constantly for sanctuary. Yet he won't trust a relationship of love, and life's traditional sanctuaries no longer offer security. So he symbolically turns to 'The End' as his "beautiful" and "only friend".

Richard Walls of *Creem* magazine wrote in retrospect that 'The End' "remains an audacious combination of impeccable musicianship (some of Densmore's finest moments), genuine poetry, and psychedelic bullshit".27 In a review in the *New York Magazine*, Richard Goldstein, one of the first to praise the song, wrote that the song "revolves around a theme of travel", both physical and spiritual, and "builds to a realization of mood rather than a sequence of events", opening with "visions of collapsing peace and harmony" and ending with "violent death".28 Densmore wrote that the song, "loosely based on classical Indian ragas", built from the subdued first two-thirds of the "hypnotic droning sound" to a "musical orgasm" in the "turbulent finale."29 Yet there is, as Goldstein also wrote, a danger of interpreting a song like 'The End' so academically because the song's value is "its freedom to imply".30 And, in his review of the debut album for the *Los Angeles Times*, Pete Johnson summarily states a common reaction, that 'The End' showed how bored Morrison "can sound as he recites singularly simple over-elaborated psychedelic *non sequiturs* and fallacies".31

"While the transport of the Dionysiac state, with its suspension of all the ordinary barriers of existence, lasts, it carries with it a Lethean element in which everything that has been experienced by the individual is drowned. This chasm of oblivion separates the quotidian reality from the Dionysiac. But as soon as that quotidian reality enters consciousness once more it is viewed with loathing, and the consequence is an ascetic, abulic state of mind. In this sense Dionysiac man might be said to resemble Hamlet: both have looked deeply into the true nature of things, they have understood and are now loath to act. They realize that no action of theirs can work any change in the eternal condition of things... Understanding kills action, for in order to act we require the veil of illusion... What, both in the case of Hamlet and of Dionysiac man, overbalances any motive leading to action, is not reflection but understanding, the apprehension of truth and its terror... The truth once seen, man is aware everywhere of the ghastly absurdity of existence."

*Friedrich Nietzsche,*
*The Birth Of Tragedy (p. 51)*

"The waltz leading to catastrophe:
swirling to spangled airy skits,
on polished floors, into an abyss,
the minor notes always recalling
that man's destiny was ruled by ultimate darkness."

*Anais Nin,*
*The Spy in the House of Love (p. 35)*

Producer Paul Rothchild repeatedly offered this interpretation of the Oedial section of the song that presented theatre to him for the first time. He explained killing the father meant killing those things instilled in you but aren't of yourself and sexually conquering the mother meant returning to your essence which can't lie to you – an end of alien concepts and a beginning of personal concepts, which are themes of the classic Oedipal story.32

In a 1969 *Rolling Stone* interview with Jerry Hopkins, when asked what this song meant to him, Morrison replied the song meant something different every time he heard it – it began as a "simple goodbye song" and its imagery was "sufficiently complex and universal" to be almost anything to anybody.33 The song, like the song, 'When The Music's Over', which would close the second album, was honed out over many nights at the Whiskey-A-GoGo, and, as the story goes, the night when Morrison added the Oedipal section was the night the group was fired. Morrison said, in the Hopkins interview, that those two songs were "constantly changing free-form pieces" and were at the "height of their effect" when the group finally put them on record.34 Pichaske echoed Morrison's view, stating that 'The End' is probably "better music than poetry, better theatre than music", and allowed The Doors to lyrically and musically perform the song as the whims of a particular performance moved them, "a script to be interpreted and reinterpreted, with much room for adlibbing".35 Morrison still is searching for the other side in a desperate land. We have become estranged, "lost in a Roman wilderness of pain", and it may be just as insane waiting for nature's purifying summer rain in this Western civilization built on the ancient foundations of Rome. Desperation leads Morrison to take the hand of a stranger – "the end".

The ensuing hint that danger waits near the "edge of town" heightens the need to take a chance by going to the edges of the world of man. Once there, Morrison moves into journey motifs, expressing his need to seek freedom, to ride "the King's highway", to "ride the snake" to the "ancient lake", to go west, to answer the call of "the blue bus". The archetypal image of the west (the end of a journey) and the Biblical symbol of the snake (the agent responsible for the expulsion from Eden) add to the growing undertone of death – and life's duality, the snake suggesting its often ancient meaning of how to return to the waters of life, the ancient lake. *Circus* magazine printed the following quote from Morrison about snakes: "We evolved from snakes and I used to see the universe as a mammoth peristaltic snake. I used to see all the people and objects and landscapes as little pictures on the facets of their skins."36

The mood shifts to a calm, eerie look at the archetypal evil in man as we take a journey with a killer down a hall in a place no longer a sanctuary – the home. Putting the killer's actions into a realistic and practical setting (awaking before dawn and putting boots on), Morrison then deviously makes the transition to the philosophical level with the human archetype of taking a "face from the ancient gallery", an action that was literally done on the ancient Greek stage. But the calmness of the mask is shattered by the emotional release when the killer completes his journey: telling his father he wants to kill him and then confronting his mother with a good ol' Morrison orgasmic scream. Bootlegs offer a more lucid, less-censored version of the obvious. In order to truly cut the ties to the past, Morrison symbolically severs or conquers ties with his parentage.

"Oedipus, his father's murderer, his mother's lover, solver of the Sphinx's riddle! What is the meaning of this triple fate? ...the same man who solved the riddle of nature (the ambiguous Sphinx) must also...break the consecrated tables of the natural order. It is as though the myth whispered to us that wisdom, and especially Dionysiac wisdom, is an unnatural crime, and that whoever, in pride of knowledge, hurls nature into the abyss of destruction, must himself experience nature's disintegration."

*Friedrich Nietzsche,*
*The Birth Of Tragedy (p. 61)*

After this, the music and Morrison move out on the edge of tension of being alive, of taking a chance to ride the king's highway, to journey to the end of the night, to break on through to the other side, to swim in mystery, to take a moonlight drive. Pichaske saw Morrison urging "a bus ride to the subconscious and to oblivion, to self-knowledge and mythic terrors, to fucking and killing brothers and sisters and fathers and mothers".37 Morrison is coaxing his "baby" to take a chance on "the blue bus", the colour suggestive of the blues tradition The Doors drew heavily upon, but a journey The Doors had only begun, evident in a response by a still quite young and not as reflective Densmore when asked what "blue bus" implied: "I never even tried to think of what in the hell the 'blue bus' means. It's just there. I can see where someone who wasn't familiar with this music would want to say, 'Now what does that damned "blue bus" thing mean?' You can tell them that if the guys in the band don't even know what it means, they don't have to worry about it."38

Taking a chance of living isn't going to be an easy ride, evident in the disquieting cacophonic climax of music with Morrison's masked chanting of "kill, kill, kill, kill".

But in the end, there is resignation. Morrison, constantly searching for sanctuary, symbolically finds it by setting free the one sure companion of life he now recognizes – death, "the end". His searching through life's "laughter" and "soft lies" has ended, and the double connotative meaning of "soft lies" underscores how the false conformity to a superficial life makes sanctuary in love (or sex) impossible. His searching through freedom has ended – his travelling through the nights to die in an attempt to be alive, to reach realms of bliss, realms of light, to reach the bright midnight. But "the end" is neither his love nor the other side; it is just a friend, the stranger's hand he needs in this desperate land. Since the other attempts have fallen short of ultimate freedom, "the end" is the last avenue to travel in order to break through to the other side.

Just as the closing song, 'The End', has built through a series of images and themes to a realization, so has the album. There weaves through the album the modern-day generic theme of alienation – a realization brought to a focal point in the last song. Unlike the huge hit single that characterized the times, 'I'm A Believer', written by Neil Diamond and sung by The Monkees, The Doors don't believe and trust the world which surrounds them with "soft lies". Their artistic imagination draws a picture which not only reflects the troubles of living in such times, but also tries to make sense of a world that doesn't make sense.

The establishment says they have the world neatly ordered, and Morrison strips away plastic facades hiding festering wounds of a society wandering in a "Roman wilderness of pain", its people desperately needing some stranger's hand while stumbling in neon grooves. The world is too perfect and has been refined of the beauty and mystery of life: our streets have become fields which never die. The times are those of Mahagonny.

The Pop culture offered freedom and brotherly love, but Morrison's images of the Pop culture offer little comfort: the Twentieth Century Fox is plastic, the Crystal Ship is fragile and expensive, and romance is short, quick and noncommittal.

In this initial flash of The Doors' artistic vision, modern life has destroyed Eden – destroyed the traditional sanctuaries of the home and of love and destroyed a coherent outlook which gave life a sense of meaning. Morrison's viewpoint was act now, search later. Life is a journey, and you live it now or miss it. The journey on the modern American Appian Way is detached and gives a false sense of security, but any journey will be painful. Life is pain, love is pain, and fear prevents people from experiencing life, from accepting what The Doors ultimately come to realize, that we are all "riders on the storm".

# chapter 2

# strange days in the summer of love

"Second, genuine art must at the same time
transcend the revolution it expresses.
It cannot be so submerged in the movement
that it forfeits its essentially subversive role.
The revolution itself must be subjected
to constant critical review;
hence, the canons of authenticity
include a fundamental estrangement of art
from its cultural setting."

*Robert G. Pielke,*
*You Say You Want A Revolution:*
*Rock Music In American Culture (p. 17)*


"We were never really protagonists of the flower movement;
in fact, we were the complete opposite...
love and peace and everything's great –
that was only half of the side of the coin.
We were providing a glimpse of the other side as well."

*Robby Krieger,*
*"No One Here Gets Out Alive: The Doors Story",*
*Jim Ladd's radio special,*
*The Inner View*

SIDE 1
Strange Days
You're Lost Little Girl
Love Me Two Times
Unhappy Girl
Horse Latitudes
Moonlight Drive

SIDE 2
People Are Strange
My Eyes Have Seen You
I Can't See Your Face In My Mind
When The Music's Over

The Summer of Love. 1967. From the West Coast, the Summer of Love had swept across the country, flower power and hippies spreading seeds of a brotherhood of love, peace and harmony on the swirling winds of a magical tension. Vietnam was polarizing the political and social climate of America, a tangible tip to the tension wrought by the Cold War and the potentially high-stakes entanglement with conflicts elsewhere in the world. The June six-day war in the Middle East where Israel made shambles of its Arab neighbours' military abilities was a blood stain compared to the blood bath that would begin in July with the civil war in Nigeria after the secession by Biafra, Nigeria's eastern region. The destabilized governments of Nigeria and Congo, Africa's two most populous nations, struggled with armed conflict – Nigeria, a civil war; Congo, a regional revolt lead by white mercenaries. The internal resolve to resist the military junta lead by Colonel George Papdopoulas that seized control of Greece in an April coup faded in December with the flight of King Constantine II and his family to Rome. Tension abounded throughout the world, though America had yet to taste how the violence of frustration would draw blood in its heartland. Nonetheless, the American youth's brotherhood of love had grown alongside a bizarre accordance of dissident and macabre times. The utopian vision of a brotherhood of love and peace characterized by the Summer of Love in 1967, to blossom in its fullest at Woodstock two years later, was about to be cracked by harsh political realities of 1968 before being shattered by the closing of the Sixties.

Promoted as a Gathering of the Tribes, a quintessential hippie happening in the Polo Field of San Francisco's Golden Gate Park in January opened this magical year of 1967. Known as "The Human Be-In", the reporting press largely misses the pun on human be-in (human being), making the same word connection as the political sit-in, and the word love-in and hippie begin appearing with considerable regularity as labels to attach to this youth movement. For the January 20 edition of the underground newspaper, *The Berkeley BARB* (Berkeley is a suburb of San Francisco), Ed Denson wrote an article, "What Happened at the Hippening", and, though he clearly liked the idea of all these folks gathering for a "Human Be-In", Denson kept repeating his theme of the irresponsibility of the organizers not knowing "how to organize on a scale that has 10,000 people anywhere doing anything". Yet to many the gathering of thousands became a bench mark of the emerging youth subculture that people could spontaneously gather and get along and that anything was possible. However, the swearing in of Lester Maddox, also in January, as the new governor of Georgia indicated that certain parts of America still valued a man who, three years earlier in defiance of the Civil Rights Act of 1964, passed out axe handles to the white customers in his restaurant so they could resist any desegregation of his public place of business.

But the seeds of the times had taken root and sprouted, and the summer opened in mid-June with a three-day festival of music, love, flowers and people, known as the Monterey Pop Festival, just south of San Francisco. Many relatively unknown rock 'n' roll artists were featured: The Jimi Hendrix Experience, Jefferson Airplane, Big Brother & The Holding Company (with Janis Joplin), The Who, Otis Redding, Ravi Shankar, Hugh Masekela, and others.[1] The first festival of its kind, Monterey strengthened the growing sense of community among youth and the alternative subculture. But in July, violent riots in the black sections of Detroit and Newark erupted.

The Beatles gave this flourishing rock culture widely acclaimed artistic authenticity with the release of their album, *Sgt. Peppers Lonely Hearts Club Band*. Arthur Penn followed with the release of his film, *Bonnie And Clyde*, starring Warren Beatty and Faye Dunaway as two ill-fated, searching young souls who are swept into a cinematic waltz of violence, bullets, and blood. Marshall McLuhan delivered, *The Medium Is The Massage*, a book that became the gospel of McLuhan's relentless preaching on how our newfangled technological communications impact society, and Ira Levin's novel integrating the evil side of witchcraft, *Rosemary's Baby*, shocked an American public who made the book a bestseller and basis of an equally successful subsequent 1968 movie. On the first Monday in October, Thurgood Marshall began his tenure as a U.S. Supreme Court Justice, the first black to do so. The magazine that would embody and nurture the emerging youth subculture, *Rolling Stone*, first appeared in November. A 17-year-old British model, Twiggy, became the fashion image, an unrealistic blend of pencil-thinness and wide-eyed vacuousness. In December, Dr. Christian Barnard performed the first successful human heart transplant in Cape Town, South Africa, though the patient died later that month.

Released during the all important Christmas movie season, Mike Nichols' film, *The Graduate*, showcased Dustin Hoffman as Benjamin Bradock, a confused, quietly rebellious college graduate whose rejection of getting a job with the college degree, adulterous affair with Mrs. Robinson, and subsequent obsessive attraction to Elaine, Mr. and Mrs. Robinson's daughter, undermine the creditability of what was the programmed American way of growing-up. The absolutely silent scenes of the University of California campus at Berkeley underscore the closing scenes when Katharine Ross, as Elaine, before running off with Ben from her own wedding, tells Ann Bancroft, who plays her mother, she won't make the same mistake mom made. The film closes with Elaine in her ruffled white wedding gown and the deshelved Ben sitting in an uneasy quiet in the back of a city bus travelling a scheduled route. The soundtrack of Simon & Garfunkel songs (i.e. 'Sounds Of Silence') further augments the theme that this spontaneous flow of desires and energy doesn't naturally head toward utopia.

The Doors' second album not only mirrors the strange days of the Sixties up to that Summer of Love in 1967, but also augurs the estranged times to follow. With expanded recording capabilities at Elektra studios (the advent of eight-track technology meant, as Ray exclaimed in a *The Source* radio special, "We can overdub?!"), The Doors recorded their second album, *Strange Days*, which was released in October 1967. The songs on this album also came from the repertoire of songs composed during the group's so-called acid fertility period when they were free from commercial demands and developed their material in front of a live audience. The complexity and quality of themes in *Strange Days* rival the artistic imagination with which The Beatles and their *Sergeant Pepper's Lonely Hearts Club Band* had revolutionized the music world a few months before at the start of the Summer of Love. Before 1967 was over, Frank Zappa released his second album, *Absolutely Free*, and the Moody Blues reemerged with *Days Of Future Past*, both, like *Sgt. Peppers* and *Strange Days*, explicitly designed albums unified around an underlining theme of expressing what lay under the shadows of the flowering youthful ideals of change and an alternative culture.

*Strange Days* doesn't offer a cozy refuge of soothing ideals or of placid, complacent sensory comfort; The Doors portray a reality of alienated people and strange days. We have become chained to a mechanized world, segmented by the clock and an alien landscape, a world separated from unknown forces that no longer fit into the smoothly running machinery of the modern way of life. In the Sixties, personal identity started becoming focused and then fixed upon numbers: social security number, phone number, driver's licence, credit card numbers, insurance policy numbers... and the list has continued to snowball. People hold onto chains – either of an established way or of a new vision – because those chains represent security and identity, but The Doors perceived either set of chains as false because neither confirmed the individual's existence or allowed passage to the "other side". Their artistic vision reflects little coherence in a culture building upon disquieting plastic images that are detached from the organic nature of life and that breed uneasy despair in even the most basic sanctuaries of life – the house and love.

Like a prism which refracts white light into a rainbow of colours, this album refracts a spectrum of the afflictions of the times. Within the album underlying themes weave together to reflect the nature of strange days: the despairing effects of existing under the shadows of the confusion of the Vietnam War and the potential of a global holocaust; the despairing effects of being a rock group, of being artists, the harbingers of unwanted messages; the despairing effects of two lovers at odds with each other because trust cannot exist; and ultimately, the despairing effects of death – death of innocence, of trust, of love, of music, of sanctuary.

This album tells a story of strangers meeting strangers in strange surroundings. To Morrison, the values of the times offered attire only for acting out a role, evident in an interview with Lizze James: he explained people trade reality for a role and give up their "ability to feel, and in exchange, put on a mask."2 Society molded individuals to be actors, the individual performing what was to be expected and acting out roles in attempts to find personal happiness. Hence, the album's cover picture which wraps around the front and the back reflects this theme: a one-point perspective of carnival-like characters performing in a dreary enclosure of a side street walled in on three sides with the fourth side sealed off by the eye of the camera.

Why make such an album, an album – as Sugerman and Hopkins wrote in *No One Here Gets Out Alive* – not as strange as the first album but still quite a "catalogue of psychic jolts and pains"?3 In response to the question, which album expressed best what The Doors were all about, producer Rothchild replied that *Strange Days* was "bulls-eye" – the album musically said everything they were trying to say and had some of Morrison's best poetry.4 Morrison told Michael Cuscuna of *Down Beat* that he was proud of this album because it told a story and that many people didn't realize what the group was doing, but that eventually this album would get the recognition it deserved.5

"It is our peculiar modern weakness to see all primitive

esthetic phenomena in too complicated and abstract a way.
Metaphor, for the authentic poet, is not a figure of rhetoric but
a representative image standing concretely before him in lieu
of a concept... We all talk about poetry so abstractly because
we all tend to be indifferent poets. At bottom the esthetic
phenomenon is quite simple: all one needs in order to be a
poet is the ability to have a lively action going on before one
continually, to live surrounded by hosts of spirits. To be a
dramatist all one needs is the urge to transform oneself and
speak out of strange bodies and souls."

> *Friedrich Nietzsche,*
> *The Birth Of Tragedy (p. 55)*

"Whereas the surrealist watches and waits for the
unpredictable manifestation of the unconscious, Rimbaud
violates his mind and ravishes the images as they form. His
poetic secrets are the result of a spiritual rape and conquest.
His art is the seizure of his own reality."

> *Wallace Fowlie,*
> *Rimbaud (A Critical Study) (p. 75)*

"[Morrison] was possessed by a vision,
by a madness,
by a rage to live,
by an all consuming fire to make art."

> *Ray Manzarek, in the video,*
> *Tribute To Jim Morrison*

Reactions to the album did reflect a lack of understanding the story
The Doors tell in the album, as the album was buried by both
comparisons to the fantastically successful first album and reactions to
the group's, especially Morrison's, persona. A 1981 review in *Creem*

offered this universal appraisal of the album in hindsight, stating that The Doors probably had too much to live up to: "Even without the instant-standard kiss of death of 'Light My Fire', there was simply a lotta promise (or threats) inherent on the debut."6

There were those who did perceive the artistic imagination of The Doors. The same review in *Creem* also said the album's "most endearing (and enduring) qualities" were its ominous themes of people being "lost, strange, confused, alienated, friendless. The Doors were peering into the sin-filled souls of hippies everywhere and offering no comfort."7 Eric Van Lustbader of *Circus* magazine recognized that the album's storyline of people "trying desperately to reach each other through the choking haze of drugs and artificial masks" builds upon the "images and characters in a series of vignettes", the whole becoming more visible as the album's story unfolds.8

By now the sound of The Doors had become distinct. In a review of this album, Steven Lowe of the classical music orientated *High Fidelity Magazine* wrote that The Doors' "sound" is unique in its relative freedom from overly distorted hurricanes of acoustical storms; they concentrate on producing a sort of undulating harmonic effect. Chords progress less by definite steps than by oozing in and out of focus.9

And so the music of this second album expresses how strange times create unfocused lives, and such is the whirlwind of strange days.

## SIDE ONE

The title cut, 'Strange Days', opens side one and swirls into an uneasy feeling that something is strange. On this song, Manzarek creates a restrained musical backdrop with the Moog synthesizer, one of its earliest uses in rock, according to Hopkins and Sugerman.10 The twang of the electronic voice processing which accents the hard syllables in Morrison's vocals effectively colours the strangeness the opening lyrics stake out, that "strange days" have found us by tracking us down. The day is when things are visible and known – but not these days, not these times. What has been suppressed behind soft lies and masks has become a hunter, tracking us down to expose and unravel the "casual joys" – the superficial delights – of our affluent society.

The Doors offer two choices: keep on playing the game or "find a new town", a new way to live. We can't retreat to the safety of a room, of home, of someone else's place of refuge; such traditional symbols of sanctuary harbour the same strangeness, because "strange rooms" are filled with "strange eyes". And Morrison intensifies this uneasy feeling when he sings about the hostess grinning as "her guests sleep from sinning". Sleep and ignore the sinning, or sleep in the comfort of sinning? No matter which, like the characters imprisoned in the cauldron of divine and hellish images of the Eagles' 'Hotel California', the guests still don't recognize the sinning for what it is. Like Old Testament prophets who signalled the coming of bad times when they spoke of sin, The Doors also warn that such acceptance of sinning alienates an understanding of ourselves.

The suppressed unknown returns to track us down, and confusion pervades us because we don't know how to deal with the unknown. Strange days create "strange hours" – a recurrent theme in many Doors' lyrics of the chains the clock imposes upon us. People "linger alone", with "bodies confused" and "memories misused" that are unable to make sense of our deep psychic past which is being suppressed. The past is becoming muddled memories with no sincere structure through which one generation can transmit to the next the knowledge of what it means being human. And we rapidly drift from strange days to an equally "strange night of stone".

Can we find safety in love? Not if bodies are confused.

Can we find safety in the past? Not if memories are misused.

Can we find safety in the mysterious? Not if the night is made of stone or if being stoned delivers us to a state as strange as the one from which we are running.

In such strange times, giving trust in any relationship is difficult, if not impossible. The next song, 'You're Lost Little Girl', begins a story which transcends more than an estranged relationship between Morrison and a lover. With a sense of high-handed compassion, the music and lyrics of this Krieger song create a melancholic, yet cynical tone, a mood Terry Rompers of *Trouser Press* magazine pointed out that is intensified by the loneliness of the minor-mode verses.11 *L.A. Free Press* writer Gene Youngblood wrote that melody's buoyancy contrasts to lyrics' weird sadness.12 Densmore detailed how Morrison's vocal has "a tranquil mood, like the aftermath of a large explosion", probably due to Rothchild's idea of Jim's girlfriend Pam performing oral sex on Jim before he sang.13

Morrison peers into the soul of the fashionably lean Twentieth Century Fox and asks a confused and lost child if she can tell him who she is. Having lost her identity, she is as estranged as the society in which she lives. But the way to find herself remains within her, a recurrent theme in The Doors' artistic vision that everybody has the knowledge and power within to break out of "strange days". Though she may say, "Impossible", and deny her own estrangement and sinning, Morrison sings that she knows "what to do".

As a way to find oneself, rock 'n' roll and The Doors invoke not only music but also love. Since the two lovers now know each other, in the third song, with Robby's commanding guitar far more confident, Jim urgently sings to his lost, little girl: 'Love Me Two Times'. Robby's song pulsates with, as Richard Riegel wrote in *Creem*, "Densmore's frenzied drumming and Krieger's sweet-sour guitar hook".14

Though surrounded by strange days, Jim urges his lost, little girl that in love they can find the rhythms of life. How good is the love? Jim sings for her to love him two times to last him through the week. But is there sanctuary in this love? No, for Jim weaves through the song Robby's lyric for his lover to love him two times because he is going away. Although Morrison drops the "s" on "times" to make the lyric sound like, "love me two time", he sings of his need to be loved twice, one for tomorrow and one for today. Love today for tomorrow because the future is uncertain, so characteristic of the plastic relationships, personal and nonpersonal, of strange days. The pulsating music and urgent lyrics create an undercurrent of a short-lived, purely sexual gratification as a way to stay afloat in the ocean of strange days. Accused of being written strictly for pure Pop (hence, commercial) reasons, the urgent and pulsating song breaks the album's solemn tone, yet it doesn't skip a beat in its message: in strange times, sanctuary isn't easily found in love.

The next song, 'Unhappy Girl', continues the story of the lost, little girl. The song's oozing tones weave in and out, suggesting that someone is out-of-sync with herself. As Sugerman and Hopkins noted, Manzarek played "the entire song backward", and Densmore created a "soft-suck rhythm sound" by playing "backward hi-hat".15 Being lost creates loneliness and unhappiness, and the unhappy girl has retreated to a sanctuary, where she is "playing solitaire" and also "playing warden" to her soul. She has locked her soul into a prison of her "own device". Concerned that she is crying, Morrison challenges her to tear away the web she has woven, to "saw through" the bars and "melt" her self-made prison. Saw implies action, not being passive about apparent limitations, about her bars. Saw is also the past tense of see: just see through the bars. Instead of being fashionably cool, warm-up and melt away the plastic facade.

Sequentially through the song, Morrison sings of the girl being "locked", "caught", and "dying" in a prison of her own device. Past tense to progressive: locked, caught, dying...but not yet dead. Imprison your soul in something you aren't, and you begin to die. But you can still experience life, can still "swim in mystery" – the answer the lost, little girl knows but doesn't recognize. Morrison refuses to become locked in this cell with his estranged lover. If loving two times hasn't helped her, then he invites her to swim in mystery – the moonlight drive.

'Horse Latitudes' leads into 'Moonlight Drive' and portrays both individuals and a world out-of-sync, a disturbed world on the ocean, caught in the "muted nostril agony" of dying. In *No One Here Gets Out Alive*, Hopkins and Sugerman wrote that Jim penned this poem in his high school years after he saw "a lurid paperback cover showing horses being jettisoned from a Spanish galleon that was becalmed in the Sargasso Sea."16 Sargasso Sea is an area of relatively still water in the north Atlantic Ocean northeast of the West Indies and lies chiefly between 25°-35° north latitude and 40°-70° west longitude. (Horse Latitudes is the name for the ocean regions located between 30° and 35° latitude in the northern and southern hemispheres.) The Sargasso Sea is a region of deep blue waters that are relatively clear and warm due to various currents of the North Atlantic which rotate around the margins of this region, notably the Gulf Stream on the west and south. The area is also abundant with brown gulfweed, a sort of seaweed that clusters in huge patches resembling meadows on the water. These peculiarities gave rise to the legends from the tales brought back by New World sailors that the Sargasso Sea was where galleons could become entangled in a snare of thickly matted islands of seaweed which were inhabited by huge monsters of the deep.

Though science and our objectivity of experience has demarcated why the Sargasso Sea is what it is, Morrison readily taps into that sea of imagination that ebbs through humans in his rendition of life's becalmed waters.

In the opening lines, the lyrics and swelling electronic confusion conjure up a strange, untranquil setting on the sea. Though the "still sea" is "sullen" and "aborted", void and dead in the eyes and minds of the sailors, the calm waters are alive and threatening, conspiring in "armour". The ocean of life's known and unknown currents has been stilled by "strange days", and those currents of life have become "sullen" (unhappy) and "aborted" (unable to enter with full maturity the sea of life). Thus, man's myth-making creates tiny monsters, something which is alive. Meaningful life, "true sailing", has been suppressed and denied. The crystal ship has become far more fragile than blissful. David Pichaske in his insightful book, *The Poetry Of Rock: The Golden Years*, noted the rhythmically static last line of the first stanza echoes that "true sailing is dead", but man must try to go on, in sailing and in life.17 Thus sacrifices are made. Men toss horses (life, an unaccepted spiritual side of life, or whatever other broad meaning related to man's psyche you wish) to the calm waters (death, the void) in hopes both to appease (to conform to) the tiny monsters and to lighten the ship and take advantage of what little wind there is, to get back in-sync with "true sailing".

With poetic precision, Morrison describes the "awkward instant" of the agony of drowning as he screams the words till they are drowned in emotional disorder and electronic feedback. The progression of adjectives and verbs mirrors the sealing over of souls by the still sea:

first they bob up and gulp for air, they become poised for a delicate moment, they see the choice(s) they have to make to survive in strange times, and then they consent to submerging, to being sealed over by the sea and the tiny monsters.

To do anything but go down might be considered sinning; the sailors on a still sea (people in strange days) deliberately jettisoned their sacrifices so to conform to the existing situation (to become more socially acceptable). They have become "carefully refined" for the tiny monsters, for those who are a part of the still sea.

If life gets out-of-sync, man breeds a few of his own tiny monsters. Pichaske wrote, "The sea kills sailing; man kills the horse."18 An ongoing process for The Doors, they occasionally bob back up above the surface of the sea of "strange days" which surround them and see a lot of horses, hence life, being jettisoned and sealed over "in mute nostril agony". Morrison then wooingly urges his lost, unhappy girl to come swim in mystery on a moonlight drive down by this same ocean where men have cast horses overboard.

How more appropriately to end side one of the album than with a cozy tryst on the beach under the moonlight?

Riegel wrote that one of the "finest heart-stops in recorded rock" is when the "gloomily romantic, itchy-crotch 'Moonlight Drive' suddenly slithers out of 'Horse Latitudes' choked raucousness".19 In a 1972 interview by John Tobler with the three surviving Doors, Manzarek said this song was the first song they recorded as The Doors, "but it was also the weakest" and they left it off the first album.20 In a subsequent interview with Pete Fornatale of *Musician* magazine, Manzarek further explained that the song was a "funkier, bluesier kind of song" at first, like a James Brown or Otis Redding song; but while recording the song for the second album, the group "fooled around for a while" before Ray said, "I got it – we're gonna do a tango... a rock tango."21

In this rock tango, Morrison offers the mystery that could free the unhappy girl from the prison of her own device. But the sinisterly laughing guitar in the background draws you into a rather disquieting love song. It is an invitation to taste more than the forbidden fruit: we aren't just in the backseat of Bob Seger's car out in the trusty woods "learning night moves"; Morrison sings of being out of the car and returning back to the darker mysteries of going down to the oceanside.

The lyrics appeal to the imagery of drugs, sex, and three universal sources of mystery: the moon (the night sky), the ocean, and the forests (which become the "wet forests", the seaweed). How can we "swim to the moon" save on a drug trip? How can we "climb through the tide" unless we are floating? How can we "penetrate" the sinisterly seductive evening "the city sleeps to hide" unless we explore the unknown?

Though Morrison echoes the "strange night of stone" image from 'Strange Days', the night for the 'Moonlight Drive' is alive: a time to swim in mystery, to step into a river of sensations and surrender to those "waiting worlds" that will be lapping at their sides. But Morrison croons that when she reaches out to hold him once they begin swimming in this mystery, he can't be her guide. Don't expect trust when relationships are based on lust and lies and masks, and not on love.

Morrison and his lover swim up to the moon (the great symbol of love and mystery) as they fall through "wet forests". The wet forests are more than just seaweed; they are the forests of both the night and the ocean, of our dark, mysterious inner self. And once past the wet forests, once Morrison breaks through to the other side, his tone no longer wooingly moans, but becomes seductively sinister, wooing her to go for a "little ride" down to the ocean side where they can get "real close" and "real tight" and "drown tonight". They have broken through to the psychic memories that are being suppressed, going down both in the backseat and through the wet forests to discover their inner selves; but the bodies are still confused, the memories are still misused, and the times are still strange.

## SIDE TWO

'People Are Strange' opens side two and restates the opening theme of side one: being lost in an estranged society. In 'Strange Days', Manzarek's Moog synthesizer provides the restrained, uneasy backdrop. In this song, Krieger's guitar moans and slithers around the lyrical portrait of estrangement. During a time guided by the visions of JFK's New Frontier, of LBJ's Great Society, and of the Woodstock Nation's brotherhood of love, Morrison sang of a painful reality that when you are a stranger, "people are strange".

The phrasing of the first stanza pauses on disquieting words: strange, stranger, ugly, alone, wicked, unwanted, uneven, and down. When people can't trust relationships and feel alone, then people become strange and faces seem ugly. When you can't find love or compassion, when you're not wanted, then women look wicked. When you are down, streets become "uneven", just like the paths one tries to follow in life.

To a stranger in a strange land, everyone seems threatening. Faces that come out of, in this song, the symbolically estranged rain offer no sense of familiarity or security. And people don't remember your name, the stamp of alienation – loss of identity, which becomes a constant companion, at times seemingly your only friend. Just as there is little security in these threatening faces when you are alone, so there is when you have seen a lover "free from disguise", of which Morrison sings in the next song.

'My Eyes Have Seen You' returns to the theme of the lost, unhappy girl. After pointing out how she is lost and unhappy, then offering her the invitation to swim in mystery, and taking her down on a moonlight drive, Morrison has seen her free of her disguise. The lyrics are simple and direct: there is no fancy image manipulating by the poet to disguise what he perceives, and Manzarek replaces the haunting organ with a crisp piano. Morrison literally may be describing somebody preparing for a shooting session under a camera's eyes, hence the "television skies" and the photographing of the soul "on an endless roll". But the lyrics are too stripped down to be specific; in this bare state the song evokes a broader meaning than just some isolated event.

The invitation in the first stanza to "stand in your door" and to "show me some more" isn't the same invitation Morrison croons in 'Moonlight Drive'. He has discovered there is more to be seen in the lost, unhappy girl than just taking her down to swim in mystery. Though the city may hide "under television skies", he has seen her free from her disguise, a very appropriate image in a town – and a society – composed of people creating illusions. The lyrics, "photograph your soul" and "memorize your alleys", suggest the alley has become part of her soul – a symbol of the urban landscape, be it a refuge of the dark side of life or a place void of the life of the streets. Although these images recall the image of "memories misused" in 'Strange Days', Morrison has seen beyond the plastic image captured on film.

The empathetic music of 'My Eyes Have Seen You' shifts to a melancholic, lost sound in 'I Can't See Your Face In My Mind'. In *IT* (*International Times*), an underground newspaper from London, Ross Hunter noted Morrison's "curious rather deadpan voice sets the mood, a kind of sad and painful truthfulness."22 After having seen the lost, little girl free from disguise, Jim discovers he can't remember her, can't picture her face in his mind. Has she returned to her "disguise", to a prison of her own device? In strange times, intimate relationships become void of any sort of union other than the very basic physical one which underlies the themes in 'Love Me Two Times' and 'Moonlight Drive'. If love merely fulfills a physical need and not a desire to share and a willingness to trust, if bodies are confused and memories are misused, what is there to remember?

Throughout the song, Jim keeps the images short, again creating a sense of meaning beyond just a single person or event, and the pregnant pauses after each stanza add to the song's haunting tone. The image of "carnival dogs" consuming lines suggests a montage of images: the carnival is a time to be something you normally aren't, and dogs are both man's best friend and a derogatory synonym; yet these are carnivorous carnival canines who, in the true American way, consume lines – lines of cocaine or of a memory. And there is the ever-present Morrison backwards pun of god and dog. The larger carnival of which the two lovers are participants is devouring any clear memory Jim has had of his lover. The lines of her face are erased as the song oozes along to the sandpaper sound of the maracas in the background. Drugs may do bizarre things to the mind, but society can play mind games just as bizarre.

The Doors' love songs often portray the inability of love in an alienated society to provide sanctuary because people don't trust or face up to each other, evident when Jim deadpans for his baby not to cry and not look at him with her eyes. In 'Unhappy Girl', her unhappiness touches Jim; but now that he has seen her free of her disguise, he cowers from any emotional attachment because he can't fulfill the relationship. He doesn't want to have to face those eyes; instead Jim sings that he hasn't been able to "find the right lie". Thus the times remain estranged as Jim sings about "insanity's horse" adorning the sky. The mute nostril agony of the drowning horse in 'Horse Latitudes' surfaces again, symbolizing a cloud of insanity.

The ironic end of this estranged relationship with the lost little girl is the Polaroid instamatic image which concludes the song as Jim croons for his baby not to cry and he won't need her picture till they say goodbye. Morrison can't remember her, but he'll take a photograph which can only capture the outer disguise to remind him who she was. The plastic memory of film – a real-life metaphor that dominates our culture.

> "...melodies reproduce the very soul and essence as it were, without the body. This deep relation which music bears to the true nature of all things also explains the fact that suitable music played to any event or surrounding seems to disclose to us its most secret meaning and appears as the most accurate and distinct commentary upon it... [M]usic is distinguished from all the other arts by the fact that it is not a copy of the phenomenon, or, more accurately, the adequate objectivity of the will, but is the direct copy of the will itself... We might, therefore, just as well call the world embodied music as embodied will."
>
> *Friedrich Nietzsche,*
> *The Birth Of Tragedy (p. 99)*

With sanctuary in a relationship disillusioned by strange days, The Doors turn to a source of refuge which is the cornerstone of Pop

THE DOORS – ARTISTIC VISION

culture: music. But what happens 'When The Music's Over'? When society has estranged the one art which appeals directly to the soul, when the rhythms of life have been shut down, then strange days become strange nights and faces become ugly. When the music is over, we drift into a "Persian night" and voices deep within cry out for a saviour to save us. The album closes with a final curtain that when the music is over, then "turn out the lights".

When a relationship is going smoothly, troubles seem so far away, as Paul McCartney sings in 'Yesterday'; but when things go sour, then the music stops playing and it seems as if someone has turned out the lights.

This song, like 'The End' which closes The Doors' first album, builds through a series of moods rather than a structured story line. Or, as Rompers suggested, the song winds "through a convoluted set of observations, instructions and invocations" that lead "to a highly charged release".23

The invocation at the opening of the song, like music, evokes one to "dance on fire". In a broad sense, fire represents being alive, free to experience forbidden and mysterious aspects of life. But when the music stops, so does the fire of life. Morrison wails that music is our only friend till the end, and a distorted guitar solo and cacophony of disorder follow. Morrison rejects the promise of the great banquet, wanting to cancel his "subscription to the Resurrection", the reward of the hard work and sacrifice ethic of either the American economic-social system or the Christian after-life. Instead he wants his "credentials" sent to the "house of detention". The "house of detention" recalls the earlier prison image of one's own device, except this is society's prison – or rather house of sanctuary for those who don't fit in, who have sinned.

66

# chapter 3

# waiting for the muse, waiting for the doors, waiting for the sun

"It is easily understood why such a feeble culture hates a strong art: it is afraid of being destroyed by it."

*Friedrich Nietzsche,*
*The Birth Of Tragedy (pp. 122-23)*

SIDE 1
Hello, I Love You
Love Street
Not To Touch The Earth
Summer's Almost Gone
Wintertime Love
The Unknown Soldier

SIDE 2
Spanish Caravan
My Wild Love
We Could Be So Good Together
Yes, The River Knows
Five To One

The Sixties were ascending to the fruition of the seeds planted in the late 1950s and early 1960s: Woodstock, Altamont, Vietnam and the war protest, the killing of college students, the ecological movement, the assassination of leaders who had dreams of brotherhood, the political reality of American democracy, and ultimately, the deaths of rock stars burning their life's flames out on the edge.

Events on the larger world stage provided background for the irrevocable path of these forces. The spirit of violence and confrontation had intensified across the planet. The Middle East seethed under a tenuous equilibrium in the aftermath of the 1967 Six-Day War as commando raids, artillery shelling, and air strikes accompanied public reprisals and threats. The brutal civil war in Nigeria that would last till January 1970 forced into the rest of the world's sensibilities the stark visual images of starving Biafran refugees, mostly innocent children. A substantial threat, at least socially, to the hard-line dictates of the power mongrels in Moscow emerged with the succession of Alexander Dubcek, a progressive Communist, as President of Czechoslovakia in January 1968. After suspending censorship, the Czech government began a liberalization of political rights Western Europe and America took for granted. In August, Soviet forces with support from other Warsaw Pact countries (Bulgaria, East Germany, Hungary and Poland) invaded Czechoslovakia to suppress "dangerous counter-revolutionary forces". The Soviet invasion of Czechoslovakia to squash this movement towards a more liberal and freer society and to reestablish the status quo did little to deter the growing impatience of the American establishment to quell the rising anti-war protests and calls for social equality. As a reminder of America's other unresolved "war", the Korean Conflict of the 1950s, North Korea's seizure of the U.S. Navy intelligence ship, the *Pueblo*, in January took eleven months of tense negotiations before the harshly treated 82-man crew (one had been killed by the boarding party) were released just before Christmas.

During that interval, a seemingly iron-clad presidency fell in the March New Hampshire primary to the flickering hope of presidential candidate Minnesota Senator Eugene McCarthy. Though McCarthy would try, in vain, to sell peace as a political policy, it was Bobby Kennedy who, for a brief period, inflamed the sputtering fires of idealism before being snuffed out in June as Martin Luther King Jr. was in April. George Wallace, the former governor of Alabama, organized a third party, the American Independent Party, and ran for president on a platform that revived the South's strong states' rights attitude to return jurisdiction to state and local governments so they could resolve their own regional and local issues, like crime, property rights, voter eligibility, public school systems, and other issues, notably those being affected by federal civil rights legislation. Eventually Richard Nixon would rise like a phoenix from the ashes of his own political expiration. His approach of moderation could do little to alter the course of the swirling forces, and a restoring of the conservative status quo, with Ronald Reagan's ascension in 1981, would wait until after recovering from the Watergate fiasco. As 1968 began, at the top of the album charts sat The Beatles' *Magical Mystery Tour*, The Rolling Stones' *Their Satanic Majesties Request*, and The Monkees *Pisces, Aquarius, Capricorn & Jones, Ltd.* By summer the charts and airwaves were filled with the sounds of Simon & Garfunkel, riding the crest of success of the soundtrack to the movie, *The Graduate*. Stanley Kubrick's film *2001: A Space Odyssey* offered a sci-fi psychedelic voyage – though arduously threatened by the ominous computer HAL – toward humanity's next phase in evolution, while Rod Sterling's co-written *Planet Of The Apes* offered a more prosaic allegory with Kim Hunter and Roddy McDowall in costumes that were as technically realistic as the opening scenes of early ape-man in *2001*. Due to its unexpected commercial success in American movie theatres, *Blow-Up* elevated the stature of Italian film director Michelangelo Antonioni beyond the world of artsy film houses. Francis Ford Coppola, considered one of the upcoming talents still under the age of 30, hired as an assistant George Lucas, fresh from University of Southern California's film school. Besides the *Godfather* films, Coppola would also direct *Apocalypse Now* and use 'The End' to open the scenes of the Vietnam War in this 1979 movie. George Lucas would create something known as *Star Wars*. On American television during the 1967-68 season, the upstart and irreverent *Smothers Brothers* (which premeried in February 1967) did the unthinkable – beat the top rated show on television, *Bonanza*, the long running American icon that incorporated much of what is endearing in the American myth: the American West of the late 1800s, a tight-knit Cartwright family, and resolve to meet any challenge to their kingdom – the Ponderosa. However, constant squabbles with higher-ups at CBS lead to the demise of the *Smothers Brothers Comedy Hour* (the brothers were fired in April 1969), and the established *Bonanza* would survive at its 9 pm Sunday time slot through the 1971-72 season – the end of the Sixties.

The Pepsi generation was replacing the Geritol crowd; their innovative voices had revolutionized the arts, their numbers and pocketbooks were revolutionizing the market place, but political clout was still a couple of decades away. Underneath this tangible turmoil, the politically implemented "New Economics" was being tested. The canon of New Economics established a national goal of sustained economic growth that creates and maintains high employment, strong production, good paychecks, and increasing profits while keeping prices reasonably stable. We just needed to constantly adjust the combination of fiscal and monetary policies – a mantra of tax-spending-credit. When the economy was overheating, impose constraints to slow the expanding by increasing taxes to curb spending, lessening tax incentives to postpone investing, tightening government spending, and making credit more expensive to limit borrowing. When the economy was sputtering, introduce incentives to stimulate the rate of growth by cutting taxes and legislating tax incentives to encourage spending and investing, increasing government spending, and making credit easy and inexpensive to stimulate borrowing. And when the culturally appropriate rate of growth is reached, moderate all these polices. Modern life was a machine; we just needed to know how to fine tune it – and from which ideology to forge the tools. Futhermore, Atlantic Richfield (ARCO) and Standard Oil of New Jersey announced in 1968 that they had discovered oil underneath the North Slope of Alaska – what would be argued as fuel to keep the engine of this machine running and would fuel the heightening debate of how to define our relationship to our dwindling natural resources.

The whirlwind of forces was spiralling in heightened anticipation of its destined final fling of energies before subsiding to a gentle breeze, to a period of recollecting energies. In this whirlwind, The Doors found themselves inside a vacuum: they were a vital source of energy, yet they were cut off from those forces.

With meteoric success comes also the inevitable conflict – if not cession – of maintaining contact with the creative and social forces upon which the artist draws. At first, The Doors' self-imposed aloofness from society had fueled their creative flames. But now, the whirlwind of success had swept the group from their roots, isolating them and all but crushing the Muse. It is not coincidental that the third and especially the fourth albums drew upon as a creative source the very whirlwind of success – the idioms of the Pop culture, a shallow source of creativity compared to what had fuelled the artistic output on the first two albums. Hence, shaped by both imposed and self-imposed influences, the third and fourth albums were not as strong conceptually as the first two. Since the summer of 1967, The Doors found themselves on a mission to deliver their artistic vision now in mass demand. They had become public property to fill the demands of deliverance *en masse* to people living in strange days. But the shamanic spirit cannot be packaged and sold as snake oil to the grasping reach of a public stumbling in neon groves. Pop could provide a quick, enticing fix for the spiritually deprived masses, eagerly receptive to any stimulus which puts them in contact with their feelings and lets them feel the momentary pulse of life's unseen forces. As Lester Bangs continually pointed out, it was all just the latest snake oil/con man scam to tantalize the American public. Though the group may have sold out so they could rattle the masses in hopes of reaching a few, the artistic vision of The Doors doesn't offer any such quick doses of soothing assurance. Plans for this third album had begun as grandiose with one side devoted to a twenty minute-plus version of a Morrison piece entitled, 'The Celebration Of The Lizard'. But it wasn't to be, as evident in Richard Goldstein's recollection of a recording session when a roughly recorded dub of 'The Celebration Of The Lizard' was played back: Ray, "gently, almost apologetically" told Jim the piece was "too diffuse, too mangy", and "Jim's face sinks".1 Without a studio version of 'Lizard', The Doors suddenly found that a lot of music was needed to fill this third album. Yet The Doors had lacked any time to develop songs with the night-after-night tension of an intimate club audience, nor had Jim had any quiet time to allow songs to flow to him.

Having been regulated to playing the standard cuts off the albums and other favourites from their original repertoire of songs, the group had cornered themselves, allowing public success to stifle the messages they had initially wanted to express. When it came time under contract to provide another album, The Doors had to produce using a creative process foreign to their normal rhythm of creating. Ray said in an interview in *Musician* magazine that they couldn't "fool around and goof off" while waiting for their Muse to arrive, but had to "call the lady down" with a plea of, "come on, give us a hand here!".2

But the artistic vision of The Doors appeared less lucid. Though the pieces still fit in the puzzle, the overall picture framed by the third album seemed hazier than the more lucid portraits rendered by the first two albums. Perhaps tired by the touring and catering to the public, The Doors might have been saying: "We have things to say, but we're tired of trying to spell them out to you, so take our half-hearted offering and make what you want from it." Perhaps the swirling forces had made them a bit dizzy? *Waiting For The Sun* evoked the typical wide range of immediate reactions. Rich Mangelsdorff asked in the Milwaukee underground newspaper, *Kaleidoscope*: "Has someone discovered that with a little printing The Doors albums can sell real big? Someone standing pat?"3 Yet Pete Johnson wrote in *The Philadelphia Inquirer* that since this album contained "the smallest amount of self-indulgent mysticism" of the group's first three albums, The Doors had "traded terror for beauty", and the "success of the swap" was a tribute to the band's "talent and originality".4 In retrospect, most reviews years later reiterated the same belief: the album was uninspired and, as Lillian Roxon wrote, "strengthened dreadful suspicion that the Doors were in it just for the money".5 The contrast of this third album with the first two is one of paradoxes. The music of the first two was studio ready when the recording began. For this third album, as Hopkins and Sugerman wrote, almost every song, mostly due to blunders by Jim, needed at least twenty takes, and 'The Unknown Soldier' required 130 starts.6 Allegedly, 'The End' and 'When The Music's Over' had each taken two takes. Starting in January of 1968, The Doors finished recording the album in May. Whereas the debut album had smouldered in the charts for half a year before soaring to the top with the release of the abbreviated 45 version of 'Light My Fire', this third album had advance orders of nearly half a million and sold 750,000 copies within ten weeks of release.

The album changed titles from *American Nights* (a poem which later appeared in Frank Lisciandro's book, *An Hour For Magic*) to *The Celebration Of The Lizard* (Morrison wanted the album cover to be in imitation lizard skin) to *Waiting For The Sun* (the title of a song left off the album, inevitably to emerge on the *Morrison Hotel* album). And Jim had wanted, as Hopkins and Sugerman noted, to recite some of his poetry between songs (a posthumous reality with *An American Prayer*); instead, printed inside the album sleeve was *The Celebration Of The Lizard*, a Morrison poem that "had refused to be wedded to music".7 'The Celebration Of The Lizard' compounds and complexifies any critical rendering of this third album. As a printed insert, the piece stands as a vivid part of the album and a reflection of Morrison's artistic vision. Yet this piece failed to be composed onto vinyl or into The Doors' artistic vision save for one or two well-executed live performances. 'The Celebration Of The Lizard' remains an attached aside, a metaphor for the frustrated Muse denied the creative input of an intimate audience every night. Mitchell Cohen wrote that the piece "in black and white, seemed silly, an unstructured *tour de force* by a mediocre poet".8 Morrison told Hank Zevallos in an interview printed in the March 1970 issue of *Poppin* that 'The Celebration Of The Lizard' was built upon the central image of a "band of youths who leave the city and venture into the desert" where each night, for pleasure and to cultivate the "group spirit", the youths "tell stories and sing around a fire".9 In an interview with Bob Chorush published in the *Los Angeles Free Press* in January 1971, Morrison said that since we identify the lizard and snake with the unconscious and forces of evil, 'The Celebration Of The Lizard' was "kind of an invitation to the dark forces", but it was "all done tongue in cheek".10

"Jim Morrison has grown to be the Sex-Death, Acid-Evangelist of Rock, a sort of Hell's Angel on the groin. Journalistic accuracy tends to depend on expediency, but the case of The Doors stretches the mass media's credibility gap to almost impossible lengths."

*Mike Jahn,*
*Jim Morrison and The Doors (pp. 8, 11)*

"And the media weren't about to be allowed to treat the Doors as Top 40 morons, even if Jim did look like jean-creaming pinup material. 'We're erotic politicians' – that gave 'em something to think about. The alternative press – now, they were different. They wanted to understand. The Doors' message that the end of the world was nigh was right on for them."

*Ian Whitcomb,*
*Rock Odyssey: A Musician's*
*Chronicle Of The Sixties (p. 341)*

Because even Doors songs that could be considered light have some purpose, usually to make fun of people who don't even realize it, the inclusion of 'Celebration' could be an apology, or a gasp for breath from under the rampaging Pop culture.

It is dubious Morrison intended 'Celebration' to be a joke – this prolonged piece has coherent structure and theme. Morrison starts at the heart of a city with lions roaming the streets, rapid dogs foaming and in heat, and a caged beast. He quickly leaves and heads south, across "the border" to begin a journey of exile that pauses in a "green hotel" where he wakes up to find a "strange creature groaning" beside him. Morrison then continues the journey to a place inside his brain, back past pain, back to a little game called "go insane". Then he and his lover are on the run, from and through a mosaic of conspicuous images. Eventually, Morrison pronounces at the end of the piece that he has lived seven years "in the loose palace of exile", but now, as night arrives, he prepares to reenter the town of his birth. Nevertheless, this elongated poetic escapade never had the chance to be creatively developed in the typical Doors' manner, nor was it taken very seriously artistically by Morrison.

Moreover, Morrison was no longer taking Morrison seriously. Jim was basking in the contemporary Americanized image of the Dionysus: allowing an everchanging crowd of groupies to pander to him, frivolously spending money on senseless things, and drinking merrily with the great American elixir, alcohol. Tales of turmoil in recording this album abounded, evident in these two recollections. Hopkins and Sugerman wrote that during the rehearsal and recording of this third album, there were "wall-to-wall hangers-on" and events like the night every guy who wanted "had a poke" at a fat girl who had no panties on and had passed out in the vocal booth with her dress pulled above her waist or when John quit in disgust as Jim lay collapsed on the studio floor in a spreading stain of his own urine.11 In an article for *The Saturday Evening Post*, Joan Didion described waiting for Morrison to arrive at a recording session. When he finally did, no one acknowledged Jim "by so much as a flicker of an eye", and after an hour or so, no one had spoken to Morrison. After some whispered conversation of frivolous suggestions between Morrison and Manzarek, silence returned to the studio. Didion wrote that Morrison lit a match and then slowly and deliberately lowered the flame to "the fly of his black vinyl pants", leaving the feeling no one would "leave the room, ever".12 This is the essence of the Morrison outlook on existence: moments suspended in time often twisted in subtle yet bizarre ways to remind us that things are never entirely what we perceive them to be.

But the tension and challenges that Morrison was presenting not only to himself but to the group and others weren't much different to the typical American way of doing things: the problem could be recognized, maybe it was discussed, maybe it wasn't, but nobody knew how to resolve it... yet everyone optimistically figured that everything would work out. Years later, writers continued the paradoxical reactions in retrospective reviews. Lester Bangs wrote that "the whole nightmare easily translated into parody" with Morrison becoming a "true clown" and wearing his Lizard King cartoon like "a bib to keep the drunk drool" from staining his shirt and that when *Waiting For The Sun* was released, the band's worth had fallen to "just this side of bubblegum".13 In contrast, David Dalton and Lenny Kaye in *Rock 100* reflected that the album expressed "a rite of natural fertility" – the music "gained texture and ornamentation" and Morrison "scooped deeper into his fantasies, rich and loamy", suggesting that his struggle was an inner one, a rebelling by the "pretensions of a pop star" against the "pretensions of an artist".14 Whether playing the tragic clown parodying the latest snake oil selling con man or the pretentious pop star duelling with the pretentiousness of the artist, neither Morrison alone nor The Doors as a unit gave any clear indication what was to be the next act on their newfound stage in life. With just a few pieces left from the earlier repertoire of songs, The Doors and producer Paul Rothchild sketched out the third album with snatches of The Doors' artistic vision. The album isn't necessarily less valid than the previous two, for it reflects The Doors' state of existence at the time. People grow and expand in many different directions throughout their lives, and art is a reflection of being human. We cannot expect an artist to maintain the same style and concepts forever. Labelling a personality type creates conflict because labels imply rigidity of existence, when actually everyone is made up of different facets interacting continually. Labels imply expected outlooks and behaviours, which create internal conflicts – and negative album reviews. Both sides of the album continue portraying the attempt to find momentary sanctuary in the embrace of love or the freedom of breaking through, but each side ends with artistic indictments: side one with 'The Unknown Soldier', a ritualistic purging of war, and side two with 'Five To One', a dark portrait of the swirling forces of the times.

## SIDE ONE

'Hello, I Love You' opens the album. On the radio special, *History Of Rock 'n' Roll*, Manzarek described how the song originated when he and Jim saw a particular black girl walking along the beach who had "a dusky, dark complexion" and was "just a little jewel walking by", and that night Jim wrote a song about walking up to a girl whom he didn't know and saying, 'Hello, I love you'.[15] The song, one of the six cuts on the original demo the group recorded for Columbia before Robby Krieger joined, echoes the passionate urgency of love portrayed in the first two albums. What is more natural than the spontaneous feeling on seeing someone who evokes a passionate greeting of "I love you" and asking what is your name?

The song, which shot to #1 in the Billboard Top 100, was the target of sharp criticism. Richard Walls labelled the song, "psychedelic bubblegum"[16], and typical was Terry Rompers' critical blast that the song was "the most blatant sell-out single of the year" and was "such a crass Top 40 (am!) single" that many fans gave up and went looking for "more committed anti-establishment groups".[17] This was some harsh commentary for a song stating the same theme found in Roy

Orbison's "pretty woman" who as she is "walking down the street" is the kind he would like to meet or in The Beatles' "lovely Rita meter maid" whom they want to know when she is free to have some tea. *Harbinger*, a Toronto underground newspaper, was a little more sensitive in its August 1968 review: the song gains "immeasurably from being heard within the context of the album, as opposed to being sandwiched between a Clearasil commercial and the weather on your favourite Top 40 station".18

Many accused The Doors of cloning Ray Davies and the Kinks' 'All Day And All Of The Night'. In an interview over ten years later, Manzarek commented on the alleged Kink-derivative, saying that the group initially thought the song was "a lot like a Kinks song", but added: "It's all rock and roll, we're all family, we're not stealing anything from them, we're sort of... [hums melody]... Yes, it is a lot like it, isn't it? Sorry, Ray."19 The simple lyrics and Krieger's pulsating, stifled guitar resound the frustrated sensual urgency. The appearance of the "queen of the angels" triggers a most natural response of not only sensual desire, but a willingness to sacrifice oneself immediately, begging to jump into her "game", a fantasy being played inside one's brain.

In the next stanza, Morrison shifts perspective, from the throbbing sensations of a longing lover to a detached third person observer. The queen of angels maintains her pedestal by staying "blind" to all the eyes she entices as she walks the streets. Ignoring eyes prevents exposing vulnerability, prevents the possibility of one of the guys making the queen of angels "sigh", which would reveal a human response, a vulnerability. To be such a Venus, she holds her head and attitude high, "like a statue" suspended in the sky. Just as a statue cannot think or feel, so she may be lying to herself about being invulnerable. Like a piece of art, as static and dead as a statue, she evokes a deep emotional response from her viewer. The throbbing urgency of passion swells up to drown Morrison's detached observations that she has wicked arms and long legs and seeing her move makes his brain scream "out this song", after which a deep swooning by Manzarek's organ takes us down and then back up. Statues may imitate sensuality, but life generates desire. The high flung imagery of this untouchable angel by the end of the song has dissolved into a more pulsating, urgent tone, if not also a more sarcastic third-person detachment, as Morrison sings about the sidewalk crouching at her feet like a begging dog (a petty god? or perhaps a modern Greek god?) and asks if anyone really hopes to make her look at him let alone "to pluck" such a "dusky jewel".

This queen of angels, no less an allusion to the city of Los Angeles also, is no longer a Twentieth Century Fox in the sky, but a dusky jewel – hard and cold to the touch, to be plucked, rhetorically close enough to what a lover really wants to do. Yet, the frustrated and longing lover is drowning in both his desire and his foolishness for even thinking she would ever look at anyone, much less him. The song closes with Morrison crooning that he wants, needs, and loves his baby, echoing the ever-eternal Top 40 triad of "I want you, I need you, I love you". Such a simple thing to say – but saying, "Hello, I love you", to a stranger is generally considered ridiculous because we attach so many complicated connotations to the word "love". Why not say it to whomever you want because it doesn't really mean anything anyway? It is just a phrase with no intrinsic meaning, any significance defined by how and why and when people use it. Here, it signifies pure and simple lust – and presents quite an enticing contrast to the wicked woman imagery of 'People Are Strange'. Just as silence often says more than words, simplicity can imply complexity. The sarcasm is made even more powerful, instead of being diminished, by the accompanying bubblegum music. Perhaps labelled as blatant Top 40/bubblegum sell-out, the song, nevertheless, restates the previous themes of love: short and urgent, but don't expect anything lasting or meaningful.

Recapitulating the theme that life is dualistic, the flip side to the 45 release of 'Hello, I Love You' was the next song, 'Love Street'. Like the dusky jewel of 'Hello, I Love You', the subject of 'Love Street', as Rompers noted, is "another vamp from the Twentieth Century Fox collection".20 Like the queen of angels strolling the sidewalk, this girl has control of her attentive audience who also seek the urgency of feeling the pulse of life, of sexuality. But in 'Love Street', the tone of passionate urgency subsides to a passive hesitancy of the anticipant lover, and this Twentieth Century Fox strolls with more sophistication, living on Love Street and having a house and garden. This traditional symbol of sanctuary, the house and garden, offers a reposing contrast to the sidewalk cruised by the queen of angels, and a more relaxing piano replaces the passionate organ of the previous song. The long vowels and the consonances that roll off Jim's tongue combine with the casual flow of the playful renderings by Robby's guitar and Ray's electric piano to create a lazy-dazy tone. This tone is far less urgent in its passion than the theme which dominates previous love songs, a view shared by Mangelsdorff who wrote, in a somewhat sarcastic tone, "I detect a tendency to resort to ballady material not in keeping with their previous robustness".21 The Twentieth Century Fox had the world locked up in a plastic box; this fox has exotic and interesting bits of ornamentation, like "monkeys", "lazy diamond-studded flunkies", and an anticipant audience of "me" and "you". More aware and manipulative than the plastic Twentieth Century Fox, she knows how to gain control on a deeper level; rather than luring them in with lust, she appeals to that deeper lure of mystery. The song slows as Morrison speaks the last stanza of lyrics, creating a tone in stark contrast to the passionate urgency of previous love songs, such as 'Light My Fire' and 'Love Me Two Times', and to the frustrated urgency of 'Hello, I Love You'. The tone is mellow. Easy going. A summer Sunday afternoon on Love Street... quite a contrast to the Moonlight Drive down by the oceanside. Morrison sticks around and plays the game for a while because it is more subtle and intriguing than foxes and statues. The song closes with Jim cruising into mellow oblivion with, "La- la-la La-la-la-la", carried along by John's perpetual soft back beat and gentle rapping of a cymbal. Yet the imagery renders 'Love Street' with the disquieting realization that Jim, though enticed by the appealing sanctuary of 'Love Street', won't surrender completely to such sanctuary. The imagery of a "store where the creatures meet" isn't exactly an invitation to a pleasant Sunday afternoon dinner.

The next song echoes the structure consistent in the first two albums: trying to find sanctuary in love followed by the desire to find meaning in freedom, in breaking through to the other side. The song, 'Not To Touch The Earth', is, as Richard Riegel in a *Creem Special Edition* wrote, "the lovers-on-the-run fragment" salvaged from 'The Celebration Of The Lizard', and the squealing dissonance between Manzarek's organ and Krieger's guitar is "particularly disturbing".22 Walls in the same special edition of *Creem* added that the song's "scattershot approach to imagery" is reminiscent of Bob Dylan: the cumulative effect of the images, though individually not too precise, is "dynamite" and the music is "prescient – new wave robotic bop".23

Krieger's leering guitar churns with the tension-strung repetition of Manzarek's organ in the introduction to create the sudden shift in focus from casual pursuing of love to trying to break through to freedom. A moment in the traditional sanctuary of the lover's house and garden is swept away by the desire to move on, to run from this life that has cut off being able to touch two sources essential for life, the earth and the sun.

The static images of 'Love Street' dissolve into the vibrant, moving images of nature, of a still moon and of shadows of trees "witnessing the wild breeze". Echoing themes in 'Moonlight Drive', these images manifest the disquieting compliancy of the lover la-la-laing along in 'Love Street'. A reviewer in the underground newspaper, *Harbinger*, astutely noted the song is a "discordant 'Moonlight Drive' plus desperation" and expresses the "apocalyptic love/death theme" which obsessed Morrison.24 The traditional source of sanctuary, the house ("upon the hill" or on Love Street) is now to be fled. The music builds with the swirling imagery, the guitar, organ, and drums crescendoing with each repeated chorus of, "Run with me". The chorus of "Run With Me" generates distance, before Morrison sketches out the "house upon the hill" in more detail as the undertone of the images and music create the usual, disquieting despair. The images of a warm mansion and rich rooms and comforts shift after getting inside, and the ensuing stanza paints a disturbing knowledge of a dead president. The theme of death is rendered vividly with the allusion to the powerful image of a slain President Kennedy in his black presidential limousine unable to outrun the speed of death. And the insanity towards which Morrison and his lover could continue to travel is further twisted more grotesquely with the image of running to the fallen head of the other great modern Western culture, running East instead of West "to meet the Czar".

"Certain roads one took emotionally also appeared on the map of the heart as travelling away from the centre, and ultimately leading to exile."

*Anais Nin,*
*The Spy In The House Of Love (p. 60)*

A repeating chorus of "Run With Me" takes the lovers and the listener deeper into Morrison's portrait of some very disturbing images of our culture. The image of "outlaws" who live by a lake recalls what Pichaske observed as The Doors' repeated use of water to evoke "death, rebirth, sexuality".25 The hard edge of the drum beat and persistent cymbal drive the song along as the imagery takes Morrison, his lover, and the listener out to the edge of lawlessness, of drowning, of baptismal, of breaking through. We reenter Eden to find the daughter of a minister is "in love with the snake", whose home is "a well" that is at the "side of the road". Evoking the unimaginable imagery of such an invitation, Morrison closes the stanza for the girl to wake up because they are almost home. Running to this home far from the rich rooms and comforts of the warm mansion upon the hill, the lovers seek to break through to the other side, to have the "gates" insight by morning and to be beyond them by evening.

The structured imagery of the previous stanzas gives way to a primal chanting to the forces of life – Morrison's chanting marching through the words, sun, burn, soon, and moon. Manzarek's organ and Krieger's guitar swirl around and down through the crescendoing Morrison chant, Densmore's drums punctuating the dissonance of the swirling forces. Finally, the pursuant lover breaks through and states he is the "Lizard King" and "can do anything". Calling upon the forces around him, the Lizard King emerges in control, without being at the mercy of sacrificing to a relationship of lust, quite an opposite to the persona in the opening two songs.

Perhaps the regal but repellent "Lizard King" image makes more sense if it is compared to why someone plays Russian Roulette. To play you go to the greatest emotional extreme possible, leading yourself to death's door and challenging the forces beyond to take you. It is the cusp of finally breaking through, the farthest you can go as a human and still come back. Every time you don't shoot yourself, you return feeling entire control over your existence, at least for a while. You are The Lizard King, capable of doing anything because, for one brief moment, you are the controlling force. Granted, one can have such moments only once in a while, but being so close to death is the most alive moment one could ever have. The toll for breaking through completely is death of the human form, so it makes sense when Jim speaks of moonlight drives and running through the forest.

Complacent existence causes spiritual death. And then again, the Lizard King may be just a reference to the archetypal image of the lizard as a guide in the dream world. Though the analysis of 'Not To Touch The Earth' easily relates to established themes, it implies a lot more. In terms of creativity, meaning, and music, this song is the most important song on the album. Because of the absence of freaks and terror in the album, this song packs a deep-seated wallop. The mansion on the hill isn't much different than the quintessential abode of sanctuary in a grade-B horror movie where somebody just happens to be wandering in a peaceful forest and enters a quaint, little farmhouse (complete with flower boxes and green shutters) to find everything as expected, except somehow their primeval instincts tell them something isn't quite right. They go into a room and find the blood and dismembered body parts. Obviously, the axe-wielding maniac is standing behind the door of the next room, but it's too late to escape because they went too far into the house and saw too much to ever be able to leave. They saw the reality of what really laid inside the house: truths that end up costing a big sacrifice, namely their lives.

The lovers have to run away from the masked realities inside the house in 'Not To Touch The Earth' because reality there continually tilts, distorts and stretches their existence until they entirely lose their grip on everything as they know it. Instead of being chopped up by a chain-saw, the sacrifice required for the knowledge gained in "the mansion on the hill" is spiritual death – death of hopes, dreams, feelings, freedom, everything that makes us human. The reality we build for ourselves in this world is but a twisted reflection of the universal meaning from which we were created, kind of like the mirrors inside a funhouse. In the everyday world, the bloody faces of dead presidents and deposed czars leer at us like psychotic murderers, only worse because we must admit that we as collective humans destroyed one of our own. Giving in to this realization and giving up trying to break through and to witness the wild breeze and to search for the well by the side of the road is what ultimately kills you. 'Tis far better to run towards the unreachable, even though we can't ever really step inside the gates. We come from that well, and despite the complexities and horrors of the existence we are born into, we always carry part of the universal spirit with us. This song expresses our urgent desire to run to the sun and moon and not to have to stand with our feet on the earth anymore. Maybe we can get there someday, guided by the outlaws at the side of the lake rather than by NASA, but the best we can do on earth is periodically to punch holes in reality and catch glimpses of what lies beyond.

The music is especially effective here, both technically and emotionally. There is not only the urgency of the lovers to get away, but also the feeling that somebody or something is chasing them while they run. The ominous tone of the music heightens the disturbing images rendered by the lyrics as the harmony builds upon an interval of notes that creates a very eerie and threatening tone to the song. The shamanic musicians understood which back door to slide through to convey their message. They switch moods with each new idea, becoming more dissonant as the journey progresses, so different from the nice music before and after this song, which further reinforces the idea of punching holes in existence. Compared to the other songs on the album, this one is representative of the brief intense moments of spiritual honesty experienced during one's attempts to escape mortality.

"It is vain to try to deduce the tragic spirit from the commonly accepted categories of art: illusion and beauty. Music alone allows us to understand the delight felt at the annihilation of the individual... The metaphysical delight in tragedy is a translation of instinctive Dionysiac wisdom into images. The hero, the highest manifestation of the will, is destroyed, and we assent, since he too is merely a phenomenon, and the eternal life of the will remains unaffected. Tragedy cries, 'We believe that life is eternal!' and music is the direct expression of that life."

*Friedrich Nietzsche,*
*The Birth Of Tragedy (pp. 101-2)*

The cacophonic moment of breaking through so adeptly rendered at the end of 'Not To Touch The Earth' and then vapourized by the flash of organ dissolves into, as Walls wrote, the "lugubrious love song", 'Summer's Almost Gone'.26 The gentle, grinning guitar of Krieger, the slightly inebriated piano sound of Manzarek, and the softly stroked cymbals of Densmore provide a dramatic shift from the tone of 'Not To Touch The Earth' and underscore Morrison's lyrical portrait of a relationship in love being merely a temporal sanctuary, like the summer slipping away. Considered less powerful than previous songs, this song, nevertheless, is an effective rendering in the overall portrait in the album, as the reviewer in Harbinger perceived, writing that the next two songs, 'Summer's Almost Gone' and 'Wintertime Love' seemed malapropos, but "an undercurrent of irrationality and foreboding" flows beneath these two song's "more conventional (banal?) nature" in relation to the rest of the album.27

With Jim's voice drawn out on the r's and n's of the opening stanza and Ray returning to the gentler tappings of the piano, the lazy-dazy summer Sunday afternoon of 'Love Street' reemerges after the momentary fleeing to the other side with the Lizard King persona. After waning through the opening lines, Jim asks where they as lovers will be when summer is gone. The swooning of wanting to light a fire or going down on a moonlight drive has yielded to a realization of compassion, of wondering where they will be, even after having triumphantly reached the edge of the lake where the outlaws live.

The lovers are more aware of what it means to be human. The summer is only a brief season, but it still means something, to enjoy basic human experiences like compassion and basking in the sun.

The next stanza frames a gentle image of carefree love, a slice of life on the southern California coast. Jim renders a picture of innocence and passiveness, the morning finding the lovers "calmly unaware" and the noon burning gold into their hair. By night, they have become active participants in this gentle world, swimming in the "laughing sea". Instead of drowning in the sea of passion, Jim is swimming in a joyful world. Instead of the lover playing the fool like a dog begging for something sweet, Morrison sings of romanticized moments, of their "good times". The tone and imagery reflect little if any quenching of passionate urgency. Yet beneath this calm unawareness and carefree goldening in the sun, there lingers both the question of when the summer is gone, where will they be and the soft, almost sad realization that winter is coming on. The music pauses after the lyric that asks where the lovers will be when summer is over, punctuating the question as both the lovers and listener contemplate the answer. Ray's soft piano sound yields to the tingling intonation of a harpsichord in 'Wintertime Love', and the carefree love of summer yields to the cold winds of winter. The lovers discover they need more than the noon sun burning gold into their hair. Jim wonders in 'Summer's Almost Gone' where they as lovers will be. In Krieger's song, 'Wintertime Love', he answers he hopes to be falling in love. Love needs contact, needs warmth; the wind is cold and he appreciates both the warmth of holding a lover and the touch of a lover. And that is why the waltz tone of the song is so appropriate. In the next stanza, Jim croons to his lover to come and dance with him, "my dear", a tone rendered far more compassionate than the wooing lover of 'Moonlight Drive' or the panting urgency of 'Hello, I Love You'. John's drumming swells with rolls rather than with punctuating beats or a gentle back beat. Though a wintertime love provides the dance of life and the warmth of sanctuary, lyrically, Jim questions if this love can endure wintertime. The images are cold and wintry as are the crisp sounds of Ray's harpsichord, creating undertones of bitter-sweet love, which, as Jay Ruby of *Jazz & Pop* noted, "reaffirm that love is dead".28

The last stanza solidifies the wintry imagery of the brevity of love. The verbal, coming, reinforces the perpetuity of the wintertime winds rendered vividly by the two adjectives, blue and freezing. The clausal structure of "love has been lost" reaffirms that the relationship has ended, the reason for Morrison again desperately yearning "to be free", a theme to be picked up by 'Spanish Caravan', the opening song on side two. There is the realization that winter will be cold no matter how warm the lover; sometimes there are periods in life where things can't or don't happen, where love is lost.

Such a winter period in American politics was occurring with the war in Vietnam, as the urgency of the shamanic-artist surfaces in a song of political unrest. 'The Unknown Soldier', a song which took its name from the national monument, marked what many considered Morrison's venture into Sixties political protest songs, or as Riegel wrote, "brazen anti-war rants".29 Morrison, quoted in *Rolling Stone*, labelled 'The Unknown Soldier' a love song "about sexual intercourse", that the violence and firing squad were just metaphors "for what's going on".30 Sure, a regimented approach to sex climaxed with an eruption of gunfire as bullets and lover unite. Manzarek offered a more even keeled explanation in a radio special produced by *The Source*: "Jim said, 'Let's do a war song'. I said, 'Everybody's doing a Vietnam song.' And he said, 'Nah, nah, this isn't a Vietnam song. This is just a song about war.'"31

"Like a mighty titan, the tragic hero shoulders the whole Dionysiac world and removes the burden from us. At the same time, tragic myth, through the figure of the hero, delivers us from our avid thirst for earthly satisfaction and reminds us of another existence and a higher delight. For this delight the hero readies himself, not through his victories but through his undoing."

*Friedrich Nietzsche,*
*The Birth Of Tragedy (p. 126)*

Hopkins and Sugerman recalled the song began in October of 1967 and was developed on the road; in two or three months "the dirge became a celebration" with a rhythm "both military (metronomic) and carnivalesque".32 Producer Rothchild stated in an 1981 interview in *Musician* that 'Unknown Soldier' was a "programmatic concept" of Jim's with so many different sections it required an "enormous amount of time to record".33 At a concert, Mitchell Cohen saw the short film which promoted the song and wrote in retrospect that the film was a "crude work and filled with Morrison-as-martyr iconography" that simulated "vomiting and political montage... yet it worked".34 Released as a single in March 1968, the song was subsequently banned by several radio chains.

The song opens with Morrison softly singing to wait till the war is over and we are a little older. With time, the war fades in memory and the soldier becomes unknown, an insight paraphrased by retrospective reviews, such as Walls in the summer 1981 issue of *Creem* who wrote that the song was a "yell of defiance, oblique yet effective", yet he suspected, "though not sadly, that for someone coming to it now it makes little sense".35

The song then shatters the lull of this opening, as the music and Morrison, in a very sarcastic nasal twinge, belt out that breakfast is where we read the news. We start the morning by consuming news, which in 1968 consisted of a large dosage of the Vietnam War and its weekly death counts, and shatters the carefree image of morning finding us calmly unaware in 'Summer's Almost Gone'. The nourishment of "television children fed" consisted of many portions of the first war carried on television. Karl Dallas of London's *Melody Maker* wrote that the song was "an apocalyptic piece which seems to sum up the Vietnam-nourished violence at the centre of American life".36 What is the fruit of such nutrients? Morrison evokes a paradox with the image of the "unborn living, living dead", people who are mentally and spiritually dead. Life isn't a sanctuary of waiting till the memory fades and the soldier becomes unknown, of wearing a protective shell of a helmet – not if what is digested at breakfast and by the children is the constant parade of allusions to death, not if a bullet from reality shatters the protective shell.

The middle of the song acts out a ritual in the ancient tradition of the shaman (The Doors probably weren't too conscious of this parallel): Morrison, the artist incarnate of the shamanic spirit, sacrifices himself in a ritual – one of military execution, the firing squad – to purge us of the burden of war. Then Morrison softly invites us to open up and "make a grave" for the spirit of all this death into our minds and to realize what has been done, to nestle this in our "hollow shoulder", an image suggesting the fake, empty compassion of our minds and hearts nurtured by television-fed images.

The song recants the breakfast and television fed images, but this time Morrison doesn't repeat the "unborn living, living dead" line, allowing the listener to fill in that hollow space before the bullet hits the "helmet's head" (not the helmet, but the head for the helmet) and The Doors close by chanting that the war is over. Although this chorus fuelled the growing social chorus to end the Vietnam War, Morrison's chanting also underscores the reality that war will not fade away. It couldn't, not with a generation having been breakfast and television fed with vivid images the Vietnam War portrayed.

## SIDE TWO

Side two begins with the need to wander. Robby's flamenco guitar, an introduction he later said was severely edited, begins the journey on

the 'Spanish Caravan'. Though 'Spanish Caravan' echoes the imagery
and desires so vividly portrayed in the debut album's opening song,
'Break On Through', this song doesn't pulsate with the same urgency.
The pace is not as hectic, not as demanding. It isn't an urgent flight
toward something unknown, but a more concrete fantasy about a
place to which to escape that isn't as intense or dangerous as the
"other side". Like in 'Love Street', there is a passive yielding to this
yearning, to have a caravan carry and take Jim away to Portugal and
Spain. "An-da-lu-si-a" rolls off Jim's tongue, the alluring bright
midnight which Jim is ever seeking when not pursuing love, and
Robby's flamenco guitar harmoniously carries the lyrics off toward this
land in southern Spain bordering on the Atlantic Ocean and the
Mediterranean Sea, an image as exotic as the girl on Love Street. After
the opening lyrics drift off with a wishful longing to be carried away,
the song pauses; then the journey swirls into a realization that this
place might be a little dangerous after all as Krieger's flamenco guitar
transforms into a driving electronic six-stringer cutting across the
swirling rhythms of Manzarek's organ with Densmore's drumming
swelling with every spin of the emerging vortex. The reoccurring
image of a ship lost at sea, so vividly painted in 'Horse Latitudes' and
alluded to in 'Wintertime Love', portrays the danger of such tripping,
that the ocean winds "find galleons lost in the sea". But these galleons
carry what Morrison seeks to pursue, the "silver and gold" in the
distant and exotic mountains of Spain, recalling the image of digging
treasures in 'Break On Through'. The gold the noon burned into their
hair in 'Summer's Almost Gone' has become, in this quest, the
promise of gold in far away mountains. Then Jim sings that he needs
to see his lover again and again, suggesting the treasure he really
wants is to attain love or happiness. Pursuit requires energy against
the currents of life, so Morrison needs to see once in a while the
treasure he seeks in order to keep going on, a rather touching
moment on Jim's part as he usually spends so much time running
from life. In sharp contrast to the urgent pursuing of his repeated
imagery of, 'Let's Run', Jim has faith the Spanish Caravan will take him
there.

The next three songs return to the pursuit of love: 'My Wild Love',
portraying an enticing lover more complex than the dusky angel of
'Hello, I Love You'; 'We Could Be So Good Together', appealing to the

times of 'Summer's Almost Gone', yet recanting the same untrusting theme rendered in the *Strange Days* album; and 'Yes, The River Knows', evoking the powers of water as an inviting cleansing, a contrast to the abducting mystery of water in 'Moonlight Drive' and 'Not To Touch The Earth'. "'Wild Love'", wrote a reviewer in *Harbinger*, was "beautifully constructed, with a lyric that again sketches around a heart which is all the ominous since it is only hinted at."37 Walls wrote that 'My Wild Love' was a "straight-ahead folkish lyric" sung as a "work song complete with hand claps and harmonic moans".38 This singing in a "chain gang chant form" captured what Ruby said was a "macabre love theme".39

Morrison is removed from the lover's trance – neither a dog begging for something sweet, nor a lazy-dazy lover laid back on 'Love Street'; neither the carefree golden boy in the summer noon sun, nor the embraced dancer in the wintertime waltz. He sees his lover as he sees his own quest for life, in terms of audacious adventure set to primal tones of a group chant. He mixes images of confronting the devil, of the devil wising up to repent, of destinations seemingly having no connections – "to the sea", "to Christmas", "to the farm", and "to Japan". When his wild love asks the people of the town she has reentered "to let her go free", she cries the same lament for breaking away as does the persona Morrison repeatedly has portrayed.

In the seventh stanza, Morrison provides as close a glimpse into this wild love's heart as can be sketched, that his wild love "is crazy", "screams like a bird", and "moans like a cat". The opposites of the cat and the bird depict the dualistic nature of life and of the wild love. The screaming of a bird strains the imagination, as does the image of moaning like a cat which hints at more than just purring. Far more complex than the dusky jewel strolling down the sidewalk and far more worldly than the vamp on 'Love Street', this wild love is crazy – and so very enticing. The song echoes the theme of a lengthy journey to reenter a town portrayed in 'The Celebration Of The Lizard', only this has been a journey by Jim's "wild love". Morrison has been on a Spanish Caravan, and now he longs for their reunion in the next song, 'We Could Be So Good Together'.

There could be little doubt of Morrison's intent in the opening line that he and his lover "could be so good together". The *carpi diem* theme of "let's live for today" continues to come through vividly in the

line about the time to wait "subtracts from joy". The deliciously latent
image of the world that the two lovers could invent, a "wanton world
without lament", envisions a lewdly sensual world without any
controls, any limits. And Morrison cleverly plays on the word, wanton,
evoking both the noun and the verb, wanting.

The four nouns – enterprise, expedition, invitation and invention
– frame an enticing picture, but there is something uneasy in the static
nature of nouns, of the allusion to expeditions of a Spanish Caravan
and a wild love, of the allusion to the invitation to the queen of angels
in 'Hello, I Love You'. Labels don't stick forever because things
change. Moreover, the image of an angel reappears at the end of this
song, of angels who fight and cry, of angels who dance and die. The
dog is no longer begging at her feet; angels are vulnerable. How
powerful the ramifications if ethereal angels are no better than
humans, if being human is one of the best deals available in the
universe. Although Morrison yearns for a "wanton world" where he
and his love can travel uninhibited and "without lament", free from
distinguishing right from wrong, he precedes these lines with a
chorus of telling her lies – "wicked lies". Again, Morrison sketches out
a sanctuary of illusion, that such a wanton world doesn't exist if lies
sustained the relationship. Yet the song closes with the hypocritical
and upbeat lyric that they "could be so good together". They could be
good together only as long as they tell each other wicked lies. If
existence requires lying to yourself to some extent to create an illusion
of sanctuary, what happens when that sanctuary is shattered? The
hypocritical tone dissolves into the easy flowing lyrics and music of
Robby's melodic song, 'Yes, The River Knows', resonating the calming
image of water in 'Summer's Almost Gone'. The mellowed tones of
the lyrics' imagery, of the drawn out vowels and consonances, of Ray's
piano, of John's soft back beat, and of Robby's percolating guitar lull
the lover and listener into Jim's gentle plea for his lover to believe that
the river "very softly" told him for her to hold him. Is this, as Ruby
noted, a deceptively tender plea to the "classic Anglo-American"
theme of suicide over the loss of a wanton world without lament with
his wild love?40 Or a realizing of answers that flow in the river of life?
The river is another primeval image, like the forest or sea. One has to
be quiet and accepting to hear these forces. The urgent passions of
youth pounding in the ears drown out messages from such other

voices. As Jim draws the listener in with the lyric, "Free fall flow river flow/On and on it goes", Ray's supple piano sound and Robby's water-soft guitar tone gentle lap at the listener floating on the light rapping of John's back beat. Yielding to the free flowing river and accepting things for what they are worth as they happen brings freedom and a more peaceful end. Although this stanza closes with an image of breathing "under water till the end" and evokes the image of the mute nostril agony of the horses in 'Horse Latitudes', the tone is more receptive, more permissive, a natural act, not filled with the youthful frustration with an older generation having made empty promises, the frustration with relationships lacking trust because of soft lies, the frustration with trying to break through the limits of being human. But Morrison doesn't forget the chains of being human. Pichaske points out the song combines "drunkenness of water with the drunkenness of wine".41 If, as the song goes on, the lover doesn't want him, then Jim will leave but he promises to drown himself "in mystic heated wine". Yielding to the luscious image of mystic heated wine, Jim, through Robby's lyrics, calmly seeks sanctuary in the magical spirits of heated wine, not the aggressive spirits of whiskey in 'Alabama Song' or of drugs that promise a trip on a crystal ship.

The Doors flow down the river of life, but not without stopping periodically to enjoy certain pleasures. They will get to the end eventually, but not desperately or urgently. As this second stanza is repeated, the song slides into a crescendo, like a major tributary into a river, the sounds swelling to drown the singer in a gentle wave of music. Flowing on the river of life and not the stream of man-made illusions brings understanding, and the shaman pauses to rise up and deliver an indictment of his society. The drums and steady bass beat which open the next song, 'Five To One', immediately shift the tone rendered in the previous songs. The daze of the mystic heated wine and the allure of being so good together dissolve away.

The poignant cry that "no one here gets out alive" captures the understood but unspoken essence of life and of the world The Doors are portraying in their albums. The guttural, unrelenting tone of Morrison in the ensuing lyrics reveals a persona now on the outside looking in, a shamanic spirit no longer swirling in the whirlwind of social and political forces of the times. The opening sexual come on of, "Now you get yours, baby/I'll get mine/Gonna make it, baby, if we try", presents a voice beckoning from a world beyond the lustful desires pulsating in 'Hello, I Love You' or of the lazy receptiveness crooned in 'Love Street' or 'Summer's Almost Gone'.

A brazen statement of political reality ensues, of "taking over" – of the old becoming old and the young becoming stronger, of they may have the guns but we have "the numbers". Morrison sings with an urgency no longer being denied, sneering that the young take over, even if the older generation isn't giving way easily – the "Us vs. Them" ideology of the Cold War, of the Sixties. Ruby wrote that the tone of the song seized "the smart-ass street-stud militant sound of the blacks like Eldridge Cleaver".42

The youth may have the "numbers" – be it bodies or marijuana joints, but they have to face reality, that their "ballroom days are over". Not only is the wintertime waltz over, but so is, as Hopkins and Sugerman wrote, "all the naive revolutionary rhetoric" that was on the streets and in the underground press during the late sixties.43 We are no longer among shadows of trees witnessing a wild breeze of 'Not To Touch The Earth'; instead, the evening shadows "crawl across the years". Morrison then delivers his parody of what Hopkins and Sugerman called the growing numbers of "hippie/flower child" who were panhandling on sidewalks outside concert halls, who carried flowers in their hands and tried to say that no one understands, but who traded in their "hours for a handful of dimes".44 The title? 'Five To One' is, as Hopkins and Sugerman noted, a statistic Jim never explained.45 But Jim did offer an explanation to Hank Zevallos in an 1970 interview pubished in *Poppin*; the song, which Morrison said he didn't think of as political, was an idea he got while waiting in the audience before starting a concert at San Jose, California: "It was one of those big ballroom places and the kids were milling around and I just got an idea for a song."46

It is difficult to take the song literally as either a blatant cry for revolution or a cutting indictment of the hippie generation; it may just be Morrison's way of expressing his aloofness to society. True to the shamanic nature of The Doors' artistic vision, the song, as noted in an insightful chapter on The Doors in *West Coast Story*, "probably was designed as some kind of ritual exorcism" to make the audience "aware of their real power".47 Karl Dallas pointed out that in the song "protest enters a new dimension, more dangerous" because the song is "less explicit" and does not wrap "all the audience's fears in a blue ribbon bow of certainty" – the song leaves "room to think, time to set".48 Because of the first two albums, most expected this album to end with, as Mangelsdorff called, "a long psychodrama counterpart" to 'The End' and 'When The Music's Over'.49 'Five To One' hardly fulfilled those expectations for many. Yet for some, 'Five To One' finally brought out The Doors' sound which they felt had been buried in the ballady melodies of the previous songs. Walls labelled 'Five To One' as "one elongated mutant spew" and forgave Morrison for the album's earlier lightweight songs.50 And the reviewer in *Harbinger* wrote: "If Morrison isn't a demon on 'Five To One', then what is he? This is Doors distilled and concentrated-spine arching music. Who'll be the first to bludgeon his parents? Pull down all the walls and ball in the smoking ruins. Bass and drums drive, guitar pierces. Morrison sings like he had a spike through his throat. Maniacal, brutal, unrelenting. Insane laugh. Jesus, what a song."51

Morrison concludes the song with a deviously drawled out portrait of the dark side of this state of drugs and free love. He moans at his honey to go home and wait for him because he has to go out to a car with some people and, not clearly recorded on the studio album, but as screamed on bootleg recordings of concerts, "get fucked up". As the band drones on with the chorus, "Get together one more time", Morrison closes the song with the very carnal intention he is going to love his girl. The popish, almost innocent 'Hello, I Love You' opening has been swept away. The Doors leave an impression of the uncalm reality brought on by such casual access to free love and drugs as a way to break through to the other side.

'Five To One' ends the album on a note of anger and confrontation, of conflict, a conflict evident in The Doors both outside and inside their music and evident in their performing and their recording, conflicts which were to be manifested in the March 1, 1969, Miami concert and in the transformation of their sound which would begin in the fourth album. The boys – the group, the sound, the artistic vision – were maturing. For many, the imagery and music in this third album diverged unexpectedly from the imagery and music rendered so vividly in the first two albums. Those albums pulsated with a real life portrait of an urgency to seek sanctuary from an alien landscape, pursuing love or trying to break through to the other side. The third album begins to reveal not only that The Doors were realizing they would have to live with the swirling whirlwind of forces in which they found themselves immersed, but also that they were being separated from those forces. Hence, the lyrics began drawing more from the imagery of nature, not of man's neon world of endless fields of asphalt.

Passionate and frustrated urgencies to find fulfillment in love or freedom became muted to tones of being patient, of enjoying the flow of the moment, of experiencing the pain of living without fighting life. That ability to deliver, as Walls called, a "chunk of lusty gloom" manifested itself in shamanic indictments of the political and social hypocrisies of the times. The album, though considered one of the weakest and least focused of The Doors' albums, lifts a well-rendered landscape out of the world of The Doors' artistic vision.

# chapter 4

# welcome to the soft parade

"Nothing can kill the revolutionary potential of rock more than crass commercialization."

*Robert G. Pielke,*
*You Say You Want A Revolution:*
*Rock Music In American Culture (p. 14)*

SIDE 1
Tell All The People
Touch Me
Shaman's Blues
Do It
Easy Ride

SIDE 2
Wild Child
Runnin' Blue
Wishful, Sinful
The Soft Parade

The Sixties were beginning the slide to a dramatic end. Leaders were being assassinated: Martin Luther King Jr. in April of 1968; Bobby Kennedy in June of 1968. The political realities of America steam rolled over the flower power of the youth: at the 1968 Democratic convention, Chicago Mayor Richard Daley demonstrated police army – Gestapo –

tactics to maintain democratic principles; though both were destined to resign in shame and scandal, Richard Nixon and Spiro Agnew were elected president and vice president in November. American involvement in Vietnam in terms of troop numbers peaked in January 1969. Half a planet away, in China, the violent turmoil of the Cultural Revolution continued to rip apart the fabric of the aging Maoist regime with bloodshed as the Chinese communist way of life, like the Western capitalist way of life, was confronted by disgruntled youth, artists, and intellectuals. Forcible vanquishing of student demonstrations disrupted many American college campuses from the April 1968 police clearing of all buildings occupied by a student sit-in at the Ivy League Columbia University to the May 1969 use of shotguns, tear gas, and a helicopter dropping a stinging chemical powder by police and National Guard on students, faculty and area residents who were occupying their self-made People's Park on the University of California campus at Berkeley. Similar student unrest confronted almost every European capital, notably the 19-day eruption in Paris in May. An unpopular disciplinary action by university officials triggered student riots that led to confrontations with police. The national student union advocated more demostrations, and the national teacher union demanded a faculty strike. Confrontations escalated, labour unions called for a general strike, and soon other organized labour joined the general strike which paralyzed President Charles de Gaulle's government, cut France off from the rest of the world, and nearly resurrected the French Revolution ghosts of anarchy and civil war. The confidently dogmatic De Gaulle survived, but a year later in April of 1969, the WW II general and hero would resign after defeat in a referendum on his proposed constitutional reforms.

During 1968, riots in American cities continued to violently express this whirlwind of swirling forces: riots over Martin Luther King Jr.'s assassination in April of 1968, a riot in Miami's black section during the mid-summer heat, and the riot with the Chicago heat of the Democratic convention in August, probably the largest and most confrontational riot in American history. After King's assassination, much more attention was given the report issued by the National Advisory Commission on Civil Disorders which had been appointed by President Johnson in 1967; headed by Otto Kerner, then governor of Illinois, the investigatory panel issued a 250,000-word report on February 29, 1968. Two of the conclusions the commission reached were that the disorders usually involved blacks reacting against symbols of white American society and not white people and that those who were rioting were seeking greater participation in the American system, not rejecting it. And the report's core tenet emphasized an axiom of racism: white racism digs and maintains the ghetto trench for the prejudicially suppressed black race. At the 1968 summer Olympics in Mexico, Tommie Smith and John Carlos, two black American athletes, won the gold (in world record time) and bronze medals in the 200-metre dash. The two stood on the awards stand with black knee-length stockings, received their medals, turned to watch the raising of one Austrialian and two United States flags (the flags of the three medal winners) as the U.S. national anthem was played, lowered their heads, and raised clenched fists (Smith his right, Carlos his left) inside black gloves. It was a bold and defiant statement both of black power ("We shall overcome") and America's disregarded impoverishment. Although they had the freedom to express such a sensational statement, Smith and Carlos were immediately suspended from the Olympic team at the insistence of the International Olympic Committee. On American prime-time television, The Mod Squad presented three rehabilitated street-wise young people – one white male, one white female, one black male – as undercover cops; they were mod, yet part of the system – marketable to television viewers, but politically correct. Showcasing a prancing and bouncing, robust Barbara Eden, *I Dream of Jeannie* led into the 1968 fall season premiere of Rowan & Martin's *Laugh-In* which offered a weekly hour of comedy in an edited *melange* perfect for the medium. But before the fall season had premiered, the news departments of the three major networks covered the Democratic National Convention in Chicago where Hubert Humphrey was nominated as the presidental candidate. The live broadcast of clashes between Chicago's police and the predominantly youthful demonstrators evoked a huge cry from the public that television had helped conspire this unnerving assault on authority, and the networks were left defending what they thought had been objective recording of what really happened. The viewing public, Nixon's so-called silent majority, was upset with what they perceived as networks broadcasting only bad news – riots, lootings, killings, the Vietnam War. Where was the good news? It was being broadcast, but storms of mayhem and blood leave more lasting impressions (and attract bigger audiences) than tranquil sunsets and sunrises. Earlier in

May, French television had been a target of the mass demonstrations because it had focused only on good news, in a sense, betraying the public with a foolish picture of their state of affairs. At Chicago, the anti-war demonstrators had the potential no march in Washington D.C. had had: the presence of television, in this case, the complete focus of the three national networks news departments. It was a demostration to an unsuspecting American public – and the television industry – of one distinctive power of this particular medium. The "tribal love-rock musical", *Hair!*, premiered on Broadway in April. Without a significant plot, the musical presented a vibrant, innovative, and entertaining version of turning on, tuning in, and dropping out. The emergence of the Theatre of Involvement followed a similar format more brazen in the reactionary artistic tradition of shocking the bourgeoisie (in the 1960s, the middle class). Though the energetic and often aggressive writers, actors and actresses laid bare the issues of the day, the anger they would predictably evoke shut down any dialogue or debate by audiences after the play. The Theatre of Involvement offered no endearing works that could survive beyond the swirling forces of the times, but when the *avant-garde* Living Theatre group performed in February of 1969 at the University of Southern California in Los Angeles, Jim Morrison planted himself in the audience. The seeds of inspiration brought quick fruition at the March 1st concert at Miami.

By 1969, one of the first waves of *The Best Of...* albums from groups of the Sixties hit the Billboard charts – The Association, The Bee Gees, Buffalo Springfield, Cream, Donovan, The Mamas and the Papas, The Rascals, and Diana Ross and The Supremes. While The Fifth Dimension's 'Aquarius/Let The Sunshine In' and songs by Creedence Clearwater Revival were being played repeatedly over radio airwaves, the tugging undercurrent of the times surfaced in two very poignant Top 40 war protest songs, 'Galveston' and 'Rudy, Don't Take Your Love To Town'. The Who unleashed *Tommy* while the fictitious and plastic Archies made millions of dollars. Led Zeppelin released their first album, a young Bob Seger was climbing the charts with 'Ramblin' Gamblin' Man', and The Beatles' *White Album* revealed what many had suspected: a fragmenting into individuals of the once cohesive Beatles. And in 1969 the first wave of rock culture heroes began dying off: author Jack Kerovac in April and Brian Jones of The Rolling Stones in July.

This phase of the rock culture, the Sixties, was about to end. The forces and issues upon which the youth had honed their creative energies were peaking and dissipating. Not only that, it was damn difficult to keep sharpening a keen creative edge against a culture of which many of the counter-culture had become a successful part. With both commercial and limited social success, the revolutionary – if not just the reactionary – edge of the counter-culture didn't have that hard stone of resistance upon which to sharpen its edge. How could millionaire musicians, like The Doors, sing about the hypocrisy of a plastic, materialistic society detached from the roots of life?

Moreover, The Doors were no longer one of the influencing, let alone, controlling forces of the whirlwind they had helped swirl into its urgent and passionate pace in the Sixties. They had become detached from their own roots, no longer firmly grounded in any rich humus of creativity. Instead, having kept pace with a swirling tour schedule, they were swept into the very plastic world so vividly rendered in their first two albums and less so in the third. In retrospect, Morrison wrote in one of his many notebooks that after he had "ploughed" his seed through the heart of America, like "a germ" in the nation's "psychic blood vein", he now embraced the "poetry of business" and became for a while a "Prince of Industry".1

Obligated to fulfill a recording contract, The Doors found themselves needing to create music for this fourth album. There were no new songs from gigging before an intimate night club audience; there were no new songs flowing to Morrison while idling away time on a rooftop or a beach. This was to be a period of transition. And after the Miami concert on March 1, 1969, The Doors, now freed of touring commitments, were clearly into a transition. Recording for this fourth album began in late 1968, but the album wasn't completed till June of 1969, though a steady string of singles were released beginning in late December of 1968 with the commercially successful 'Touch Me'. Part of this transition was that *The Soft Parade* would include separate writing credits for individual songs. Krieger said Morrison wanted separate credits because, among other reasons, he thought the lyrics in Robby's song, 'Tell All The People', were too political.2 In a radio special produced by *The Source*, Ray offered this paraphrasing of Jim: "I ain't saying that: 'Can't you see me growing/get your guns/follow me down'."3 Jim told Jerry Hopkins in a 1969 *Rolling Stone* interview that initially the group did things in the interest of unity, but since the unity wasn't "that much in jeopardy", people should know "who was saying what" because he and Robby had very different visions of reality.4 For many, it didn't matter who was saying what; the album was panned as a sell-out. And the growing erratic behaviour of Morrison provided an easy target at which to aim – and make stick – such criticism. The consensus opinion was that during this period Morrison was basically a disinterested, drunken asshole, a view Jim seemed to share in a passage from one of his notebooks, writing that being drunk was a "good disguise" and that he drank so he could "talk to assholes" which, he wrote, included himself.5 In a *Rolling Stone* article about the making of the Morrison myth, Mikal Gilmore summarized what has been repeatedly written about Jim at this time: Morrison had gone from being one the "smartest, scariest and sexiest heroes" in rock 'n' roll to a "heart-rending alcoholic and clownish jerk".6 The impression that The Doors no longer appeared in control of their work and that no one was taking them seriously anymore seemed quite apparent after the bawdy March 1st concert in Miami's Dinner Key Auditorium which brought warrants for Jim's arrest on charges of "lewd and lascivious behaviour in public by exposing his private parts and by simulating masturbation and oral copulation". The Lizard King, a self-proclaimed erotic politician, was about to meet the hard, cutting edge of judicial – and political – reality. With the release of *The Soft Parade*, reviewers had more than just the music tempering their perspectives of this latest Doors' album. Though writing for *Creem* in the summer of 1981, Richard Riegel encapsulated the general reaction, writing that if *Waiting For The Sun* had made many older hippies question their view of The Doors "as Avatars of the *avant-garde*", then *The Soft Parade* had finished any interest in the group.7 Lester Bangs was less cordial, proclaiming The Doors' "artistic stock had hit an all-time low", the group had abandoned their "original promise", and they – especially Morrison – had "turned what they represented into a joke".8 In an 1981 interview with *Musician*, Manzarek said the group was ready to move on to their next phase and to do something different, like recording with horns and strings.9 The use of strings from the Los Angeles Philharmonic and horns of local jazz musicians generated a swell of critical response. In the underground newspaper, *Northwest Passage*, Rob Cline wrote: "The Doors, while trying to explore new musical horizons, fell flat on their asses. Does a rock 'n' roll group really need violins and trombones? The Doors are the best when getting it on straight and hard as witness their first 2 albums."10

David Walley in *The East Village Other* took direct aim, stating that the album was "badly messed up by the syrupy arrangements of Paul Rothchild" and could be retitled, *The Rothchild Strings Play The Doors*.11 Miller Francis, Jr., in the underground newspaper, *The Great Speckled Bird*, felt "that a misfire in poetic 'Art Rock' like *The Soft Parade* comes on so fucking pretentious, like something written rather than something sung."12 Many in the underground felt betrayed, yet there were those who had hated the first albums but insisted this fourth one marked the maturity of the group away from teenybopdom. A reviewer in the Ottawa underground newspaper, *Octopus*, wrote that: "I always hated the Doors and Jim Morrison and found their previous albums boring. This time it is different. The sensual, animal, back to the hills, down on it sound is emphasized by the light use of strings and horns... [The Doors] have progressed, this album is not just for the teen queens to get horny over, it is an interesting, tough and important album."13

Did they sell-out? In an 1981 interview, the person some accused of gumming up the lucid Doors sound with the syrupy resonance of strings and horns, Paul Rothchild, said that the intention of this album was "to hit the mass, mass market, with horns, strings, the full orchestra treatment", but they consciously recorded "in an attempt to explore all the idioms available", although he agreed that 'Touch Me' was a compromise which alienated part of The Doors' original audience while gaining "an enormous number of new fans".14 He also said in another interview that to get Jim interested while making *The Soft Parade* was "like pulling teeth".15 Ray, years later in a radio special produced by *The Source*, said that in retrospect using horns and strings "probably wasn't the best idea we ever had, but we enjoyed doing it".16 In an interview with *Guitar World* in 1994, Robby Krieger said he didn't "really like orchestrating the songs" on this album and would never have done it – it had been Rothchild's idea.17 Without much of any repertoire of songs from which to draw, The Doors and Rothchild could produce, at best, a fuzzy sketch of The Doors' artistic vision on the fourth album. If on the album cover the group seemed a distant image behind the camera stationed on the tripod, their music seemed just as distant, the album a collection of seemingly unrelated still life portraits. The Doors' artistic vision in the previous albums was more active and pervasive; this time, the vision isn't as focused on society and remains behind the camera for the next photographic opportunity. The Doors and Rothchild rendered a hastily drawn portrait of the very pop idioms of which they were so critical. The songs are technically simple, unimaginative snatches seemingly covered in the blues, like the cover of the album. Trying to impose a critical rendering that some sort of thematic structure underlies *The Soft Parade* isn't fair to The Doors' artistic vision. The cohesive artistic rendering in this fourth album was the idiomatic exploration of Pop. The Doors and Rothchild produced an album that would sell, a definite sell-out in terms of artistic vision and creative value.

Momentary sanctuary in a sell-out: like the persona in the previous albums moving from the momentary sanctuary of a lover to the freedom of breaking through, so the artistic spirits rest momentarily in the risky sanctuary just this side of bubblegum pop before returning to rich humus in which to nurture their roots. Bangs, perhaps the most critical and appraising writer of Jim Morrison, reflected in an 1981 article for *Creem* titled, "Jim Morrison, Oafus Laureate", that the "bubblegum/parody" of the third and fourth albums may have been "entirely intentional, premeditated, one juncture in a vast strategy" to reveal that "machismo equals bozo in the drag", that rock stars were just "huge oafus cartoons", and that Morrison's games of "poet" and "shaman" were "two more gushers of American snake-oil".18 Yet Dave DiMartino offered a retrospective appraisal that Morrison "never dealt with specifics" and gave answers that were neither true nor false "because they were abstract and primitive simultaneously" – abstract because the lyrics dealt "with 'soft parades', words that fit together nicely but meant little", and primitive because the lyrics dealt "with the basest of emotions and never taking them to their logical conclusions".19 The Doors, and especially Morrison, could paint lucid portraits with mere impressions which were musically and lyrically drawn from the vast and complex matrix of metaphors our culture uses to define reality.

"Only as an esthetic product can the world be justified to all eternity – although our consciousness of our own significance does scarcely exceed the consciousness a painted soldier might have of the battle in which he takes part. Thus our whole knowledge of art is at bottom illusory... Only as the genius in the act of creation merges with the primal architect of the cosmos can he truly know something of the eternal essence of art. For... he is at once subject and object, poet, actor, and audience."

*Friedrich Nietzsche,*
*The Birth Of Tragedy (p. 42)*

"Most people were as incapable of entering Jim's kingdom as a camel passing through the eye of a needle. But they would suffice as his audience; actor and spectator – the world was divided into the two."

*Ian Whitcomb,*
*Rock Odyssey: A Musician's Chronicle*
*To The Sixties (p. 339)*

Such impressions touch what everyone suspects but doesn't know how to express in concrete terms, for people understand easier the subconscious metaphors which circumvent prejudices imposed upon the conscious mind by the environment. And Riegel hinted at such a realization when he noted that the album marked Morrison's changing to a "newer rock 'n' roll persona", that Jim was finally seeing life from a "musician's eye viewpoint" and was "mutating into a bluesman".20 It is not difficult to slide such an artistic persona under the term shaman, or as some critics wrote, shamanic bluesman. By this album, the overtones and poetic imagery of the artistic vision are far less introspective and self-enclosing, less urgent and less angry. In short, more melancholy. There are few if any answers, and the outward trappings and confusion of this society aren't going to change, but one gets the impression that these shamanic spirits have approached a truce with mortality: "Life kind of sucks, society is screwed up, and that's the way things are going to be, but I don't care because I'm enjoying some of the simple pleasures of being alive; I'm feeling okay about things, so the futility can just wait until I have enough energy to define it in my mind." Artistically, then, *The Soft Parade* is an ambiguous transformation to the blues

103

outlook, evoking undefined feelings without striving to be one thing in particular. Lyrically, Morrison is into this transformation, but musically, the others haven't caught up. This album, musically different than the style of the other five, becomes a compilation of musical *cliches* and rip-offs. The seriousness of the lyrics of these songs, especially of those written by Morrison, is hard to determine. The words probably would have been much more effective with music that had organically grown with the lyrics, but they lose a lot of impact in this setting. To say that this discrepancy adds more tension to the message gives credit that is undeserved, given that this album wasn't really planned. When the music's good, enjoy it, and when the words are good, enjoy them, but trying to link the two together isn't necessarily valid. This album wasn't created to be interpreted in that way. It was a creation painstakingly pieced together by Rothchild. Morrison told John Tobler in an interview at the Isle of Wight Festival in England that the album "kinda got out of control" and took too long to make and that an album, like a book of stories strung together, should have "some kind of unified feeling and style", but *The Soft Parade* lacks that.21 However, patterns and relationships do emerge which render a transition in The Doors' artistic vision. The rebellious cries for action are mellowing into the acceptance of the way life is. The cries of social anguish are becoming more reflective, more mirror-like in their renderings. The rush of the anxious, uninhibited lover who has transcended through the passive, detached lover is transforming into a shamanic bluesman. Beginning to understand his own feelings and limitations as a human, the youthful shaman has become closer to other people, at least on the most basic levels. The artistic vision, which before had rejected plastic people and society, now becomes more accepting. Life is becoming a "soft parade" – well, compared to the previous albums, a softer parade – of shamanic insights and artistic renderings.

## SIDE ONE

*The Soft Parade* opens with a full blast of horns and a proclamation of alternative leadership in 'Tell All The People'. Reactions to the song ranged from Francis writing that the song "is night club shuck"22 to Mitch Kapor writing in the *View From The Bottom*, a New Haven underground newspaper, that the same song "is our great synthesis of erotic politician with Christ image martyr rock".23 Penned by Krieger, the song reflects his style of simple and ambiguous textures: tell the people to "follow me down". Down to where? The music scales upward with the horns, but the lyrics don't suggest the people are being led to the mountain top as they stop to look at the wonder at their feet. Though we usually live looking up toward success, seeking the appearance of external completeness, life's real wonder and meaning may lie in travelling down into facing yourself, into honesty, into spiritual freedom and Morrison's image of other weird scenes from inside the gold mine. Morrison, the crooning erotic politician, sings to follow him "across the sea" to "molded flowing revelry". During a time of deep social unrest, the song offered the allure of simple resolution. But like most Doors' songs, there flows an undercurrent of uncertainty and uneasiness about this erotic politician promising the people he can "set them free". The lyric urging us to take his hand and then bury our "troubles in the sand" may suggest the easy removal from sight the problems of modern existence, yet the lyric also sketches an image of the ostrich-with-its-head-in-the-sand way of dealing with troubles. Bury can suggest death, and the ensuing call to "get your guns" doesn't exactly reassure that the journey across the sea will be peaceful. Rejecting social restraints doesn't necessarily mean you automatically become totally honest with yourself; there is a blind limbo in there somewhere... Though hippies were filling rifle barrels with flowers, The Doors weren't using olive branches to illustrate their artistic vision. Pichaske, wary of this decree to follow in this trip across the sea, wrote that this new world was dangerous – "insofar as a new awareness destroys old preconceptions, it threatens death and destruction".24 But so does voluntary blindness and lying to yourself. The Doors' artistic vision persistently probes the problem of which do you follow. To get to this promise land of "molded flowing revelry" requires crossing the sea, a place where there has been more than one unnerving breaking through to the unknown, as in 'Moonlight Drive' and 'Horse Latitudes'. As the 1960s drew to a close, political leaders were being assassinated, the United States seemed adrift as it became more bitterly divided, and Krieger's 'Tell All The People' portrayed a rather simplified saviour – a political statement Morrison seemingly didn't want credit for. And the portrait The Doors paint of breaking through to the other side, to a promised land, is hazier than the previous portraits, for what they are running from isn't as clearly defined. As they have done in their previous albums, The Doors shift their perspective from breaking through to rendering a portrait of love. 'Touch Me' opens with more Kriegersque lyrics, vague and ambiguous images which allude to something to which we can all relate but aren't clear on what it is. In an interview with Robert Matheu in 1981, Robby explained the song originally was "hit me", not "touch me", but Jim wouldn't sing that lyric.25 Densmore expounded on this, writing that Robby had written, "Come on, come on, come on, now, HIT me, babe!", from one of the many rumoured domestic squabbles between him and his girlfriend, but had offered no resistance when Jim suggested the change to "touch me".26 Whether it's touch or hit me, the song portrays a passion intense enough to take not only a lover's physical but also emotional punches because the love will go on till the rain stops and the stars fall. Nevertheless, a mellowing Morrison wanted to tone the lyric down to "touch me", a line he had used in previous live performances of 'When The Music's Over' as recorded on bootlegs: "Something wrong, something not quite right/Touch me baby/All through the night". The song evoked probably The Doors' most popish expression of love, as the sweet strings of violins swelled in the background with Morrison's crooning. Bob (Turk) Nirkind in a Detroit underground newspaper, *The South End*, offered a typical reaction: with strings and horns replacing the raw power of The Doors, 'Touch Me' loses the forcefulness the group had demonstrated in the past, and "the words do zero for the image" established by The Doors.27 Francis was more blatant about The Doors' sell-out, rhetorically asking if 'Touch Me' could "be sung with a straight face in a super-elegant night club to a drunk set of plastic middle-aged Muzak-lovers, with identically the same sound?".28 But, why not enjoy the good feelings when they happen, even if it means acknowledging something as syrupy as loving someone till the rains stops and the stars fall? How long can you survive trying to always outfox plastic Twentieth Century Foxes? Beneath the horns and strings, The Doors generate a controlled frenzy of sound, and as J. Kordosh of *Creem* wrote: "Curtis Amy ends the whole mess with an equally manic sax solo."29 The closing jazz solo on sax by Amy musically frees the individual from the controlled musical frenzy of The Doors and the accompanying instrumentals. A twist of humour brings the entire triad of sound and lyrics to a blunt ending: "Stronger than dirt!". The gang-chanted finale quotes the then-popular

TV commercial slogan of Ajax household cleaner. Ajax-cleansed and freed from his lover and whatever promise that may have been broken, Morrison slides into the other side as the shamanic bluesman in 'Shaman's Blues' and weaves together a fragmented message of impending impressions to his lover. Reviewers reacted accordingly, typified by Rich Mangelsdorff who wrote in his review in *Kaleidoscope* that 'Shaman's Blues' was "one of those half-assed things where you can guess at what The Doors are, rather than feel it direct".30 Francis labelled the song "at best an embarrassment",31 yet Patricia Kennely reviewed the song as a "scatty-sounding amalgam of jazz and blues": much stretching and bending of free, choppy segments with many jazzy vocal and instrumental licks.32 As for 'Shaman's Blues' fitting-in to mainstream Top 40, forget it. Our present mental and spiritual states don't frame daily existence on values, metaphors, or an outlook that can comprehend or appreciate the landscape the shamanic spirit (or for that matter, the artistic spirit) moves through. You have to be able to economically shape and market your art if you want to fit-in, to survive on our modern landscape. Thus, the shamanic world is difficult to communicate in modern languages or thoughts which have diminished the capacity and ability to represent such realities. And Morrison was more unconscious than conscious of the shamanic landscape from which he spoke.

Instead of calling forth a persona of a street-wise, smart-ass rebel taunting with the reactionary rhetoric of cynicism and detachment, Morrison evokes a tone which reveals an honesty that is more sensitive and meaningful. The voice is quite human as he sings about there never being someone else "like you" or someone who does the "things you do" and then croons for another chance. This isn't the detached, cynical lover who rendered a plastic image of the 'Twentieth Century Fox' or who taunted the unhappy and lost, little girl in 'Strange Days'. There is no sarcastic portrait of a prison of one's own device or a world locked up inside a plastic box. Rather, there is an invitation to get back together: he asks if she has an evening she could "lend" – a much softer sounding and rendered yearning than the taunting and demanding lover of earlier songs. Yet, though wiser, he is still on the outside looking in at his lover; he knows her moods and her mind, repeating the lyric, "And your mind" (four times on the album, six on the CD), before adding, "And you're mind". She is his, as he is hers, to a certain extent because she has given a piece of herself to him by letting him get close enough to understand her mind.

In 'Shaman's Blues', the subtle undercurrent of uncertainty surfaces like crashing waves upon the shores of the listener's ears with such images as "train yard nursing penitentiary". This image depicts the dualism of life, of trapping one's own freedom in a prison when forming relationships which are necessary for spiritual wholeness in that they comfort and nurse the soul, if just for a brief moment. After a Manzarek organ riff which swirls around with the image that has just been flashed into the listener's mind, Morrison hits, more than touches, the listener with a rather stark image of feeling the close and hot pursuit of "cold grinding" jaws of a grizzly bear. Does this image make sense from someone singing the blues of being alone? Not really, unless a shamanic voice is trying to express an image of intense fear he knows his lover must face up to – or run from, not much different than the image of strange days returning to track us down. Being alone, outside the nursing penitentiary of the relationship, the lover has to face herself again. Humans are basically alone, left to choose between trapping themselves in a briefly soothing relationship or fighting their own inner grizzlies. This is not that far removed from the "run with me" chant conjured up in 'Not To Touch The Earth'.

And Morrison nicely brings an abrupt shift to that image of running with the ensuing lyric of stopping and whispering "in Saturday's shore" that all the world is a "saviour". The lover can hide from the grizzly by immersing herself in the external world. Saturday is freedom, but Monday provides the sanctuary and security of the weekly routine. Are you going to stand on Saturday's shore or are you going to take the swim on a Moonlight Drive? The edge of transition in 'Tell All The People', the ambiguity of seeing the wonder at their feet as they prepare to follow their saviour across the sea, is cast in a more personal light.

Morrison also is standing on Saturday's shore, at the edge of the sea, the edge before entering a baptism or a drowning, but he isn't burying all his troubles in the sand. Like all edges in The Doors' portraits of life, this one is a place to confront what it means to be human: will you stop and remember the pain? Living means pain, and the blues not only sing of this, they embrace it as part of the experience of living.

Throughout the song reoccurs the plea to stop – a stark contrast to the passionate urgency so vividly expressed in previous albums. The tone of slowing and stopping has already been hinted at in the previous two songs. In 'Shaman's Blues' the stopping signals a moment for reflecting: stop "to consider" and stop to "remember". It is the blues – the detached lover pleading for his love not to forget, not to make a mistake. Running away from yourself only leads you in circles. The path to breaking through isn't one you blindly stumble upon while running from grizzlies; it comes with honest self-awareness, from stopping and reflecting. The frustrations of both shaman and lover seem to cry out in the stanza where Jim, lonely for his lover, wonders if she thinks about how he feels while he is "on the meadow" while she is "on the field". The meadow renders an image of nature, whereas field depicts an image of land manicured by man, such as the image of streets being "fields that never die" from 'The Crystal Ship'. The shaman/lover, separated from his world and lover, wanders detached from the fields of man, from the neon groves, yet his lover can't break through to the meadow. She remains on the field. And he finds the essence of the blues: he is alone, and he cries. Having broken through to the other side, the shaman finds he hasn't left behind all that makes him human. According to Densmore, the spoken coda which ends the song was created by sliding in and out ad-lib bits from various vocal takes of Jim's.33 The amorphous ride out of the song leaves for a departure to anywhere, including a vague allusion of the "bridesmaid" to the coda queen/bride image at the closing of side one in 'Easy Ride'.

This stark and disquieting closing to 'Shaman's Blues' slides into an equally wicked laugh which opens 'Do It'. Kennely suspected the song was "studio concoction music" better suited for "something a bit more serious".34 Of 'Do It' Nirkind wondered if anyone could explain why The Doors did this "electric, buzzing song" with the "most inane lyrics ever put on an album" by the group.35 Perhaps the child-like chanting by the boys which precedes Morrison's wicked laugh is a subtle way of saying the song was all in fun; besides, the bubblegum pop fits the repeated calling to the "children" in the song... until you hear the song effectively rendered in concert by one of The Doors tribute bands (The Doors never performed the song live). And then the power of the music hits you.

The song recalls the simplified message of salvation sung in 'Tell All The People' as Morrison sings repeatedly for the children please to listen to him because they you will eventually "rule the world". The erotic politician, having learned something about being human, is no longer preaching that ultimate revolution is what we want now! or that one can leave the world behind by breaking through to the other side. No, children, you will inherit the world, so listen. To what? That "you got to please me"? And what pleases the me? A wild love? A journey to the other side? How about an "easy ride"?

Side one opens with a calling for people to take a journey "across the sea", and side one closes with the return to the journey image, recanting the *carpi diem* theme to a lover to seize the day and take an 'Easy Ride'. Robby's laughing guitar, Ray's prancing organ, and John's upbeat drumming create a simple and carefree texture, and Jim's light and crisp vocals are dominated by long vowels and rolling consonants of the lyrics. The Doors may be rendering the appearance of a light-hearted trip through love, but there emerges the impression they are portraying something deeper than an "easy ride". Instead of enjoying the moment, Jim returns to a campy, sarcastic look at a relationship, echoing the flightiness of 'I Looked At You' from the debut album. He knows what will get a reaction and will take that risk of exploring the mask that she wears. The Doors frequently portray masks covering deeper emotions, and the "costume of control" yields to the passion of excitement unfolding to the exploring fingers of the lover. Just as the lover in 'Shaman's Blues' knows her moods and mind, this lover is equally confident, knowing the "joy" unfolding beneath her "costume of control" will easily overcome the vague defensive struggle put up by her pride.

The comparison of her eyes to "polished stone" alludes to the mask of the costume of control, the calculated cool of the Twentieth Century Fox, the aloofness of the queen of the angels. But Jim has seen the Twentieth Century Fox/queen of angels free of her disguise(s), which doesn't necessarily mean there is substance underneath. Costume of control yields to joy, and the ensuing "burning glass" image nicely captures the melting stone, the transparency of the mask, the "light my fire" urgency below every costume of control. And the sounds she is making don't come with a frown; he doesn't have to see the smile – he can hear it. Instead of closing the song with the lovers drifting off into the sunset, Morrison evokes the image of having broken through on the highway to the bright midnight. He invites the "coda queen" to be his bride, the "coda queen" merging the imagery of a coda, an independent closing to a musical piece, with the allusion to the queen of angels. And Jim reveals she can now "rage in darkness" at his side. She has broken through from the field to the meadow, and the *carpi diem* theme is resounded in full passionate resonance of seizing "summer in your pride" and taking "winter in your stride". The pride which vaguely had fought the unfolding joy can now seize the power of summer. And the seasons have been absorbed by the lovers, instead of marking the passage of love through a summertime love into a wintertime waltz as they did in the album, *Waiting For The Sun*. But do the *cliched*, Opryland ripoffs render the song in a sarcastic tone? Is Jim mocking his lover because he is able to strip her mask so easily, giving him an easy ride, a brief encounter in his meadow, and knowing she will return to the field? The hand clapping through this lyric amplifies the upbeat tone of the guitar, organ and drums. Unabashed, Morrison rides the calculated excitement of passion, but it is an "easy ride", one for the moment. The same undercurrent of uneasiness, of momentary delight, of a laughing guitar also laps at the shores of this image of an "easy ride", as The Doors fade away, Morrison crooning, "Easy, easy, easy, easy, easy, easy, easy/Ee-ee-ride/All right".

## SIDE TWO

Side one closes with Morrison almost laughing an upbeat "all right", and side two opens with Morrison restating "all right", but in a considerably different tone. The pulsating, deliberate deliverance of Densmore's drumming, Manzarek's organ, and Krieger's guitar in 'Wild Child' makes a dramatic shift from the tightly composed orchestrated opening on side one and the laughing, light tone rendered in 'Easy Ride'. The coda queen, after becoming her shamanic lover's bride, has emerged as a "wild child", in one sense a product of their union. She is "full of grace", but this grace isn't the calculated coolness and costume of control of the Twentieth Century Fox or the long-legged, agile, dusky jewel strolling along the beach.

This grace is free of any self-imposed prison or masks that need exploring. This "wild child" offers what the opening song on side one alluded to – a saviour of the people. The "cool face" image that closes the opening stanza reveals a mask of neither polished stone nor burning glass. This "cool face" isn't feverish with passionate urgency; it is balanced with wisdom the Twentieth Century Fox on Love Street has yet to learn.

"To understand tragic myth we must see it as Dionysiac wisdom made concrete through Apollonian artifice. In that myth the world of appearance is pushed to its limits, where it denies itself and seeks to escape back into the world of primordial reality."

*Friedrich Nietzsche,*
*The Birth Of Tragedy (p. 132)*

Free from disguise, she is a "natural child", yet, true to The Doors' portrayal of life being dualistic, she is also a "terrible child". Neither her mother's nor father's child, she was born "screamin' wild", resonating like the coda queen raging in darkness at Morrison's side. Morrison undercuts the music with the spoken line about "an ancient lunatic" reigning in "the trees of the night", an image that hints at the world forsaken by modern society, but not by him and his "wild child" coda queen. The imagery also echoes the shadowy picture rendered in 'Not To Touch The Earth' of the shadows of trees beneath a still moon witnessing a wild breeze. The shaman on the meadow is no longer alone; his lover has become, as portrayed on *Waiting For The Sun*, the "wild love" who has eluded Morrison on the previous albums, but who isn't just a fleeing companion as in 'Not To Touch The Earth'. The Doors etch out their belief we have to face our fears and not cower in hesitant action, to experience the journey of living, often expressed in the appeal to return to primal intuitions and urges. The "wild child", not chained to anything, is free to experience life, dancing on her knees with a "Pirate Prince" by her side. Not necessarily the Prince of Darkness, Morrison draws upon the dualistic image of Prince Charming as a pirate, capable of taking her on a "Spanish Caravan". Instead of grizzlies, "hunger" is at her heels. "Freedom" is in her eyes because she can face her deepest fears – she can stare into the eyes of the "hollow idol". The void, the abyss, the ancient cave of human existence which we believe we have evolved away from and no longer should look into – this wild child not only can face it, but can stare into it, "full of grace", and return as a "saviour" of the people. This portrait generated many reviews that Morrison was singing his revolutionary rhetoric and finally evoking his usual apocalyptical images. Kennely labelled 'Wild Child' a real Doors song: "Hypnotic, dark, surreal, evil."36 Nirkind wrote that the music – "Krieger's whining guitar and Densmore's rapid spot-drumming" – seems "to groove on Morrison's talking-singing ode to revolution"37, a view echoed by Mangelsdorff: "wail and cry with drive and Morrison riding the lethal horse of anarchy right at you, with a grim treasure under his arm".38 But not everyone sensed the same terror, as exemplified by Francis who thought the song sounded like Morrison wrote it hoping "it would be quoted about him someday – it sounds like a 'hip' press release".39 Or by Kordosh who stated the song emerged "as an uncomfortably stupid paean to ideas" The Doors had shot down on earlier albums.40 Bangs, rendering Morrison in the caricature of a Bozo Dionysus, wrote that one such Bozo moment in The Doors records was "the mock-portentousness of the 'Do you remember when we were in Africa?' coda" that ended 'Wild Child'.41 Nonetheless, this spoken closing punctuates the pulsating music of the song and harks back to the coda queen who is raging in darkness as side one closes. The image-laden, Morrison-written 'Wild Child' dissipates quickly in the upbeat, less image-laden, Krieger-written 'Runnin' Blue', complete with Robby's vocal debut on the chorus. Kennely wrote that Robby's singing made "you properly appreciate Jim Morrison".42 Francis wrote that 'Runnin' Blue' is "astonishing in its arrogance"43, and Mangelsdorff expounded on this: "Poor Otis dead and gone" singsongs Morrison, with a Redding horn-section blast rising up on out, cut to Dylan parody, complete with mock nashvilley backdrop, then BST [Blood, Sweat & Tears] horn-section jibes. All the while, Morrison's ego (rebounding from the Miami debacle?) stretches itself in almost Maileresque fashion across the scene, looking for the home where the psyche finds soothing broth.44

Offering homage to the recently deceased Otis Redding, Morrison sang the opening lyrics to the song, "Poor Otis dead and gone/Left me hear to sing his song/Pretty little girl with the red dress on", during a live performance of 'When The Music's Over' during a three-day engagement at Winterland in San Francisco in late December 1967 (he sang these lyrics just before the final refrain of 'When The Music's Over'). Redding died in a plane crash on December 10, 1967, and had been scheduled to perform at Winterland along with The Doors. On this album, the song recants the journey motif, but the crisp confidence expressed in the previous songs, like 'Tell All The People' or 'Easy Ride', has evaporated. Now The Doors sing about stopping, backing down, turning around slowly, and remembering, like in 'Shaman's Blues' – but The Doors don't slow down because they have "the runnin' blues". Like Otis looking for that dock in the bay, The Doors conjure up a vision of looking for sanctuary, maybe back in L.A. And the dock in the bay brings back the image of an edge, of "Saturday's shore", of a place where one crosses over. The sanctuary being sought isn't the same one being sought with the urgent, passionate running evoked by 'Break On Through' or 'Not To Touch The Earth'. This running seems to be in circles, running towards a past that always returns to the present. And this running in circles exposes vulnerability, of "runnin' scared" and "runnin' blue", of going so fast and wondering what to do. Do? Like the image of acceptance in the album's closing song, The Doors recall the images of the "easy ride" – don't fight that "runnin' blue". Sometimes you have to retrace your steps to find where you lost yourself. The cost of not doing so is to become permanently vulnerable and battered by external forces. The urgent, jazzy rhythm of 'Runnin' Blue' to get back to the dock in the bay dissolves into the meditative allure rendered in 'Wishful, Sinful'. Of the shift, Nirkind sarcastically noted we get "Jim Morrison, dark politician, crooning" in the comforts of "another refugee from Top 40 radio".45 The 45 single had the typical antithetical B-side song, 'Who Scared You', which sounded like a studio-blues concoction that badly emulated Blood, Sweat & Tears and was strained through lyrics whose ambiguity and piece-meal nature probably contributed to keeping the song off the album. Of the opening image of water, Pichaske wrote that blue was an "amorphous image" in Doors songs: sometimes it suggested "faith and potentiality", sometimes the traditional sense of "feelin' blue", but was aligned often with water "to connote death, and/or sexuality"46. Although the "cooling water" slows the tempo, the song sketches out a similar portrait of the impending impressions rendered by the shamanic bluesman in 'Shaman's Blues'. The song's opening image, "wishful crystal", resurrects on the horizon from this dock by L.A. the fragile ship of thrills, 'The Crystal Ship', hinting at the disquieting imagery underscoring the tone of the song.

The next stanza alludes to the terrible, yet natural child: a "wishful sinful" love that is "beautiful to see" and is where Jim wants to be.

Having left her to wander and seek out the dock in the bay, the lover might be longing for that dancing with the coda queen in the ancient forests of Africa. Ironically, the violins swell up, musically rendering the popish remorse of longing for a lost love, but the sexual pun on "came" in the closing line of the stanza doesn't elude the crooning Morrison.

He is on the dock looking into the sea, and he "can't escape the blue" – of the water or the feeling – of being separated from his "wishful sinful wicked" lover. The allusion to drowning is a powerful one, reinforced by the paradoxical image of rising magic while the sun, shining "deep beneath the sea", calls him to sink to the dark depths of that sea, and in the background, the soft woodwinds tow gently at the listener. The 'Moonlight Drive' Jim urgently had wooed to his lover in *Strange Days* has been reversed. Like the lonely shamanic bluesman in 'Shaman's Blues', he laments that he loves to hear both the wind and his lover crying – a lamenting for more tears to cover everything in wicked blue or the desire to hear her screamin' wild? As in previous albums, The Doors close *The Soft Parade* with a resolution, and that song, 'The Soft Parade', garnered the most reactions of any Doors' song. Francis wrote that the song contained "some of the most atrocious attempts at poetry" outside a college writing class and that in the spoken introduction Morrison sounds like a Hollywood version of a down home fundamentalist preacher: "None of this means a fucking thing, but it does show the narcissist preacher behind the rock star's image".47

"[T]he dangerous narcissism of adolescence... comes always in the wake of the very sensibility that makes the writing of poetry possible... It lives more in the realm of ambition than of poetic achievement through an unwillingness to be diminished or humbled. The narcissism of adolescence... continues in the making of lyric poets who are eternal adolescents, eternally unadaptable, forever incapable of fixing themselves into a pattern of life. The essentially romantic trait of narcissism is its inevitable obsession with the indefinite and the unlimited."

*Wallace Fowlie,*
*Rimbaud (A Critical Study) (p. 239)*

More succinctly, Kordosh wrote that he couldn't remember The Doors doing a "more juvenile song".48 But Kapor thought the song saved the album, noting that musical constancy linked the loosely structured poetic images; moreover, he appreciated what he called "Morrison's newly found sense of humour".49 Kennely wrote that The Doors built the song "on tidal shifts of music and kinetics, declamatory poem trips", stringing sections together like "contrasting beads of melody and surreality".50 Terry Rompers in a retrospective review was more explicit; he wrote that the song begins with the "unbearably dopey" speech about not being able to petition the Lord with prayer, moves into a "beautiful quasi-oriental section before changing gears abruptly into jivey upbeat California philosophy" which is followed by a jazzy segment and then a "heavily rhythmic section that sounds like badly mixed Booker T [Washington]", and that after some more kindred changes "lurch into view", Morrison proclaims the "almost obligatory closing pronouncement" about whipping horses' eyes and making them sleep and cry – "Another amazing piece of convoluted brilliance, and one of the Doors' finest recordings."51 In contrast, Riegel wrote this song helped end the "obligatory *tour de force* cut" for a Doors album because the song was a "crazy collage of discordant elements" which included Morrison "exorcising more of his Southern-Calvinist demons by portraying a hellfire preacher" and "rattling off his favourite things in the Babylon" he had found in Los Angeles: "For the Doors, psychedelia had already turned into nostalgia, and we waited to see what their next album would bring."52 Attempting to tie together the themes in longer Doors' songs based on what he called the "psycho-mythic narrative" technique of Morrison, Pichaske explained that this type of narrative was "prone to unravelling" because it was so diffused and subtle it lost focus: "In the last analysis", wrote Pichaske, the song "offers less insight into the magic of Doors' theatre, than a key to its failure: the drama is ultimately a dead-end process, for one soon runs out of myths and characters, and loses himself easily in loose connections."53 In a 1981 interview with BAM, producer Rothchild stated that a lot of the song was composed with bits of poetry out of Jim's notebooks that he and Jim thought fit rhythmically and conceptually.54 And loose connections do piece together to render an artistic vision The Doors were trying to express. 'The Soft Parade' begins with what opened the album on 'Tell All The People', the allusion to a saviour. Morrison oratorically recites a time in seminary school when a person preached we "can petition the Lord with prayer" and then screams we can't. Bangs wrote that "the drunken yowling sermon 'Yew CAN-NOT pe-TISH-SHON the lo-WARD with PRAY-yer'" was another of what he considered a great Bozo moment on The Doors' records.55 Brash and arrogant in his rebellious stance, Morrison, as a seminary student, pronounces his freedom from the schooling he believes has betrayed him and finds he has broken through – to the realization that what he has been led to believe to be security isn't and that he is now adrift. Plaintively Morrison laments for "sanctuary" and for "soft asylum". Just when The Doors render a picture that gets your head and blood pounding with anger against the soft lies of society, they plunge you into the depths of personal vulnerability and fear. The once harsh imagery and sounds have yielded to softer images and sounding words, the long vowels and sustained consonants, like r and n, flowing from the blues of being alone.

The sanctuary that has been sought is only fleeting, because any commitment to a relationship, like trying to petition the Lord, becomes meaningless in an alienated society. What is left is the realization of vulnerability. The song becomes upbeat as Morrison draws quick sketches of images, snatches of life, fragments which piece together in a disconcerting tone, like snapshots from Los Angeles, from "peppermint miniskirts" and "chocolate candy" to the "champion sax" image which alludes nicely to the Curtis Amy sax solo in 'Touch Me'. The unexpected twist of loving one's neighbour until "his wife" comes home lingers for a moment within the listener's mind before the music shifts into the next series of images. With the paradoxical backdrop of soft brushing of the drums by Densmore, Morrison sings through a series of images not necessarily soft. The "polished stones" of the mask in 'Easy Ride' reemerge in the lyric about "winter women" who are "growing stones", an image which may also suggest infertility of being pregnant with stones. And their carrying of babies to the river echoes the image in 'Tell All The People' of "milky babies revelry" across the sea – but carrying them to what? Death or baptism? Life is dualistic.

The impression that this part of the song generates of a leather-clad (even bearded) Morrison skipping through a Sesame Street-like venue beckoning to a bunch of cutesy kids almost kills the montage of images before Morrison stops at the street corner to pronounce, "The Monk Bought Lunch". Since you can't petition the Lord with prayer, might as well pay some attention to more relevant day-to-day things, like eating.

As the other three Doors musically wind into the heart of 'The Soft Parade', Morrison underscores them with a rap about this section being the "best part of the trip". The fragmentary nature of drug trips is reflected not only in the fragmentary nature of this song, but also in the overall Doors' artistic vision – fragmentary till pieces are put together to form an overall picture. The trip Morrison is about to paint isn't from a hallucinogenic drug, but from the drug The Doors believe to be the most deceiving and destructive of all drugs. In their previous albums, The Doors have rendered a picture of modern life chained to our mechanized world being segmented by time and an alien landscape. It is a world being separated from life's unknown forces that don't fit into the smoothly running machinery of our modern way of life. 'The Soft Parade' reveals a less acrimonious attitude and a reluctant acceptance of this way of life, that "successful hills are here to stay" and "everything must be this way". The tone in the imagery of "gentle street where people play" and "welcome to the soft parade" is quite a shift from the scream in 'When The Music's Over' that we want the world now and from the smart-ass revolutionary of 'Five To One'. Here is one of those peaceful, accepting moments, far removed from the anxious night. But beneath the peace is the realization that people sweat, save and build all their lives for "a shallow grave", yet there has to be something else, somehow to defend this way. Acceptance of the soft parade doesn't mean that The Doors were condoning it or that accolades would replace the disquieting mechanical imagery of The Doors' artistic vision, evident in the subsequent image of listening to the engines of the soft parade hum. Passive resignation to the way everything must be, to the easy ride of successful hills, doesn't change the mechanized reality of modern life; it just makes for a smoother, quieter running engine, a soft parade. But engines can chew you up or run you over. The Doors depict an organic, yet mechanical machine that gives the illusion of humming, for it is really a disjointed conglomeration of disquieting images. Traditionally a shaman relies on fellow animal powers to aid him, and Morrison appropriately counters his acceptance of the soft parade with the calling of a "cobra" on his left and a "leopard" on his right. The imagery suggested by the exotic, poisonous cobra snake and the equally exotic, dangerous leopard cat transcends simple one-to-one symbolic correspondence; the two become larger than mere animals. And these creatures vibrate with energy far more alive than the energy of the curious creatures on 'Love Street'. Then he slides into imagery reminiscent of 'Wild Child': a "deer woman" dressed in a silk dress and girls who have "beads around their necks" and have kissed the exotic "hunter of the green vest", a hunter who has grappled "with lions in the night". Again, The Doors render an artistic vision of facing the primal past which lies beneath the costume of control, beneath the soft parade – a vision of following the shaman down, the wild child back to Africa. This is not the imagery from the soft parade of successful hills, of suburbia sprawled under the neon grooves, of fields of asphalt that never die. But this return to our primal past begins to end as the lights become brighter and the pulse of our modern world interjects – the moaning radio. The anxiety and anger rendered by The Doors haven't been entirely lost. The struggle against society continues, but without the need for one side to be right and the other wrong. Both are going to exist, but the bluesman now can slide between the field and the meadow when he needs to and realizes as a human, he can't survive entirely on his own inner energy. For Morrison, dog was a reverse pun of god, and his subsequent lyric, "calling to the dogs", reflects the shaman still calling to the other world of spirits, of power animals. But Morrison croons on that it is becoming harder to describe sailors who journey to the other side "to the underfed", to those who no longer know freedom, who are sweating and saving for a shallow grave, who are television children fed, who quell hunger for primal passions. Though the pathways to the landscape the shaman travels are becoming dimmer, there is an acceptance that the soft parade must be this way.

Besides the nice sounding combination of sounds in "tropic corridor" and "tropic treasure", the images recall similar imagery in 'Break On Through'. And the "mild Equator" suggests man's constant attempts to create the ideal temperate environment in which to live – the soft and mild parade. But Morrison recants themes of 'Tell All The People' and 'Wild Child': the need for "someone" or "something new" or "something else" to help us get through, lines which underlie the closing chanting chorus of "Calling on the dogs... Calling on the gods". Morrison brings this fragmentary trip through the soft parade to a close by standing again in the meadow, calling to his lover on the undying fields of city asphalt, as three overlays of lyrics weave a cacophony of confusion. (The recording of this song The Doors made for the NET

[National Education Television] special, *Critique*, in 1969, doesn't have the overlays of vocals and offers a clearer rendition of this coda, though it is not exactly what Morrison vocalized for the studio recording.) The two lovers will meet at "the crossroads" on the "edge of town" under the "evening sky". The soft parade, the moaning radio, and the brightness of the neon grove yield to the darkness the wild child found so liberating, to the evening sky – a softer image of the bright midnight Morrison had so urgently sought in the debut album or of the sensuously sinister moonlight drive of 'Strange Days'. But the guns of liberation/death in the album's opening song return when Morrison cries to "bring your gun" and we shall "have some fun!" If we are going to wrestle with lions in the night, come prepared. The spoken closing image of whipping the horses' eyes to make the horses "sleep and cry" is as arbitrary a closing coda as the one to 'Wild Child', except that it hauntingly echoes the morbid treatment rendered the horses by the sailors afloat on the dead calm seas in 'Horse Latitudes'. Cry suggests tears, which stirs one last ripple through the imagery of water rendered so prominently throughout the album. The intensity of the ending manages to be compelling without the anger, escapist without the fear or frustration, urgent without the danger. The Doors frame the album upon a pattern quite consistent with the previous albums, but the tone, which underscores the Top 40 production, reveals a shift in the shade of meaning The Doors were rendering in their artistic vision. A more mellowed tone has heightened the pictures The Doors were drawing. Moreover, the shamanic bluesman has revealed wisdom and insights the previous albums haven't: the persona from which The Doors have rendered their previous portraits of life has come to terms with his own vulnerability and is more at peace with it, now both susceptible and ready for love, for taking the risk of trusting someone with his deepest secrets. And the next album, *Morrison Hotel*, expresses the ascension into what the blues often embrace – the fulfillment of love.

# chapter 5

# the hard rock cafe &
# morrison hotel

"Dionysiac art, too, wishes to convince us of the eternal delight of existence, but it... makes us realize that everything that is generated must be prepared to face its painful dissolution. It forces us to gaze into the horror of individual existence, yet without being turned to stone by the vision: a metaphysical solace momentarily lifts us above the whirl of shifting phenomena. For a brief moment we become, ourselves, the primal Being, and we experience its insatiable hunger for existence. Now we see the struggle, the pain, the destruction of appearances, as necessary, because of the constant proliferation of forms pushing into life, because of the extravagant fecundity of the world will... Pity and terror notwithstanding, we realize our great good fortune in having life – not as individuals, but as part of the life force with whose procreative lust we have become one."

*Friedrich Nietzsche,*
*The Birth Of Tragedy (pp. 102-3) Pictures of front and back*
*covers of the album, Morrison Hotel (Elektra Records,*
*released February 1970)*

SIDE 1
Roadhouse Blues
Waiting For The Sun
You Make Me Real
Peace Frog
Blue Sunday
Ship Of Fools

SIDE 2
Land Ho!
The Spy
Queen Of The Highway
Indian Summer
Maggie M'Gill

The meteoric success of 'Light My Fire' in the heated Summer of Love had rocketed The Doors out of night club gigging into a swirling schedule which came to a crashing halt after the raucous Miami Dinner Key concert. After baring their souls and delivering their message through the unseen rhythms of the electric heart of rock 'n' roll, The Doors were yearning – and needing – to return those souls to some earthy roots. But 1969 was hardly a reposing period. On July 20, America answered the challenge issued by President John F. Kennedy: Neil Armstrong and Buzz Aldrin took the first human steps on the moon. Technology had made the "Moonlight Drive". On November 20, the federal government conceded some of the dangers of this moonlight drive with techonology: federal legislation outlawed DDT and initiated a two-year phase out of the once hailed miracle chemical to eradicate unwanted insect pests. By the end of the year, otherwise significant events would emerge in the monetary spotlight from behind the mid-summer shadow of Armstrong's and Aldrin's walks on the moon. On a farm in upstate New York in August, removed from mainstream America, the Woodstock festival brought to fruition the seeds of flower power which blossomed over the overt mass drug usage at the gathering before the chill of The Rolling Stones' free Altamont festival held in California in December brought a killer frost to those pastoral ideals. The gruesome *Tate* and *La Bianca* murders in Los Angeles in August eventually led to the arrest of Charles Manson and members of his "family". Hoping the courtroom would rectify the unruly display at the Democratic National Convention, the American justice system began the trial of the Chicago 8 in September. As the initial test of the criminal offence of intent to incite a riot as defined in the 1968 Civil Rights Act, the trial would become both a farce and insult to America's sense of impartiality. With the conviction of Black Panther leader Bobby Seale for contempt of court, the "8" were reduced to the Chicago 7.

Meanwhile, a rather quiet scientific event was engineered by a group of young Harvard University Medical School scientists: they isolated from a living organism, for the first time, a gene, the basic building block of life. Landing on the moon and isolating a gene from a living organism, science had broken on through to the other side. Now that we were there, what was next?

In October, the New York Mets, their first year of existence in 1962 as probably the worst team ever in American baseball, won the World Series. But after the St. Louis Cardinals traded outfielder Curt Flood, he did the inconceivable – sued America's pastime, Major League Baseball.

Flood challenged the traditional view that major league baseball was like a large company with divisions in each major city whose owners could shuffle players as they wished under the "reserve clause"; he contended that by not allowing him to work where he wanted, just like any other worker in America, Major League Baseball was violating federal antitrust laws. Though Flood would lose in court, the sport of baseball, with the subsequent emergence of free agency and very lucrative television contracts, would become the big business of entertainment. Fears of "runaway inflation" followed by recession shaped government economic policy which hoped to deter rising unemployment and higher costs to borrow money.

As Congress pondered how to re-tune this New Economics engine, the Banking Committee of the House of Representatives examined the effects on the housing industry caused by the prime lending rates jump from 7.5% to 8.5%. In some still distant future quietly slumbered the double digit figures of the late 1970s, which would pale these figures of the 1960s. Repeatedly serious commentators of American society were pointing out that never before had so many Americans had it so good

123

economically, but the presence of television unabashedly presented to the impoverished the stark contrast between their day-to-day world and the images of advertising. The resultant frustration was further fuelled by television also displaying to the haves how the have nots lived. Vietnam wasn't the only source of agitation coming into the American living room every evening. Troops were actually being withdrawn from South Vietnam – by both sides, as the Nixon administration pursued "peace with honour" at the laggard peace talks in Paris. On September 3, Ho Chi Minh, the president of North Vietnam, died aged 79.

In November, news reports of a civilian massacre by American soldiers at the South Vietnam village of My Lai in March of 1968 prompted charges to be eventually brought against Lt. William Calley, who was in charge of the unit at that time.

In the film *True Grit*, John Wayne's one-eyed, hard drinking Rooster Cogburn depicted Old West Americana ideals of dogmatically administrating justice with his gun while aiding a fiesty, independent young woman's determination to bring her father's murderer to justice. Meanwhile, Paul Newman and Robert Redford delighted millions with their charming, rebellious portrayal of Old West outlaws in *Butch Cassidy And The Sundance Kid*. Portraying a young Texan spirit who rides into New York City with idealistic ambitions of making it, Jon Voight joined Dustin Hoffman to tell the story of two lost youthful souls, Joe Buck and Ratzo Rizzo, who ride out the alienation of America's modern urban landscape by learning how to trust each other and share compassion in *Midnight Cowboy*. Though the public was somewhat misled by the film's title, which is a term for "male hustler", and equally surprised by the film's ruthless realism, the movie became a box office hit despite its "X" rating, regarded as a commercial handicap back then, and then received the Oscar for Best Picture. Barbra Streisand made her big screen debut (an Oscar winner) in the lively *Funny Girl* film adaptaion of the Broadway musical, but the line between what had been considered mainstream Hollywood films and pornograghy was blurring with the importation of such films as the Swedish *I Am Curious (Yellow)* and *Fanny Hill* and subsequent forgettable releases by Hollywood film studios themselves.

The preeminent doctrine of the marketplace now focused on youth and sex. In July, the movie, *Easy Rider*, opened, and ominously, Capt.

America tells Billy, "We blew it". In the fall of 1969, public television premiered a children's show called, *Seasame Street*. And thus began the debate over its presenting the rudiments of American education and values in commercial-like formats – snippets and snatches of images that would capture the pre-schooler's attention. On television the edited rhythm is natural to the medium – as it is on the concert stage or in the sports arena; in the classroom or living room of life, the rhythm isn't as fluid.

In June The Doors had begun playing concerts again that were...well... concerts. In September of 1969, The Doors headlined the Toronto Rock 'n' Roll Revival festival which featured the last-minute addition of the Plastic Ono Band fronted by John Lennon and Yoko Ono. A NET TV special (which never aired) focused on The Doors, allowing a slightly pouchy and heavily bearded, cigar-toking Jim Morrison to introduce songs from *The Soft Parade* and poetry from his just privately published *The Lords And The New Creatures*.

In the 1969 *Rolling Stone* interview, Jerry Hopkins asked Morrison if he believed rock was dead. Jim replied that what was called rock and roll "got decadent", was revived by the English and became "articulate", and finally "became self-conscious, involuted and kind of incestuous", which marks "the death of any moment" when the energy or belief dissipates.1 So a similar judgement could be cast upon The Doors, for they were reflecting, as always, in part, the larger forces of the culture around them.

In 1970, with successive releases of the last three Beatles' albums, *Abbey Road*, *Hey Jude* and *Let It Be*, the articulate phase to which Jim had referred was about to shift to the even more self-conscious focus of rock as a business from the early 1970s on. The Doors needed a return to some roots, to reaffirm their own beliefs. The group, especially Morrison, had more than once alluded to a yearning to do gigs again at the Whiskey, in the tight, sweaty atmosphere of a club. In the excitement and electricity of the mass hysteria of a concert, as Morrison told Hopkins, with so many people gathered together, what you do doesn't matter that much.2 Lizze James indicated from her interviews with Jim during this period that he had "talked excitedly" about doing a TV special on the history of the blues.3

Moreover, pressures to showcase Morrison were building. Morrison's film, *HWY*, would be the focal point of a couple of film festivals. Talk circulated of Jim going solo, both on record and as a film star, heir to the swashbuckling image of Douglas Fairbanks, which didn't quite fit the pouchy, mellowed, cigar-toking, bearded beat poet on the NET TV special.

Added to all this, Elektra Records wanted another album, hopefully, as Sugerman and Hopkins pointed out, a live album in time for the Christmas season of 1969, less than six months after the release of *The Soft Parade*.4 And the depressing aftermath of the Miami fiasco was slowly hardening into the reality of the energy and time needed for judicial defence. But what The Doors had been missing for the preparation of the third and fourth albums wasn't for this fifth album: time to work on sculpturing and rendering portraits from their artistic vision.

According to Sugerman and Hopkins, The Doors began rehearsing in September of 1969 and started recording tracks in November.5 Three days after *Morrison Hotel* was released in February 1970, The Doors achieved, as the March 4 issue of *Variety* reported, a first for an American rock group – a fifth straight gold ($1,000,000-seller) album.6 *Morrison Hotel* quickly climbed Billboard's Top LPs chart, stopping behind Simon & Garfunkle's *Bridge Over Troubled Water*, The Beatles' *Abbey Road* and *Hey Jude*, *Led Zeppelin II*, and Crosby, Stills, Nash & Young's *Deja Vu*.

The album stayed only 27 weeks on the charts. Besides the pronounced presence of *Bridge Over Troubled Water* and The Beatles' last three albums, Chicago were beginning to toot their horns, Creedence Clearwater Revival were delivering a distinct sound, and young Michael Jackson was leading the Jackson 5 into the charts. It was as simple as 'ABC'. Into these calming waters of "letting it be" and being a "bridge over troubled water", Elektra released the single, 'You Make Me Real'.

Billboard billed the song a "rousing rocker" and "perfect discotheque item that's loaded with sales appeal" that would quickly find a "high spot" on their Hot 100 chart.7 The song charted at #97 on Billboard's Top 100 for April 11, peaking at #50 on May 7 before slipping out of the hottest hundred tunes in America two weeks later. Like the diminished chart performance, the heated anticipation of the reviewers for the second, third, and even fourth albums had cooled for the reception of this fifth album. Kind of. Lester Bangs, in his review of the album for *Rolling Stone*, thought it might have been a "fine album", but couldn't judge it apart from the previous ones and concluded that so much of its music came from the "same extremely worn cloth" as the music on the other albums and that The Doors' artistic "well of resources" had become a standing lake that was slowly drying up.8 A reviewer in the lesser read underground newspaper from Tallahassee, *Amazing Grace*, drew the same comparison, writing that the album was "the same basic Doors' sound... you've been hearing for three years. Had this been their second or third LP, it would have been a smasher".9 Patricia Kennely, writing for *Jazz & Pop*, stated *Morrison Hotel* would have been a "great second album", but musically was neither inspired nor dazzling, just "competent, very workmanlike rock": the album had "good polyfuckrhythms, but sad to say, some pretty faggy-sounding piano work", and it had a "Fanny Farmer Valentine quality that is not only lacy but craven"10. In the context of the rest of The Doors' work, the sound may be the same worn cloth, but the music is never exactly the same colour or pattern.

More than one reviewer celebrated the absence of strings and horns, the music now stripped down to what many perceived as the hard, churning driving sound the group excelled at on their own – but this time with guest bassists Ray Neopolitan and Lonnie Mack and on harmonica, John Sebastian (late of The Lovin' Spoonful). *Fusion*, then an underground publication out of Boston, in a January 1971 issue retrospective of 1970, labelled *Morrison Hotel*, "Drinking man's album of the year"11. An earlier review of the album in a May 1970 issue offered a more introspective assessment that the album presented a "continual shifting of Morrisonian blues off of musically dark poetics", portraying the "assertive density, the graveyard, strep-throat vocals and the existential abrasiveness" that was expected from The Doors.12 Dave Marsh, though somewhat harsh towards some of the album, wrote in *Creem* that The Doors were "truly the most American rock 'n' roll band" he had ever heard: "Like this country, when they're good, they're unbeatable, when they're awful, they're horrifying. And sometimes, they're horrifyingly good."13 In probably the most comprehensive review of any Doors' album at the time, Chris Reabur (a pseudonym for Bruce Harris) in *Jazz & Pop* levelled his critical review to a more even keeled assessment, writing that at the core of Morrison's song writing was a "basic sense of order" and that it was dubious Jim tolerated "blank visions of empty chaos in his lyrics"; having faith in Morrison's integrity as an artist, Reabur wrote that Jim "does not throw words around in his work but rather tends to be simplistic, direct, and painfully concise"14. The subtitles of side one and side two of the album underscore Reabur's point. Reabur noted that *Hard Rock Cafe* (side one) denotes a kind of house, that *Morrison Hotel* (side two) is "the hotel of Jim Morrison's mind", and that this hotel (the album) is a house with "many visitors, many different views and ways of life."15 Cruise to the Hard Rock Cafe roadhouse before checking into Morrison Hotel. Hopkins and Sugerman recollected that Ray and his wife found in L.A.'s skid-row district a real Morrison Hotel with rooms for $2.50 a night.16 Maybe the boys couldn't return to the Whiskey, but they still could rub elbows with good ol' folks, the blue-collared people, the ones rooted to life's realities. More than one critic took a stab at this image portrayed by the front and back cover photos of *Morrison Hotel* and *Hard Rock Cafe*, respectively, and by the inner sleeve picture. Kennely, whose relationship with Morrison, according to Hopkins and Sugerman, had soured, wrote with a sharp edge: "Oh fie. Where are the DOORS, those musical brats?" before she answered "certainly not on the jacket" nor on the inside foldout photo of the "scummy bar" with The Doors trying to look "equally scummy and not making it by a country mile" and with Morrison looking like "he just missed the urinal"17.

With preliminary pronouncements that The Doors (notably Morrison) were returning to their earlier sound, Kennely echoed how many reacted – that she had "expected more from Dionysus"18.

Morrison was too intellectual to be simply rock, but too rock to be purely intellectual. Jim's relationship to his listeners seemed similar to kids watching an adult movie: they laugh when the adults laugh, even though they don't understand the humour, and they identify with the raw emotion portrayed, even though they don't understand how or why it is really affecting them. Thus, Jim's popularity started to drop when the kids finally got bored. Some of the grown-up critics and fans gave up too, embarrassed by the overdramatic display of personal emotion by Jim which made them feel like voyeurs. And some just may have resolved The Doors were mainly portraying a personal struggle and emotional evolution that couldn't carry anyone else along. According to Reabur, the "best way to discover" The Doors is through those who dislike them the most because such attempts to prove what is wrong with The Doors always point out what makes The Doors so great: "The best picture of The Doors' brand of insanity is best drawn by the sane man who hates them."19 Like maybe Stephen Halpert writing in his article, titled, "Get Back: The Doors Are Closed", in the March 20, 1970, issue of *Fusion*: "For years we suffered from [Morrison's] oedipal hangups, and some of us even ate it up. For years we listened to his poetry, as trite and meaningless as the language could produce... "

With the release of *Morrison Hotel* we've finally crashed, the past albums and style rejected, and what do you think they're trying to tell us, that Morrison's finally gotten into rock and playing us funky roadhouse blues... but Morrison's grovelling, his cracked, whiskey voice milking it out, freaking around in stupidity, perpetrating a shallow legend. Morrison was the product of a frantic, confused decade... He was our most subjective rock performer, substituting musical ability for psychological release. [He] is full of upper class torment and anger. He is an actor of the grotesque, the Lizard King of The Doors, very much part of hallucinogens, an ambiguous poet, and not much of a performer. Who needs it?20

Marsh countered that Jim "doesn't bother trying to justify his mental voyeurism" but "simply writes a song about it" and the other Doors "back him perfectly"21. Reabur expanded this view writing that Morrison was always "more a prophet than a pied piper" and that though Jim couldn't show us how to live, he could show us "how not to live": "*Morrison Hotel*, for all its flurries of autobiography, is really more directly an album about America, about you and me only by inference."22 Furthermore, Reabur framed his review upon the perception that the album was built on two central image patterns of roads and houses, and this imagery portrayed "a vision of America in all its savage splendour and awesome beauty"23.

"As the critic gained ascendancy in theatre and concert, the journalist in the schoolroom, and the newspaper in society, art degenerated into the lowest kind of amusement and esthetic criticism into the cement of a social group that was vain, distracted, egotistic, and totally unoriginal... Never has there been so much loose talk about art and so little respect for it."

*Friedrich Nietzsche,*
*The Birth Of Tragedy (p. 135)*

"The great mark of the genius is to reveal to each critic what he is looking for."

*Wallace Fowlie,*
*Rimbaud*
*(A Critical Study) (p. 127)*

The same basic Doors' pattern emerges, tempered by the realizations the blues bring. This is no longer the reckless, freedom pursuing lover of the first album trying to find an island in his lover's arms and country in her eyes or seeking a soul kitchen to warm his mind by. Nor is this the detached lover singing to an unhappy girl locked in a self-made prison to join him and swim in mystery. Nor the passive lover of Love Street, content to wait and see what will happen. This is a shamanic bluesman, more aware and mature of what being human and being sensual means. Jim removed the personal sanctuary of the beard, and a more relaxed Doors' sound drew a portrait rendered in the tones of the blues.

Musically, it can be called blues, but the entire picture rendered by the album doesn't demonstrate the birth of full-fledged bluesmen, lyrically or musically. A tentative attitude and approach to the blues tint the album. In the real world of jazz blues, one of the most important underlying feelings is reverence for age, a respect for experience, knowledge, and wisdom you can only attain after a whole lifetime of playing and learning – of experiencing life at all stages. The greatest emphasis is on the sharing of knowledge between generations, because people need a structure of knowledge to understand what they feel. We experience emotion from the day we are born, and we can play our music and evoke the spectrum of being human, but nobody understands life until they have experienced and learned all of its twists and turns. The blues are about the lifelong struggle to come to peace with oneself – a struggle that The Doors experienced, but that never really reached a true fruition. The Doors perform all the technical aspects and are in touch with the underlying emotional currents of life as they render the blues, but they aren't truly bluesmen at this stage of their artistic lives. In this album, the pop idiomatic production of *The Soft Parade* aside, The Doors seem caught between being their old psychedelic, poetically ambiguous selves or all-out bluesmen. What results is old Doors' images being forced into an incongruous musical framework. They are trying to return to some kind of roots, but cannot reconcile this search with their artistic evolution toward mature blues – which they are beginning to truly feel, beginning to break through to. True blues, although tempered by age to the point that their nuances seem almost imperceptibly subtle, still pack a strong emotional punch. It is a punch The Doors as a group would never learn how to deliver, as the swirling whirlwind of the Sixties would rock its own punch on Morrison.

## SIDE ONE
*Hard Rock Cafe* rocks, opening with a trip to the 'Roadhouse Blues', a song many felt was a blast to The Doors' earlier sound, garnering such critical adjectives as raunchy, sweaty, dirty, funky, and so on. Lester Bangs in *Rolling Stone* wrote that the "angry hard rock" of this song was what The Doors excelled at – the raw funk of "jagged barrelhouse piano, fierce guitar, and one of the most convincing raunchy vocals" Morrison ever recorded.24 'Roadhouse Blues' paints a picture based upon, as Reabur pointed out, the two central images of the album – roads and houses.25 The Doors render another portrait of the journey motif, only we are not on a crystal ship, nor are we drifting or running down a highway to wherever.

We have some control, if we keep our "eyes on the road" and a "hand upon the wheel". According to Sugerman and Hopkins, the opening lines Jim had said to his perpetually on-and-off again girlfriend, Pamela, as she drove to a cottage Jim had bought behind a country bar and club in Topanga Canyon, located just northwest of L.A.26 You better keep your eyes on the road and a hand on the wheel after you leave the free-wheeling interstate highways of L.A. and drive on the tightly curved Topanga Canyon road winding through the mountains north of Malibu. Like all journeys The Doors take you on, this one offers risk and danger, a risk willingly taken not only to go to the roadhouse but also, as Reabur noted, to leave something. Out in the hills, you can find bungalows and take life slow as the music rocks on. The roadhouse offers "a real good time", not a synthetic scene of plastic Twentieth Century Foxes hanging out on the Strip or angelic queens strolling on Venice Beach. Here is sanctuary away from the soft parade of "peppermint miniskirts" and "chocolate candy". The roadhouse and bungalows in the back are the sanctuaries The Doors have found the most comforting during these strange times. Paul McCartney would sing, "let it be", in an anthem The Beatles would soon release, but for Jim, life rolls, as he repeatedly sings in the chorus, "Let it roll". And the roadhouse also rolls, since it is, as Reabur wrote, "a house with wheels, a kind of road house itself"27. The bungalow in Topanga Canyon is far away from the warm mansion at the top of the hill in 'Not To Touch The Earth'.

The tightness of the song's rocking blues rhythm is musically itself a real good time. Robby's guitar and John Sebastian's harmonica roll and bounce through a musical interlude after Jim says, "Do it, Robby, do it". This is a considerably different do it than the studio filler from an album ago. The minor mode tone of taking the highway to the end of the night has been transformed into a rhythmical blues of "go down slow" in a bungalow "all night long", driven along by the steady, pulsating bottom of the bass guitar.

The earlier urgent 'Moonlight Drive' wooing of the unhappy girl lost in a prison of her own device has matured to the deeper understanding of an adult trapped by commitments made in life. Jim sings to the 'Ashen Lady' to give up her vows: she needs to free herself from the values which have made her ashen and a prisoner of her own twentieth century plastic box. Such changing also could save the city which is just a larger plastic box. Even though the city supposedly provides security, how certain is that security? Morrison sings about waking up in the morning and getting himself a beer because the future is always uncertain and the end is constantly near; of this attitude, Marsh wrote, "How fuckin' American can you get?... Have mercy. There is none."28

So why not wake up in the morning and, as Jim sings, have a beer? But not always; sometimes you have to keep your eyes on the road and hand on the wheel to get to the next roadhouse because each house is only temporary. The Doors render a more mature portrait of life's temporalness without the heavy tones cast by such previous portraits as 'The End'. Death may be the next stop down the road, that next night, that day – inevitably some next moment, for as we roll down the road of life, we draw nearer to that end.

The Doors roll on to pause and reflect. A leftover song from the third album, *Waiting For The Sun* offers a moment of, as a reviewer in *Fusion* noted, "curious relaxation and becalmed innocence"29. There reemerges the image of breaking through to the other side at the ocean's edge, but instead of rendering the image in the darker, urgent tones of sliding into the wet forests of the "Moonlight Drive", Jim renders an image of dawning light and innocence, an innocence not of ignorance but of pure feeling, of racing down to the sea. The sea has been the scene where horses drowned in mute nostril agony, where lovers took a moonlight drive, where everything was covered in wishful, sinful blue; now the urgent running has become standing "on freedom's shore" – the rolling becomes a waiting for the sun. But the sun is "scattered"; the light of innocence, of freedom, of love, of trust, of security – scattered.

Eden hasn't been destroyed, just shattered, fragmented, and scattered in these strange days. Yet we have to live our lives, and part of that living is waiting for such things as someone to come along and "hear my song" and "tell me what went wrong". The blues roll on as The Doors wait momentarily for a resolution.

Though Morrison sings about this being the "strangest life" he has ever known and echoes the lucid picture of estranged relationships rendered in *Strange Days*, the next song, 'You Make Me Real', portrays a moment where Jim has found a real good time. Bangs labelled the song as a "thyroid burst of manufactured energy" as played by any of the multitude of mediocre groups.30 Reabur wrote that "though masquerading as another bangbang rock 'n' roll excursion into Morrison's 'cock psychology'", the song restated, "in its own moronic way", the theme to let it roll.31

Morrison opens the song with the first two laments of the standard Pop triad: he wants and needs his lover. Because he loves her? Nah... because he isn't "real enough" without her. Jim enjoys the simplicity of the moment because she makes him real, makes him "feel like lovers feel", and makes him cast off "mistake and misery". He sings of being free of the past, of the old securities and insecurities. This relationship does what waiting on freedom's shore didn't, what being in island of her arms didn't, what hanging around 'Love Street' didn't, what cruising on a crystal ship or down a highway to the bright midnight didn't; this relationship makes Jim free because it makes him real.

The imagery is short and concise, the music pulsating and driving. This isn't the Ashen Lady of 'Roadhouse Blues' being wooed to give up her vows, nor is this the unhappy girl being played along through the estranged relationship on *Strange Days*, nor the plastic Twentieth Century Fox, nor the vamp living on 'Love Street', nor the ambivalent lover in 'Shaman's Blues'. This one is different because she makes him feel real. Jim isn't wanting to glide with her into the mysterious sea of a Moonlight Drive; he sings, "So let me slide into your tender sunken sea", which is just beyond freedom's shores. Listening to Jim slur through this line justifies Reabur's observation it should be awarded the "all-time great Morrison slur, 'So lemme tie a binder rounder, don't you see'."32

The haughty, urgent arrogance in 'Light My Fire' and 'Hello, I Love You', the passive hesitancy in 'Love Street', the ambivalent almost passionless sarcasm in the love songs on *The Soft Parade* have become confident self-assuredness with the passionate rhythms of life. The focus is still on what I can get, but there has been a recognition that love, though temporal, isn't trite. Love isn't as plastic as the people who play with it.

But life rolls, and The Doors roll us through a journey in the next song, 'Peace Frog'. Labelling the song, "apocalypse-with-a-beat", Richard Riegel wrote that Morrison "raided his recent autobiography for images" which represented the "national convulsions" evoked by the incessant Vietnam War.33 Though calling 'Peace Frog' a throwaway protest song and concluding the title was at best a "bad joke", Reabur thought the song portrayed an America beyond the good guys vs. the bad guys found in the contemporary movie, *Easy Rider*, and rendered a "much more terrifying America, a land of death and violence and horror"34. According to Densmore, Krieger had "this great rhythm guitar lick", but Morrison didn't have "anything lyrically to complement it"; eventually though, Rothchild had Jim record two poems on top of each other – one poem as a metaphor of Jim's life, the other of Pam.35

Alluding to both national and personal confrontations of a violent, if not bloody, nature, Morrison yanks away the blanket of peace and security America snuggles under and portrays a scene of blood in the streets and blood rising to follow him. The almost sarcastic tone of the dubbed-in back-up Morrison vocals of "She came" shifts with the next stanza.

Though there is some serious pain being inflicted in our society as a whole, we remember – and find sanctuary in – moments of loving, trusting intimacy, in momentary pauses on the road of life with someone who can make or has made us feel real; for Jim, that someone came around "the break of day" and then drove away with "sunlight in her hair".

Though they may have burned gold into their hair in 'Summer's Almost Gone', they are no longer as innocent as they were then. The Doors return to a rather vivid image of water which has been more archetypal in previous songs, of blood in streets running like "a river of sadness". The river of blood running "down the legs of the city" (the legs of L.A. Woman?) slides us deep into purging and rebirth. The city the Ashen Lady needs to help save is pretty deep in blood, a stark and messy contrast to the neat neon groves of our urban environment. But between these American streets running with blood, "she came". Along the streets of Morrison's own life, of his own memories are the times she came with him in town, at dawn, at Eden, on freedom's shore, in the bungalow. But she came and then drove away, "sunlight in her hair".

Just as he felt comfortable with the rhythm of the roadhouse blues, so Morrison does with this rolling lover, a variation of the wild love. He understands enough to etch the ensuing image of dead Indians "scattered on dawn's highway" and litany of blood with a rhythm and tone minus his usual acrimonious electronic bitterness.

Reabur explained that some of that blood in the streets results from accidents caused by careless travellers "who don't keep their eyes on the road and their hands upon the wheel" and that on the highway of the dawn of America, we find a dead Indian: the birth of our nation (careless travellers from the Old World?) brought blood, and, as Reabur wrote, "blood is the rose of her flag which sometimes is striped red, red, and red"36. Even the sanctuary of The Doors' beginning, Venice Beach, is stained with blood, as is the "bloody red sun of phantastic

L.A.".". Phantastic, alluding to the direct Latin derivative, phantasm, suggests a vision created by imagination, like both L.A. and the blood being bled so profusely by a nation in internal turmoil.

America laid beneath her patch-worked blanket of tranquillity, but, as Reabur wrote of the somewhat naive hopefulness of the Sixties; "We were wanting for the sun, but when it came, it filled the sky with blood."37 The implication of whose fingers have been chopped off leaves you wondering what kind of grip the lover, the queen of angels, or America has left. And then Morrison puts a twist on the traditional image of the rose, singing "blood is the rose of mysterious union" – union with his lover, union of egg and sperm to make new blood, new life which will roll through America.

Instead of a journey to the other side, to escape, to seek sanctuary, 'Peace Frog' portrays a journey to reflect on personal and national events, be it the riotous 1968 Democratic Convention in Chicago to Morrison's stage bust at New Haven in December of 1968 to the early childhood memory of an accident Morrison's family came upon on the highways of America. Interestingly, and probably legally intelligent, there was no allusion to the Miami fiasco. The barrelhouse rhythms of this opening set at Hard Rock Cafe comes to a reposing moment in 'Blue Sunday', a moment more than one critic jabbed at as Bangs did, calling it an "insipidly 'lyrical' piece" that was "crooned in Morrison's most saccharine Hoagy Carmichael style"38. Or "Perry Como" style, according to Kennely.39 The song is simple, content with finding true love "on a blue Sunday" and having her look at him and tell him he is the only one. Jim has left Saturday's shore of 'Shaman's Blues' and comfortable slides into this blue Sunday. The blues accept and embrace life's joys and pains. There is reposing peace to be found on a clear, maybe wishful, sinful blue Sunday. The Doors have come a long way since the hectic, intransigent pace characterized by the song 'I Looked At You' on the first album. There are signs of burgeoning maturity, of admitting, without necessarily a bitter tone, one's vulnerabilities. Instead of fleeing from moments of sanctuary in a lover's arms to moments of breaking through on some heady journey, Morrison sings he has found his girl. The passionate desire to slip into her "tender sunken sea" has been complimented by the comfort that she waits for him "in tender times". There is the realization that this girl is "the world", that "my girl is mine". This is a different mine than the sarcastic twist rendered in 'Shaman's Blues'. She has yielded, and by inference of the song's tone, so has he; that is why she is his – and he is hers. Morrison's drifting off in his "la-la-la"-ing at the end recalls the same ending to 'Love Street', but this feels more comfortable, less reluctant to yield to the vulnerabilities of life, to the blues. Just as 'You Make Me Real' is followed by an "apocalypse-with-a-beat" portrait of America, so is 'Blue Sunday'. 'Ship Of Fools' didn't garner much critical attention, the most notable perhaps being Kennely's labelling the song "ecology-rock,"40 but the song concisely depicts the American trip. The image, "ship of fools", became part of America's consciousness when Katherine Anne Porter's first novel, *Ship Of Fools*, was published in 1962. Best know for her short stories, Porter (1890-1980) weaves together a rich tapestry of threads that detail and intertwine the fascinating and the mundane of the novel's spectrum of characters in this drifting micro-world of humanity. The novel, which she notates at the end of the book took her twenty years to write, is about the voyage of a German ship from Mexico to Germany in 1931 just before the rise to power of Hitler and the Nazis. The movie version of Porter's story was a box office hit in 1965. And after the photographs from the Apollo moon flights came back, especially the earthrise photographs, most artistic minds readily perceived the image that earth was just an shimmering island, a vibrant spaceship in the vast sea of the universe. The "ship of fools" image has been rendered in many different shades by many different artists; as Porter noted in the paragraph that prefaced her novel, earth as a ship on its voyage to eternity is a simple, universal image that transcends the ages. In this Doors song the image of such a ship is cast into drug imagery, just as in 'Crystal Ship'. Morrison opens with the very apocalyptic image of the humanity dying out with nobody "left to scream and shout". Similar to the early 1960s anthem of twist and shout? For The Doors, the human race is becoming passive, numb eyes stuffed in cars that crawl past the evening that the city sleeps to hide, forsaking the rhythms of Eden, rhythms that early rock 'n' roll had awakened. But something more sinister is happening: modern life is on the ultimate drug trip to oblivion. Though people have walked on the moon, our smog will get us soon. We're hooked on a drug called technology. The same magic that put us on the moon generates the smog that will kill us.

The technology which can take us to other worlds is destroying our own world, just as the abuse of any drug does. The crystal ship is no longer some personal journey to go hear the scream of the butterfly; earth is that crystal ship – our only ship. And Jim sings how everyone is hanging out, up, down, and in and holding on fast, and he hopes "our little world" somehow survives. The imagery alludes to a drug trip, an unsteady and a dangerous one at that, given the fragility of our fair sister who has been stabbed in the side of the dawn with fences and dragged down.

While we wait on freedom's shore for the next flash of Eden, for maybe a new crystal ship, the ship of fools arrives. The prophetic attitude of talking about sin from earlier Doors' works has mellowed to an acceptance that this is our only ship; there won't be any saviour, any 'Mister Good Trips' who will bring us a "new ship". So we better climb on board and make the best of going home, a home that as a ship of fools is not too enticing. Morrison's lyrics sweep an undertow of uneasiness beneath the rolling, bouncy rhythm of the music, as he repeats the first stanza fading with the call to climb on board. The lyrics deliver a similar apocalyptic image as 'When The Music's Over', but the music rendering this image is far different. Maybe the music isn't over and it isn't time to turn out the lights at the Hard Rock Cafe – yet. Living the blues means learning to embrace and celebrate the pains and joys of living in the scattered sun and on this ship of fools.

## SIDE TWO

The Doors close the set at Hard Rock Cafe and check into Morrison Hotel. Just as side one opens rolling down the road to find a real good time, side two opens with the theme of travel. 'Ship Of Fools' moves into 'Land Ho!' and a portrait of a sailor waiting on freedom's shore, itchy to get rolling on the seas, to walk in foreign lands. Marsh called the song a "carnal rock 'n' roll sea chanty."41 No longer a mystery to be feared, the sea has become a route to the other side; as David Pichaske wrote, the song is an old tale of the sea, of "man's need to escape every now and then"42. Grandpa puts his grandson on his knee to tell this young boy's eggshell fragile mind some tales, and the old man awakens the restless blood of yearning to get rolling again because he is "going crazy" from being at one spot and needs to "walk on foreign sands". Foreign sands? Like maybe Tangie Town? Though the imagery in this song is of the northern seas and not the Tropic Corridor or Africa, the song suggests the same exotic tone in 'Spanish Caravan'. This old man has travelled to other sides; still, he is "graceful", having returned "with silver in his smile", rather than gold from the mountains of Spain. This isn't quite the same grace the wild child in *The Soft Parade* was full of. The hectic pace of neon groves of fields that never die left behind in the bungalows behind the roadhouse in the album's opening song seem so distant to the rolling, natural rhythms of the simple pleasures this voyager of the world enjoys, like smoking "a briar pipe", walking "for country miles", and singing songs.

He sings "songs of shady sisters", which conjure up the smouldering imagery of a real good time in a bungalow or at Tangie Town, yet Grandpa found his girl with the sunlight in her hair – grandma. He sings songs of "old time liberty" because he has sailed from freedom's shore and walked on foreign sands. He sings songs of love and death and "songs to set men free". The Doors can hear the songs the old man sings; they're singing the same ones. Are they singing the same blues? Or is this just Popeye rock? A Popeye documentary that isn't strong enough to capture the same blues feelings of this old sailor? The journey images and other parallels to the previous Doors' songs are good, but are these images annoyingly inane cartoon portraits of America that render an impression of still-lifes rather than an unfolding of a journey? Is 'Land Ho!' a snapshot version of some travelogue-type book, or is it an extension of the freedom sought in 'Break On Through'? The image of "old time liberty" becomes more specific, as Jim sails off with a story from the past – the "three ships and sixty men" alluding to Columbus's voyage with the Pinta, Nia, and Santa Maria. Charting "for ports unread", this voyage doesn't suggest that the ship is dangerous or too fragile, like the crystal ship, but rather that the sea harbours the dangers of north winds that blow till half the crew is dead. Although dangerous, the seas aren't so strange: grandpa has sailed the frozen seas of those north winds.

Morrison closes the song with the rollicking acceptance of letting life roll and seeing what happens. If he gets a dollar bill, then he will buy some booze and drink his fill. If he gets "a number two", then he will go home and marry his lover – just like grandpa did grandma. And in the closing refrain, Jim sings that if he gets back home and feels all right, then he will love his baby – an expression of passion and sincerity that a similar closing refrain to 'Five To One' lacked. There is no need to get fucked up first before coming home to make love to his lover.

But then the rollicking, rhythmical acceptance of 'Land Ho!' slows into the deliberate, foreboding tone of 'The Spy'. Jim opens the song with a stark contrast to the imagery of 'Love Street' and other previous love songs like 'Light My Fire', 'Love Me Two Times', 'Hello, I Love You', and 'Touch Me': he is "a spy in the house of love". Marsh wrote that the song "sounds like south side Chicago on LSD".43 The earlier persona has matured, accepting the limitations, if not more intricate dynamics, of love; Jim is willing to be a spy, rather than a conquering lord or Lizard King. Such understanding diminishes the tone once so cynical of the easy ride, of the lost little girl.

The unsettling image of sleeping in strange rooms in 'Strange Days' is hinted at when Jim croons that he knows the dream his lover dreams. Despite Densmore's soft brush drumbeat, the sanctuary this house provides for sleeping and dreaming is not all that comforting since the spy knows "your deepest secret fear". Unlike the lover in 'Strange Days' who preyed on those fears and taunted his lover, or the lamenting shamanic bluesman wanting to make his lover "mine" because he knows those fears, this lover knows how to sooth with the word she longs to hear, but Jim doesn't clearly indicate how he will use that word. He stealthily moves through the song, and this portrait of comfortable knowledge and smug awareness leaves the slightly uncomfortable sensation of what will he do with that knowledge and awareness. How safe is THIS house of love? This bungalow where the lovers go down slow? This room in Morrison Hotel? The imagery of this lyric may well have been borrowed from Anais Nin's 1954 novel, *A Spy In The House Of Love*. Benjamin Franklin V and Duane Schneider in their retrospective book, *Anais Nin: An Introduction*, wrote that the novel, typical of Nin's works, explored the "psychological anguish of a female character, Sabina", detailing her attempts to understand her difficulties and "reach a state of wholeness or contentment that leads to happiness in life"44. Nin (1903-1977) uses a kaleidoscope of organic and inorganic imagery to portray Sabina's sensual and psychological pursuit to impale her sense of trapped obligation and to feel, even if only momentarily, the freedom a man has "to enjoy without love"45 – yet all the while seeking that allusive sanctuary of love. Like the lyrics of The Doors and particularly Morrison, Nin offers the reader more than a lifting of the veil for the voyeur's eyes: the swirling imagery that portrays Sabina's variation of being a "back door man" occasionally mingles with the emotional and psychological comets and shooting stars that grace the internal universe of being human. In the Doors song, the spy in Morrison's house of love knows the secrets, the deepest fears and dreams, and intonates a sense of control. In Nin's novel, Sabina is completely insecure with her behaviour. She feels like "a spy in the international house of love", and she compares her feelings to the tensions she sees in the lives of spies in the movies: their constant fear of exposing themselves with careless behaviour and their "need for continuous pretending, quick improvisations of motivations, quick justifications of their presence here or there"46.

Whether or not Morrison actually read this novel, he certainly shared Nin's artistic perspective. From interviews with and articles by Nin (especially a 1973 interview)47 printed in *A Woman Speaks: The Lectures, Seminars, And Interviews Of Anais Nin* (1975), Nin uses language quite kindred to ideas Morrison expressed, notably in his interviews with Lizze James between 1968-70. Both talk about how the individual inherits his or her cultural concept of morality; how guilt is induced by the religion, family, and whoever has had prestige over an individual; how people willingly trade in freedom and play roles and wear masks; and how each individual needs to rid himself or herself of those things that are not genuine to him or her. And The Doors have clearly depicted such social role playing and trading-in of freedom with the meticulously arranged second album, *Strange Days* – a follow up to the themes rendered in 'The End' which closed the debut album. As portrayed in both the works of The Doors and Nin, to confront alien concepts and search for personal concepts invites a journey of adventure. To Nin this sense of adventure is "tremendously necessary" for us to transcend the sense of tragedy and loss we experience in life and that once we accept that experience can be painful, that relationships end, and that we will be challenged: "as long as we have a place that says this is our life and it's going to go on, then we won't have any of this tremendous pessimism or suicidal impulses"48. The music of The Doors, evident in the lyrics of Morrison, was reflecting such awareness that modern life wasn't just a sequence of apocalyptic experiences whirling toward some decisive, unavoidable finale. Life is a process, and know where the roadhouses are, as life rolls on...

Leaving the sedated, uneasy tone of 'The Spy', The Doors pick up the beat to musically render Jim's portrait of his 'Queen Of The Highway'. Ray said this song was "a great song" – it was about Jim and Pam, "an American Frontier Indian swirl, a love dance, a mating ritual"; it was about the Indians starting "all over again" with a new generation, but, as Ray added, Jim and Pam "unfortunately... never had any children"49. Morrison opens the song by recalling the theme of the roadhouse blues – his lover is "a princess" and also a "queen of the highway". Queen of wherever she roams, she isn't the vamp staking out her kingdom by playing mind games on Love Street or the Strip or by strolling the sidewalks of Venice Beach. She is the wild love, but tempered, like the girl with the sunlight in her hair in 'Peace Frog'. Just as America brings together a patchwork of vivid images, the ensuing fragments of vivid images are held together by the relationship of the two lovers. The road goes to "Madre", Spanish for mother. The fields of Andalusia in 'Spanish Caravan'? First flash of a return to the womb, to Eden? This suggestion of innocence quickly yields to the imagery of the beauty and the beast. Can she tame the blind tiger? Only he can save her, but can he win her love? Now wedded, the princess is "a good girl", and she and the blind tiger stand in the meadow "naked as children" and "wild as can be". Far from freedom's shore and the frozen northern seas, the black leather shaman and his lover, the queen of the highway, have returned to the meadow, to the innocent vulnerability of naked children. And since blood is the rose of mysterious union when he slides into her tender sunken sea, life rolls on as the soon to be off-spring start the cycle all over.

Life brings the roaming lovers, the angry tiger and his restless princess, back to innocence, to trust in love and in each other, and to start the cycle of life again. The final stanza reiterates that life is a cycle, that this innocence doesn't last. Death's pall swirls back as the illusion of "son of a frontier Indian swirl" resurrects the earlier image of scattered Indians on dawn's highway. With the duality so characteristic of The Doors' artistic vision, Jim balances this swirling with the beautiful lyric, "Dancing through the midnight whirlpool/Formless". This image draws from the imagery of the bright midnight, of dancing on fire, of breaking through to the other side.

At last, formless and dancing. Celebrating life while being free from it. Old time liberty. But it's just a moment that Jim hopes will last "a little while longer", because eventually the moment shifts. Again, as Reabur pointed out, there is the "threat the human race is dying out"50. The shadow of the 'Ship Of Fools' slides underneath the formless dancing and casts a realization that moments, like light or flashes of Eden, shift. Seasons also shift, and The Doors render a portrait of a season they hadn't rendered before – the season of autumn, of "Indian Summer". There had been summertime loves and wintertime waltzes, but the quiet moments of the autumn of love had eluded them. A time to reflect, to harvest the fruits of a summer love, rather than to lament the wintry absence of its warmth or to hop off in pursuit of the next sultry sanctuary of lust. The music slows, the lyrics rendering simple brush strokes of what Jim realizes – that he loves her "the best" and "better than all the rest". Syrupy? Too saccharine? Who hasn't felt such moments? How else could you communicate that moment better? Not at that moment. But the song isn't as settling as its tone suggests. "Indian summer" harks back to the scattered Indians on dawn's highway. And Jim sings he loves her better than the rest he had met in the summer, but things, like summer, aren't going to remain this calm. And the opening riffs of 'Maggie M'Gill' sweep away this Indian summer tranquillity. For Marsh, 'Maggie M'Gill' paints a picture of the "seamy side of rock 'n' roll", with Morrison "writing like Tennessee Williams for a rock and roll song"51. Side two opens with warm tales from grandpa the sailor, but closes with daddy getting drunk and leaving Maggie nothing; she has to leave the warm mansion at the top of the hill and sail her own frozen seas. Reabur perceived Maggie M'Gill as "the archetypical American heroine, a rural woman" in a frontier-Western type setting who, "with no other course left her", pursues "what a frontiersman might have called a 'life of sin'"52. She goes "down to Tangie Town" where people "really like to get it on". Tangie Town is not on Love Street, nor is it hiding beneath television skies. In 'Roadhouse Blues' we leave town for the hills; in 'Maggie M'Gill' we return from the hills to town, to the city's roadhouses, to the bungalows in the back. We have gone through the Hard Rock Cafe and arrived at Morrison Hotel. Reabur wrote that Maggie M'Gill makes the journey to Tangie Town, and though what she "finds seems ugly, sordid, tawdry", this is the end of the road: "If you can't get it on in Tangie Town, there ain't nowhere you'll be able to get it on."53 The wild child returns to the city to get it on. The Ashen Lady gives up her vow. No longer depicting modern existence with harsh hypocritical tones, The Doors offer a portrait rendered with an understanding tone of what it means to be human. If you're feeling sad and blue, society has taught us to go buy something to relieve that depression, something like a "brand new pair of shoes". But Morrison wants shoes that help us travel to something that money can't buy – Tangie Town. The repetition of the word "down" and the raucous music of this song have brought down the previous ethereal high renderings of love. Indian summer doesn't keep the house on the hill warm all the time.

Getting it on, like sliding into the tender sunken sea of the queen of the highway, starts the cycle all over: mom meets dad in the back seat of a "rock 'n' roll car". Come back from the wet forests of a moonlight drive, and there still are the blues of getting it on in the back of the modern sanctuary of the car with music made for rockin' 'n' rollin'. The great American frontier has rolled into rock 'n' roll, but life still delivers the blues. Maggie isn't another lover in the alternating questing for sanctuary The Doors have been portraying; rather, The Doors render a portrait of another soul who also has been singing the blues, lovingly sketched out in the next to last stanza.

The shamanic bluesman who began emerging in *The Soft Parade* seems to be more grounded in the realities of life, more accepting of the roadhouses, the crystal ship of fools, the Blue Sundays and Indian summers, the grandpas who sailed as whalers and the Maggie M'Gills; he now is able to sit at the Hard Rock Cafe and drink that mug of understanding with Maggie M'Gill. The theme which had begun emerging in the album, *Waiting For The Sun*, and was so resoundingly stated in 'Roadhouse Blues' closes the set in *Morrison Hotel* as Morrison sings for Maggie to roll on. Let it roll. You don't need crystal ships or plastic boxes of Twentieth Century Foxes or stores on Love Street or highways to a bright midnight. Life will take you on the journeys and to the sanctuaries if you just let it roll.

# chapter 6

# l.a. woman,
# you're my woman

"We must step resolutely into the thick of those struggles which are being raged right now between the insatiable thirst for knowledge and man's tragic dependency on art."

"We have only to place Faust, who storms unsatisfied through all the provinces of knowledge and is driven to make a bargain with the powers of darkness, beside Socrates in order to realize that modern man has begun to be aware of the limits of Socratic curiosity and to long, in the wide, waste ocean of knowledge, for a shore."

"The chances are that almost every one of us, upon close examination, will have to admit that he is able to approach the once-living reality of myth only by means of intellectual constructs. Yet every culture that has lost myth has lost, by the same token, its natural, healthy creativity. Only a horizon ringed about with myths can uniform a culture. The forces of imagination and of Apollonian dream are saved only by myth from indiscriminate rambling."

*Friedrich Nietzsche,*
*The Birth Of Tragedy (pp. 96, 109, 136)*

"Nietzsche killed Jim Morrison, I had once said rather melodramatically to some startled friends in Berkeley."

*John Densmore,*
*Riders On The Storm: My Life With Jim Morrison*
*And The Doors (p. 3)*

SIDE 1
The Changeling
Love Her Madly
Been Down So Long
Cars Hiss By My Window
L.A. Woman

SIDE 2
L'America
Hyacinth House
Crawling King Snake
The WASP (Texas Radio And The Big Beat)
Riders On The Storm

The Sixties were about to close: peace accords to end the Vietnam War "with honour" were finalized in January 1973, nine months before the U.S. Senate formed a committee to investigate something known as the "Watergate Break-In". With the resignation of President Richard Nixon, the United States was ready to be driven by a Ford, rather than a Lincoln. The resurgence of the status-quo would wait another decade.

But the painful ending of the Sixties continued as the spring of 1970 brought the murdering of American youths on the college campus of Kent State (Kent, Ohio) and Jackson State (Jackson, Mississippi). On May 4, Ohio National Guard opened fire and killed four people during an anti-war demonstration at Kent State University who had nothing to do with the demostrating.

On May 15, state highway patrolmen opened fire at Jackson State College and killed two. These killings were followed by the autumn drug-overdose deaths of rock music idols, Jimi Hendrix (September 18) and Janis Joplin (October 4).

As the downspin began of the whirlwind of forces that had swirled through the Sixties, the country was weary from what seemed to be a nightmarish onslaught on the American Dream. In January of 1970, the jury convicted five of the Chicago 7 on crossing state lines with intent to promote riots, but acquitted the seven of conspiring to actually cause riots. In February, a Bank of America branch in Santa

Barbara, California, was burned down, and in March a townhouse in Greenwich Village was destroyed by the explosion of a bomb factory of the radical underground militant group, the Weathermen who, in 1971, would explode a bomb in the Senate wing of the Capital Building in Washington D.C. Somewhat lethargic to another manned-moon flight, the nation became riveted with the unscripted drama of the crippled Apollo 13 mission in April 1970 as NASA performed during its finest hour. While the nation was still recovering from the three-man crew's dramatic and successful return to Earth, President Richard Nixon carefully explained why the U.S. had launched an "incursion" into Cambodia on April 29, and there followed massive anti-war demonstrations highlighted by the presence of many Vietnam veterans. The August killing of Judge Harold Haley and three of his four kidnappers during an escape attempt at one of the last monuments by architect Frank Lloyd Wright, the Marin County Civic Center in California, led to the nationwide manhunt for college-educated, street-wise, ex-UCLA philosophy instructor, Black Panther activist, Angela Davis (a physical manifestation of the long-legged "dusky jewel" in 'Hello, I Love You'). She would be acquitted in 1972 by an all-white jury of charges of murder, kidnap, and criminal conspiracy. In September, the Presidential Commission on Campus Unrest concluded that the gap between the youth and the establishment posed a threat to American stability; Vice-President Agnew denounced the commission's findings, and President Nixon did nothing to acknowledge them. In November began the court-martial of Lt. William Calley for the massacre of Vietnamese civilians at My Lai. In December, the Supreme Court ruled constitutional the federal law lowering the voting age to 18, and the Twenty-sixth Amendment to the U.S. Constitution became law when the 38th state, ironically Ohio, to ratify it did so on June 30, 1971 – small consolation to the average aged soldier of 19 years-old fighting in Vietnam. In January of 1971, Charles Manson and three women accomplices were found guilty of the Sharon Tate and La Bianca murders; and in March, Lt. Calley likewise was found guilty of premeditated murder of 22 people at My Lai while his superiors were exonerated.

By May, several weeks of anti-war protesting in Washington D.C. culminated with mass arrests which reached 12,000.

The clear-cut political labels of "hawk" and "dove" continued both to intensify and to blur as America grappled with the growing confusion stirred by the images and issues of Vietnam. This ambiguous public view seemed mirrored even in two movies which depicted differing views of war and which were box office hits for 1970: George C. Scott recreated in an Oscar-winning role the enigmatic WW II American hero, General George S. Patton Jr. in *Patton*, which won the Oscar for Best Picture; and Robert Altman's *M\*A\*S\*H* used the Korean War to make a satiric, irreverent statement about the Vietnam conflict and war. Besides the Vietnam War, a faltering American economy of rising inflation and joblessness also confronted President Nixon who countered with fiscal austerity while promoting federal legislation to clean up the environment mess America was stewing in. As his first act for the new decade, on January 1, 1970, Nixon signed into law the *National Environmental Quality Improvement Act*. On April 22, the first "Earth Day" took place as a nationwide teach-in on environmental awareness and responsibility.

On June 3, the *Endangered Species Conservation Act* became law. And in December, the Environmental Protection Agency (EPA) was established by merging several federal agencies overseeing environmental issues. The political and legislative actions of 1970's "Year of the Environment" would radically alter the *laissez faire* way people had conducted business at the exploitation of America's natural resources. We could no longer just wantonly stab the Earth in the side of the dawn and drag her down with fences; at least the American compartment of this ship of fools would try to clean up the smog before it got us.

It was a time of juggling principles and aspirations. Political and social administrating could no longer tinker with the cursory worn-out seams of the economic fabric that tied society together or just replace parts of what had been a durable engine of economic success with which to drive a society. The automobile companies, the standard American industrial barometer, were struggling due to a major strike, slipping sales, and the assault by imported smaller cars. Detroit responded with the unthinkable for American highways – subcompacts; American Motors introduced the Gremlin, and Ford soon followed with the Pinto. Forces larger than patching thread-bare social fashions or fine tuning a sputtering economic/political engine were overtaking the languishing status quo.

On the evening of January 12, 1971, the world of American television changed: Norman Lear's *All In The Family* premiered, and Carroll O'Connor's Archie Bunker ushered in a real-life irreverence never before seen on American public prime-time television. While two other prime-time family shows, the *Brady Bunch* and *The Partridge Family*, are forever affixed to that early 1970s aura with their 1950s sitcom demeanor, *All In The Family* portrayed relationships – the bickering, the prejudices, the frailties, the warts, the humour of a squabbling low-income family – that transcend the times. Based on the British television show, *Till Death Do Us Part*, the Bunker household was not the Pondersosa of Bonanza, and viewers responded favourably to what they saw. The stalwart *The Ed Sullivan Show* was gone by the start of the fall season of 1971, and *Bonanza* by the start of the fall of 1972. Even in the world of rock 'n' roll, things were falling apart. The imminent demise of The Beatles was all but done with the release of solo albums by McCartney, Lennon, and Harrison before the summer of 1971.

The feuding and dissension among The Beatles, the complacency of successful groups from the Sixties, and The Doors themselves underscored the events of the last couple of years, signalling that the times were a-changing. The L.A. and San Francisco sounds were withering back into the social humus of change, as the blossoming of a new sound began unfolding. Social commentary was yielding to the pleasantries of Pop. Rock was becoming calculated showmanship; the Lizard King was yielding to the snake-oil artist of a young Alice Cooper. In June of 1971, Bill Graham closed what had been an energetic forum for early rock 'n' roll bands – his Fillmore East (New York City) and Fillmore West (San Francisco); Graham said rock musicians were becoming too greedy and wanted more lucrative venues, like sports arenas. The influx into the rock scene pulsed with the music of The Osmonds, The Jackson Five fronted by a pre-pubescent Michael Jackson, The Partridge Family, John Denver, James Taylor, Carole King, Carly Simon, Cat Stevens, The Carpenters, Three Dog Night, Grand Funk Railroad, Black Sabbath with a young Ozzy Osbourne, Chicago, Jethro Tull, Santana, and Elton John. Rob Houghton, in a March 1971 review of this last Doors album, made a comment about The Doors' sound, yet his off-the-cuff sarcasm was such a prognostic statement of what rock music would do, writing that if Pabst Blue Ribbon, a beer company, were smart, they would contract The Doors for a bunch of commercials: "They would increase sales by as much as a hundred per cent mostly by me."1 There was one last burst of creative expression in this so-called "Golden Age of Rock" before the recording industry finally formulated a rock sound, and rock 'n' roll became the ever self-conscious business of rock music. And before 1971 was over, the unassuming but ubiquitous Smiley face had conquered the market place. As Morrison's trial for "lewd and lascivious behaviour" in Miami unfolded, Elektra released two albums after *Morrison Hotel*: a double live album, *Absolutely Live*, in July 1970 and a compilation of hits, *13*, in November 1970 for the Christmas sales season. Disillusioned as he was dragged through the very real experience of the American judicial process, Morrison was no longer the boisterous lion in the night, but he could still rattle off the quotable snips, like the one Danny Sugerman paraphrased: "First Janis, now Jimi; you're drinking with number three."2 Bearded again, Morrison also was rounded at the edges – physically, mentally, and emotionally. Aging had done to Dionysus what nothing else had: grounded him to the reality of being human on Earth, a grounding that would bury him as Jim's heart ceased on July 3, 1971, three months after the release of the sixth original Doors' album, *L.A. Woman*. This album had become a long awaited enterprise for The Doors, for it would fulfill their contract with Elektra, an obligation which had become increasingly burdensome, especially for Morrison, who never learned to accept such imposed limitations. Jim had become a prisoner of not only his own devices but also forces he couldn't begin to control. He repeatedly had expressed his desire to escape the frustration of fulfilling what was expected of Jim Morrison, lead singer of The Doors, also evident in a writing from his notebooks where Jim wondered which of his "cellves" would be remembered.3 Moreover, all of The Doors openly had expressed the desire to return to where they felt they had originally derived their music – the blues.

But those weren't the blues spun from the souls of slaves adrift in a strange land with no roots save their own people. The blues with which The Doors rendered their artistic vision came from the souls of struggling artistic spirits adrift in their own culture and land. In the hands of The Doors, that blues evoked a rather chilling impression.

Though separate from the trends of pop and rock music, The Doors, since their beginning, had been mirrors, their lives and music – their artistic vision – reflecting the whirlwind of forces swirling in the 1960s and early 1970s. And they continued to reflect the times in their final album as a foursome. Bruce Harris, in University Review, wrote what was a consensus opinion of The Doors, that the group was "never much involved in the mainstream of rock music" and was "always more of a monument than an influence": "Unaffected by trends and fads, they are simply making music."4 As if to underscore this aloofness, The Doors cut their last album in their own rehearsal studio across the street from Elektra. Ray said they knew the sound quality in that studio: "We had that room down; we would make it sound really good."5 But the group didn't perform up to producer Paul Rothchild's expectations which Ray even admitted. In a 1981 interview, Rothchild recollected that there were two good songs, 'Riders On The Storm' and 'L.A. Woman', but the rest of the album was "dogmeat" with no heart in the music. He stated that he had his "head down on the console for the first time in my career", the group was "very lethargic", and nobody was listening to anybody's ideas; he resolved the only way the group would unify to make this record was "if they lost me as a whipping master"6. So The Doors moved a jukebox, pinball machine, and sofa into the downstairs of their rehearsal studio, engineer and now co-producer Bruce Botnick moved a recording console and portable eight-track machines into group manager Bill Siddens' office upstairs and then strung cables down to the first floor through the windows, and Elvis Presley's bassist Jerry Scheff and rhythm guitarist Marc Benno were hired to play. On the decision to use eight-track rather than sixteen-track recording machines, Densmore wrote that this move backward in technology forced the group to record "only genuinely great material... like our first album: raw and simple"7. These changes in instrumentation affected the interplay between the usual parts. Though still a Doors' sound and style, the roles of the different instruments became more distinct. Whereas Ray and Robby had woven all the lines between themselves before, interchanging melody and bass lines, etc., these lines no longer were so intimately woven together. The bass always played the bass lines, the rhythm guitar always played block chords, Robby played snatches of countermelodies and melodic accents, and Ray became more or less a lead/rhythm player, filling in with more sophisticated harmonies and occasional melodies. There was a lot of good music that couldn't have been done before because, with more players, individual lines could be technically more involved. The result was that the sound was fuller, but the texture wasn't as deep nor nearly as intimately tied to the hearts of the artists as it was before. The boys and their music were maturing. The reviews of the album split into the usual established viewpoints. Nick Tosches in Fusion offered an insightful perspective encompassing more than just the album: "With *L.A. Woman*, The Doors aesthetic hovers on (over?) the brink of *fin de vie*... no one else could validly commit either the theatricality of 'Love Her Madly' or that of the words/music to the refrain of 'The WASP' without producing some kind of laughable poo-poo. The Doors, on the other hand, create, in these two songs, works of total raunch by the very fact of their exaggerated heavy-handedness. Anybody can be subtle with a profundity but it takes some kind of a medicine man to be pushy with a vacuity."8

To say Morrison was consciously being a shaman or, as the modern mind generally synonymizes, a medicine man is to give Jim undue credit; he was more unconscious than conscious of the landscapes he was travelling beyond the profane, the so-called real world.

That doesn't mean Jim wasn't a shamanic spirit, nor does that diminish the power of Jim's poetic vision. Jim's relationship with the creative spirit allowed him to tap into some very deep impressions that as a whole reflected a significant portrait of our society. Especially in this last album, the lyrics seem to be more like a free association outburst of poetic images as they crossed Jim's mind. Though these poetic images don't necessarily shape the same coherent work of art portrayed by the piecing together of the earlier poetic images, they remain emotionally provocative.

The dissociated quality creates a subtle, but still powerful impact because you are never quite sure what is going to hit you next or how it will affect you. The images are vacuous, but substantial, leaving room to interpret them differently every time you hear them. This is a significant point of maturity when the artist can manipulate the images in a way that doesn't diminish their impact. One of the starkest images from the album was on the yellow sleeve jacket over the record: a figure of a woman crucified to a utility pole, her head bowed below the dingy sky of L.A., bowed below the wires carrying one of the invisible forces which we bow to and which fuels the world of electronic music. Eden, Eve, the source of fertility, our saviour – nailed to a modern tree. This theme, a consistent one in The Doors' artistic vision, emerges in a stark visual image. And Andrew Lloyd Webber and Tim Rice's *Jesus Christ Superstar* had become a rock opera (pumping new life into what had became in the hands of modern religious organizations a rather lifeless spirit) as 1970 yielded to 1971. It was a time for a resurrection, for the Sixties to become the Seventies, for Mr. Mojo to get rising.


## SIDE ONE

The album opens with the personification of Morrison as a "changeling", and the music renders a rich texture to the short, concise images as the lyrics etch out this imagery of change in 'The Changeling'. Morrison sings about the urban world of living uptown, downtown, and all around and where survival focuses on one thing – having money and having none. This is a considerable distance from the earlier days of stumbling in the neon groves as cars crawl by stuffed with eyes. Though this urban world isn't Eden, The Doors seem at home in this plastic world so permanent in its temporalness.

Amidst the plastic landscape of the city, Jim becomes the essentials for living: the air we breathe, the food we eat, the friends we greet. Change – so necessary to survive – is easy, because Morrison sings he has "never been so broke" that he couldn't break away from town. Love the city, this L.A. Woman, and then seek sanctuary in worlds away from her, in bungalows where people go down slow to the Texas Radio and the Big Beat, out on the perimeter in a forest of azure, in the free flowing of being a changeling. The term, changeling, derives from two meanings of the root, change.

From the folklore of Northern European, usually the birth of a handicapped or other exceptionally abnormal child was explained away with the story of a changeling – a fairy substituted for a human baby. The substituted fairy could have been a fairy baby or an elder fairy who was no longer useful to the fairy tribe. This explanation of exchanged spirits led to some horrible infanticides or abuse of children in attempts to rid the body of the unwanted spirit. It also explains the Archaic meaning of the word – a simpleton, idiot, or imbecile. But changeling also refers to one who is apt to change – be it as a traitor of loyalty or as a vagabond to the shifting world of opportunities and demands. Though Jim's ostracized relationship with his parents blends with the fairy mythology of changelings, the song reflects the expediency of changing – of having money, of having none, of flowing with the swarming streets, of leaving town on a midnight train. When Morrison sings of leaving town on a "midnight train", it is another journey into the bright midnight to seek out bliss, to seek out the other side. The insect-like busyness of the "swarming street" contrasts to the implied ease of the "midnight train" out of town, yet a "midnight train" shades the song with the same foreboding hue any journey into the night portrayed in a Doors song – it is a trip into the unknown, a trip on which the fading refrain and accompanying clapping easily takes you. According to Hopkins and Sugerman, the lyric for 'The Changeling' was written in 1968, and the images in the lyric do reflect the rich artistic rendering so inherent in the first three albums.9

Typical of their presentations on albums, The Doors juxtapose this song about a journey with a song about love, as the group slides back into what many labelled a song reminiscent of the earlier, more commercial Doors' sound. Robby penned 'Love Her Madly', a funky blues with a bouncy bass line. The song was released as a single in late March 1971, topped out at #11 in mid-May, and then disappeared off the Billboard Top 100 charts a month later. Characteristic of The Doors, the 45 rpm single was backed by the Doors' cover of Willie Dixon's gravelly blues number, '(You Need Meat) Don't Go No Further'. Houghton wrote in *Creem* that though 'Love Her Madly' was a "great boogying song", it wasn't a "fantastic piece of music", but when "sandwiched between The Jackson Five and Steve Stills, it shines"10. But it doesn't shine with the same flame of the earlier come on to "light my fire" urgency; the flame has mellowed to a more resigned funky blues lament of, "Don't you love her madly?" and "Don't you need her badly?" Like The Doors' repeated seeking of life in the arms of love and then in freedom and then back to love, this lover also has been a changeling, having walked out the door a "thousand times before". But there is a plastic tone to this love and these lovers. Instead of burning with the urgency of a youthful lover, the yearning to "be her daddy" hints at the business-like relationship with a sugar daddy who provides for services rendered – treasures for pleasures. The popish, upbeat song bouncing along with cursory lyrics sketches a transparent portrait of love compared to the earthy, blues-rendered portrait of 'Maggie M'Gill' an album earlier and to the gritty urban tone of 'L.A. Woman' that closes side one. A Krieger lyric usually has at least one ambiguous image which transcends the apparent innocence of the song. The "seven horses" who "seem to be on the mark" underline the "deep blue dream" imagery which draws us to the edge of blue in 'Wishful Sinful', a shoreline of a sea where horses have gone down in mute nostril agony. But the melodies are upbeat, "happy" – major key all the way, a contrast to the usual minor mode renderings. The contrast between the upbeat music and self-depreciating words that superficially seem to be simple bravado gives the song a kind of hysterical, desperate air. Like the hysterical laugh people emit when something so bad happens they don't know how to deal with it any other way. A lost, helpless laugh. The lover has been forced to face the question of whether the affair (and, more largely, anything in the world) really meant something since it all is destined to change.

Jim sings the closing refrain in such a light, funky tone and leaves the subtle impression that madly can easily become maddening, the chill of a cold lover in a darkened room. Or the growing realization that accepting life as it is and being adaptable doesn't mean you can continue having easy access to your own private meadows away from the fields. Or the possibility of the lover losing his mental grip. Within the context of this album, there is the subtle hint beneath the sing-song tone that he just might not be able to cope with the realization that changeability makes life meaningless. The sing-song tone shifts dramatically when The Doors follow with what David Pichaske called a "standard, very conventional blues" composition,11 'Been Down So Long', a stark psychological sketch of life as a prisoner. Hugh Noname, a pseudonym reviewer who surfaced in the London underground newspaper, *IT*, wrote that the song "pounds the head relentlessly with no apologies to the late" Richard Faria, whose book provided the title and refrain for 'Been Down So Long'12. The book,

*Been Down So Long It Looks Like Up To Me*, published in 1966 two days before Faria's death in a motorcycle accident, catalogues the events of college student (then, campus hippie), Gnossos Pappadopoulis. The book's cataloguing of our culture's banality, as Maybelle Lacey wrote in her review of the book in *Library Journal*, "rolls with its own momentum", but "coarse language and the last possible word in sex and physiological descriptions does exceed all limits of good taste"13. At that time. Basically a culturally saturated cynic whose actions reflect his lingering adolescent perspective of the world, Gnossos probably provided a kindred spirit with whom Morrison identified. Jim also challenges the then current limits of good taste of pop music with his raunchy vocal opening about being "down so Goddamn long". In this song, the standard Doors' theme of being prisoners of our own devices becomes a starker image of a prison in a far different tone, different texture, different sketch of isolation. The absence of Manzarek's keyboards allows the relentless downbeat of the bass to drag against Krieger's stifling, frustrated pulsating guitar, etching an aggressive musical backdrop for the anger and apprehension the lyrics evoke. On a literal level, this song depicts a simple, gutsy blues portrait of a prisoner lamenting to the warden to open the lock while longing for one of the most basic ways to reverse feeling entrapped and to gain a sense of freedom, of control through the implicit sexual come on for his baby to get down on her knee and give her love to him.

Just as the lost little girl played warden to her soul in a self-made prison, The Doors have become prisoners of their own devices, especially Morrison having become the public performer so caricaturized on the cover of *Strange Days*. Morrison can just as easily be lamenting to his own self-made warden to break the lock and key to free his soul. The erotic politician, the lion in the night, the Dionysus of the Sixties, the unabashed lover in 'Back Door Man' unabashedly reveals a side of innocence, of being human, of feeling entrapped, when he pleads to "let the poor boy be".

But Jim's struggle hasn't been the same as those of the lovers about which he has sung. His age and experience brings not only the chauvinistic yearning for a lover on her knees, but also the hard reality of the Miami trial. The very real potential of jail certainly influenced this picture rendered by The Doors' artistic vision; the free flowing spirit bouncing from seeking love to breaking through to the other side is beginning to recognize the blues of lamenting, more in a neurotic sense than a helpless one, pleading to forces beyond one's control to "set me free". The songs's aggressiveness suggests that the frustrated spirit is about to lash out at something. Setting yourself apart, as Jim (and the group) did, leaves you without anything permanent to hold on to. It becomes a struggle, forcing you to become a changeling, and changes bring about fundamental doubts about the meaning of existence as a human. The struggling shamanic spirit may be saying he doesn't know which way to turn anymore – down or up. For the moment, he may be asking himself for enough freedom to reach out and touch something solid.

"The poet is the one exposed to all attacks, the one whose state of intoxication drives him constantly to the brink of catastrophe [and makes him] 'totally vulnerable'. The 'method' which permits the creation of poetry necessitates at the same time such an awareness of human experience, such a clear vision into the world of men and nature, that the poet's strength is offset by a new human vulnerability."

*Wallace Fowlie,*
*Rimbaud (A Critical Study) (p. 171)*

"[Morrison] didn't understand ["being a spectacle"]... [Miami] was the ultimate confrontation in that Jim lost for the first time."

*Bill Siddens, Doors' manager,*
*in Westwood One Radio Special,*
*"Rock & Roll Never Forgets: Jim Morrison"*

What's more immediate and tangible than a blow job? Or afterwards, the cold lover in the darkened room of 'Cars Hiss By My Window'?

The portrait of internal alienation in 'Been Down So Long' shifts to one of external alienation in the bluesy, 'Cars Hiss By My Window'. If the tones of the previous songs haven't, the tone of this song interjects you into the steamy, smoke-filled dark night club scene where the voice of the urban blues becomes the oracle.

With the absence of keyboards, the brooding guitar and bass melodies backed by the soft back beats of Densmore's drumming – all having an uncanny similarity to John Lee Hooker's 'Nightmare' – set the tone for Morrison to shift from one prison to another, from the desire for the lover at his command to the emptiness of a cold lover. The lyrics, Hopkins and Sugerman noted, were lifted from one of Jim's Venice Beach notebooks.14

The implied image of a traditional symbol of sanctuary, the house, again becomes a strange room, penetrated by the relentless waves of cars hissing by the window. This image implies more than just incessant waves of cars; it suggests snakes, an image akin to the imprisoned Lizard King telling his lady to get down on her knees in the previous song, only this Lizard King isn't the crawling king snake on side two who rules his den. The beach puts us on the edge of water and in a world where transition happens, where one form yields to another, where the deep blue dream of 'Love Her Madly' becomes a soft parade of waves and headlights shining on the wall. And this lover isn't walking out the door. The alienation between these lovers, as Morrison croons that he can't hear his baby though he calls and calls, is a different alienation than the inability to communicate as between the two lovers in *Strange Days* – those were two people living on surface images, surface love. This song, so much simpler in musical tone, laments a far deeper rift between two people, a psychological rift that transcends any superficial sarcasm about a plastic Twentieth Century Fox living on Love Street or being a prisoner of her own device. The song begins to touch the fears that can chill a human soul.

The long, drawn out vowels and consonants of stanza one shift to the shorter, harder vowels and consonants found in the last stanza: started, trembling, sonic, boom, cold, kill, and darkened.

The trembling windows in this prison send trembling shivers along the spine. The uncertainty is no longer an anxious waiting for the next journey to the new and unknown, for the next escaping;

there is a chilling reality of expected anticipation from repeated experience, like the waves and cars. This relationship isn't superficial; it has the power to explode more forcefully and cause more devastation than previous portrayed relationships. Though more subtle, these images are more powerful than the blatant sarcasm in earlier songs because you don't know when or how the scene will explode. The suddenness of a "sonic boom" punctuates the growing possibility that in this darkened room this cold girl might kill him.15 Not only emotionally, but very possibly physically. Even when the sonic boom occurs, there is no faltering in the mood or progression of the song – or the flow of waves and cars. Though Jim doesn't admit his control has been upset by unexpected forces, there is the undercurrent reality that it has. As he closes the song with a vocalized electric guitar blues solo, the windows within the lover's soul start trembling with the chilling reality that when this music is over, he may well have his lights turned out. Whereas Morrison was mostly aloof from the lovers with whom he associated in previous songs, usually condescending, here he admits that others have the power to destroy him – or at least that he recognizes his personal vulnerability. The younger Lizard King thought he could control his den, as he tries to reassert on side two, but the changeling knows he can't control his metamorphoses.

Side one opens with a changeling singing he has never been so broke that he couldn't leave town and closes with a return to town – a funky, blues ode to Los Angeles, 'L.A. Woman'. A discordant organ crescendo signals the return to town, and then guitar, drums, and keyboards take us on, what Terry Rompers called, "a perfect California car song: bright, steady and energetic"16. But this is more than just another car song. The lover persona Jim sang about in previous albums has been, as Pichaske noted, anthropomorphized into the city, "a stroke of genius" allowing The Doors "to infuse the song with typical sexuality while maintaining an essentially sociological theme"17. Robert Pielke, in his book *You Say You Want A Revolution*, echoed a similar assessment: the city (metaphorically representing the state) is personified as a whore whose hair is burning and whose wanderings are confined to freeways, midnight alleys, and topless bars. The imagery is as dominated by the dark as the Beach Boys' is by light; neither give any promise of ending.

We are confronted with the unmistakable indications of destruction, disease, disaster, and disillusionment.18 And as Pielke noted, the music in a minor key complements this lyrical tone of negation.19 In this melancholic valentine to Los Angeles, the relationship with love and life has transcended the one-on-one personal level, and, for The Doors, as Pichaske wrote, L.A. "becomes a city of night inhabited by lonely, lost angels (pun intended) with the blues"20. Los Angeles, the city of light is, for Jim, "a city of night", a phrase, according to Hopkins and Sugerman, he borrowed from a novel by John Rechy.21 Rechy's book, *City Of Night*, published in 1963, depicts a vagabond world of sexual deviance and homosexuality. The story is a – as Lloyd W. Griffin wrote in his review of the book in the *Library Journal* – "cool, level, extremely graphic account of a piece of sub-cultural America as true, unfortunately, as the facets of America revealed by Tom Wolfe or Robert Frost", and follows an unnamed narrator who "has seen it all and has struggled unsuccessfully to break away from a life of loneliness and loss, terror and the search for reality in a hostile (indifferent) and unreal world"22. Besides several of the book's phrases and images which must have stimulated Morrison's own creative imagination and surfaced in various lyrics Jim wrote, what also must have appealed to him was the vivid, descriptive tour, both physical and psychological, from Times Square in New York City to Pershing Park in Los Angeles to the Navy docks of San Diego to San Francisco to the grandest parade of masks, the Mardi Gras in New Orleans that Rechy portrays of this frenzied, wanton sub-culture which Morrison no doubt had journeyed, if but casually, through in the mid-1960s. Like Rechy's unnamed narrator who perpetually seeks solitude from world of sexual hustling in the cities of night only to return, a behaviour quite natural for people seeking self-meaning and security, so Jim continually returns to his city of night, L.A. Woman. In this song, instead of expressing the cynicism exemplified in earlier albums or the lamenting of blues in recent songs, Jim accepts his unresolved relationship, wondering if Los Angeles is "a lucky lady" or "just another lost angel". The image is no longer a lost little girl; it is a woman, a little lady, an image of considerably more depth than girl.

We return to L.A. for a Sunday afternoon drive, but this isn't a trip down Love Street as we drive through L.A. Woman's suburbs into her

The six studio albums: The Doors (January, 1967).

Strange Days (October, 1967).

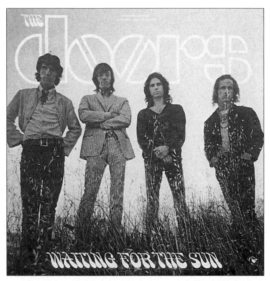

Waiting For The Sun (July, 1968).

The Soft Parade (July, 1969).

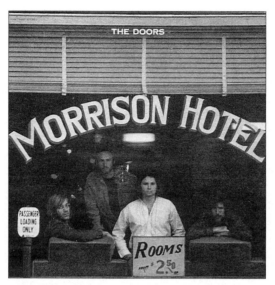

Morrison Hotel (February, 1970).

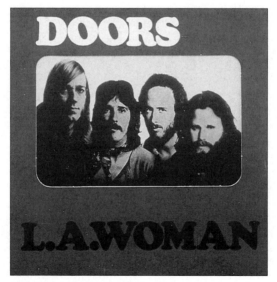

L.A. Woman (April, 1971).

The Doors, as they appeared on early Elektra promo shots, 1967.

The Doors playing at an outdoor concert in California, summer 1967.

1968 promo shot: the image emerging.

Ray Manzarek and Jim Morrison during a concert on August 4, 1968 in
Philadelphia.

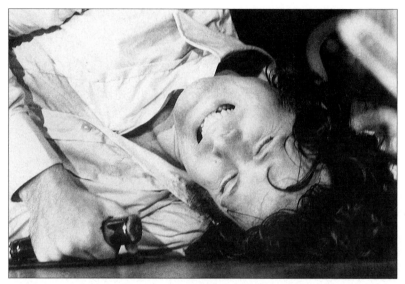

In concert in Copenhagen, September 17, 1968.

Jim Morrison, as he appeared shortly before his death.

Jim Morrison's grave in Paris, now a shrine for fans.

The remaining members of The
Doors: John Densmore,

Robby Krieger,

and Ray Manzarek, in 1995.

blues – into the blues of twentieth century L.A., of twentieth century America, of the Western dream. And Ray's ragtime piano melody dances us right into those blues.

In the 'Soft Parade', The Doors accept that successful hills are part of life's landscape; but in 'L.A. Woman', the San Gabriel mountains of the Angeles and San Bernardino National Forest which surround Los Angeles, hills of western pine forests which frequently renew themselves via fire, those hills, the beautiful hair of the L.A. Woman, "are filled with fire". The hills are changing, and yet they aren't. Echoing the opening lines from 'Light My Fire', Morrison sings that if they say he never loved L.A., "you know they are a liar". Come on, L.A., city of light try to set the night on fire.

The song then creates a lusty urban scene that so easily slithers out from the darkened night club scene into the free flowing imagery of driving down the freeway and roaming "midnight alleys" past "cops in cars" and "topless bars". Having detached themselves from the strange times in order to render a vivid portrait of those strange days, The Doors now comfortably roll along on them. Having photographed alleys of society with the eye of a critical shamanic spirit, of artists trying to hold a mirror up to their society, The Doors now roam those alleys, even as they marvel at having never seen "a woman so alone". As with many aspects of his life, Jim had a love/hate relationship with L.A. Sugerman wrote that Morrison lived longer in L.A. than anywhere else, loved the city harder than anyone he knew, and said goodbye in a "love letter, a delicious song of longing and lust"23. Hopkins and Sugerman later wrote in *No One Here Gets Out Alive* that 'L.A. Woman' was Jim's "despairing salute" a city he now perceived as "diseased and alienated".24

In his review of the album, Bruce Harris wrote that The Doors' music reflects their vision of American as a museum of disease.25 Morrison stated the same in a personal letter to *Creem* editor, Dave Marsh, writing that he had "always seen Los Angeles as a microcosm of the States, a genetic blue-print"26 In this song, The Doors create a museum-like image of L.A. penetrated by freeways, a prison of love and blues, of alienation and disease. A city of light that is a city of night. Freeways that exit into midnight alleys. Suburbs (secure American homes) that sprawl around the "motel money murder madness" of Los Angeles (an image that condenses the imagery of the

Eagles' 'Hotel California' and Pink Floyd's 'Money' into a simple phrase of alliteration which underscores the disease afflicting not only the outwardly appearing beauty of L.A. Woman, but America and life in the twentieth century). Money the stuff that survival seems to be dependent upon, the stuff the changeling has and doesn't have. And when the mood changes from "glad to sadness", the shift is effortless. But Mr. Mojo is going to rise, he's going to keep on risin', keep on resurrecting. Hopkins and Sugerman noted in the same tone of jest they believed Jim used when he said "Mr. Mojo" was not only part of an anagram for his name, but also the name he would use when contacting L.A. after he had escaped to Africa.27 In his book, *Riders On The Storm*, Densmore recalled how Morrison showed the group how he derived "MR MOJO RISIN" from "JIM MORRISON" and John wrote that since mojo was a black slang word for sexual prowess, he would "steadily increase the tempo back up to the original speed, *a la* orgasm"28. Or was mojo inspired by the greasy and diminutive character, Oswald Mojo who married Pamela, a British girl who turned out to be an oil heiress, in Faria's *Been Down So Long It Looks Like Up To Me*? Like the acceptance in 'Ship Of Fools' that this world is our only home, so Jim accepts that L.A. is his woman. L.A. Woman is a changeling, just as Jim is, and there is tension in his acceptance that he doesn't know what change will bring, what different identity she or he will assume next. Just as the narrator in Rechy's novel oscillated between breaking through to the other side and seeking out the peace of solitude, Morrison (and The Doors) has likewise throughout the previous albums, but in 'L.A. Woman' the group reaches a level of understanding and establishes a relationship with his city of night that Rechy's narrator didn't. L.A. is Jim's home, but also an extension and reflection of himself, as he has become of her.

## SIDE TWO
Having closed side one with a resigned yet funky ode of blues to 'L.A. Woman', The Doors open side two with a marching drum cadence (reminiscent of 'Unknown Soldier') in 'L'America'29. Written and recorded months earlier for Michelango Antonioni's Zabriskie Point (a 1970 movie), the song had been rejected by Antonioni. Though

spared from being part of what movie critics almost universally panned as a bomb by the Italian film director, The Doors' artistic vision seemed quite similar in focus to Antonioni's. Arthur Schlesinger Jr. wrote in his review of the movie in Vogue that the "iconography of the American landscape" fascinated Antonioni: Antonioni's vision of America was of "a land of nightmare" where nature, though beautiful, was dead.30 The images and impulses of America that Antonioni clumsily pieced together, The Doors draw into a more fluid impression, their music exposing what the film couldn't. After Densmore had explained how Morrison tried telling Antonioni the apostrophe after the "L" was short for Latin America or anywhere south of the border, John described the recording session with Antonioni, surmising that the song was too much for the director since he didn't understand the "cryptic references to money (beads) and grass (gold – as in Acapulco)" and the song, with its "dark, dissonant chords" of the cold steel resonance of Robby's guitar overshadowing Jim's strong singing, summarized the movie.31 Indeed, the music of 'L'America' casts a foreboding tone over the image of going "down to Lamerica", a journey into the museum, not away from it on some midnight train. Or perhaps the midnight train leaves 'L.A. Woman' and journeys into 'L'America'. We can't escape; we can't run and hide. This 'L'America' is the America into which the Sixties has began to dissolve. The lyric about trading "beads for a pint of gold" recalls the cynical image in 'Five To One' of walking with flowers in your hand while trading "hours for a handful of dimes". Though we could be trading money for dope to buy our escape to the other side, the implication of this image transcends more than a literal rendering by the slang. The motel money murder madness of 'L.A. Woman' is a pint of gold, the yellow metal which drives people crazy, traded for the beads of hippies, of flower children, of Native Americans, of hope, of love, of innocence. The journey of innocence has drifted into the sins of the Western dream, becoming the 'Spanish Caravan' sailing back to Madre to search for silver and gold in the mountains of Spain. Beads are museum pieces of periods of history, but gold – that's an eternal pursuit in the Western dream.

Manzarek drapes a curtain of disquieting uneasiness with his organ, sounding like very unfriendly raindrops, made even uneasier by Krieger repeatedly playing a descending four-note guitar line.

Rather than a typical minor mode, the music is in an unusual one with a lot of funky rhythmical syncopation. The unusual overlying and mixing of these lines creates a weird dissonance, a dissonance just as revealing of the confused state of America as was the cacophonic rendering of *The Star-Spangled Banner* by Jimi Hendrix at Woodstock. 'L'America' is one of The Doors' most innovative pieces musically. The rainman offers the epitome of what many labelled as Morrison therapy: the rainman can "change your weather" and "luck", and then "teach you how to... [through the suggestion of rhyme, intercourse] find yourself". Fucking equals finding salvation, freeing oneself, breaking through to the other side. Or maybe this is subtle sarcasm, Jim playing the lyric off of what people expected. This album, on one level, represents a struggle between the old arrogance of the younger Lizard King and the new doubts plaguing the older changeling. Some of the sarcasm seems to be a little self-directed, toward the younger, more naive, and angrier self.

"It may be claimed that a nation, like an individual, is valuable only in so far as it is able to give to quotidian experience the stamp of the eternal. Only by so doing can it express its profound, if unconscious, conviction of the relativity of time and the metaphysical meaning of life. The opposite happens when a nation begins to view itself historically and to demolish the mythical bulwarks that surround it. The result is usually a definite secularization, a break with the unconscious metaphysic of its earlier mode of existence, with all the accompanying dismal moral consequences."

*Friedrich Nietzsche,*
*The Birth Of Tragedy (p. 139)*

Jim, now older, begins to realize he can't take shelter in his Lizard King persona like he used to because he has matured enough to recognize his vulnerabilities – and the foolishness of being forever the Lizard King and all it implied – although legions of subsequent fans don't. The older Lizard King now comes as a rainman. The organ

interlude between this stanza and the third stanza echoes the organ
melody of 'Strange Days', a reminder that these strange days haven't
been washed away. Yet 'friendly strangers' come to town, and despite
being put down, their ways captivate the women, leaving the
impression they will "come again" like the "gentle rain". The sexual
pun of "come" alludes to the implied sexual rhyme of the previous
stanza, but the urgency of earlier songs has quieted to a gentle rain.
The conquest of the Lizard King reentering the town has become a
seduction of the townsfolk, or at least the women.

'L'America' may be a museum, but it also will change. The Doors
then slide us into a disquieting image of sanctuary, presenting the
museum-like 'Hyacinth House' of disjointed images. The lyric
suggests Jim was just throwing out images, some which may refer to
earlier images, but these probably aren't meant to be interpreted, just
to evoke gut responses. The 'Hyacinth House' seems to be a
fabricated image, another version of the house on 'Love Street'.
Neither of those houses offers sanctuary or imprisonment, seemingly
just something to pass through with the curiosity of wondering what
they are "doing to please the lions this day".

In his book, *Riders On The Storm*, Densmore draws a connection
with the Greek Hyacinth myth, but somehow the disjointed images of
Jim's lyrics are almost too mundane (or perhaps just neutral with no
specific feeling intended) to invoke any sense of despair and tragedy
as in the myth. The Lizard King sees that "the bathroom is clear" and
bemoans the loss of the Jack-of-Hearts; what a come down. Or maybe
just an allusion to the "jack o' diamonds is a hard card to play" line in
a Richard Faria poem.32 But the almost moanful tone in which
Morrison sings underscores a sense of resignation to the mundane.

This temporal node of sanctuary, the 'Hyacinth House', could be a
museum of Jim himself, a place he tentatively meanders through,
wondering what they will do to please the young lion and looking at
old images in a different light, unsure of how he feels about his
control of his existence. He realizes he needs a "brand new friend",
who doesn't "bother" or "trouble" or "need" him – perhaps a friend
like, as Jim closes the song, "the end". However, this isn't the same
End as it once was, for Morrison is acknowledging the blues of being
human in twentieth century America. Part of the blues of being born
into the museum of 'L'America' can be expressed in love – or sex, as

165

expressed in The Doors' cover of bluesman John Lee Hooker's 'Crawling King Snake'. In reviewing the album, Richard Riegel wrote the song had been "Hooker's pre-higher-education treatment of Morrison's obsessive 'Celebration Of The Lizard' theme"33. For Houghton, this cover of the song presented "Morrison at his most reptilian"34. Jim's gravelly rendition of the much smoother, even delivery by Hooker reveals an internal aggression and frustration pent up in Morrison, a feeling if Hooker ever felt in his younger days, he came to terms with. Nonetheless, the musical arrangement of this song isn't as aggressive as in other songs, like Willie Dixon's 'Back Door Man'. The portrait rendered by the music is confident, but not as urgent as in previous portraits. 'Crawling King Snake' was from The Doors' early repertoire of gigging, and Morrison's rendition of Hooker's lyrics of a "crawling king snake" who rules his den and mate suggests the earlier images of cars hissing by the den-like room of 'Cars Hiss By My Window' and of the wanton lover in 'Been Down So Long' seeking control of his lover. Instead of headlights on the walls in the cold, darkened room, the two lovers crawl "just like the spider on the wall".

The lyric evokes a vivid picture of the evil tempter from the Garden of Eden, a powerful symbol of Nature's forces. The changeling rainman dons the persona of masculine sexuality, of the Lizard King, if just momentarily before the more mature Morrison acknowledges the vulnerabilities he now recognizes, like trusting a "maiden with wrought-iron soul". It is time to ride the storm, and the electric piano ending to 'Crawling King Snake' preludes the forthcoming 'Riders On The Storm'. We move from the blues of a man who was born in the Mississippi Delta and couldn't write or read into the 'The WASP (Texas Radio And The Big Beat)' of a Southern-aristocratic, college-educated Morrison. According to Hopkins and Sugerman, the lyrics were published in the 1968 Doors' souvenir book,35 and another version surfaces in the recording of The Doors' Denmark television appearance. The lyric also formed part of a well-honed reinterpretation on the posthumous album, *An American Prayer*.

As trite as the technique of speaking lyrics over music can be, The Doors deliver a potent impression with the primal drum beat and bass line, one that is, as Rompers wrote, "hypnotic and convincing"36. In a lighter tone, Meltzer of *Rolling Stone* wrote: "I'll be a monkey's uncle if 'The WASP' doesn't showcase Morrison's finest command of spoken jive to date", comparing Morrison's timing to "the equal of George Burns in his prime"37. Instead of the wet forest of 'Moonlight Drive' or a deep blue dream, this song oozes "cool and slow with plenty of precision" out of the Virginia swamps, a glancing allusion to one of the states Jim's Navy family lived in and the state where he graduated from high school. The "big beat" has a "narrow and hard to master" back beat – organic yet precise, not the contrite self-conscious pop and rock music of which Morrison had become so critical.

"Man today, stripped of myth, stands famished among all his pasts and must dig frantically for roots, be it among the most remote antiquities. What does our great historical hunger signify, our clutching about us of countless other cultures, our consuming desire for knowledge, if not the loss of myth, of a mythic home, the mythic womb? Let us ask ourselves whether our    feverish and frightening agitation is anything but the greedy grasping for food of a hungry man. And who would care to offer further nourishment to a culture which, no matter how much it consumes, remains insatiable and which converts the strongest and most wholesome food into 'history' and 'criticism'?"

*Friedrich Nietzsche,*
*The Birth Of Tragedy (p. 137)*

The "Western dream" promises precision and predictability, a dream which some call "heavenly in its brilliance", but is shrouded in the shadow of disquieting melodies and tones and images. The music (and lyrics) weave, as Rompers noted, "a dense, malevolent spell,"38 as friends gather on a "thin raft", construct "pyramids in honour" of escaping, and arrive in "the land where the Pharaoh died". Then The Doors take us away, the third stanza painting a sharp contrast of primal images to the Pharaohs and the Western dream: a forest with "brightly feathered" Negroes calling for us to live with them in azure forests. We are on a perimeter where there aren't any stars, in forests of sky blue azure, a deep blue dream. Out on this edge, we are "stoned – Immaculate", free from moral blemish, free from fault, undefiled, pure. Primal and free. The wild child. Leaving town to be the changeling. Breaking through to the other side. A wanton world without lament? The music isn't over out here on the perimeter: it's a cool and slow beat, it's "soft-driven", it's "slow and mad" and sounds "like some new language". Like the secret alphabets of 'Soul Kitchen'. But there are disquieting images in this forest of azure. No stars for guidance, for navigation, for orientation. And the drug imagery of being stoned to get to that forest of azure is no more reassuring than the journey to a strange night of stone in 'Strange Days'. From living in such an alienated landscape created by the Western dream, Morrison draws forth some of the deepest fears of man: heartaches, no God, the hopeless night, hungry souls, and a lover reminiscent of the lover in 'Cars Hiss By My Window' – a "maiden with wrought-iron soul".

And the shamanic voice of the artistic spirit speaks forth to let it be known that "no eternal reward" can forgive us "for wasting the dawn". We have ruined Eden, Earth, our fair sister, Gaia, the Garden, and we have ruined L.A. – a city of dawn, of light, a flash of Eden as we wait for the sun down at the edge of the ocean. The song ends, trailing off with the very cool image of wandering in the Western Dream with "the hopeless night" and a "maiden with wrought-iron soul". We are left with the image of a girl who, though still innocent, is quite mechanical, quite precise, quite cold – hardly the warm plastic of the twentieth century foxes and vamps of earlier songs. The little girl has grown into and become the iron bars of the prison of her own device. The lost angel has become a maiden with a wrought-iron soul. Jim has begun to come to terms with his vulnerabilities: he can accept them and can peacefully (and confidently) return to some of his earlier images and personas without the internal and external conflict. But he is no longer the Lizard King; he's the changeling, who at the beginning of the album couldn't tell up from down. At first, Jim's conflicts seem so immediate, but gradually they become distant. By 'The WASP', Jim has accepted circumstances of his existence which frees him to return to his meadow, to an earlier poetic image he can now deliver with a more mature understanding, and 'Riders On The Storm' prognosticly seals off this return to the meadow. The last Doors' song on this album was, as Ray said in the radio programme, *History of Rock 'n' Roll*, the last one Jim ever sang, the last one The Doors recorded, and the last one for the album.39 Labelled as a "lazy paced rocker" by *Variety*,40 'Riders On The Storm' was released just before Jim's announced death, the song never rising higher that #14 on Billboard's Top 100 and lasting only three months on the chart. Many labelled the song, "nightclub cocktail piano music", or any combination of those words, which reflected what a disenchanted Rothchild had told The Doors – their studio playing sounded like "cocktail lounge music" – before he decided not to produce this album.41 But the entire album creates, suggests, and caters to the darkened atmosphere of a nightclub, so 'Riders On The Storm' sounds even more seductively alluring with its cocktail piano tinge, like sliding into the mysteries lapping at our sides in a moonlight drive. We're going down by the ocean side, going get real close, get real tight, as the opening waves of thunder draw you in to take a journey as a rider on the storm with the killer on the road. Life in the Western dream isn't necessarily pleasant, and the images in the opening stanza of 'Riders On The Storm' reflect the standard Doors' theme of life as a journey we are tossed into. There is a blues attitude that these are the dues of being alive, of being born into this twentieth century world of L'America, of being thrown into this world "like a dog without a bone" or "an actor out on loan". Morrison's standard pun of dog as backwards god slides in as does the suggestion we are all but acting out a part in this life, souls on loan to this world.

But this world can be harsh, evident in the soft, quiet presentation of the deadly reality of killer hitchhikers on the freeways of L.A., of L'America, on the highways to the bright midnight. The image of the killer's brain "squirming like a toad" evokes a far different tone and feeling than the usual parade of snake images; it is an image that doesn't immediately fit into our normal scheme of symbols. Someone can easily rationalize, as many have, that the rhyming of toad with road is forced and another example of Morrison's mediocre poetry. But even after one has rationalized this image, one is still left reacting to it. That is why the image, like so many other images The Doors created in their music, is effective. The image is as blunt and rational as death, and the gentle undercurrent of the song's music and lyrics now harbours the threatening edge of death.

Not every stranger is a friendly rainman who will come like a gentle rain. Yet you will find yourself in a tragic way if you do give this stranger a ride. Whether we like it or not, everyone is on the 'Ship Of Fools', a crystal ship of sorts. Everyone is a rider on the storm. Everyone is on a journey that continually risks losing security, losing "sweet family". The journey on this road is vividly dangerous, and Jim quietly appeals to a previous theme, as Hopkins and Sugerman wrote, "a cry to love and Pamela", Morrison's longtime girlfriend.42 In this appeal to the girl to take her lover "by the hand" and "make him understand", love becomes more than just another short term sanctuary; it gives life meaning. This is quite different than a similar appeal in 'When The Music's Over'. The water-like sounding harmonies of Robby's guitar and Ray's electronic piano backed by John's soft, steady, uptempo drum beat render a seductively alluring contrast to the threatening nature of the storm, its thunder peeling behind the portrait The Doors are painting. The continuously spiralling bass line echoes the storm's turbulent nature, and Ray's descending electronic piano runs create the cadence of a gentle rain, quite a different feeling of rain than the one created in 'L'America'.

As Rompers noted, The Doors didn't end with a bang, but with a rainstorm,43 the final piano lines and the waves of thunder of 'Riders On The Storm' rendering a feeling not far from waiting quietly on the shoreline for the next transition in life's journey. The Doors have broken through and come back. Rather than leaving with the bang so many expected of such raucous, rebellious, erotic politicians seemingly bent on sinister intent, like a gentle rain that falls, they leave as they began: artistic spirits trying to render their artistic vision for others to hear, to see, to feel, to share. The allure of slowly fading into the storm and its potentially drowning waters seals this closing poetic statement by The Doors with Jim Morrison. Jim just fades away into the storm: how could he possibly follow that up? The blues, hence the music, on this album are more confident and mature than previously. Not necessarily true bluesman, The Doors do demonstrate a better grasp on the impact of the interplay between the words and the music. Their artistic outlook has settled down from the earlier anger and arrogance; thus the music has room to grow and become deeper, which it does. The emotion is much more subtle, making it more powerful. This subdued impact is closer to the true essence of the blues than raw anger and sarcasm ever can be in the same way that ambiguous images are more powerful than pointedly crafted portraits. A piece that portrays strong, pointed feeling evokes immediate response. Once that moment of connection is broken, the emotion subsides. With a piece that is more subtle, emotional reaction doesn't occur right away, its impact usually causing you to feel many different reactions. Because you can't just experience the immediate emotion and purge yourself of it, it sticks with you and works upon you in ways you may not expect or understand. It is like the difference between the explosive anger that causes you to lash out at something, and the quiet, enduring anger that gradually motivates you to change something about yourself or the circumstances of your life. To let that kind of emotion work upon you, you have to accept it and try to understand how it is affecting you. The true bluesmen has experienced enough to do this, and this depth of understanding is reflected in his music. The Doors were beginning to be able to command the power of such subtlety. The doors of perception they were beginning to cleanse – to open – have and reveal a subtlety far deeper than the earlier ones they had broken through.

"[In the Sixties] if you wanted to try something totally out of the ordinary, then you had the freedom to do it. If you succeeded you reached the heights of ecstasy, and if you failed, your brothers and sisters were around to pick you up and support you. That was security. I think today people are looking for other things as their source for security...[m]oney being the biggest factor...when the pursuit of [money] gets in the way of the real issues – like respect for another person, common decency – that's really important. Money has never been solid ice to stand on – look at The Depression – yet people keep focusing on that as their protection from the woes of the world."

*Ray Manzarek,*
*in interview with Mark Hendrickson,*
*"The Legend Lives On...And On"*

171

Rock 'n' roll opened a lot of doors and exposed minds in numbers never before realized to levels of awareness, of consciousness, of perceptions at a scale never possible before.

The Doors rendered an artistic vision for the consciousness, painting many scenes which had remained behind the closed doors of the facades of twentieth century foxes, of soft parades, of living in these strange days of twentieth century America. As long as the world of man remains a world demanding conformity and grinding away behind plastic images and values imposed upon our existence, the artistic vision rendered by The Doors remains a vivid portrait of the landscape we move across.

# chapter 7

# let it roll

"For it is the lot of every myth to creep gradually into the narrows of supposititious historical fact and to be treated by some later time as a unique event of history... It is the sure sign of the death of a religion when its mythic presuppositions become systematized, under the severe, rational eyes of an orthodox dogmatism, into a ready sum of historical events, and when people begin timidly defending the veracity of myth but at the same time resist its natural continuance – when the feeling for myth withers and its place is taken by a religion claiming historical foundations. This decaying myth was now seized by the newborn genius of Dionysiac music, in whose hands it flowered once more, with new colours and a fragrance that aroused a wistful longing for a metaphysical world."

*Friedrich Nietzsche,*
*The Birth Of Tragedy (p. 68)*

"The deepest problem before America is moral or psychological. Since much of the current uneasiness reflects a search less for solutions than for meaning, remedies depend for their effectiveness on the philosophy or values which inspire them. The student unrest is impressive, not because some of it is fomented by agitators, but because it includes some of the most idealistic elements of our youth. In fact, much that disquiets us today gives cause for hope, for it reflects not cynicism but disappointed idealism."

*New York Governor Nelson Rockefeller, 1968*

The validity of music isn't grounded in the concreteness of isolating the composition and dissecting it down into tangible components. The music's validity is as much rooted in the audience's response to it as in the performer's artistic endeavours to create it. Analysis of rock 'n' roll doesn't validate the revolution of which it is a large part. What is IS.

Rock 'n' roll has not only swept away so many social taboos (i.e., the validity of racial segregation, of Victorian sexual norms, of "time is money" ethics of the 8-to-5 work day, etc.), but also opened up access to rhythms and awareness, patterns and knowledge that have been buried beneath the crunch of patterns and rhythms of civilization. What kind of knowledge does our modern mentality of the Western dream offer our young? Knowledge derived from the ethics of business? Knowledge derived from the ethics of authoritarian religions or political ideologies? How long can a culture continue to pass on such knowledge before the children perceive the ludicrousness of it?

Rock 'n' roll started merging knowledge and awareness that had been expelled. A revolution of values and consciousness had began. But revolution is neither a solution nor does it achieve solutions; it is a process. As a more mature Morrison would realize, evident in his interview with John Tobler at the Isle of Wight Festival in 1970, "You have to be in a constant state of revolution, or you're dead...[revolution] has to be every day."1 For a revolution to avoid becoming the status quo, it must remain revolutionary. If a revolution achieves "victory", it immediately kills the revolution. The ultimate purpose of any worthwhile revolution is not victory, but the emergence of a process that enhances a culture's relationship with life. And when a revolution is under way, there are plenty who want heard what they have to say. But one easily stuck criticism (and often desired) of rock is that its lyrics are unintelligible. Transcribe 'Tutti Frutti' or try to pin down any intrinsic meaning to 'Louie, Louie'. Yet The Doors made it clear that they wanted people to listen to what their music was saying. An interviewer in the BBC's special, *The Doors Are Open*, asked Ray Manzarek if he wanted people to like The Doors; Ray replied, "I'd like them to listen; I'd like them to give the music a chance and...[pauses]...just to listen."

The Doors claimed their roots were in the blues, but the blues they grew out of were the manicured lawns of suburbia and the many plastic dogmas of the middle class, not the mud of the Mississippi Delta or the urban grit of the inner city of the north. That doesn't mean the blues The

Doors played were any less than what is considered blues; rather, the sound lacked gregarious grounding to the rhythms of life outside of Western man's mechanical world. The blues of a John Lee Hooker, a Willie Dixon, a Muddy Waters, and so on roll with a pace that celebrates and embraces the urgency of passion, of frustration, of pain, of anger, but the rhythm remains rooted to a more natural rhythm of life. In the music of The Doors, which also celebrates and embraces the urgency of passion, frustration, pain, and anger, the blues are nurtured by four musicians grounded to America's artificial pace of a fragmented, sped-up, mass-produce-and-consume rhythm. Middle-class angst. Nonetheless, The Doors' artistic orientation was shamanic, not commercial. Change was inevitable as the six albums evolved. You can't sing revolution all your life. Hence, The Doors would mature. The writings from Morrison's later years, especially the last section in *Wilderness*, reveal a definite shift in Jim. The blossom of a more mature poet was unfolding, but its stem was about to be cut from the roots of life, the scissors of fate already beginning to be closed by his folly of being a jerk. Who Jim Morrison was as a person, a friend, a buddy whom people palled around with, and who Jim Morrison dead rock idol aren't essentially the same, nor can anyone set the correct image of who Jim was, is, or will be. We are witnessing a birth and growth of a legend. Only a germ of truth is needed to "What the new rebels are doing is jeering at the mass of us for not knowing that beneath the solid middle-class house there is a cellar stacked with dynamite. But with no training as mining engineers or fire-watchers, they go down there with lighted matches and hail the subsequent explosions as art. ...out of this explosion of 'total honesty, total freedom' may come such a tyrannical reaction, an impulse to censor and police and restrain, that the Rebels – or, let us hope, the sons and daughters of the Rebels – will pull back in time and save their free society by recognizing that the first guarantee of liberty is the willingness not to demand too much of it. The fly-wheel of liberty is responsibility." Alistair Cooke2

"Without conflict, change is impossible; but without satisfactory resolution, the changes won't last. It is the overriding task of this current generation of revolutionaries to resolve the potentially destructive conflicts bequeathed to them, while encouraging the healthy tensions."

*Robert G. Pielke,*
*You Say You Want a Revolution*

*Rock Music In American Culture* (p. 210) nurture the image people choose to perceive and believe. The public image of Jim Morrison, lead singer of The Doors and young Dionysus of the Sixties rock scene, is a function of the public perceptions and values at whatever moment. Yet Jim never wavered from the statement he made in the original 1967 Elektra Records biographical sheets: "But the main thing is that we are The Doors."3

To those who have read our words, thank you. I close with a translation of words written by Friedrich Nietzsche and published in 1872 in his book, *The Birth Of Tragedy*, a book Jim Morrison said is "the one volume to read if you hope to understand his thoughts":4 "Though the favourites of the gods die young, they also live eternally in the company of the gods. Of what is noblest on earth we cannot reasonably expect that it have the durable toughness of leather."5 After all the reading and listening and writing I have done on The Doors, there are two statements I will definitely make about Jim Morrison: he is quite dead, and he is very much alive.

"The Poet makes himself a seer by a long, gigantic and rational derangement of all the senses. All forms of love, suffering, and madness. He searches himself. He exhausts all poisons in himself and keeps only their quintessences. Unspeakable torture where he needs all his faith, all his super-human strength, where he becomes among all men the great patient, the great criminal, the one accursed – and the supreme Scholar – because he reaches the unknown! Since he cultivated his soul, rich already, more than any man! He reaches the unknown, and when, bewildered, he ends by losing the intelligence of his visions, he has seen them. Let him die as he leaps through unheard of and unnameable things: other horrible workers will come; they will begin from the horizons where the other one collapsed!"

*Arthur Rimbaud*
*letter to Paul Demeny (15 May 1871)6*

# chapter 8
# acknowledgements

## GETTING IT STRAIGHT...

A fter graduating from high school, I went to college in the summer of 1973 and found in the library of Ball State University a cosmos of information on The Doors written by others eons removed from the world of small town USA in America's heartland. My mind was expanded. Ever since, I have been revising both many assumptions I have made and a lot of information I have gathered about The Doors. In short, correcting mistakes. But getting it straight isn't all that easy, evident in the following three examples.

(1) Doors keyboardist Ray Manzarek was born in 1939. But somewhere in some early rock 'n' roll reference book the year of his birth was cited as 1935, and, henceforth, a preponderance of other authors and reference books use 1935.

(2) Another example is from the widely circulated Sunday American newspaper supplement, *Parade Magazine* (September 17, 1995). In a small article titled "Parade's Special Intelligence Report/When Jim Morrison Brought Drama – and Controversy – to the Rock Stage", an upcoming 10-part PBS television documentary, *Rock & Roll*, was previewed by featuring the segment about The Doors' Miami concert on March 1, 1969, and Morrison's subsequent bust (p. 21). The article stated Morrison was arrested on onstage; however, warrants weren't issued till March 5 while The Doors were vacationing in the Caribbean, and Morrison eventually turned himself in on April 3 after he had returned to the States. And the article spells producer Paul Rothchild's name as "Rothschild", the more common spelling for the surname.

(3) In *The Lizard King: The Essential Jim Morrison* (published in 1992), Jerry Hopkins, who had been writing about The Doors for 25-plus years, wrote that 'Running Blue' was released as a single from the album, *Morrison Hotel* (p. 129). 'Runnin' Blue' is song number two on side two of *The Soft Parade*, the album that preceded *Morrison Hotel*. The reason I include this minor miscue from Hopkins (and not more grievous miscues by others who have written on The Doors or on Morrison) is I have always had a high regard for Hopkins because of his insistence on presenting information as accurately as possible.

Though we live in an age of information, it is also a world of deadlines and myriad layers of diversions and intents, and survival isn't always to the meticulous. As Hopkins wrote about Oliver Stone's attempt to tell The Doors' story on film, a gonzo journalistic attitude doesn't allow facts to get in the way of a good story. Yet, I welcome comments, suggestions, additions, corrections, etc.

I am deeply indebted to Kerry Humpherys for allowing me access to his extensive archives of Doors material. Kerry is the editor-in-chief of *The Doors Collectors Magazine* (a quarterly) and sells various types of Doors-related items from an extensive catalogue. Kerry can be contacted at: TDM Inc. P.O. Box 1441, Orem, Utah 84059-1441 U.S.A. Phone: (1) 800-891-1736.

I want to acknowledge the other major Doors fanzine, which has been a valuable source of information also Rainer Moddemann's *Doors Quarterly Magazine*. Rainer can be contacted at: Am Oelvebach 5, D. 4150 Krefeld-Stratum 12, Germany.

Finally, thank you to Danny Sugerman, who offered encouragement and much appreciated praise while also helping this book move toward publication. Ray Manzarek, who told me, "Good work!" and encouraged me to find a publisher. And Penny Braybrooke, General Manager at Castle Books, who believed this book warranted being published and has always been supportive.

# FOOTNOTES

Introduction
A DOOR OPENS...

1  John Tobler, "The doors in a nutshell; 64 quick questions", *ZigZag*, September 1972, p. 29.
2  *History of Rock 'n' Roll*, aired 29 April 1978, WOWO Radio, 1190 AM, Fort Wayne, IN.
3  John Densmore, *Riders On The Storm: My Life With Jim Morrison* and The Doors (New York: Delacorte Press, 1990), p. 46.
4  *History of Rock 'n' Roll*.
5  Tobler, p. 29.
6  Mike Jahn, *Jim Morrison And The Doors* (an unauthorized book) (New York: Grosset & Dunlap, 1969), p. 54.
7  *The Inner View: No One Here Gets Out Alive: The Doors Story* (4-hour radio special), aired 1979; host: Jim Ladd.
8  Densmore, p. 79.
9  Jim Morrison, *Wilderness: The Lost Writings Of Jim Morrison, Volume I* (New York: Villard Books, 1988), p. 205.
10 Jahn, *Jim Morrison And The Doors*, p. 35.
11 Pete Johnson, "Doors Rattle Hinges at Whiskey-A-GoGo", Los Angeles Times, 18 May 1967, Part IV, p. 13.


Chapter 1
BREAKIN' ON THROUGH: THE DEBUT ALBUM

1  Don J. Hibbard and Carol Kaleialoha, *The Role Of Rock* (Englewood Cliffs, NJ: Prentice-Hall, Inc., 1983), p. 48.
2  Ibid., p. 43.
3  Lizze James, "Lizze James Interview with Jim Morrison", printed in Danny Sugerman and Benjamin Edmonds, eds, *The DOORS: The Illustrated History* (New York: William Morrow and Company, 1983), p. 65.
4  Lester Bangs, "Jim Morrison, Oafus Laureate", *Creem Special Edition: The Doors*, Summer 1981, p. 29.

5 Nik Cohn, *Rock From The Beginning*, (New York: Stein and Day, 1969), p. 236.

6 Gene Youngblood, "Doors reaching for outer limits of inner space", *Los Angeles Free Press*, 1 December 1967, pp. 6, 15.

7 Irwin Stambler, *Encyclopedia Of Pop, Rock & Soul* (New York: St. Martin's Press, 1974), p. 167.

8 John Densmore, *Riders On The Storm: My Life With Jim Morrison And The Doors*, (New York: Delacorte Press, 1990), p. 129.

9 Wallace Fowlie, *Rimbaud And Jim Morrison: The Rebel As Poet* (Durham, NC: Duke University Press, 1993; paperback edition 1994), p. 123.

10 Fred Powledge, "Wicked Go the Doors", Life, 12 April 1968, p. 86B.

11 Lizze James, "Jim Morrison: Ten Years Gone", *Creem Special Edition: The Doors*, Summer 1981, p. 18.

12 Robert Somma, "Banging Away At The Doors Of Convention", *Crawdaddy*, October 1968, p. 20.

13 Paul Williams, "Rothchild Speaks", *Crawdaddy*, July/August 1967, pp. 20, 21.

14 Densmore, p. 102.

15 John Rechy, *City Of Night* (New York: Grover Press, Inc., 1963), p. 43. The unnamed narrator of the story describes a scene with Pete, a familiar and street wise figure in the world of Times Square in New York City: "[Pete] added hurriedly, 'I don't dig that scene – I guess I'm too Restless.' He made it, instead, from place to place, week to week, night to night." Also of note is Rechy's use of the label, "the Other Side", when the unnamed narrator describes the sexual boundary of the Hollywood world of vagrants and wanderers (p. 200-201).

16 Richard Goldstein, ed., *The Poetry Of Rock* (New York: Bantam Books, 1969), p. 81.

17 David R. Pichaske, *The Poetry Of Rock: The Golden Years* (Peoria, IL: The Ellis Press, 1981), p. 82.

18 Goldstein, *The Poetry Of Rock*, p. 81.

19 John Tobler, "The doors in a nutshell; 64 quick questions", *ZigZag*, September 1972, p. 28.

20 Bertolt Brecht, *The Rise And Fall Of The City Of Mahagonny*, translated by W.H. Auden and Chester Kallman, original trans. 1960 (Boston: David R. Godine, 1976), p. 18.

21 Ibid., p. 9.
22 "Opening the Doors", *The East Village Other* (New York underground newspaper), 1-15 July 1967, p. 11.
23 Paul Williams, "Music without the Myth", *Rolling Stone*, 11 September 1981, p. 34.
24 Densmore, p. 103.
25 Ibid.
26 Jerry Hopkins and Danny Sugerman, *No One Here Gets Out Alive*, (New York: Warner Books, Inc., 1980), p. 60.
27 Richard Walls, "The Doors" (record review), *Creem Special Edition: The Doors*, Summer 1981, p. 48.
28 Richard Goldstein, "The Doors Open Wide", *New York Magazine*, reprinted in Sugerman's *The DOORS: The Illustrated History*, p. 21.
29 Densmore, p. 122.
30 Goldstein, "The Doors Open Wide", reprinted in *The DOORS: The Illustrated History*, p. 21.
31 Pete Johnson, "Popular Records: Latest Stones Album Best Yet", *Los Angeles Times*, Calender section, 26 February 1967, p. 30.
32 Mike Jahn, *Jim Morrison And The Doors* (an unauthorized book) (New York: Grosset & Dunlap, 1969), p. 46.
33 Jerry Hopkins, "The Rolling Stone Interview: Jim Morrison", *Rolling Stone*, 26 July 1969, p. 18.
34 Ibid., p. 17.
35 Pichaske, p. 78.
36 Salli Stevenson, "An Interview With Jim Morrison" (Part I), *Circus*, January 1971, p. 44. Quote is reprinted in Eric Van Lustbader's "Jim Morrison: Riding Out The Final Storm", *Circus*, September 1971, p. 39.
37 Pichaske, p. 78.
38 Powledge, p. 90.


Chapter 2
STRANGE DAYS IN THE SUMMER OF LOVE

1 'Light My Fire' would become the #1 selling single in America the week of July 29; in June, The Doors were just another one of many bands from Los Angeles and the West Coast, and they didn't

warrant any particular attention for the organizers of Monterey to recruit them. Bands that appeared at Monterey Pop Festival (June 16-17-18, 1967) included:

The Association
Big Brother & The Holding Company (with Janis Joplin)
The Blues Project
Booker T. & The MGs w The Mar-Keys
Buffalo Springfield
The Byrds
Canned Heat
Country Joe & The Fish
The Electric Flag
Eric Burdon & The Animals
Grateful Dead
Hugh Masekela
Jefferson Airplane
The Jimi Hendrix Experience
Laura Nyro
Lou Rawls
The Mamas & The Papas
Otis Redding
The Paul Butterfield Blues Band
Quicksilver Messenger Service
Ravi Shankar
Scott McKenzie
Simon & Garfunkel
The Steve Miller Blues Band
The Who

2   Lizze James, "Jim Morrison: Ten Years Gone", *Creem Special Edition: The Doors*, Summer 1981, p. 21.

3   Jerry Hopkins and Danny Sugerman, *No One Here Gets Out Alive*, (New York: Warner Books, Inc., 1980), p. 130.

4   Vic Garbarini, "Blues for a Shaman: Doors' Producer Paul Rothschild (sic)", *Musician*, August 1981, p. 56.

5   Michael Cuscuna, "Behind the Doors", *Down Beat*, 28 May 1970, p. 13.

6   J. Kordosh, "Strange Days" (record review), *Creem Special Edition: The Doors*, Summer 1981, p. 48.

7   Ibid.
8   Eric Van Lustbader, "Jim Morrison: Riding Out The Final Storm", *Circus*, September 1971, p. 37.
9   Steven Lowe, "The Lighter Side", *High Fidelity Magazine*, January 1968, p. 98.
10  Hopkins and Sugerman, *No One Here Gets Out Alive*, p. 128.
11  Terry Rompers, "Looking Through the Doors", *Trouser Press*, September/October 1980, pp. 1-2.
12  Gene Youngblood, "Doors reaching for outer limits of inner space", *Los Angeles Free Press*, 1 December 1967, p. 6.
13  John Densmore, *Riders On The Storm: My Life With Jim Morrison And The Doors*, (New York: Delacorte Press, 1990), p. 132.
14  Richard Riegel, "Tongues of Knowledge in the Feathered Night (The Blue Bus Is Double Parked): The Doors On Record", *Creem Special Edition: The Doors*, Summer 1981, p. 10.
15  Hopkins and Sugerman, *No One Here Gets Out Alive*, p. 128.
16  Hopkins and Sugerman, p. 19.
17  David R. Pichaske, *The Poetry Of Rock: The Golden Years* (Peoria, IL: The Ellis Press, 1981), p. 81.
18  Ibid.
19  Riegel, p. 10.
20  John Tobler, "The doors in a nutshell; 64 quick questions", *ZigZag*, September 1972, p. 28.
21  Pete Fornatale, "Strange Days: Doors' Organist Ray Manzarek", *Musician*, August 1981, p. 48.
22  Ross Hunter, "Sounds: Strange Doors", *IT* (*International Times*, London), 5-19 January 1968, p. 12.

Chapter 3
WAITING FOR THE MUSE, WAITING FOR THE DOORS, WAITING FOR THE SUN

1   Richard Goldstein, "The Shaman As Superstar", *New York Magazine*, reprinted in *The DOORS: The Illustrated History*, pp. 75-76.
2   Pete Fornatale, "Strange Days: Doors' Organist Ray Manzarek", *Musician*, August 1981, p. 49.

3   Rich Mangelsdorff, "Doors Stuck?", *Kaleidoscope* (Milwaukee underground newspaper), 23 August – 12 September 1968, p. 6.

4   Pete Johnson, "Waiting for the Sun", *The Inquirer* (Philadelphia newspaper), reprinted in *The DOORS: The Illustrated History*, p. 100.

5   Lillian Roxon, *Rock Encyclopedia* (New York: Grosset & Dunlop, 1969), p. 152.

6   Jerry Hopkins and Danny Sugerman, *No One Here Gets Out Alive*, (New York: Warner Books, Inc., 1980), p. 179.

7   Ibid., p. 191.

8   Mitchell Cohen, "Remembering Morrison", *Fusion*, June 1974, p. 19.

9   Hank Zevallos, "Jim Morrison" (interview), *Poppin*, March 1970, p. 47.

10  Bob Chorush, "The Lizard King reforms: taking the snake and wearing it; An interview with Jim Morrison", *Los Angeles Free Press*, 15 January 1971, p. 24.

11  Hopkins and Sugerman, *No One Here Gets Out Alive*, pp. 172, 174. Also see pp. 161-64 in *Riders On The Storm: My Life With Jim Morrison And The Doors*, (New York: Delacorte Press, 1990) for John Densmore's account of this tumultuous time of recording.

12  Joan Didion, "Waiting for Morrison", *The Saturday Evening Post*, 20 January 1969, p. 16.

13  Lester Bangs, "The Doors", *The Rolling Stone Illustrated History Of Rock & Roll*, Jim Miller, ed. (New York: Rolling Stone Press, 1976), p. 262.

14  David Dalton and Lenny Kaye, *Rock 100* (New York: Grosset & Dunlap, Publishers, 1977), p. 166.

15  *History of Rock 'n' Roll*, aired 29 April 1978, WOWO Radio, 1190 AM, Fort Wayne, IN.

16  Richard C. Walls, "Waiting For The Sun" (record review), *Creem Special Edition: The Doors*, Summer 1981, p. 51.

17  Terry Rompers, "Looking Through the Doors", *Trouser Press*, September/October 1980, p. 2.

18  "The Doors" (record review of 'Waiting For The Sun'), *Harbinger* (Toronto underground newspaper), August 1968, p. 21.

19  Fornatale, p. 49.

20  Rompers, p. 2.

21 Mangelsdorff, p. 6.
22 Richard Riegel, "Tongues of Knowledge in the Feathered Night (The Blue Bus Is Double Parked): The Doors On Record", *Creem Special Edition: The Doors*, Summer 1981, p. 12.
23 Walls, p. 51.
24 Harbinger, p. 21.
25 David R. Pichaske, *The Poetry Of Rock: The Golden Years* (Peoria, IL: The Ellis Press, 1981), p. 80.
26 Walls, p. 51.
27 Harbinger, p. 21.
28 Jay Ruby, "Pop Record Reviews: The Doors, Waiting For the Sun", *Jazz & Pop*, December 1968, pp. 56-57.
29 Riegel, p. 13.
30 Jonathan Cott, "Doors, Airplane in Middle Earth", *Rolling Stone*, 26 October 1968, p. 12.
31 *The Source: The Doors Special Encore* (3-hour radio special), Show #NBC 82-23 (New York: NBC Radio's Young Adult Network), aired 2-4 July 1982. In his book, *The Lizard King: The Essential Jim Morrison*, Jerry Hopkins wrote that 'Unknown Soldier' was from Morrison's writings when he lived in Venice Beach the summer of 1965, right after graduating from UCLA (pp. 93, 95).
32 Hopkins and Sugerman, *No One Here Gets Out Alive*, pp. 149-50.
33 Vic Garbarini, "Blues for a Shaman: Doors' Producer Paul Rothschild (sic)", *Musician*, August 1981, p. 54.
34 Cohen, p. 19.
35 Walls, p. 51.
36 Karl Dallas, "Jim Morrison – Is He The American Mick Jagger?", *Melody Maker*, 3 August 1968, reprinted in *Contemporary Literary Criticism*, Sharon R. Gunton, ed. (Detroit: Gale Research Company, 1981), p. 287.
37 Harbinger, p. 21.
38 Walls, p. 51.
39 Ruby, p. 57.
40 Ibid.
41 Pichaske, p. 80.
42 Ruby, p. 57.
43 Hopkins and Sugerman, *No One Here Gets Out Alive*, p. 152.
44 Ibid.

45 Ibid.
46 Zevallos, p. 50.
47 Rob Burt and Patsy North, ed., *West Coast Story* (London: Phoebus Publishing Company, 1977; published in U.S.A. by Chartwell Books Inc., Secausuc, NJ.), p. 40.
48 Dallas, reprinted in *Contemporary Literary Criticism*, p. 287.
49 Mangelsdorff, p. 6.
50 Walls, p. 51.
51 Harbinger, p. 21.


Chapter 4
WELCOME TO THE SOFT PARADE

1 Jim Morrison, *Wilderness: The Lost Writings Of Jim Morrison, Volume I* (New York: Villard Books, 1988), p. 206.
2 Robert Matheu, "Through The Doors Again: Manzarek, Krieger & Densmore Today", *Creem Special Edition: The Doors*, Summer 1981, p. 59. In his book, *The Lizard King: The Essential Jim Morrison*, Jerry Hopkins wrote that Morrison didn't want people to think he wanted others to follow him because he neither trusted leaders nor want to be a leader (p. 120).
3 *The Source: The Doors Special Encore* (3-hour radio special), Show #NBC 82-23 (New York: NBC Radio's Young Adult Network), aired 2-4 July 1982.
4 Jerry Hopkins, "The Rolling Stone Interview: Jim Morrison", *Rolling Stone*, 26 July 1969, p. 17.
5 Morrison, Wilderness, p. 207. Compare this poem by Morrison to Wallace Fowlie's translation of Arthur Rimbaud's poem, *Evening Prayer* [Oraison du soir] (p. 69).
6 Mikal Gilmore, "The Legacy of Jim Morrison and The Doors", *Rolling Stone*, 4 April 1991, p. 33.
7 Richard Riegel, "Tongues of Knowledge in the Feathered Night (The Blue Bus Is Double Parked): The Doors On Record", *Creem Special Edition: The Doors*, Summer 1981, p. 12.
8 Lester Bangs, "The Doors", *The Rolling Stone Illustrated History of Rock & Roll*, Jim Miller, ed. (New York: Rolling Stone Press, 1976), p. 262.

9 Pete Fornatale, "Strange Days: Doors' Organist Ray Manzarek", *Musician*, August 1981, p. 50.

10 Rob Cline, "Record Reviews", *Northwest Passage* (Bellingham, WA underground newspaper), 19 August 1969, p. 20.

11 David Walley, "The Elektra Company, or How One Learns to Love the Bombs", *The East Village Other* (New York underground newspaper), 10 September 1969, p. 12.

12 Miller Francis Jr., "Callin' on the gods", *The Great Speckled Bird* (Atlanta underground newspaper), 20 October 1969, p. 18.

13 KT, "Records" (review of *The Soft Parade*), *Octopus* (Ottawa, Canada, underground newspaper), vol. 2-11 (1969), p. 26.

14 Vic Garbarini, "Blues for a Shaman: Doors' Producer Paul Rothschild (sic)", *Musician*, August 1981, p. 56.

15 Blair Jackson, "Paul Rothchild: The Doors' producer recalls the agony and the ecstasy of working with The Doors", *BAM*, 3 July 1981, p. 19.

16 *The Source: The Doors Special Encore* (3-hour radio special), NBC Radio's Young Adult Network, 1982.

17 Alan Paul, "Strange Days" (interview with Krieger), *Guitar World*, March 1994, p. 112.

18 Lester Bangs, "Jim Morrison, Oafus Laureate", *Creem Special Edition: The Doors*, Summer 1981, p. 29.

19 Dave DiMartino, "Morrison in Miami: Flesh and Memories", *Creem Special Edition: The Doors*, Summer 1981, p. 31.

20 Riegel, p. 12.

21 From John Tobler interview with Jim Morrison at Isle of Wight Festival, 1970, on *Opening The Doors Of Perception* ("over one hour of rare and intriguing dialogue") [CD]. (Transcript of interview is printed in Jerry Hopkin's *The Lizard King: The Essential Jim Morrison*, see p. 235.)

22 Francis, p. 18.

23 Mitch Kapor, "Soft Parade", *A View From The Bottom* (New Haven, CT underground newspaper), 7 August 1969, p. 13.

24 David R. Pichaske, *The Poetry Of Rock: The Golden Years* (Peoria, IL: The Ellis Press, 1981), p. 80.

25 Matheu, p. 59.

26 John Densmore, *Riders On The Storm: My Life With Jim Morrison And The Doors*, (New York: Delacorte Press, 1990), p. 190.

27 Bob (Turk) Nirkind, "The Doors – Follow Them Down", *The South End* (Wayne State University, Detroit, underground newspaper), 21 August 1969, p. 8.
28 Francis, p. 18.
29 J. Kordosh, "Soft Parade" (record review), *Creem Special Edition: The Doors*, Summer 1981, p. 51.
30 Rich Mangelsdorff, "Music Wheel", *Kaleidoscope* (Milwaukee underground newspaper), 12-25 September 1969, p. 15.
31 Francis, p. 18.
32 Patricia Kennely, "Pop Record Reviews: The Doors, The Soft Parade", *Jazz & Pop*, October 1969, p. 41.
33 Densmore, p. 205.
34 Kennely, p. 41.
35 Nirkind, p. 8.
36 Kennely, p. 41.
37 Nirkind, p. 8.
38 Mangelsdorff, p. 15.
39 Francis, p. 18.
40 Kordosh, p. 51.
41 Lester Bangs, "Jim Morrison: Bozo Dionysus a Decade Later", *Musician*, August 1981, p. 44.
42 Kennely, p. 41.
43 Francis, p. 18.
44 Mangelsdorff, p. 15.
45 Nirkind, p. 8.
46 Pichaske, p. 80.
47 Francis, p. 258.
48 Kordosh, p. 51.
49 Kapor, p. 13.
50 Kennely, p. 41.
51 Rompers, p. 3.
52 Riegel, p. 12.
53 Pichaske, p. 79.
54 Jackson, *BAM*, 3 July 1981, p. 19.
55 Bangs, *Musician*, p. 44.

Chapter 5
THE HARD ROCK CAFE & MORRISON HOTEL

1  Jerry Hopkins, "The Rolling Stone Interview: Jim Morrison", *Rolling Stone*, 26 July 1969, p. 16.
2  Ibid., p. 15.
3  Lizze James, "Jim Morrison: Ten Years Gone", *Creem Special Edition: The Doors*, Summer 1981, p. 18.
4  Jerry Hopkins and Danny Sugerman, *No One Here Gets Out Alive*, (New York: Warner Books, Inc., 1980), p. 269.
5  Ibid.
6  "Archies' 'Jingle, Jingle' Wins 'Em a Gold Disk; Doors Cop 5th Straight", *Variety*, 4 March 1970, p. 43.
7  "Spotlight Singles: Top 60 Pop Spotlight" (Doors – "You Make Me Real"), *Billboard*, 4 April 1970, p. 60.
8  Lester Bangs, "Morrison Hotel", *Rolling Stone*, 30 April 1970, p. 53.
9  "Morrison Hotel", *Amazing Grace* (Tallahassee, FL underground newspaper), vol. 1, no. 5 (1970), p. 12.
10 Patricia Kennely, "Pop Record Reviews: The Doors, Morrison Hotel", *Jazz & Pop*, May 1970, pp. 54-55.
11 "Records 70", *Fusion* (Boston underground publication), 22 January 1971, p. 24.
12 "Albums" (review of Morrison Hotel), *Fusion* (Boston underground publication), 1 May 1970, p. 20.
13 Dave Marsh, "Morrison Hotel – The Doors", *Creem* (Detroit), vol. 2, no. 10 (February 1970), p. 25.
14 Chris Reabur, "Morrison Hotel Revisited", *Jazz & Pop*, September 1970, p. 22. "Chris Reabur" was a pseudonym for Bruce Harris.
15 Ibid., p. 23.
16 Sugerman and Hopkins, *No One Here Gets Out Alive*, p. 270. For a detailed account of the photograph session with Henry Deitz at Morrison Hotel and Hard Rock Cafe see John Densmore's account in *Riders On The Storm*, p. 244.
17 Kennely, p. 55.
18 Ibid.
19 Reabur, p. 22.
20 Stephen Halpert, "Get Back: The Doors Are Closed", *Fusion* (Boston underground publication), 20 March 1970, p. 38.

21 Marsh, p. 52.
22 Reabur, p. 22.
23 Ibid.
24 Bangs, "Morrison Hotel", *Rolling Stone*, p. 53.
25 Reabur, p. 23.
26 Sugerman and Hopkins, *No One Here Gets Out Alive*, p. 271. See also Hopkins, *The Lizard King: The Essential Jim Morrison*, p. 129.
27 Reabur, p. 23.
28 Marsh, p. 52.
29 Fusion, 1 May 1970, p. 20.
30 Bangs, "Morrison Hotel", *Rolling Stone*, p. 53.
31 Reabur, p. 23.
32 Ibid.
33 Richard Riegel, "Tongues of Knowledge in the Feathered Night (The Blue Bus Is Double Parked): The Doors On Record", *Creem Special Edition: The Doors*, Summer 1981, p. 14.
34 Reabur, p. 23.
35 John Densmore, *Riders On The Storm: My Life With Jim Morrison And The Doors*, (New York: Delacorte Press, 1990), pp. 244-45. In his book, *The Lizard King: The Essential Jim Morrison*, Jerry Hopkins wrote that, in one of Morrison's notebooks, Manzarek found "Abortion Stories", which included the litany of blood sung in 'Peace Frog' (p. 129).
36 Reabur, p. 23.
37 Ibid.
38 Bangs, "Morrison Hotel", *Rolling Stone*, p. 53.
39 Kennely, p. 55.
40 Ibid.
41 Marsh, p. 52.
42 David R. Pichaske, *The Poetry Of Rock: The Golden Years* (Peoria, IL: The Ellis Press, 1981), p. 82.
43 Marsh, p. 52.
44 Benjamin Franklin V and Duane Schneider, *Anais Nin: An Introduction* (Athens, OH: Ohio University Press, 1979), p. 113.
45 Anais Nin, *A Spy In The House Of Love* (New York: Pocket Books, 1994; copyright 1959 by Anais Nin), p. 56.
46 Ibid., p. 82.
47 Anais Nin, *A Woman Speaks: The Lectures, Seminars, And*

*Interviews Of Anais Nin*, edited by Evelyn J. Hinz (Chicago: The Swallow Press Inc., 1975), pp. 255-56. Compare Nin's ideas to Morrison's responses in Lizze James's interviews as used in her article, "Jim Morrison: Ten Years Gone", *Creem Special Edition: The Doors* (Summer 1981, pp. 16-23) and as reprinted in *The DOORS: The Illustrated History*, edited by Danny Sugerman and Benjamin Edmonds – see "Part I: Lizze James Interview with Jim Morrison" pp. 64-67 and "Part II: Lizze James Interview with Jim Morrison" pp. 122-24.

48 Ibid., p. 220.

49 Pete Fornatale, "Strange Days: Doors' Organist Ray Manzarek", *Musician*, August 1981, p. 50.

50 Reabur, p. 24.

51 Marsh, p. 51.

52 Reabur, p. 24.

53 Ibid.

Chapter 6
L.A. WOMAN, YOU'RE MY WOMAN

1 Rob Houghton, "L.A. Woman" (record review), *Creem Special Edition: The Doors*, Summer 1981, p. 54.

2 *The Doors: A Tribute To Jim Morrison* (Burbank, CA: Warner Home Video, Inc., 1982).

3 Jim Morrison, *Wilderness: The Lost Writings Of Jim Morrison, Volume I* (New York: Villard Books, 1988), p. 209.

4 Bruce Harris, "L.A. Woman: The Doors", University Review, reprinted in *The DOORS: The Illustrated History*, p. 173

5 Pete Fornatale, "Strange Days: Doors' Organist Ray Manzarek", *Musician*, August 1981, p. 50.

6 Vic Garbarini, "Blues for a Shaman: Doors' Producer Paul Rothschild (sic)", *Musician*, August 1981, p. 57.

7 John Densmore, *Riders On The Storm: My Life With Jim Morrison And The Doors*, (New York: Delacorte Press, 1990), p. 256.

8 Nick Tosches, "The Doors", *Fusion* (Boston underground publication), 25 June 1971, p. 49.

9 Jerry Hopkins and Danny Sugerman, *No One Here Gets Out Alive*,

(New York: Warner Books, Inc., 1980), p. 320.

10  Houghton, p. 54.

11  David R. Pichaske, *The Poetry Of Rock: The Golden Years* (Peoria, IL: The Ellis Press, 1981), p. 83.

12  Hugh Noname, "Doors: LA Woman", *IT* (*International Times*, London underground newspaper), 26 August – 9 September 1971, p. 18.

13  Maybelle Lacey, (book review of Richard Farina's *Been Down So Long It Looks Like Up To Me*), *Library Journal*, 1 April 1966, p. 1924.

14  Hopkins and Sugerman, *No One Here Gets Out Alive*, p. 320.

15  Is the lyric, "A cold girl'll kill you", or is it, "Ah, cold girl I'll kill you"? Either line certainly adds a sinister twist to the meaning of the lyric. But such altering between what may have been written to be the lyric and what was sung would not have been beyond Morrison's artistic liberty – or intent. Listener discretion is advised.

16  Terry Rompers, "Looking Through the Doors", *Trouser Press*, September/October 1980, p. 4.

17  Pichaske, p. 84.

18  Robert G. Pielke, *You Say You Want A Revolution: Rock Music In American Culture* (Chicago: Nelson-Hall, 1986), p. 241.

19  Ibid.

20  Pichaske, p. 84.

21  Hopkins and Sugerman, *No One Here Gets Out Alive*, p. 320.

22  Lloyd W. Griffin, (book review of John Rechy's City of Night), *Library Journal*, July 1963, pp. 2228-29.

23  Danny Sugerman, "A Shaman's Journey Through The Doors", *Creem Special Edition: The Doors*, Summer 1981, p. 39.

24  Hopkins and Sugerman, *No One Here Gets Out Alive*, p. 320.

25  Harris, reprinted in *The DOORS: The Illustrated History*, p. 173.

26  Reproduction of Jim Morrison's personal letter to Dave Marsh, editor of *Creem, The Doors Collectors Magazine*, Spring 1994 (Issue #4), p. 32.

27  Hopkins and Sugerman, *No One Here Gets Out Alive*, p. 343.

28  Densmore, p. 259.

29  'L'America' also appears as 'Lamerica', 'LAmerica', 'L'america', and 'lamerica' in some of Morrison's handwritten poetic tidbits: – in a different poem, untitled, "Lamerica" appears in the first

three lines and then "lamerica" appears in the rest of the poem (*Wilderness: The Lost Writings Of Jim Morrison, Volume I*; pp. 7-8); for two different poems, the titles were, "LAMERICA" (Wilderness; pp. 26, 45); for a different poem, the title was, "LAmerica" (Wilderness; p. 87); in a different poem entitled, "L'America", "L'america" appears in the first line and the "Lamerica" appears in the rest of the poem (*The American Night: The Writings Of Jim Morrison, Volume II*; p. 140). Morrison's enunciation is, "la-mer-e – ca". Therefore, should it be, "La'merica"? Morrison's intent is to shift our perception of "America" – and hence all the typical implied images and meanings with that word – to a different viewpoint with the exotic and strange sounding 'L'America'.

30  Arthur Schlesinger Jr., "Movies" (review of Antonioni's Zabriskie Point), *Vogue*, 1 April 1970, p. 116.

31  Densmore, p. 255.

32  Richard Farina, *Long Time Coming And A Long Time Gone* (New York: Random House, 1969), opening page.

33  Richard Riegel, "Tongues of Knowledge in the Feathered Night (The Blue Bus Is Double Parked): The Doors On Record", *Creem Special Edition: The Doors*, Summer 1981, p. 15.

34  Houghton, p. 54.

35  Hopkins and Sugerman, *No One Here Gets Out Alive*, p. 320.

36  Rompers, p. 4.

37  Meltzer, "L.A. Woman" (record review), *Rolling Stone*, 27 May 1971, p. 48.

38  Rompers, p. 4.

39  *History of Rock 'n' Roll*, aired 29 April 1978, WOWO Radio, 1190 AM, Fort Wayne, IN.

40  "Top Singles Of The Week" (Doors... "Riders on the Storm"), *Variety*, 16 June 1971, p. 46.

41  Blair Jackson, "Paul Rothchild: The Doors' producer recalls the agony and the ecstasy of working with The Doors", *BAM*, 3 July 1981, p. 20. Densmore, in *Riders On The Storm*, remembered Rothchild calling this song "cocktail jazz" (p. 251).

42  Hopkins and Sugerman, *No One Here Gets Out Alive*, p. 324.

43  Rompers, p. 4.

Chapter 7
LET IT ROLL

1   From John Tobler interview with Jim Morrison at Isle of Wight
    Festival, 1970, on *Opening The Doors Of Perception* ("over one
    hour of rare and intriguing dialogue") [CD]. (Transcript of
    interview is printed in Jerry Hopkin's *The Lizard King: The
    Essential Jim Morrison*, see p. 233.)
2   Alistair Cooke, "Focus on The Arts" in *Section One/The Year In
    Focus, The 1968 World Book Year Book: A Review Of The Events Of
    1967* (New York: Field Enterprises Educational Corporation, 1968),
    p. 55.
3   Danny Sugerman and Benjamin Edmonds, eds, *The DOORS: The
    Illustrated History* (New York: William Morrow and Company,
    1983), p. 9.
4   Mike Jahn, *Jim Morrison And The Doors* (an unauthorized book)
    (New York: Grosset & Dunlap, 1969), p. 73.
5   Friedrich Nietzsche, *The Birth Of Tragedy & The Genealogy Of
    Morals*, translated by Francis Golffin (New York: Doubleday
    Anchor Books, 1956), p. 125.
6   *Rimbaud: Complete Works, Selected Letters*, translated by Wallace
    Fowlie (Chicago: The University of Chicago Press, 1966), p. 307.

# DISCOGRAPHY & FILMOGRAPHY

The discography has been broken up into the following:

A. Audio Recordings (chronological listing);
B. Radio and television specials on The Doors (alphabetical listing);
C. Videos (alphabetical listing).

I owe many thanks to Kerry Humpherys who shared with me his extensive personal collection of Doors recordings.

Consult Rainer Moddemann's *The Doors* (Germany: Heel, 1991) for extensive discography on foreign produced recordings.

The following recordings were referred to in regards to The Doors' recordings of 'Back Door Man', 'Cars Hiss By My Window', 'Crawling King Snake', 'Light My Fire', 'Little Red Rooster', and 'Who Do You Love':

*Coltrane, John.* The Best of John Coltrane [CD]. Altantic, 1541-2, 1970. (For comparison to the dual solos in 'My Favourite Things' which inspired the structure of dual solos in 'Light My Fire'.)

*Dixon, Willie.* I Am The Blues [album]. Columbia, PC 9987. Reissued on CD by Mobile Fidelity Sound Lab, MFCD 872 (Columbia, copyright 1970). Original Master Recording series. (Includes 'Back Door Man' and 'The Little Red Rooster'.)

*Hammond, John Jr.* The Best of John Hammond [CD]. Vanguard, VCD-11/2, 1986/87; reissue of 1970 double album. (Includes 'Who Do You Love' and 'Backdoor Man' and Chuck Berry is credited as writer of 'Backdoor Man'.)

*Hooker, John Lee.* John Lee Hooker: The Legendary MODERN Recordings 1948-1954 [CD]. Virgin Records America (Flair), 7243 8 39658 2 3, 1993. (Includes 'Crawling King Snake'.)

*Hooker, John Lee.* The Hook: 20 years of hits & hot boogie [CD].

195

Chameleon Records, D2-74794, 1989. VeeJay Hall of Fame Series. (Includes 'Crawlin' Kingsnake' and 'Nightmare'.)

*Howlin' Wolf (Chester Burnett).* Howlin' Wolf: His Greatest Sides, Vol. 1 [cassette]. Chess Records (MCA Records), CHC-9107, 1983. (Includes 'The Red Rooster' and 'Back Door Man'.)

# SINGLES

'Break On Through'/'End Of The Night'
*45 rpm single, Elektra, 45611, January 1967.*

'Light My Fire'/'The Crystal Ship'
*45 rpm single, Elektra, 45615, April 1967.*

'People Are Strange'/'Unhappy Girl'
*45 rpm single, Elektra, 45621, September 1967.*

'Love Me Two Times'/'Moonlight Drive'
*45 rpm single, Elektra, 45624, November 1967.*

'The Unknown Soldier'/'We Could Be So Good Together'
*45 rpm single, Elektra, 45628, March 1968.*

'Hello, I Love You'/'Love Street'
*45 rpm single, Elektra, 45635, June 1968.*

'Touch Me'/'Wild Child'
*45 rpm single, Elektra, 45646, December 1968.*

'Wishful, Sinful'/'Who Scared You'
*45 rpm single, Elektra, 45656, February 1969.*

'Tell All The People'/'Easy Ride'
*45 rpm single, Elektra, 45663, May 1969.*

'Runnin' Blue'/'Do It'
*45 rpm single, Elektra, 45675, August 1969.*

'You Make Me Real'/'Roadhouse Blues'
*45 rpm single, Elektra, 45685, March 1970.*

'Love Her Madly'/'Don't Go No Further'
*45 rpm single, Elektra, 45726, March 1971.*

'Light My Fire'/'Love Me Two Times'
*45 rpm single, 'Spun Gold' Series, E-45051, April 1971.*

'Touch Me'/'Hello, I Love You'
*45 rpm single, 'Spun Gold' Series, E-45052, April 1971.*

'Riders On The Storm'/'The Changeling'
*45 rpm single, Elektra, 45738, June 1971.*

'Tightrope Ride'/'Variety Is The Spice Of Life'
*45 rpm single, Elektra, 45757, November 1971.*

'Ship With Sails'/'In The Eye Of The Sun'
*45 rpm single, Elektra, 45768, May 1972.*

'Get Up And Dance'/'Treetrunk'
*45 rpm single, Elektra, 454793, July 1972.*

'The Mosquito'/'It Slipped My Mind'
*45 rpm single, Elektra, 45807, August 1972.*

'Riders On The Storm'/'Love Her Madly'
*45 rpm single, 'Spun Gold' Series, E-45059, September 1972.*

'The Piano Bird'/'Good Rockin''
*45 rpm single, Elektra, 45825, November 1972.*

'L.A. Woman'/'Roadhouse Blues'
*45 rpm single, 'Spun Gold' Series, Elektra, 45122.*

'People Are Strange'/'Break On Through'
*45 rpm single, 'Spun Gold' Series, Elektra, 45123.*

'Love Her Madly';
'Riders On The Storm'/'Touch Me';
'Light My Fire'
*45 rpm EP, Elektra, EPE 230 MX 165842, 1980 (Australian release).*

'Roadhouse Blues' (stereo)/'Roadhouse Blues' (mono).
*45 rpm promotional single, Elektra/Asylum Records,
E-46005-A, 1978.*

'Roadhouse Blues'/'Albinoni Adagio'
*45 rpm single, Elektra, E-46005, January 1979.*

'Hello, I Love You';
'Love Me Two Times'/'Ghost Song';
'Roadhouse Blues' (both from *An American Prayer*).
*45 rpm double single. Elektra, K 12215, 1979 (English pressing).*

'The End'/'The Delta'
(Carmine Coppola and Francis Coppola).
(in conjuncture with Francis Coppola's movie, *Apocalypse Now*)
*45 rpm single, Elektra K 12400 (EF-90166), 1979.*

'Gloria'/'Love Me Two Times'
*33 1/2 rpm single from* Alive, She Cried. *Elektra, E 9774T,
1983 (English pressing).*

'Gloria' (clean edit)/'Gloria' (dirty album version).
*33 1/2 rpm promotional single, 1983. Elektra/Asylum Records,
EAOR 4942.*

'Love Me Two Times'/'Moonlight Drive'
(Inc. 'Horse Latitudes').
*33 1/3 rpm promotional single, Elektra/Asylum Records,
EAOR 4955, 1983.*

'Light My Fire' (Side A: album version, 1985/Side B: edit of live version, Live at the Hollywood Bowl, 1987).
*33 1/2 rpm promotional single. Elektra/Asylum/Nonesuch Records, 5245.*

'Break On Through';
'Love Street'/'Hello, I Love You';
'Touch Me'
*33 1/2 rpm promotional copy. Elektra Entertainment, 7559-66556-0, 1991 (English pressing).*

'Light My Fire'/'People Are Strange' & 'Soul Kitchen'
*33 1/2 rpm single. Elektra Entertainment, 7559-66537-0, 1991 (English pressing).*

'Riders On The Storm'/'Roadhouse Blues' (live)
& 'Love Her Two Times' (live).
*33 1/2 rpm single. Elektra, 7559-66509-0, 1991 (English pressing).*

'The Unknown Soldier' (The Doors)/'A Soldier's View Of Vietnam'
(Doc Kennedy).
*33 1/2 rpm. Elektra/Asylum/Nonesuch Records, PR 8001, no date (circa 1980s). (A Special Limited Edition 12 inch single from 98 KZEW in support of the Vietnam Veterans Memorial Fund of Texas.)*

'Break On Through' (from Stone's film, *The Doors*).
*CD single. Elektra, PRCD 8314-2, 1991.*

'Light My Fire' (3:04)/'Love Me Two Times' (3:15).
*CD single. Elektra, 45051-2, no date.*

'The Ghost Song'
*CD single. Elektra, EKR 205CD 7559-66119-2, 1995 (English pressing). Includes 'The Ghost Song', 'Roadhouse Blues' (live), 'Love Me Two Times' (live), Jim Morrison Interview (1:25 in length).*

# ALBUMS/COMPACT DISCS

The Doors [album]. *Elektra Records, EKL-74007 Mono, EKS-74007 Stereo, January 1967.*
> Side 1: Break On Through (To The Other Side); Soul Kitchen; The Crystal Ship; Twentieth Century Fox; Alabama Song (Whiskey Bar); Light My Fire
> Side 2: Back Door Man; I Looked At You; End Of The Night; Take It As It Comes; The End

The Doors [cassette], *TC5-4007.*
The Doors [8-track tape]. *ET8-4007.*
The Doors [album]. *Mobile Fidelity Sounds Lab, MFSL 1-051, 1980. Half-Speed Production & Mastering; Original Master Recording series.*
The Doors [CD]. *Elektra/Asylum Records, 74007-2, November 1983. [The version pressed by PolyGram in West Germany lists Robby Krieger as 'Bobby Krieger']*
The Doors *[24KT Gold Plated CD]. DDC Compact Classics, Inc. (Northridge, CA), GZS-1023, July 1992. (Pressed in Japan.)*


Strange Days [album]. *Elektra Records, EKL-74014 Mono, EKS-74014 Stereo, October 1967.*
> Side 1: Strange Days; You're Lost Little Girl; Love Me Two Times; Unhappy Girl; Horse Latitudes; Moonlight Drive
> Side 2: People Are Strange; My Eyes Have Seen You; I Can't See Your Face in My Mind; When The Music's Over

Strange Days *[cassette], TC5-4014.*
Strange Days *[8-track tape], ET8-4014.*
Strange Days *[CD]. Elektra/Asylum Records, 74014-2, September 1985.*
Strange Days *[24KT Gold Plated CD]. DDC Compact Classics, Inc. (Northridge, CA), GZS-1026, October 1992. (Pressed in Japan.)*


Waiting For The Sun [album]. *Elektra Records, EKL-74024 Mono, EKS-74024 Stereo, July 1968.*

Side 1: Hello, I Love You; Love Street; Not To Touch The Earth; Summer's Almost Gone; Wintertime Love; The Unknown Soldier
Side 2: Spanish Caravan; My Wild Love; We Could Be So Good Together; Yes, The River Knows; Five To One
Waiting For The Sun *[cassette], TC5-4024.*
Waiting For The Sun *[8-track tape], ET8-4024.*
Waiting For The Sun *[cassette], 60156-4, August 1982.*
Waiting For The Sun *[CD]. Elektra/Asylum Records, 74024-2, August 1985.*
Waiting For The Sun *[24KT Gold Plated CD]. DDC Compact Classics, Inc. (Northridge, CA), GZS-1045, October 1993. (Pressed in Japan.)*

The Soft Parade [album]. *Elektra Records, EKS-75005, July 1969.*
Side 1: Tell All The People; Touch Me; Shaman's Blues; Do It; Easy Ride
Side 2: Wild Child; Runnin' Blue; Wishful, Sinful; The Soft Parade
The Soft Parade *[cassette], TC5-5005.*
The Soft Parade *[8-track tape], ET8-5005.*
The Soft Parade [CD]. *Elektra/Asylum Records, 75005-2, May 1988.*

Morrison Hotel [album]. *Elektra Records, EKS-75007, February 1970.*
Side 1: Roadhouse Blues; Waiting For The Sun; You Make Me Real; Peace Frog; Blue Sunday; Ship Of Fools
Side 2: Land Ho!; The Spy; Queen Of The Highway; Indian Summer; Maggie M'Gill
Morrison Hotel *[cassette], TC5-5007.*
Morrison Hotel *[8-track tape], ET8-5007.*
Morrison Hotel *[CD]. Elektra/Asylum Records, 75007-2, May 1985.*

Absolutely Live [double album]. *Elektra Records, EKS-9002, July 1970.*

201

Side 1: Who Do Love; Medley – Alabama Song/Back Door
Man/Love Hides/Five To One
Side 2: Build Me A Woman; When The Music's Over
Side 3: Close To You; Universal Mind; Break On Thru #2
Side 4: The Celebration of the Lizard; Soul Kitchen
Absolutely Live *[cassette]*, *C2-9002*.
Absolutely Live *[8-track tape]*, *T8-9002*.


13 *[album]*. *Elektra Records, EKS-74079, November 1970.*
Side 1: Light My Fire; People Are Strange; Back Door Man;
Moonlight Drive; The Crystal Ship; Roadhouse Blues
Side 2: Touch Me; Love Me Two Times; You're Lost Little Girl;
Hello, I Love You; Land Ho; Wild Child; The Unknown Soldier
13 [cassette], TC5-4079.
13 [8-track tape], ET8-4079.


L.A. Woman *[album]*. *Elektra Records, EKS-75011, April 1971.*
Side 1: The Changeling; Love Her Madly; Been Down So Long;
Cars Hiss By My Window; L.A. Woman
Side 2: L'America; Hyacinth House; Crawling King Snake; The
WASP (Texas Radio And The Big Beat); Riders On The Storm
L.A. Woman *[cassette]*, *TC5-5011*.
L.A. Woman *[8-track tape]*, *EET8-5011*.
L.A. Woman [CD]. *Elektra/Asylum Records, 75011-2,*
*March 1985.*
L.A. Woman *[CD]*. *HMV Classic Collection (London), C88 1-6.*
*Includes a 12-page booklet with text by Max Bell and reprints of*
*three reviews of album. 2500 pressed.*
L.A. Woman *[24KT Gold Plated CD]*. *DDC Compact Classics, Inc.*
*(Northridge, CA), GZS-1034, March 1993. (Pressed in Japan.)*


Other Voices *[album; without Jim Morrison]*. *Elektra Records,*
*EKS-75017, November 1971.*
Side 1: In The Eye Of The Sun; Variety Is The Spice Of Life; Ships
w/ Sails; Tightrope Ride

Side 2: Down On The Farm; I'm Horny, I'm Stoned; Wandering Musician; Hang On To Your Life


Weird Scenes Inside The Gold Mine *[double album]. Elektra Records, 8E-6001, January 1972.*
Side 1: Break On Through; Strange Days; Shaman's Blues; Love Street; Peace Frog/Blue Sunday; The WASP (Texas Radio And The Big Beat); End Of The Night
Side 2: Love Her Madly; Spanish Caravan; Ship Of Fools; The Spy; The End
Side 3: Take It As It Comes; Runnin' Blue; L.A. Woman; Five To One; Who Scared You; (You Need Meat) Don't Go No Further
Side 4: Riders On The Storm; Maggie M'Gill; Horse Latitudes; When The Music's Over
Weird Scenes Inside The Gold Mine *[cassette], C2-6001.*
Weird Scenes Inside The Gold Mine *[8-track tape], T8-6001.*


Full Circle *[album; without Jim Morrison]. Elektra Records, EKS-75038, July 1972.*
Side 1: Get Up And Dance; 4 Billion Souls; Verdilac; Hardwood Floor; Good Rockin
Side 2: The Mosquito; The Piano Bird; It Slipped My Mind; The Peking King And The New York Queen


The Best Of The Doors [Quadraphonic album]. *Elektra Records, EQ-5035, September 1973.*
Side 1: Who Do You Love; Soul Kitchen; Hello, I Love You; People Are Strange; Riders On The Storm
Side 2: Touch Me; Love Her Madly; Love Me Two Times; Take It As It Comes; Moonlight Drive; Light My Fire
The Best of The Doors *[cassette], TC5-5035.*
The Best of The Doors *[8-track tape], ET8-5035.*


Morrison, Jim (Music by The Doors). An American Prayer

*[album]. Elektra/Asylum Records, 5E-502, November 1978;*
*re-issued 1995 with CD version and with bonus tracks (see CD*
*listing).*

> Side 1: Awake (Ghost Dance, Dawn's Highway, Newborn
> Awakening); To Come Of Age (Black Polished Chrome/Latino
> Chrome, Angels And Sailors, Stoned Immaculate); The Poet's
> Dream (The Movie, Curses Invocations)
> Side 2: World On Fire (American Night, Roadhouse Blues,
> Lament, The Hitchhiker); An American Prayer

An American Prayer [cassette], 5C5-502.
An American Prayer [8-track tape], 5T8-502.
An American Prayer [CD], 61812-2.
  bonus tracks: Babylon Fading, Bird Of Prey, The Ghost Song


Greatest Hits *[album]. Elektra/Asylum Records, 5E-515,*
*October 1980.*

> Side 1: Hello, I Love You; Light My Fire; People Are Strange; Love
> Me Two Times
> Side 2: Break On Through; Roadhouse Blues; Not To Touch The
> Earth; Touch Me; L.A. Woman

Greatest Hits [cassette], 5C5-55.
Greatest Hits [8-track tape], 5T8-515.


Alive, She Cried *[album]. Elektra/Asylum Records, 60269-1,*
*October 1983.*

> Side 1: Gloria; Light My Fire; You Make Me Real
> Side 2: Texas Radio & The Big Beat; Love Me Two Times; Little
> Red Rooster; Moonlight Drive

Alive, She Cried *[cassette], 60269-4.*
Alive, She Cried *[CD]. Elektra/Asylum Records, 60269-2,*
*June 1984.*


Classics *[album]. Elektra/Asylum Records, 60417-1, May 1985.*

> Side 1: Strange Days; Love Her Madly; Waiting For The Sun; My
> Eyes Have Seen You; Wild Child; Crystal Ship; Five To One

Side 2: Roadhouse Blues (live); Land Ho!; I Can't See Your Face In My Mind; Peace Frog; The WASP; The Unknown Soldier
Classics [cassette], 60417-4.

The Best of The Doors *[double album]*. *Elektra/Asylum Records, 60345-1, June 1987.*
    Side 1: Break On Through; Light My Fire; The Crystal Ship; People Are Strange; Strange Days; Love Me Two Times
    Side 2: Five To One; Waiting For The Sun; Spanish Caravan; When The Music's Over
    Side 3: Hello, I Love You; Roadhouse Blues; L.A. Woman; Riders On The Storm
    Side 4: Touch Me; Love Her Madly; The Unknown Soldier; The End
The Best of The Doors *[cassette]*, 60345-4.
The Best of The Doors *[2 disc CD]*. *Elektra/Asylum Records, 9 60345-2, July 1987.*
  Disc 1: sides 1 & 2 of double album
  Disc 2: sides 3 & 4 of double album

Live at the Hollywood Bowl *[album]*. *Elektra/Asylum Records, 60741-1, June 1987.*
    Side 1: Wake Up; Light My Fire
    Side 2: The Unknown Soldier; A Little Game; The Hill Dwellers; Spanish Caravan
Live at the Hollywood Bowl *[cassette]*, 60741-4.
Live at the Hollywood Bowl *[CD]*. *Elektra/Asylum Records, 60741-2, July 1987.*
  bonus track: an edit of the live version of 'Light My Fire'

The Doors: An Oliver Stone Film (soundtrack) *[album]*. *Elektra Entertainment, 61047-1 (European release only), March 1991.*
    Side 1: The Movie; Riders On The Storm; Love Street; Break On Through; The End

Side 2: Light My Fire; Ghost Song; Roadhouse Blues; Heroin (performed by Velvet Underground & Nico); Carmina Burana: Introduction (performed by Atlanta Symphony Orchestra and Chorus, conducted by Robert Shaw); Stoned Immaculate; When The Music's Over; The Severed Garden (Adagio); L.A. Woman

The Doors: An Oliver Stone Film (soundtrack) *[CD]. Elektra Entertainment, 61047-2, March 1991.*
The Doors: An Oliver Stone Film (soundtrack) *[cassette], 61047-4.*

In Concert *[3 albums]. Elektra/Asylum Records, 7559-61082-1 (European release only), May 1991. [Compilation of the live recordings from Absolutely Live, Alive, She Cried, and Live At The Hollywood Bowl.]*
Side 1: House Announcer; Who Do You Love; Medley – Alabama Song/Back Door Man/Love Hides/Five To One; Build Me A Woman
Side 2: When The Music's Over; Universal Mind; Petition The Lord with Prayer; Medley – Dead Cats Dead Rats/Break On Through #2
Side 3: The Celebration Of The Lizard; Soul Kitchen
Side 4: Roadhouse Blues; Gloria; Light My Fire (including Graveyard Poem)
Side 5: You Make Me Real; Texas Radio & The Big Beat; Love Me Two Times; Little Red Rooster; Moonlight Drive
Side 6: Close To You; The Unknown Soldier; The End
In Concert *[2 disc CD]. Elektra/Asylum Records, 61082-2, May 1991. [Compilation of the live recordings from Absolutely Live, Alive, She Cried, and Live At The Hollywood Bowl.]*
Disc 1: sides 1, 2 & 3 of triple album
Disc 2: sides 4, 5 & 6 of triple album
In Concert *[cassette], 61082-4.*

# MANZAREK

Manzarek, Ray. The Golden Scarab (A Rhythm Myth)
*[album]. Mercury Records, SRM 1-703, 1974.*
    Side 1: He Can't Come Today; Solar Boat; Downbound Train;
The Golden Scarab
    Side 2: The Purpose Of Existence Is?; The Moorish Idol; Chose
Up And Choose Off; Oh Thou Precious Nectar Filled Form (or)
A Little Fart

Manzarek, Ray. The Whole Thing Started with Rock &
Roll Now It's Out of Control *[album]. Mercury Records,*
*SRM-1-1014, 1974.*
    Side 1: The Whole Thing Started With Rock & Roll Now It's Out
Of Control; The Gambler; Whirling Dervish; Begin The World
Again
    Side 2: I Wake Up Screaming; Art Deco Fandango; Bicentennial
Blues (Love It Or Leave It); Perfumed Garden

Nite City (Ray Manzarek, keyboards and vocals). Nite
City *[album]. 20th Century Records, T-528, 1977.*
    Side 1: Summer Eyes; Nite City; Love Will Make You Mellow;
Angel W/No Freedom
    Side 2: Midnight Queen; Bitter Sky Blue; Caught In A Panic; In
The Pyramid; Game Of Skill

Ray Manzarek's Nite City. Golden Days Diamond Nights
*[album]. 20th Century Fox Records, 6370 263, 1978 (W. Germany*
*pressing).*
    Side 1: Riding On The Wings Of Love; The Dreamer; Holy Music;
Ain't Got The Time
    Side 2: Die High; Blinded By Love; Barcelona; America

Manzarek, Ray. (Carl Orff's) Carmina Burana *[album].*

*A&M Records, SP-4945, 1983.*

Manzarek, Ray. 'The Dance (Tanz)'/'The Wounds Of Fate (Fortune Plango)' & 'Boiling Rage (Estuans Interius)' [from Carl Orff's *Carmina Burana*]. *33 1/3 extended, promotion, 1983. A&M Records, SP-17255.*

Manzarek, Ray. The Golden Scarab (A Rhythm Myth) *[CD]. PolyGram Records, 314 512 445-2, 1992. [Includes 3 cuts from The Whole Thing Started With Rock & Roll Now It's Out of Control.]*

McClure, Michael and Ray Manzarek. Love Lion *[CD]. Shanachie Entertainment Corp., 5006, 1993. McClure's poetry and Manzarek's musical accompaniment.*

# KRIEGER & DENSMORE

Butts Band. Butts Band *[album]. Blue Thumb Records, BTS-63.*
  Side 1: I Won't Be Alone Anymore; Baja Bass; Sweet Danger; Pop-A-Top
  Side 2: Be With Me; New Ways; Love Your Brother; Kansas City

Butts Band (with Robby Krieger and John Densmore). Hear & Now! [album]. *Blue Thumb Records, BTSD-6018, 1975.*
  Side 1: Get Up, Stand Up; Corner Of My Mind; Caught In The Middle; Everybody's Fool; Livin' And Dyin'
  Side 2: Don't Wake Up; If You Gotta Make A Fool Of Somebody; Feelin' So Bad; White House; Act Of Love

Krieger, Robbie. Robbie Krieger & Friends *[album]. Blue*

*Note, BN-LA564-H, 1977.*
Side 1: Gumpopper; Uptown; Every Day; Marilyn Monroe
Side 2: The Ally; Low Bottomy; Spare Changes; Big Oak Basin
Krieger, Robbie. Robbie Krieger & Friends *[CD]. World
Pacific (A Blue Note Label), CDP 7 96101 2, 1991.*

Krieger, Robby. Versions *[album]. Passport Records, PB 6017,
1982.*
Side 1: Tattooed Love Boys; Her Majesty (w/ Densmore on
drums & Manzarek on keyboards); East End, West End; Crystal
Ship (w/Densmore on drums & Manzarek on melodica); Street
Fighting Man
Side 2: Reach Out I'll Be There; Gavin Leggit; Underwater Fall;
I'm Gonna Tell On You (w/ Densmore on timbales); Harlem
Nocturne

The Krieger-Densmore Reggae Bonanza. 'Kinky
Reggae'/'Get Up Stand Up' *33 1/3 extended, promotion
copy, 1983. Rhino Records, RNTI 403. (Recorded in 1975.)*

Krieger, Robby. Robby Krieger *[album]. Cafe Records, CAFE
730, 1985. Mobile Fidelity Sound Lab, Original Master Recordings
series. w/ Arthur Barrow, Bruce Gary, Don Preston.*
 Side 1: Bag Lady; Reggae Funk; Bass Line Street
 Side 2: Costa Brava; Noisuf

Krieger, Robby. Robby's Hobby. *33 1/3 extended. Macola
Record Co., MRC-0928, 1986.*
 Side 1: Nasti Kinki (short radio mix); Nasti Kinki (radio mix)
 Side 2: Nasti Kinki (dance version); Nasti Kinki (instrumental)

Krieger, Robby. No Habla *[album]. I.R.S., IRS-80024, 1989.*
Krieger, Robby. No Habla *[CD]. I.R.S., IRSD-80024, 1989.*
 Wild Child; Eagles Song; It's Gonna Work Out Fine; Lonely

Teardrops; Love It Or Leave It; The Big Hurt (Dolores); Piggy's Song; I Want You, I Need You, I Love You; You're Lost Little Girl

Krieger, Robby. Door Jams *[CD]. I.R.S. (International Record Syndicate, Inc.), IRSD-82014, 1989.*
Gavin Leggit; East End, West End; Her Majesty; Reach Out, I'll Be There; I'm Gonna Tell On You; Spare Changes; Big Oak Basin; Reggae Funk; Crystal Ship; Underwater Fall; Bass Line Street; Bag Lady; Low Bottomy; The Ally

Robby Krieger Organization. RKO Live! *[CD] Albany, NY: One Way Records, Inc., 1995.*
Revelation; Back Door Man; Blue Note Shuffle; Spanish Caravan/Spain; Riders On The Storm; So What; African Daisy; Gavin Leggit; Light My Fire

# OTHER NOTEWORTHY RECORDNGS

Mike Curb & The Waterfall. The Doors Songbook *[album]. Forward Records Corp., ST-F-1020.*
Side 1: Break On Through; Crystal Ship; Hello I Love You; Love Me Two Times; Light My Fire
Side 2: People Are Strange; Touch Me; Love Street; Unknown Soldier

Various artists. *Elektra/Asylum September Releases [double album]. Elektra/Asylum Records, EK-PROMO-21. 'Light My Fire' (6:50) is #5 on side 3. Some of the other songs included are David Gates, 'Clouds' and 'Sail Around The World'; Queen, 'Liar' (off debut album); Jackson Browne, 'These Times You've Come' and 'Redneck Friend'; and Linda Ronstadt, 'Love Has No Pride' and 'Sail Away'*

Various artists. 12 Terrific Tunes *(Elektra/Asylum Sampler)* *[album]. Elektra/Asylum Records, PROMO 1/79 STEREO, 1979. 'Roadhouse Blues' (off of* An American Prayer*) is #6 on side 1.*

Apocalypse Now (Original Motion Picture Soundtrack) *[double album]. Francis Ford Coppola, director. Elektra, DP-90001, 1979. 'The End' is #1 on side 1.*

Guitar Speak *[CD]. No Speak, X2 0777 7 13193 27, 1988. Last track is 'Strut-A-Various' by Robby Krieger.*

Various artists. Requiem For The Americas: Songs From The Lost World *[album]. Produced by Jonathan Elias. Enigma, 7 73354-1, 1989. 'The Journey' and 'The Chant Movement', poetry readings by Jim Morrison, #1 and #2 on side 2.*
Various artists. Requiem For The Americas: Songs From the Lost World *[CD]. Enigma, 73354-2.*

Rock Concert: 'Rock Stars Live!' Volume 1. *Carrere Music (Time-Warner Company), 9548-31216-2, 1992. Track 14 is 'Love Me Two Times'*

Rock And Roll Hall Of Fame *[CD]. DPRO-04676 (not for sale). Compilation by Gregg Geller, Rock and Roll Hall of Fame Foundation Inc. (Eighth Annual Induction Dinner. Tuesday, January 12th, 1993. The Century Plaza Hotel, Los Angeles.) Includes 'Light My Fire' and 'Break On Through' performed by 3 surviving Doors and Eddie Vedder of Pearl Jam.*

# RADIO & TELEVISION SPECIALS

The Classic Artist Series: The Doors, A Tribute To Jim Morrison *(3 hours)*. *Colorado Springs, CO: Unistar, aired 14-16 June 1991. (Repacking of The Doors 25th Anniversary Radio Special, aired 20-22 April 1990, host: Ed Sciaky.)*

Classic Call: The Doors (2 hours). *Hollywood, CA: Premier Radio Network, aired week of 14 September 1987. Host: Billy Juggs.*

Classic Cuts *(individual 1 hour shows) New York: MJI Broadcasting.*
Week of 11 May 1992: *first 10 minutes, Ray Manzarek with 'Hello, I Love You' and 'Back Door Man';*
Week of 31 August 1992: *first 10 minutes, Ray Manzarek with 'L.A. Woman';*
Week of 26 October 1992: *last 8-9 minutes, Ray Manzarek with 'Riders On The Storm';*
Week of 28 December 1992: *last 10 minutes, Ray Manzarek with 'Break On Through' and 'The WASP (Texas Radio And The Big Beat)';*
Week of 11 January 1993: *first 11-12 minutes, Ray Manzarek with 'Love Me Two Times' and 'Roadhouse Blues';*
Week of 22 March 1993: *last 8 minutes, Ray Manzarek with 'Touch Me' and 'Hello, I Love You'*

The Continuous History Of Rock And Roll: The Doors Profile *(2 hours). Show #32. New York: Rolling Stone Magazine Productions, aired 15-16 May 1982.*

The Doors: From The Inside With Jac Holzman *(6 hours). Valley Isle Productions Ltd. and Media America, Inc., 1988. Produced by Sandy Gibson.*

THE DOORS – Setting The Record Straight *(7 hours). Culver City, CA: Westwood One.*
  *Show #91-42 (1 hour), aired week of 14 October 1991;*
  *Show #91-43 (1 hour), aired week of 21 October 1991;*

*Show #91-44 (1 hour), aired week of 28 October 1991;*
*Show #91-45 (1 hour), aired week of 4 November 1991;*
*Show #91-46 (1 hour), aired week of 11 November 1991;*
*Show #91-47 (1 hour), aired week of 18 November 1991;*
*Show #91-48 (4 hours), aired week of 25 November 1991.*

The Doors Special *(1 hour). Show # 164. New York: MJI Broadcasting, aired week of 12 February 1990.*

The Doors 25th Anniversary Radio Special *(3 hours). New York: Unistar, aired 20-22 April 1990. Host: Ed Sciaky.*

The Doors: Wanted Dead Or Alive *(2 hours). Culver City, CA: Westwood One, aired week of 24 June 1985.*

Goodnight America *(ABC-TV midnight specials). 1 May 1974.*

History of Rock 'n' Roll (personal tape recording). *Aired 29 April 1978, WOWO Radio, 1190 AM, Fort Wayne, IN.*

In Concert – The Doors: Live In Seattle *(2 hours). Show #91-50. Culver City, CA: Westwood One, aired week of 9 December 1991.*

The 'In' Sound (U.S. Army radio broadcasts). *These were 25 minute shows; the following broadcasts included 5-minute interviews with Ray Manzarek: 3 July 1967; 10 July 1967; 16 October 1967; 23 October 1967; 15 January 1968.*

In the Studio: 'The Doors', THE DOORS *(1 hour). Show # 135. Burbank, CA: Album Network and Bullet Productions, aired week of 21 January 1991. Host: Ray Manzarek.*

In the Studio: 'The Doors, L.A. WOMAN *(1 hour). Show #146. Burbank, CA: Album Network and Bullet Productions, aired week of 8 April 1991. Host: Ray Manzarek.*

In the Studio: 'The Doors, STRANGE DAYS *(1 hour). Show # 145. Burbank, CA: Album Network and Bullet Productions, aired week of 1 April 1991. Host: Ray Manzarek.*

Inner View: The Doors – Part 1 *(1 hour). Series #14, Show #1. Beverly Hills, CA: Inner View, 1976. Host: Jim Ladd.*

Inner View: The Doors – Part 2 *(1 hour). Series #14, Show #2. Beverly Hills, CA: Inner View, 1976. Host: Jim Ladd.*

Inner View: The Doors – Part 3 *(1 hour). Series #14, Show #3. Beverly Hills, CA: Inner View, 1976. Host: Jim Ladd.*

Inner View: The Doors – Part 4 *(1 hour). Series #14, Show #4. Beverly Hills, CA: Inner View, 1976. Host: Jim Ladd.*

The Inner View: No One Here Gets Out Alive: The Doors Story *(4 hours). Aired 1979. Host: Jim Ladd.*

Legends Of Rock 1987: The Legend Of The Doors, Part One *(2 hours). NBC Radio Entertainment, aired week of 7-13 December 1987.*

Legends Of Rock 1987: The Legend Of The Doors, Part Two *(2 hours). NBC Radio Entertainment, aired week of 14-20 December 1987.*

Legends Of Rock 1989: The Legend Of The Doors, Part One *(2 hours). NBC Radio Entertainment, aired week of 20-26 November 1989. (Repacked repeat of 1987 special.)*

Legends Of Rock 1989: The Legend Of The Doors, Part Two *(2 hours). NBC Radio Entertainment, aired week of 27 November - 3 December 1989. (Repacked repeat of 1987 special.)*

Off The Record Special – Featuring: The Doors *(1 hour). Show #91-12. Culver City, CA: Westwood One, aired in March 1991 (repeated week of 16 December 1991). Host: Mary Turner.*

Pioneers In Music: The Doors *(1 hour). Show #37. New York:*

*D.I.R. Broadcasting Corp., aired week of 31 March 1986.*

Profiles In Rock: Jim Morrison & The Doors *(1 hour). Program # PRB-802-9. Studio City, CA: Watermark, aired 31 May - 1 June 1980.*

Rock & Roll Never Forgets – 'Jim Morrison' *(5 hours). Culver City, CA: Westwood One, aired week of 25 July 1983.*

Rock Scope: Jim Morrison & The Doors *(2 hours). Sacramento, CA: Sangre Productions, 1981.*

Royalty Of Rock: Doors I *(1 hour). New York: RKO Radio Networks, 1983.*

Royalty Of Rock: Doors II *(1 hour). New York: RKO Radio Networks, 1983.*

The Source: The Doors Special *(2 hours). Show #NBC 81-9. New York: NBC Radio's Young Adult Network, aired 4-6 December 1981.*

The Source: The Doors Special Encore *(3 hours). Show #NBC 82-23. New York: NBC Radio's Young Adult Network, aired 2-4 July 1982.*

Supergroups Presents 'Light My Fire': commemorating the 20th anniversary of The Doors *(3 hours). Los Angeles: ABC Rock Radio Network, aired 20-25 May 1987. Hosts: Ray Manzarek, John Densmore, Robbie Krieger; produced by Denny Somach Productions.*

Superstar Concert Series – The Doors *(1 1/2 hour). Show #91-27. Culver City, CA: Westwood One, aired 6-7 June 1991.*

Superstar Concert Series – The Doors In Vancouver BC *(1 1/2 hour). Show #91-49. Culver City, CA: Westwood One, aired 7-8 December 1991. Repackaged as Superstar Concert Series – The Doors IN Vancouver – 1970 (1 1/2 hour), show #92-27, aired weekend of 4-5 July 1992.*

'Three Hours For Magic': The Jim Morrison Special *(3 hours)*. *New York: London Wavelength, 1981. Frank Lisciandro; produced by Jon Sargent.*

'Three Hours for Magic': Jim Morrison. *1-sided promo disc of radio special produced by Jon Sargent and distributed by London Wavelength, New York City.*

A 20th Anniversary Salute To The Doors (2 hours). *New York: Radio International, aired 10-26 April 1987. Host: Robby Krieger; produced by Jon Sargent.*

UP CLOSE: The Doors *(2 hours). Media America Radio, Near Perfect Productions, 1994.*

# VIDEOS & FILMS

The Best Of 60s (video of various footage and of the complete NET show, *Critique*, on The Doors). (No acknowledged label.)

Beyond The Doors (fictional drama of Jimi Hendrix, Janis Joplin, Jim Morrison). Unicorn Video, Inc., 1989.

Break On Through (3-minute promotional film). Los Angeles: Elektra Records, 1966.

The Doors. A Feast Of Friends (40-minute documentary film). Los Angeles, 1969.

The Doors (video of footage from concert in Stockholm 1968, BBC special *Doors Are Open*, Doors' film *Feast of Friends*, and *Beat Club*). (No acknowledged label.)

The Doors: A Tribute To Jim Morrison. Burbank, CA: Warner Home Video, Inc., 1982.

The Doors: An Oliver Stone Film. Van Nuys, CA: LIVE Home Video, 1991.

The Doors Are Open: The Roundhouse, London, Sept. 1968. Douglas Music Video (manufactured and distributed by Warner Reprise Video, a division of Warner Bros. Records), reproduction of BBC show first broadcasted on 17 December 1968 by Granada Television International Limited.

The Doors: Dance On Fire. Universal City, CA: MCA Home Video, 1985.

The Doors: Light My Fire [video single]. New York: A*Vision Entertainment, 1988.

The Doors: Live At The Hollywood Bowl. Universal City, CA: MCA Home Video, 1987.

The Doors: Live In Europe 1968. New York: HBO Video, 1988.

The Doors: The Soft Parade, A Retrospective. Universal City, CA: MCA Home Video, 1991.

McClure, Michael and Ray Manzarek. Love Lion. New York: Mystic Fire Video, 1991.

Morrison, Jim, Frank Lisciandro, and Paul Ferrara. HWY (50-minute film). Los Angeles, 1969.

The Unknown Soldier (3-minute promotional film). Los Angeles: Elektra Records, 1968.

# SELECTED BIBLIOGRAPHY OF WORKS CITED

'Albums' (review of Morrison Hotel). *Fusion* (Boston), 1 May 1970, p. 20.

'Archies' 'Jingle, Jingle' Wins 'Em a Gold Disk; Doors Cop 5th Straight' *Variety*, 4 March 1970, p. 43.

Bangs, Lester. 'Jim Morrison: Bozo Dionysus a Decade Later' *Musician*, August 1981, pp. 40-45.

Bangs, Lester. 'Jim Morrison, Oafus Laureate' *Creem Special Edition: The Doors*, Summer 1981, pp. 24, 29.

Bangs, Lester. 'Morrison Hotel' (record review). *Rolling Stone*, 30 April 1970, p. 53.

Book Review Digest: Sixty-Second Annual Cumulation (March 1965 to February 1966). Josephine Samudio, ed. New York: The H.W. Wilson Company, 1966. 'Farina, Richard: Been Down So Long It Looks Like Up To Me' on pp. 360-61.

Book Review Digest: Fifty-Ninth Annual Cumulation (March 1963 to February 1964). Dorothy P. Davison, ed. New York: The H.W. Wilson Company, 1964. 'Rechy, John: City Of Night' on p. 837.

Brecht, Bertolt. *Gesammelte Werke* (19 volume work published in German). *Frankfurt am Main*, 1967; Band 2 contains, 'Aufstieg und Fall der Stadt Mahagonny'.

Brecht, Bertolt. The Rise And Fall Of The City Of Mahagonny. Translated by W.H. Auden and Chester Kallman, original trans. 1960. Boston: David R. Godine, 1976.

Burt, Rob and Patsy North, ed. West Coast Story. London: Phoebus Publishing Company, 1977. (Published in U.S.A. by Chartwell Books

Inc., Secausuc, NJ.) (Entry on The Doors, pp. 38-42.)

Chorush, Bob. 'The Lizard King reforms: taking the snake and wearing it; An interview with Jim Morrison' *Los Angeles Free Press*, 15 January 1971, pp. 23-24.

Cline, Rob. 'Record Reviews' (*The Soft Parade*). *Northwest Passage* (Bellingham, WA), 19 August 1969, p. 20.

Cohen, Mitchell. 'Remembering Morrison' *Fusion*, June 1974, pp. 18-19.

Cohn, Nik. *Rock From The Beginning*. New York: Stein and Day, 1969. (The Doors are discussed on pp. 235-36.)

*Contemporary Literary Criticism*. Edited by Sharon R. Gunton. 'Morrison, Jim: 1943-1971' on pp. 285-96, Vol. 17. Detroit: Gale Research Company, 1981.

*Contemporary Authors*. Edited by Francis Carol Locher. 'Morrison, James Douglas: 1943-1971' on pp. 450-52, Vols. 73-76. Detroit: Gale Research Company, 1978.

Cott, Jonathan. 'Doors, Airplane in Middle Earth' *Rolling Stone*, 26 October 1968, pp. 1, 12.

'Curb Inks Morrison In New Now Artist-To-Film Movie' *Billboard*, 2 May 1970, p. 3.

Cuscuna, Michael. 'Behind The Doors' *Down Beat*, 28 May 1970, pp. 13, 32.

Dalton, David and Lenny Kaye. Rock 100. New York: Grosset & Dunlap, Publishers, 1977. (Entry on The Doors, pp. 163-66.)

Densmore, John. Riders On The Storm: My Life With Jim

Morrison And The Doors. New York: Delacorte Press, 1990.

Didion, Joan. 'Waiting for Morrison' *The Saturday Evening Post*, 20 January 1969, p. 16.

DiMartino, Dave. 'Morrison In Miami: Flesh And Memories' *Creem Special Edition: The Doors*, Summer 1981, pp. 30-32.

The Doors. The Doors/Complete (songbook). Leo Alfassy, piano arrangements. New York: Music Sales Corporation, 1970. Includes reprint of 'Stage Doors' by Harvey Perr as introduction.

The Doors. Morrison Hotel (songbook). Herbert Wise, ed.; Leo Alfassy, piano arrangments. New York: Music Sales Corporation, 1970.

'The Doors' (record review of *Waiting For The Sun*). Harbinger (Toronto), August 1968, p. 21.

Farina, Richard. Been Down So Long It Looks Like Up To Me. New York: Dell Publishing Co., Inc. (paperback version of Random House hardbook, 1966), 1967.

Farina, Richard. Long Time Coming And A Long Time Gone. New York: Random House, 1969.

Fornatale, Pete. 'Strange Days: Doors' Organist Ray Manzarek' *Musician*, August 1981, pp. 46-51, 60.

Fowlie, Wallace. Rimbaud. Chicago: The University of Chicago Press, 1965 (First Phoenix Edition [paperback], 1967). This is a rewrite of two earlier works, Rimbaud: The Myth of Childhood and Rimbaud's Illuminations.

Fowlie, Wallace. Rimbaud And Jim Morrison: The Rebel As Poet. Durham, NC: Duke University Press, 1993 & 1994.

Francis, Miller, Jr. 'callin' on the gods' (review of *The Soft Parade*). *The Great Speckled Bird* (Atlanta), 20 October 1969, p. 18.

Franklin V, Benjamin and Duane Schneider. *Anais Nin: An Introduction*. Athens, OH: Ohio University Press, 1979.

Garbarini, Vic. 'Blues for a Shaman: Doors' Producer Paul Rothschild (sic)' *Musician*, August 1981, pp. 52-57.

Gerstenmeyer, Heinz. Jim Morrison And The Doors: Die Songtexte der Studio-LPs (English lyrics to studio albums). Munchen, Germany: Schirmer/Mosel, 1992.

Gilmore, Mikal. 'The Legacy Of Jim Morrison And The Doors' *Rolling Stone*, 4 April 1991, pp. 30-31, 33-34, 62.

Goldstein, Richard, ed. The Poetry Of Rock. New York: Bantam Books, 1969 (first published 1968). ('Twentieth Century Fox', p. 85; 'Horse Latitudes', p. 142; 'The End', pp. 143-44.)

Griffin, Lloyd W. (book review of John Rechy's City Of Night). *Library Journal*, July 1963, pp. 2228-29.

Halpert, Stephen. 'GET BACK: The Doors Are Closed' *Fusion* (Boston), 20 March 1970, p. 38.

Hendrickson, Mark. 'The Doors: The Legend Lives On...And On' (interview with Ray Manzarek). *Only Music*, December 1987, pp. 32-35, 53.

Hibbard, Don J. with Carol Kaleialoha. The Role Of Rock. Englewood Cliffs, NJ: Prentice-Hall, Inc., 1983.

Hopkins, Jerry. The Lizard King: The Essential Jim Morrison. New York: Charles Scribner's Sons, 1992.

Hopkins, Jerry. 'The Rolling Stone Interview: Jim Morrison'

*Rolling Stone*, 26 July 1969, pp. 15-24.

Hopkins, Jerry and Danny Sugerman. No One Here Gets Out Alive. New York: Warner Books, Inc., 1980.

Houghton, Rob. 'L.A. Woman' (record review). *Creem Special Edition: The Doors*, Summer 1981, p. 54.

Hunter, Ross. 'Sounds: Strange Doors' (record review of Strange Days). *IT (International Times*, London), 5-19 January 1968, p. 12.

Jackson, Blair. 'Paul Rothchild: The Doors' Producer Recalls The Agony And The Ecstasy Of Working With The Doors' *BAM*, 3 July 1981, pp. 18-20, 25.

Jahn, Mike. Jim Morrison And The Doors (an unauthorized book). New York: Grosset & Dunlap, 1969.

James, Lizze. 'Jim Morrison: Ten Years Gone' *Creem Special Edition: The Doors*, Summer 1981, pp. 16-23.

Jilek, Ed. 'Records' *The Paper* (Michigan State University, East Lansing, MI.), 9 May 1967, p. 12.

Johnson, Pete. 'Doors Rattle Hinges At Whiskey-A-Go-Go' *Los Angeles Times*, 18 May 1967, Part IV, p. 13.

Johnson, Pete. 'Popular Records: Latest Stones Album Best Yet' *Los Angeles Times*, Calender section, 26 February 1967, p. 30. (Includes record review of *The Doors* under the subtitle, 'Doors Open Up')

Kapor, Mitch. 'Soft Parade' (record review). *View From The Bottom* (New Haven, CN), 7 August 1969, p. 13.

Kennely, Patricia. 'Pop Record Reviews: The Doors, Morrison

Hotel' *Jazz & Pop*, May 1970, pp. 54-55.

Kennely, Patricia. 'Pop Record Reviews: The Doors, The Soft Parade' *Jazz & Pop*, October 1969, pp. 40-41.

Kerouac, Jack. On The Road. New York: Penguin Books, 1976 (first published New York: Viking Compass Editin, 1959; copyrighted Jack Kerouac, 1955, 1957).

Kordosh, J. 'Soft Parade' (record review). *Creem Special Edition: The Doors*, Summer 1981, p. 51.

Kordosh, J. 'Strange Days' (record review). *Creem Special Edition: The Doors*, Summer 1981, pp. 48, 51.

Krieger, Robby. 'Take It As It Comes' (reprint of Manzarek handwritten sheet music of song). *The Doors Quarterly Magazine*, Issue 32, June 1995, pp. 29.

KT. 'Records' (review of The Soft Parade). *Octopus* (Ottawa, Canada), vol. 2-11 (1969), p. 26.

Lacey, Maybelle. (Book review of Richard Farina's Been Down So Long It Looks Like Up To Me). *Library Journal*, 1 April 1966, p. 1924.

Laurence, Paul. 'Ray Manzarek' (interview). *Audio*, December 1983, pp. 40-45.

Lisciandro, Frank. Jim Morrison: An Hour For Magic. New York: Delilah Communications Ltd., 1982.

Lisciandro, Frank. Morrison: A Feast Of Friends. New York: Warner Books, Inc., 1991.

Lowe, Steven. 'The Lighter Side/The Doors: Strange Days'

(record review). *High Fidelity Magazine*, January 1968, p. 98.

Ludlow, Liz and Jesse Nash. 'Robbie Krieger' (interview). Masters Of Rock: The Life And Times Of Jim Morrison, Winter 1990, Vol. 1, No. 3, pp. 21-23.

Mangelsdorff, Rich. 'Doors Stuck?' (record review of *Waiting For The Sun*). *Kaleidoscope* (Milwaukee), 23 August - 12 September 1968, p. 6.

Mangelsdorff, Rich. 'Music Wheel' (record review of *The Soft Parade*). *Kaleidoscope* (Milwaukee), 12-25 September 1969, p. 15.

Marsh, Dave. 'Morrison Hotel – The Doors' (record review). *Creem* (Detroit), vol. 2, no. 10 (February 1970), p. 25.

Matheu, Robert. 'Through The Doors Again: Manzarek, Krieger And Densmore Today' *Creem Special Edition: The Doors*, Summer 1981, pp. 56-66.

Miller, Jim, ed. The Rolling Stone Illustrated History Of Rock & Roll. New York: Rolling Stone Press, 1976. (Entry on The Doors by Lester Bangs, pp. 262-63.)

'Morrison Hotel' (record review). *Amazing Grace* (Tallahassee), vol. 1, no. 5 (1970), p. 12.

Morrison, Jim. The American Night: The Writings Of Jim Morrison, Volume II. New York: Vintage Books, 1990.

Morrison, Jim. 'Anatomy Of Rock' *Jazz & Pop*, September 1970, pp. 18-19.

Morrison, Jim. 'from DRY WATER' *The Los Angeles IMAGE*, 3-16 October 1970, p. 20.

Morrison, Jim. Jim Morrison's An American Prayer. Baton Rouge: B of A Company, Louisiana, 1984.

Morrison, Jim. 'Jim Morrison Raps..' eye, October 1968, pp. 53-55.

Morrison, Jim. 'Jim Morrison's Tribute To Brian Jones' *Datebook*, November 1969, pp. 15-17.

Morrison, Jim. The Lords & The New Creatures. New York: Simon and Schuster, Touchstone Book edition, 1971 paperback edition of 1970 printing.

Morrison, Jim. The Lords & The New Creatures. New York: Simon and Schuster, First Fireside Edition, 1987.

Morrison, Jim. 'The Lost Writings Of Jim Morrison' (excerpts from *Wilderness: The Lost Writings Of Jim Morrison*). *Rolling Stone*, 6 October 1988, pp. 69-70.

Morrison, Jim. (opening lines to 'Soft Parade'). The Los Angeles IMAGE, 3-16 October 1969, p. 8.

Morrison, Jim. 'poems from DRY WATER' *ROCK*, 2 February 1970, p. 4.

Morrison, Jim. Reproduction of personal letter to Dave Marsh, editor of *Creem*. The Doors Collectors Magazine, Spring 1994 (Issue #4), pp. 28-33.

Morrison, Jim. 'Sounds For Your Soul' (reprint poem from *The Doors Program Book*). 16 Spec, Summer 1968, p. 54.

Morrison, Jim. Wilderness: The Lost Writings Of Jim Morrison, Volume I. New York: Villard Books, 1988.

Nietzsche, Friedrich. The Birth Of Tragedy & The Genealogy

Of Morals. Translated by Francis Golffin. New York: Doubleday Anchor Books, 1956.

Nin, Anais. A Spy In The House Of Love. New York: Pocket Books (a division of Simon & Schuster), 1994 (first published Chicago: The Swallow Press Inc., 1959; copyrighted Anais Nin, 1954).

Nin, Anais. A Woman Speaks: The Lectures, Seminars, And Interviews Of Anais Nin. Edited by Evelyn J. Hinz. Chicago: The Swallow Press Inc., 1975.

Nirkind, Bob (Turk). 'The Doors – Follow Them Down' (record review of *The Soft Parade*). *The South End* (Wayne State, Detroit), 21 August 1969, p. 8.

Noname, Hugh. 'Doors: LA Woman' (record review). *IT* (*International Times*, London), 26 August – 9 September 1971, p. 18.

'Opening The Doors' (review of WOR-Stereo's Birthday Anniversary Rock Show at the Village Theatre). *The East Village Other* (New York), 1-15 July 1967, p. 11.

Parmalee, Patty Lee. Brecht's America. Salt Lake City, Utah: no publisher, 1970 (an unpublished literary study, 2 volumes, 493 pages, located in libraries of Indiana University).

Paul, Alan. 'Strange Days' (interview with Krieger). *Guitar World*, March 1994, pp. 58-62, 64, 66, 68, 112, 186, 189.

Perr, Harvey. 'Stage Doors' (concert review). *Los Angeles Free Press*, 8 August 1969, p. 26.

Pichaske, David R. The Poetry Of Rock: The Golden Years. Peoria, IL: The Ellis Press, 1981. (Chapter 5 on The Doors on pp. 75-84.)

Pielke, Robert G. You Say You Want A Revolution: Rock Music In American Culture. Chicago: Nelson-Hall, 1986.

Porter, Katherine Anne. Ship Of Fools. *Boston: An Atlantic Monthly Press Book* (Little, Brown and Company), 1962.

Powledge, Fred. 'Wicked Go The Doors' *Life*, 12 April 1968, pp. 86A, 86B, 89-94.

Reabur, Chris. 'Morrison Hotel Revisited' *Jazz & Pop*, September 1970, pp. 20-24. 'Chris Reabur' was a pseudonym for Bruce Harris.

Rechy, John. City Of Night. New York: Grover Press, Inc., 1963.

'Records 70' *Fusion* (Boston), 22 January 1971, p. 24.

Riegel, Richard. 'Tongues Of Knowledge In The Feathered Night (The Blue Bus Is Double Parked): The Doors On Record' *Creem Special Edition: The Doors*, Summer 1981, pp. 8-15.

Rimbaud, Arthur. Rimbaud: Complete Works, Selected Letters. Translation, Introduction and Notes by Wallace Fowlie. Chicago: The University of Chicago Press, 1966.

Rimbaud, Arthur. A Season In Hell And The Illuminations. Translated by Enid Rhodes Peschel. New York: Oxford University Press, 1973.

Rompers, Terry. 'Looking Through The Doors' *Trouser Press*, September/October 1980, front cover, pp. 1-4. (Fold-up tabloid so that front cover is half of last page.)

ROLLING STONE / Rock Almanac: The Chronicles Of Rock & Roll. New York: Collier Books, 1983.

Root, Robert L., Jr. 'A Listener's Guide To The Rhetoric Of

Popular Music' *Journal Of Popular Culture*, Summer 1986, pp. 15-26.

Roxon, Lillian. Rock Encyclopedia. New York: Grosset & Dunlop, 1969. (Entry on The Doors, pp. 150-53.)

Ruby, Jay. 'Pop Record Reviews: The Doors, Waiting For The Sun' *Jazz & Pop*, December 1968, pp. 56-57.

Schlesinger, Arthur Jr. 'Movies' (review of Antonioni's Zabriskie Point). Vogue, 1 April 1970, pp. 116, 118.

Somma, Robert. 'Banging Away At The Doors Of Convention' *Crawdaddy*, October 1968, pp. 17-20.

'Spotlight Singles: Top 60 Pop Spotlight' (Doors – 'You Make Me Real'). *Billboard*, 4 April 1970, p. 60.

Stambler, Irwin. Encyclopedia Of Pop, Rock, & Soul. New York: St. Martin's Press, 1974. (Entry on The Doors, pp. 166-69.)

Stevenson, Salli. 'An Interview With Jim Morrison' (Part I). *Circus*, January 1971, pp. 42-45.

Sugerman, Danny. 'A Shaman's Journey Through The Doors' *Creem Special Edition: The Doors*, Summer 1981, pp. 37-38.

Sugerman, Danny, ed. The Doors: The Complete Illustrated Lyrics. New York: Hyperion, 1991.

Sugerman, Danny, ed. The Doors: The Complete Lyrics. New York: Delta Book (Dell Publishing of Bantam Doubleday Dell Publishing Group), 1992. Paperback version with revisions of *The Doors: The Complete Illustrated Lyrics* (Hyperion, 1991).

Sugerman, Danny and Benjamin Edmonds, eds. The DOORS: The Illustrated History. New York: William Morrow and Company, 1983.

Tobler, John. 'The doors In A nutshell; 64 Quick Questions'

(interview with 3 Doors). *ZigZag*, September 1972 (No. 25), pp. 28-29.

Tobler, John. Interviews With The Four Doors On Opening The Doors Of Perception ('over one hour of rare and intriguing dialogue') [CD]. Raven, (RVCD-33), no date. Transcription of interview with Jim Morrison is printed in Jerry Hopkin's *The Lizard King: The Essential Jim Morrison*, see pp. 231-36.

'Top Singles Of The Week' (Doors...'Riders on the Storm'). 16 June 1971, p. 46.

Tosches, Nick. 'The Doors' *Fusion* (Boston), 25 June 1971, pp. 47-49.

Van Lustbader, Eric. 'Jim Morrison: Riding Out The Final Storm' *Circus*, September 1971, pp. 37-41. (Also Circus, 31 January 1981, pp. 24-30.)

Walley, David. 'The Elektra Company, Or How One Learns To Love The Bombs' *The East Village Other* (New York), 10 September 1969, p. 12.

Walls, Richard C. 'The Doors' (record review). *Creem Special Edition: The Doors*, Summer 1981, p. 48.

Walls, Richard C. 'Waiting For The Sun' (record review). *Creem Special Edition: The Doors*, Summer 1981, p. 51.

Whitcomb, Ian. Rock Odyssey: A Musician's Chronicle Of The Sixties. Garden City, New York: Dolphin Books, 1983. (Scattered references to The Doors; interesting account of Morrison on pp. 336-42.)

Williams, Paul. 'Music Without The Myth' *Rolling Stone*, 11 September 1981, p. 34.

Williams, Paul. 'Rock Is Rock: A Discussion Of A Doors Song' ('Soul Kitchen'). *Crawdaddy*, May 1967, pp. 42-46.

Williams, Paul. 'Rothchild Speaks' (interview). *Crawdaddy*, July/August 1967, pp. 18-25.

Youngblood, Gene. 'Doors Reaching For Outer Limits Of Inner Space' (record review of Strange Days). *Los Angeles Free Press*, 1 December 1967, pp. 6, 15.

Zevallos, Hank. 'Jim Morrison' (interview). *Poppin*, March 1970, pp. 46-53.

# chapter 10
# the scene:
## notes, stories & tidbits
## on the lyrics

In an attempt to outline the scene of the late 1960s in which The Doors recorded and released their music, the following information is broken into units corresponding to each of the six studio albums. The segment for each particular album includes the following information: notes, stories, tidbits, etc. on the individual songs of that album which include sales chart histories as recorded by BILLBOARD magazine; lists of concurrent popular albums and singles; yearly lists of best-sellers and other popular books; yearly lists of popular movies; American fall television programing (the start of a new American television season).

The various notes, stories, and other tidbits on the songs recorded by The Doors (with Jim Morrison) attempt to site possible sources or inspirations for lyrics, cross-reference lyrics and lines in the songs with other printed poetry by Jim Morrison, and discusses ambiguities.

The following were used as sources for the lyrics.

First and foremost, I relied upon the actual recordings, which I began trying to transcribe in the 1970s when I was an undergraduate in college and started researching for printed versions of the lyrics. To clarify fuzzy passages, I turned to live recordings, especially those on bootlegs. The printed lyrics on inner sleeves of albums and in the songbooks, *The Doors/Complete* (1970) and *Morrison Hotel* (1970), provided initial written formats, though these sources proved unreliable for accuracy.

Years later, Danny Sugerman edited *The Doors: The Complete Illustrated Lyrics* (Hyperion, hardback edition, 1991; Dell, paperback revised edition, 1992). Though the book provided verification of ambiguous passages and presented an enlightening edition of the lyrics with essays from that time period, it is not a thoroughly accurate transcription of the lyrics as recorded on the six studio albums. But this printed edition controls the copyrights of the lyrics and remains the sole resource (American published) of complete printed lyrics.

In 1993, I met Heinz Gerstenmeyer, a German who began in 1977 trying to transcribe the lyrics as The Doors had recorded them. In 1992, Heinz's book of the English lyrics for the studio albums, *Jim Morrison & The Doors: Die Songtexte Der Studio-LPs*, was published out of Germany, although it too has incongruous parts, many of which Heinz indicated were due to the demands by the previous copyrighted edition.

Nevertheless, Heinz's transcriptions and personal correspondences provided the most complete and challenging work to which to compare my transcriptions of Doors lyrics.

There probably can be no definite work that reproduces these lyrics with complete accuracy. Jim Morrison mumbled, screamed, slurred, dropped, and, as Heinz repeatedly has said, 'swallowed' words that cannot be transcribed; moreover, given the spontaneity of Morrison's artistic liberty, a handwritten lyric doesn't necessarily mean he sang it that way. Listeners should use discretion – and their own imaginations.


# ACKNOWLEDGEMENTS

As credited on Elektra recordings, all songs are written by The Doors (lyrics by Jim Morrison or, where noted, Robby Krieger) except: the songs on the fourth album, *The Soft Parade*, and the fifth album, *Morrison Hotel*, where individual songs were credited; 'Alabama Song', music by Kurt Weill and lyrics by Bertolt Brecht (Warner/Chappell Music ASCAP); 'Back Door Man', written by Willie Dixon (Hoochie Coochie Music BMI); 'Crawling King Snake', written by John Lee Hooker and Bernard Besman (LaCienega Music, BMI).

*Sources for poetry of Jim Morrison cited as cross references to the lyrics are:*

(1) Jim Morrison, *The Lords And The New Creatures* (poems) (New York: Simon and Schuster, Touchstone Book edition, 1971 paperback edition of 1970 printing);

(2) Jim Morrison, *Wilderness: The Lost Writings of Jim Morrison,* Volume I (New York: Villard Books, 1988);

(3) Jim Morrison, *The American Night: The Writings Of Jim Morrison,* Volume II (New York: Vintage Books, 1990);

(4) Frank Lisciandro, *Jim Morrison: An Hour For Magic* (New York: Delilah Communications Ltd., 1982).

*The texts used for printed versions of lyrics are as follows:*

(1) Heinz Gerstenmeyer, ed., *Jim Morrison & The Doors: Die Songtexte Der Studio-LPs* (English lyrics to studio albums) (Munchen, Germany: Schirmer/Mosel, 1992);

(2) Heinz Gerstenmeyer, personal correspondences;

(3) Danny Sugerman, ed., The Doors: The Complete Illustrated Lyrics (New York: Hyperion, 1991);

(4) Danny Sugerman, ed., *The Doors: The Complete Lyrics* (New York: Delta Book [Dell Publishing of Bantam Doubleday Dell Publishing Group], November 1992); paperback version with revisions of *The Doors: The Complete Illustrated Lyrics* (Hyperion, 1991);

(5) my own transcription and annotation of lyrics of The Doors' six studio albums.

Unless otherwise noted, any reference to *The Doors: The Complete Lyrics* is valid for the previous edition, *The Doors: The Complete Illustrated Lyrics.*

A comparison of several lyrical transcriptions in Jerry Hopkins and Danny Sugerman's *No One Here Gets Out Alive* (New York: Warner Books, Inc., 1980) to the later transcriptions in Danny Sugerman's edited *The Doors: The Complete Lyrics* reveals differences, which exemplify the uncertainty of trying to transcribed these lyrics – which is further indicated with differences in some of the lyrical transcriptions in John Densmore's *Riders On The Storm: My Life With Jim Morrison And The Doors* (New York: Delacorte Press, 1990).

Fred Baggen of The Netherlands is an adamant connoisseur of the bootlegs, and I am indebted to him for the information concerning lyrics that Morrison interjected on live recordings that I have not listened to.

The BILLBOARD chart information used in this book is copyright by BPI Communications Inc. and is used courtesy of BILLBOARD magazine.'BillboardR' is a registered trademark of BPI Communications.

THE DOORS [album].
*Elektra Records, EKL-74007 Mono, EKS-74007 Stereo, January 1967.*

Side 1:
Break On Through (To The Other Side)
Soul Kitchen
The Crystal Ship
Twentieth Century Fox
Alabama Song (Whisky Bar)
Light My Fire
Side 2:
Back Door Man
I Looked At You
End of the Night
Take It As It Comes
The End

Producer, Paul A. Rothchild
Production Supervisor, Jac Holzman
Engineer, Bruce Botnick
Additional Musicians: Larry Knechtal, bass

The Doors *[cassette]. TC5-4007.*
The Doors *[8-track tape]. ET8-4007.*
The Doors *[album]. Mobile Fidelity Sound Lab, MFSL 1-051, 1980.*
*Half-Speed Production & Mastering; Original Master Recording series.*
The Doors *[CD]. Elektra/Asylum Records, 74007-2,*

*November 1983.*
*[The version pressed by PolyGram in West Germany lists Robby*
*Krieger as "Bobby Krieger."]*
The Doors *[24KT Gold Plated CD]. DDC Compact Classics, Inc.*
*(Northridge, CA), GZS-1023, July 1992. (Pressed in Japan.)*

In a 1972 interview by John Tobler with the three surviving Doors, Krieger said that he wrote the lyrics for 'Light My Fire' and the rest of the songs were Morrison's lyrics (*ZigZag*, September 1972, p. 29).

November 1966 – according to John Densmore in *Riders On The Storm*, The Doors do recording and mixing sessions for THE DOORS at Sunset Sound Recording Studios in Los Angeles. September and October, according to Riordan & Prochnicky's *Break On Through*.

BILLBOARD's TOP LP'S

| | | | |
|---|---|---|---|
| Mar. 25, 1967 | #163 | Mar. 3 | # 63 |
| Apr. 1 | #153 | Apr. 6 | # 60 |
| Apr. 8 | #151 | Apr. 13 | # 52 |
| Apr. 15 | #128 | Apr. 20 | # 51 |
| Apr. 22 | #123 | Apr. 27 | # 49 |
| Apr. 29 | #118 | May 4 | # 49 |
| May 6 | #103 | May 11 | # 49 |
| May 13 | # 93 | May 18 | # 51 |
| May 20 | # 92 | May 25 | # 44 |
| May 27 | # 91 | June 1 | # 46 |
| June 3 | # 89 | June 8 | # 45 |
| June 10 | # 77 | June 15 | # 35 |
| June 17 | # 51 | June 22 | # 30 |
| June 24 | # 20 | June 29 | # 22 |
| July 1 | # 17 | July 6 | # 21 |
| July 8 | # 17 | July 13 | # 20 |
| July 15 | # 10 | July 20 | # 11 |
| July 22 | # 9 | July 27 | # 13 |
| July 29 | # 9 | Aug. 3 | # 14 |
| Aug. 5 | # 5 | Aug. 10 | # 15 |
| Aug. 12 | # 5 | Aug. 17 | # 17 |
| Aug. 19 | # 4 | Aug. 24 | # 20 |

| | | | | |
|---|---|---|---|---|
| Aug. 26 | # 4 | | Aug. 31 | # 20 |
| Sept. 2 | # 4 | | Sept. 7 | # 24 |
| Sept. 9 | # 4 | | Sept. 14 | # 27 |
| Sept. 16 | # 2 | | Sept. 21 | # 30 |
| Sept. 23 | # 2 | | Sept. 28 | # 27 |
| Sept. 30 | # 3 | | Oct. 5 | # 32 |
| Oct. 7 | # 3 | | Oct. 12 | # 32 |
| Oct. 14 | # 4 | | Oct. 19 | # 40 |
| Oct. 21 | # 4 | | Oct. 26 | # 40 |
| Oct. 28 | # 3 | | Nov. 2 | # 45 |
| Nov. 4 | # 3 | | Nov. 9 | # 47 |
| Nov. 11 | # 3 | | Nov. 16 | # 46 |
| Nov. 18 | # 4 | | Nov. 23 | # 67 |
| Nov. 25 | # 5 | | Nov. 30 | # 63 |
| Dec. 2 | # 5 | | Dec. 7 | # 68 |
| Dec. 9 | # 6 | | Dec. 14 | # 65 |
| Dec. 16 | # 11 | | Dec. 21 | # 60 |
| Dec. 23 | # 12 | | Dec. 28 | # 51 |
| Dec. 30 | # 23 | | Jan. 4, 1969 | # 49 |
| Jan. 6, 1968 | # 23 | | Jan. 11 | # 48 |
| Jan. 13 | # 30 | | Jan. 18 | # 51 |
| Jan. 20 | # 31 | | Jan. 25 | # 64 |
| Jan. 27 | # 35 | | Feb. 1 | # 93 |
| Feb. 3 | # 35 | | Feb. 8 | # 93 |
| Feb. 10 | # 47 | | Feb. 15 | #106 |
| Feb. 17 | # 53 | | Feb. 22 | #125 |
| Feb. 24 | # 50 | | Mar. 1 | #151 |
| Mar. 2 | # 50 | | Mar. 8 | #151 |
| Mar. 9 | # 50 | | Mar. 15, 1969 | #148 |
| Mar. 16 | # 51 | | Mar. 23 | # 59 |
| | | | | *out of charts* |

## BILLBOARD's TOP LP'S & TAPE

| | |
|---|---|
| Sept. 20, 1980 | #189 |
| Sept. 27 | #154 |

| | |
|---|---|
| Oct. 4 | #143 |
| Oct. 11 | #133 |
| Oct. 18 | #130 |
| Oct. 25 | #129 |
| Nov. 1 | #128 |
| Nov. 8 | #138 |
| Nov. 15 | #137 |
| Nov. 22 | #157 |
| Nov. 29 | #167 |
| Dec. 6 | #196 |
| Dec. 13 | #194 |
| Dec. 20 | #191 |
| Dec. 27 | #191 |
| Jan. 10, 1981 | #192 |

BREAK ON THROUGH
'Break On Through' b/w 'End Of The Night' was released by Elektra as a 45 rpm single (# 45611), January 1967.

BILLBOARD's HOT 100
Apr. 8, 1967 #126 (That's it!)

According to Densmore, Krieger stated that Paul Butterfield's 'Shake Your Money Maker' inspired the guitar melody for 'Break On Through' (*Riders On The Storm*, pp. 86-87). Densmore described the drumbeat he used as a fast bossa nova rhythm from Brazilian music (pp. 102-3).

In *The Lords And The New Creatures* (poems), Morrison writes about a door to "the other side" where the soul can free itself (p. 90). In *The American Night*, Morrison writes about going to morning's "other side" (p. 12). In the piece titled, 'The Celebration Of The Lizard', Morrison writes about releasing control and "breaking through" (*The American Night*, p. 41; and inside sleeve of the album, *Waiting For The Sun*).

Morrison no doubt read John Rechy's 1963 novel, *City Of Night*, and borrowed some of Rechy's imagery (see notes to song, 'L.A. Woman' on sixth album, *L.A. Woman*). The Rechy's nameless narrator uses the label, "the Other Side", to describe the sexual boundary of the

Hollywood world of hustling vagrants and wanderers where the most active members are confident that "unreciprocating vagrants and wanderers" who come to this hustling world will eventually "cross the sexual boundary that separates them now – and they wait almost vengefully for the crossing of that line – to the Other Side – their side" (pp. 200-201).

The recorded chorus, "She gets," omits a final word, high, which was censored from the studio version but which was often explicitly resounded in live recordings.

The imagery of the lyric about making the scene from week to week, day to day, and hour to hour is practically verbatim from Rechy's novel, *City Of Night*. The unnamed narrator of the story describes a scene with Pete, a familiar and street wise figure in the world of Times Square in New York City, who comments about shacking up with someone permanently to avoid the difficulties of hustling during the bitter cold of winter: "[Pete] added hurriedly, 'I dont dig that scene – I guess I'm too restless.' He made it, instead, from place to place, week to week, night to night" (p. 43).

## SOUL KITCHEN
Lyric as written by Jim Morrison is published in *The American Night* (pp. 101-102).

John Densmore, in his book *Riders On The Storm*, states the song was a tribute to Olivia's, a small soul food restaurant Morrison frequented during his stay on Venice Beach (p. 40). But Morrison probably intended to suggest the obvious sexual metaphor of warming his head next to her oven: of staying all night in her "soul kitchen" and warming his "mind" next to her "gentle stove".

In the first stanza, do the street lights share or shed their "hollow glow"? In *The Doors: The Complete Lyrics*, it is shed (p. 26). Densmore, in *Riders On The Storm*, transcribes the lyric with shed (p. 101). Gerstenmeyer, in a personal correspondence, argues that "shed" should be "share", but had to print shed in his book (p. 13). Part of Gerstenmeyer's argument is based on examining a Morrison handwritten copy of this lyric. In *The American Night*, the verb printed in the line is share (p. 101). Even after listening to live recordings, I still hear shed (shared?), though either word would fit within the context of the lyrics.

## THE CRYSTAL SHIP
'Light My Fire' b/w 'The Crystal Ship' was released by Elektra as a 45 rpm single (# 45615), April 1967.

In *Riders On The Storm*, Densmore stated that Morrison wrote this song "in the middle of breaking up with an early girlfriend" before the group had their first gig (p. 96).

## TWENTIETH CENTURY FOX
Given Morrison's admiration for the French poet Arthur Rimbaud, this lyric is a wonderful contrast to Rimbaud's "Venus Anadyomne" (see Wallace Fowlie's translation in *Rimbaud: Complete Works, Selected Letters*, p. 41).

## ALABAMA SONG (WHISKEY BAR)
(music by Kurt Weill (1900-1950), lyrics by Bertolt Brecht (1898-1965), Warner/Chappell Music ASCAP)

Lyrics were written in English and are printed in *Bertolt Brecht, Gesammelte Werke*, a 19 volume work published in German (Frankfurt am Main, 1967

Band 2, 'Aufstieg Und Fall Der Stadt Mahagonny', p. 504).

Brecht did not use "Whiskey Bar" as a subtitle for this song.

According to Manzarek in an interview with John Tobler of *ZigZag* magazine, the group was inspired by this song on an album he had of Brecht and Weill songs ("The Doors In A Nutshell; 64 Quick Questions", September 1972, p. 28). Densmore, in *Riders On The Storm*, wrote that he thought the song was "a bit odd" when Manzarek first played it to the group off the original cast album for Mahagonny, but realized its relevancy as the group began creating their own arrangement of the song (p. 78).

Jim Morrison sings the first stanza of the song, "Oh, show me the way / To the next whiskey bar", which is the way the lyric appears in Brecht's complete works and in W.H. Auden and Chester Kallman's translation, *The Rise And Fall Of The City Of Mahagonny*. The next stanza, Morrison sings, "Oh, show me the way/To the next little girl"; in Brecht's complete works the lyric is "pretty boy" and in Auden/Kallman's translation it is "Mister Right" (p. 34). Both Gerstenmeyer and Parmalee note that in the songplay, "Mahagonny", Brecht used "pretty girl" instead of "pretty boy" in the second stanza; but in the opera, *The Rise And Fall Of The City Of Mahagonny*, Brecht changed the lyric to "pretty boy" because the song is sung by the whores after they arrive in Mahagonny. A third stanza, which The Doors don't include, begins with the lyrics, "Oh, show us the way to the next little dollar!"

*The following is based on information from these sources:*

 – personal correspondences with Heinz Gerstenmeyer;
 – Bertolt Brecht, *The Rise And Fall Of The City Of Mahagonny* (Boston: David R. Godine, 1976; translated by W.H. Auden and Chester Kallman, original trans. 1960); Patty Lee Parmalee, Brecht's America (*Salt Lake City, Utah*: no publisher, 1970; unpublished literary study, 2 volumes, 493 pages, located in libraries of Indiana University).

Auden and Kallman wrote that The Rise and Fall of the City of Mahagonny "must offend and repel its audience" to succeed – by portraying how in a Paradise-city modern capitalism "destroys human choice" and "panders to the darkest and most cruel aspects of individual and community", the musical accuses the audience, "members of that society, with self-cannibalism" (p. 9). Auden and Kallman interpret Mahagonny's change from a "suckerville" of oppressive dictates of financial rules to a "vast panorama of sensual pleasure which also collapses" as representing for Brecht two faces of our capitalism that required either "a grinding obedience which produces empty 'pleasure' or an equally oppressive freedom based on the ability to pay" or both: "Whatever cannot be translated into money...[has] no meaning, no value, no effect in Mahagonny... Neither God nor nature can destroy or reform Mahagonny. Only its own internal contradictions can do that..." (pp. 17-18).

Brecht wrote five Mahagonny poems in the early 1920s, and, according to Auden/Kallman, published these songs in 1926 in *Taschenpostille* ("pocket breviary") and then republished them in a larger edition entitled, *Hauspostille* ("domestic breviary"); *Hauspostille* had some melodies for the lyrics, apparently composed by Brecht himself (p. 10). In the spring of 1927, Weill approached Brecht to collaborate on a show for the Baden-Baden Festival of Modern Music. The two reworked five songs from *Hauspostille* and added a new finale to create *Das Kleine Mahagonny*, a one-act show they called a

"Songspiel", a "play upon the term Singspiel (that is, *opera comique* or ballad opera)" (Auden/Kallman, p. 10). The show premiered, according to Gerstenmeyer, on July 17, 1927, at the Baden-Baden Musicweeks, 'Alabama Song' being introduced by Lotte Lenya. From 1927-29, Weill and Brecht continued reworking the piece into an opera which became *Aufstieg Und Fall Der Stadt Mahagonny (The Rise And Fall Of The City Of Mahagonny)*, which premiered, according to Gerstenmeyer, in Leipzig on March 9, 1930, again with Lotte Lenya as Jenny, one of the main characters. In essence, the works were more a continuous work, not an original with later revisions. But the work must have appealed to both Weill and Brecht's desire to incite a reaction from their culture, for both shows caused riots, notably provoking the people in the fledging Nazis movement. Parmalee noted, after researching the reviews of these premieres, "the bourgeoisie, who expected to see classical opera in its opera house, was certainly convinced that it was seeing communist propaganda" (pp. 285-86).

Auden/Kallman indicated that the three songs, 'Off To Mahagonny', 'Who Lives In Mahagonny', and 'God in Mahagonny' were written before 1922, and that "the two most famous songs, the 'Alabama' and 'Benares' pieces, were written around 1925" (p. 10). According to Parmalee, Weill and Brecht wrote interchangeably on the text and music for the subsequent shows, and, thus, it would be difficult to separate the music as that of Weill and the lyrics as that of Brecht (p. 288). Kind of like The Doors.

LIGHT MY FIRE

'Light My Fire' b/w 'The Crystal Ship' was released by Elektra as a 45 rpm single (# 45615), April 1967.

BILLBOARD's HOT 100

| May 27, 1967 | #131 | July 29 | # 1 |
| June 3 | # 98 | Aug. 5 | # 1 |
| June 10 | # 61 | Aug. 12 | # 1 |
| June 17 | # 50 | Aug. 19 | # 2 |
| June 24 | # 24 | Aug. 26 | # 4 |
| July 1 | # 19 | Sept. 2 | # 4 |

| July 8 | # 12 | | Sept. 9 | # 8 |
| July 15 | # 8 | | Sept. 16 | # 18 |
| July 22 | # 3 | | Sept. 23 | # 23 |

*out of chart*

| Aug. 31, 1968 | # 91 |
| Sept. 1 | # 91 |

In *The Doors: The Complete Lyrics*, this song's by-line is, "Lyrics by Robby Krieger and Jim Morrison" (p. 30). Robby Krieger wrote most of this lyric.

In an interview published in *Masters Of Rock: The Life And Times Of Jim Morrison* (Winter 1990), Krieger explained that one day Morrison told the group to go home and write some songs since the group needed more songs; Robby didn't think he could, but he knew he would have to write a pretty "heavy" song about earth, air, fire, or water to impress Morrison and finally came up with the line about "light my fire" (p. 21). Densmore, in *Riders On The Storm*, narrates a longer version of the first session the group had with Krieger's idea (pp. 61-64).

The stanza about love becoming a "funeral pyre" – or just the second line about wallowing in the mire – is usually credited to Morrison. Manzarek, in an interview published in *Musician* (August 1981), said Jim added the verse about love becoming a "funeral pyre" (p. 48). Densmore described the first rehearsal of the song in his book, *Riders On The Storm*, and when Morrison got to the second stanza, Densmore wrote that Jim stopped and asked Krieger, "Where's the rest of it?" Robby responded he got stuck on the second verse; Jim mulled about it while Ray and John kept playing the embryonic rhythm and then sang the line about wallowing in the mire before adding "the rest of the lyrics Robby had written" (p. 64). In an interview published in the July 3, 1981, issue of *BAM*, Paul Rothchild recalled his least favourite line in the song was the one about wallowing in the mire and he told Jim so without knowing Jim was the one who had contributed that lyric to Krieger's song (p. 20).

The heart of the song is driven by instrumental solos which were based, according to Densmore and Krieger, on chords similar to John Coltrane's jazz version of 'My Favourite Things'. The rudimentary structure from which Manzarek and Krieger build their interplay between the organ and guitar is quite similar to that between Coltrane's soprano sax and McCoy Tyner's piano on their rendition of Ricard Rogers and Oscar Hammerstein II's song. The song became one of America's best known songs from the musical *The Sound Of Music* when Julie Andrews sang it in the 1965 film version. Julie Andrews (the wholesome "Mary Poppins" image stuck to her with no less tenacity than the "young lion/Dionysus" image did to Jim Morrion) sings Rodgers-&-Hammerstein's innocuous 'Favourite Things'; Jim Morrison sings Robby Krieger's fervent 'Light My Fire'; and the two are fused by John Coltrane's soul-probing sax.

In *Riders On The Storm*, Densmore explains how in later concerts Krieger began incorporating the melody from The Beatles' 'Eleanor Rigby' into his guitar solo which inspired Densmore to develop both a short exchange of his drumming with Krieger's soloing and cues to signal the end of both Krieger's and Manzarek's solos (pp. 142, 195). Michael Hicks writes a more detailed account of this evolution in his unpublished *The Evolution Of 'Light My Fire'*. The essay offers an informative, detailed analysis of how the song evolved, much like the evolution of songs by other American musicians such as Ives and Louis Armstrong who composed by "eclecticism and quotation", using "whatever musics were at hand". Hicks writes the song was "a chain of allusions that kept lengthening until the group, if not the song, collapsed under the weight of its fame". (My copy of this article by Hicks, an associate professor of music at Brigham Young University in Utah, originated from Kerry Humpherys' Doors archives.)

In an interview with Alan Paul that was printed in *Guitar World*, March 1994, when asked about his solo in 'Light My Fire', Krieger responded that this solo was typical, though he played it different every time: "To be honest, the one on the record is not one of my better versions. I only had two tries at it" (p. 64). For a more detailed musical analysis of Krieger's technique on this solo and other Doors songs, see Keith Wyatt's article, "Inside The Goldmine" (Krieger's guitar style), published in the March 1, 1994, issue of *Guitar World* (pp. 70, 72, 74, 76, 78).

Paul Williams, in his discussion of this album in "Rock Is Rock: A Discussion Of A Doors Song" which was printed in *Crawdaddy* (May 1967), wrote "Is there really any point in saying something like, 'The instrumental in "Light My Fire" builds at the end into a truly visual orgasm in sound' when the reader can at any time put the album onto even the crummiest phonograph and experience that orgasm himself?" (p. 43).

There is a transcription of the lyrics and music in the September 1988 issue of *Guitar* (pp. 35-44).

## BACK DOOR MAN
by Willie Dixon (1915-1992)
(C) 1961, 1989 HOOCHIE COOCHIE MUSIC
(BMI)/Administered by BUG
All Rights Reserved. Used by Permission.

*The following versions of the song are printed:*
(1) as sung by Jim Morrison;
(2) as sung by Willie Dixon on, *I Am The Blues* (album, Columbia, PC 9987, 1970; reissued on CD by Mobile Fidelity Sound Lab, MFCD 872, Original Master Recording series). For a good review of this album and Dixon, see Don Heckman's "Pop: The Early Blues Sound Better Than Ever" in *The New York Times*, Sunday edition, April 5, 1969 (section II, p. 36).

Krieger stated that the group wanted to do 'Back Door Man' after he had heard John Hammond Jr. do the song (Doe and Tobler, *The Doors In Their Own Words*, p. 20; quote from 1968). Densmore, in *Riders On The Storm*, wrote Hammond inspired their cover of "Back Door Man" (p. 51). John Hammond Jr. is the son of John Hammond, who was a prominent figure at Columbia records. Hammond Sr. was responsible for the signing of Billie Holiday, Aretha Franklin (before she left to find stardom elsewhere), Pete Seeger, and Bruce Springstein; in 1961, he signed what, at first, was called "Hammond's Folly" – Bob Dylan – and produced Dylan's debut album and, according to the record sleeve, his second album, *The Freewheelin' Bob Dylan*. John Hammond Jr. is credited for bringing the Hawks (a group which included Robie Robertson and whhich would later become The Band) down from Canada to the States in 1964 before Dylan used them as his band for the first tour of playing his music electric.

In an interview with Alan Paul that was printed in *Guitar World*

(March 1994), Krieger was asked how faithful to the original version of 'Back Door Man' the group tried to be, and he replied that they "probably weren't good enough musicians to play exact copies" and they knew Morrison would never sing the song anywhere close to the original (p. 62).

BACK DOOR MAN
(Willie Dixon)
    (C) 1961, 1989 HOOCHIE COOCHIE MUSIC
    (BMI)/Administered by BUG
    (altered lyrics, Jim Morrison)

[yelps, grunts]
Yeah! Yeah! Come on! Yeah
I am a...
Yeah, I'm a back door man
I'm a back door man
The men don't know
But the little girls understand

'ell, all you people, they're trying to sleep
I'm out there making with my midnight creep
Yeah, 'cause I'm a back door man
The men don't know
But the little girls understand
All right, yeah

You men eat your dinner,
Or eat your pork and beans
I eat more chicken
Any man ever seen, yeah, yeah
I'm a back door man – wha
The men don't know
But the little girls understand

Well, I'm a back door man!
I'm a back door man
Well, baby

245

I'm a back door man
The men don't know
But the little girls understand


BACK DOOR MAN
(Willie Dixon)
(C) 1961, 1989 HOOCHIE COOCHIE MUSIC
(BMI)/Administered by BUG

The following lyrics are transcribed from *Willie Dixon, I Am The Blues* [album] (Columbia, PC 9987); reissued on CD by Mobile Fidelity Sound Lab, MFCD 872 (Columbia, copyright 1970) on the Original Master Recording series.

Footnotes compare this transcription with the lyrics as printed on the sheet music provided by BUG MUSIC and with the lyrics as sung by Howlin' Wolf (Chester Burnett, 1910-1976) and by John Hammond Jr., a contemporary of The Doors.

The four versions of the song – Dixon's, Howlin' Wolf's, Hammond's, and The Doors' – all vary. A comparison of The Doors' version of this song to those recorded by Dixon, Howlin' Wolf, and Hammond reveals how Howlin' Wolf's version influenced both Hammond and Morrison in phrasing of delivery and borrowing of additional lyrics which Dixon didn't use.

*Recordings consulted were: The Best Of John Hammond* [CD] (Vanguard, VCD-11/12, 1987; reissued of 1970 double album); *Howlin' Wolf: His Greatest Sides, Vol. 1* [cassette] (Chess Records [MCA Records], CHC-9107, 1984).


I-I-I-I am the...the back door man
I-I-I-I am the back door man
Well, the men don't know
But the little girls, they understand1

When evrybody is, ah, trying to sleep
I'm somewhere making my midnite creep
And every morning when the rooster crow
He's telling me that it is the time to go2

I am the back door man
I am the back door man
Well, the men don't know
But the little girls, they understand3

Well, they took me to the doctor shot full of hole
'N the nurse, she cried, "Save his soul"
I was accused of murder in first degree
The judge wife cried, "Let the man go free"4

I am the back door man
I am the back door man
Well, the men don't know
But the little girls, they understand3

I was accused of murder in the first degree
The judge wife cried, "Let the man go free"
The cop's wife cried, "Don't take him down"
I'd rather be in six feet of ground5

I am the back door man
I am the back door man
Well, the men don't know
But the little girls, they understand

I-I-I-I am the back door man
I-I-I-I am the back door man
Well, the men don't know
But the little girls, they understand

Oooh
I-I-I-I am
I-I-I-I am
Back door man

1 *The lyrics as printed on the sheet music provided by*
*BUG MUSIC are:*

Oh yeah, I'm your back door man

Oh yeah, I'm your back door man
The men don't know
But the little girls understand.

Howlin' Wolf varies the first stanza with, "I-I-I-I am...a back door man". John Hammond sings the same opening as Howlin' Wolf, except the opening two lines are "I am...whoa, back door man / I-I-I am...Lord, a back door man."

2 The lyrics on the sheet music provided by BUG MUSIC print the closing line as, "He's telling me that you got to go". Howlin' Wolf pretty much sings the lyrics in this stanza as Dixon does, except he closes the stanza with, "Something tell me I got to go". John Hammond only sings the first two lines of this stanza before singing his 3-line chorus for the song, "Whoa, I am...Lord, a back door man / Well, the men don't know / But the little girls understand."

3 The chorus as printed on the sheet music provided by BUG MUSIC is, "Oh yeah, I'm your back door man / The men don't know / But the little girls understand". Howlin' Wolf phrases the opening line of the chorus with the phrasing Dixon uses at the end: "I am... back door man."

4 This stanza as printed on the sheet music provided by BUG MUSIC is:

They took me to the doctor shot full of holes
And the nurse's cried please save his soul
I'se accused of murder in the first degree
The judges wife plead Let him be.

Howlin' Wolf sings this verse as,

They take me to the doctor shot full of hole
The nurse cried, "Please save his soul"

248

'Cused for murder, first degree
Judge wife cried, "Let the man go free."

John Hammond just sings the last two lines and then adds his 3-line chorus.

5 Dixon does not make it clear who is saying, "I'd rather be in six feet of ground": the cop's wife or the back door man. The lyrics as printed on the sheet music provided by BUG MUSIC are just the two lines, "The cops wife cried Don't take him down/I'd rather you give me six feet of ground."

Although Howlin' Wolf also doesn't make it clear who wants the six feet of ground, he does add a twist of humor to his version of this verse along with the pork 'n' beans and chicken lyric that Morrison borrows:

Same doctor, cop's wife cried, "Don't take him down"
I'd rather be there's six feet in the ground
When you come home, you can eat your pork 'n' beans
I eats more chicken...any man seen

At this point of the song, John Hammond sings the two lines from the previous stanza about being taken to the doctor shot full of holes and then adds his 3-line chorus. Hammond then adds another stanza, "Well, you men eats your dinner, ah, cold dozen beer/I eats more chicken, any man seen", before ending the song with his 3-line chorus.

## END OF THE NIGHT

'Break On Through' b/w 'End Of The Night' was released by Elektra as a 45 rpm single (#45611), January 1967.

The song was one of the six songs recorded by group (before Robby Krieger joined) on a demo at Aura Records (a subsidiary of World Pacific Studios) in Los Angeles on September 2, 1965.

The lyric about taking "the highway to the end of the night" is an image Hopkins and Sugerman wrote Jim borrowed from the novel, *Journey To The End Of The Night*, written by "the French Nazi apologist and adamantine pessimist, Louis-Ferdinand Ce'line" (p. 60). According to producer Paul Rothchild, this line was originally, "take a trip into the end of the night", but Morrison in the studio decided to change it because trip had been "violently overused" (Paul Williams' interview in

*Crawdaddy,* August 1967, p. 25).

## TAKE IT AS IT COMES

In *The Doors Quarterly Magazine* (Issue 32, June 1995, p. 29), appears a reproduction of the sheet music to the song, 'Take It As It Comes'. It is credited to "R. (Speed) Krieger". According to the *DQ* article, the sheet music was hand written by Ray Manzarek in 1966 and submitted to ASCAP so The Doors could have copyright control of their songs.

In *No One Here Gets Out Alive*, Hopkins and Sugerman wrote that Morrison didn't want to do meditation like Densmore and Krieger were, but Jim attended one of the lectures to look into the Maharishi's eyes and "see if he was happy"; Morrison decided the Maharishi was and dedicated this song to him (p. 92).

## THE END

Lyric as written by Jim Morrison is published in *The American Night* (pp. 111-113).

In a 1969 *Rolling Stone* interview with Jerry Hopkins, to the question what did the song, 'The End', mean to him, Morrison replied that he didn't know what he was trying to express and that every time he heard the song, it meant something else. Morrison explained the song began as a "simple goodbye song", but he thought the song's imagery was "sufficiently complex and universal" the song "could be almost anything you want it to be" (July 26 1969, p. 18). Densmore, in *Riders On The Storm*, recalls during his narrative of the first session the group had with Krieger's idea for 'Light My Fire' that Morrison introduced one of his new songs – the lyrics that would become the opening of 'The End'; Densmore wrote, "A chill ran up my spine. These weren't lyrics, they were an epitaph" (p. 62).

In an interview published in the December 1983 issue of *Audio*, Manzarek stated that album version of "The End" was a combination of the only two takes the group did of the song. The splice was made in the Oedipal section, at the beginning of the line about the killer awaking before dawn; though there is a sound change between these two cuts, Manzarek said the splice works because at this point of the song the "whole tone of the piece changes" (p. 44).

In a personal correspondence, Gerstenmeyer expresses similar difficulty with transcribing the passage about the "blue bus" following

the Oedipal section and transcribes the passage as (which is different
from what was printed in his book on p. 33).1

And meet me at the back of the

> Blue bus (d'you know)
> Blue rock, on the
> Blue bus, (do ne)
> Blue rock
> Come on, yeah...

I transcribed the last four lines of this passage as

> To the blue rock
> On the blue bus
> To the blue love
> Come on, yeah.

There ensues an instrumental passage under which is barely
audible a distant vocal, perhaps Morrison's infamous mantra, "Kill the
father, fuck the mother". These passages were not transcribed in *The
Doors: The Complete Lyrics*, either the Hyperion hardcover (First
Edition, 1991) or Delta paperback edition (1992).

There is the story of Morrison returning to the studio after or
before the recording of "The End" and spraying the studio down with
a fire extinguisher. There are three different accounts of this story:
Jerry Hopkins' *The Lizard King: The Essential Jim Morrison* (p. 71);
James Riordan and Jerry Prochnicky's *Break On Through* (p. 115), and
Jerry Hopkins and Danny Sugerman's *No One Here Gets Out Alive* (p.
100). In *Riders On The Storm*, Densmore mentions this story in his
recollection of the recording sessions for 'The End' (pp. 88-89).

What aging does to one's perspective – two recollections of the
recording 'The End' by producer Paul Rothchild in separate interviews
14 years apart.

In an interview with Paul Williams published in *Crawdaddy* (August
1967), Rothchild explained that 'The End' was always changing and
Morrison used it as an open canvas for his bits and pieces of poetry and
images along with things he just wanted to say, but after the group

recorded the song and could hear it on record, the song became the statement they wanted to make and they then performed it that way, with slight variations (p. 19).

In an interview with Blair Jackson published in *BAM* (3 July 1981), Rothchild responded to Jackson's comment about Morrison's statement that 'The End' and 'When The Music's Over' were free-form pieces that became static when they were recorded by saying "that's very hip, but not quite accurate". Rothchild said he had seen the group do 'The End' no fewer than 100 times and the song had a very specific form and wasn't that different when The Doors performed it before and after they had recorded it: "What is on the record is exactly the way The Doors wanted you to hear 'The End'" (pp. 18-19).

STRANGE DAYS [album].
*Elektra Records, EKL-74014 Mono, EKS-74014 Stereo, October 1967.*
> Side 1:
> Strange Days
> You're Lost Little Girl
> Love Me Two Times
> Unhappy Girl
> Horse Latitudes
> Moonlight Drive
> Side 2:
> People Are Strange
> My Eyes Have Seen You
> I Can't See Your Face in My Mind
> When The Music's Over

Producer, Paul A. Rothchild
Production Supervisor, Jac Holzman
Engineer, Bruce Botnick
Additional musicians: Doug Lubahn (of Clear Light), bass
Paul Beaver, Moog Synthesizer

Strange Days *[cassette]*, *TC5-4014.*
Strange Days *[8-track tape]*, *ET8-4014.*
Strange Days *[CD]. Elektra/Asylum Records, 74014-2,*

*September 1985.*
Strange Days *[24KT Gold Plated CD]. DDC Compact Classics, Inc. (Northridge, CA), GZS-1026, October 1992. (Pressed in Japan.)*

In a 1972 interview by John Tobler with the three surviving Doors, Krieger said that he wrote the lyrics for 'You're Lost Little Girl' and 'Love Me Two Times' and the rest of the songs were Morrison's lyrics (*ZigZag*, September 1972, p. 29).

August-October 1967 – The Doors do recording sessions for STRANGE DAYS at Sunset Sound Recording Studios in Los Angeles.

BILLBOARD's TOP LP'S

| | | | |
|---|---|---|---|
| Dec. 2 | # 5 | Dec. 7 | # 68 |
| Nov. 4, 1967 | #100 | June 15 | # 99 |
| Nov. 11 | # 4 | June 22 | # 95 |
| Nov. 18 | # 3 | June 29 | # 81 |
| Nov. 25 | # 3 | July 6 | # 80 |
| Dec. 2 | # 3 | July 13 | # 72 |
| Dec. 9 | # 3 | July 20 | # 70 |
| Dec. 16 | # 4 | July 27 | # 57 |
| Dec. 23 | # 4 | Aug. 3 | # 57 |
| Dec. 30 | # 9 | Aug. 10 | # 54 |
| Jan. 6, 1968 | # 9 | Aug. 17 | # 42 |
| Jan. 13 | # 18 | Aug. 24 | # 38 |
| Jan. 20 | # 23 | Aug. 31 | # 37 |
| Jan. 27 | # 22 | Sept. 7 | # 40 |
| Feb. 3 | # 22 | Sept. 14 | # 32 |
| Feb. 10 | # 27 | Sept. 21 | # 32 |
| Feb. 17 | # 27 | Sept. 28 | # 38 |
| Feb. 24 | # 31 | Oct. 5 | # 47 |
| Mar. 2 | # 31 | Oct. 12 | # 53 |
| Mar. 9 | # 46 | Oct. 19 | # 55 |
| Mar. 16 | # 64 | Oct. 26 | # 89 |
| Mar. 23 | # 98 | Nov. 2 | # 94 |
| Mar. 30 | # 94 | Nov. 9 | #102 |
| Apr. 6 | # 94 | Nov. 16 | #131 |
| Apr. 13 | # 97 | Nov. 23 | #130 |

| Apr. 20 | # 96 | Nov. 30 | #137 |
| Apr. 27 | # 95 | Dec. 7 | #142 |
| May 4 | # 97 | Dec. 14 | #142 |
| May 11 | # 92 | Dec. 21 | #137 |
| May 18 | # 88 | Dec. 28 | #133 |
| May 25 | # 88 | Jan. 4, 1969 | #168 |
| June 1 | #100 | Jan. 11 | #188 |
| June 8 | #105 | | |

## YOU'RE LOST LITTLE GIRL

In *The Doors: The Complete Lyrics*, song's by-line is, "Lyrics by Robby Krieger" (p. 70). In an interview with Robert Matheu that was printed in *Creem Special Edition: The Doors* (Summer 1981), Krieger stated he composed the song, "You're Lost Little Girl" (p. 59).

In *Riders On The Storm*, Densmore narrated part of the recording session for this song, detailing how Morrison's vocal has "a tranquil mood, like the aftermath of a large explosion", probably due to Rothchild's idea of Jim's girlfriend Pam performing oral sex before Jim sang (p. 132).

## LOVE ME TWO TIMES

'Love Me Two Times' b/w 'Moonlight Drive' was released by Elektra as a 45 rpm single (# 45624), November 1967.

### BILLBOARD's HOT 100

| Dec. 9, 1967 | # 75 |
| Dec. 16 | # 59 |
| Dec. 23 | # 48 |
| Dec. 30 | # 38 |
| Jan. 6, 1968 | # 30 |
| Jan. 13 | # 25 |
| Jan. 20 | # 40 |

In *The Doors: The Complete Lyrics*, song's by-line is, "Lyrics by Robby Krieger" (p. 72). In Robert Matheu's interview printed in *Creem Special Edition: The Doors* (Summer 1981), Krieger stated he composed the song, 'Love Me Two Times' (p. 59).

Throughout the song, Morrison drops the "s" on times to make the lyric sound like he is asking his baby to love him "two time". And this rendering is similar on live recordings. Not until the closing lines of the song does he clearly enunciate times with an "s". Although it clearly appears to be times, the twist with the meaning, two-time, is somewhat enticing.

## UNHAPPY GIRL

'People Are Strange' b/w 'Unhappy Girl' was released by Elektra as a 45 rpm single (# 45621), September 1967.

Sugerman and Hopkins noted that Manzarek played "the entire song backward", and Densmore created a "soft-suck rhythm sound" by playing "backward high-hat" (*No One Here Gets Out Alive*, p. 128). Densmore, in *Riders On The Storm*, wrote that producer Rothchild had Manzarek overdub his piano chord changes backward as Ray listened to the song backward, and then Rothchild played it forward (p. 128).

## HORSE LATITUDES

Lyric as written by Jim Morrison is published in *The American Night* (p. 156).

In the selection, "SELF-INTERVIEW", that opens *Wilderness*, Morrison wrote that he wrote 'Horse Latitudes' when he was in high school (p. 2).

There is a different poem entitled, "HORSE LATITUDES", published in *Wilderness* (pp. 94-95).

Horse Latitudes is the name for the ocean regions located between 30° and 35° latitude in the northern and southern hemispheres. These regions separate the easterly trade winds on the equator sides from the prevailing westerly winds on the polar sides; hence, these parts of the oceans are characterized by calm and very light winds and clear and warm weather. The name supposedly originated from 18th century sailors whose ships to the New World became becalmed and who threw overboard horses not only to lighten the load but also to conserve water and food supplies that could not be extended.

Sugerman and Hopkins, in *No One Here Gets Out Alive*, detail the recording technique used to create the sound effects for this song. Producer Rothchild and engineer Botnik "created a backdrop of *musique concrete*: varied the speed of tape recording white noise by hand-winding it, electronically altered the recording of already strange sounds of The Doors playing musical instruments in unusual ways, and created other strange sounds like a Coke bottle dropped into a metal trash can, coconut shells beating on a tile floor, and friends wailing their lungs raw" (pp. 127-28).

In a book of quotes edited by Andrew Doe and John Tobler, *The Doors In Their Own Words*, Morrison said the song was about Spanish sailing ships becoming stuck in the Doldrums and the men had to lighten the vessels by throwing their major cargo overboard – horses for the New World. Morrison imagined that the horses must have started kicking and chucking when brought to the edge of the boat and that "it must have been hell" to watch as the horses lost strength after swimming for a while and slowly sunk away (p. 23, quote attributed to 1968).

In *Jim Morrison And The Doors*, Mike Jahn wrote that song depicts "the Doldrums, where sailing ships from Spain would get stuck" and the sailors, to lighten the vessel, threw some of their cargo overboard, the major cargo being horses for the New World (p. 60).

The Doldrums is the name of the region of the north part of the south Atlantic Ocean northeast of Brazil of South America and southwest of the Grain Coast of Africa (Guinea, Liberia, Sierra Leone area).

In *No One Here Gets Out Alive*, Jerry Hopkins and Danny Sugerman wrote that, in high school, Jim penned the poem (which became this lyric) after being inspired by a "lurid paperback cover" depicting horses being cast overboard from a Spanish ship becalmed in the Sargasso Sea (p. 19).

Sargasso Sea is an area of relatively still water in the north Atlantic Ocean northeast of the West Indies and lies chiefly between 25°-35° north latitude and 40°-70° west longitude. The Tropic of Cancer lies just north of 20° latitude. The Sargasso Sea is a region of deep blue waters that are relatively clear and warm due to various currents of the North Atlantic which rotate around the margins of this region, notably the Gulf Stream on the west and south. The area is abundant with brown gulfweed, a seaweed that clusters in huge patches resembling meadows on the water. These peculiarities gave rise to the legends from the tales brought back by New World sailors that the Sargasso Sea was where galleons could become entangled in a snare of thickly matted islands of seaweed which were inhabited by huge monsters of the deep.

## MOONLIGHT DRIVE

'Love Me Two Times' b/w 'Moonlight Drive' was released by Elektra as a 45 rpm single (# 45624), November 1967.

The song was one of the six songs recorded by group (before Robby Krieger joined) on a demo at Aura Records (a subsidiary of World Pacific Studios) in Los Angeles on September 2, 1965.

Lyric as written by Jim Morrison is published in *The American Night* (pp. 97-98).

In a 1972 interview by John Tobler with the three surviving Doors, Manzarek said this song was the first song they recorded as The Doors, "but it was also the weakest" and they left it off the first album (*ZigZag*, September 1972, p. 28). In a subsequent interview with Pete Fornatale of *Musician* magazine, Manzarek further expanded that the song was a "funkier, bluesier kind of song" at first, like a James Brown or Otis Redding song; but while recording the song for the second album, the group "fooled around for a while" before Ray said, "I got it – we're gonna do a tango... a rock tango" (August 1981, p. 48).

## PEOPLE ARE STRANGE

'People Are Strange' b/w 'Unhappy Girl' was released by Elektra as a 45 rpm single (#45621), September 1967.

### BILLBOARD's HOT 100

|  |  |  |  |
|---|---|---|---|
| Sept. 16, 1967 | #102 | Oct. 21 | # 17 |
| Sept. 23 | # 65 | Oct. 28 | # 12 |
| Sept. 30 | # 44 | Nov. 4 | # 14 |
| Oct. 7 | # 32 | Nov. 11 | # 18 |
| Oct. 14 | # 23 | Nov. 18 | # 40 |

In advertisements in the village *Voice*, promoting the upcoming Doors' June 12 through July 2, 1967, engagement at Steve Paul's *Scene East* (New York City), appears also, "The INCREDIBLE TINY TIM...365 NIGHTS A YEAR". According to Tiny Tim, Jim Morrison approached him during this time he opened for The Doors and suggested he should do a certain Doors' song: 'People Are Strange'. But, as Tiny Tim lamented, a week later the group had a hit single with "Light My Fire" and nothing ever become of the idea. Actually, Jim probably understood the appropriateness of that idea... (Anthe Rhodes, "Sometimes I Feel Like a Lonesome Little Rainbow: Tiny Tim and some classic Hollywood moments" in *Shepherd Express*, 29 August - 5 September 1991, p. 10.)

In an interview with Alan Paul that was printed in *Guitar World*, March 1994, Krieger describes how Morrison came up with the lyrics. Jim had shown up at Krieger's house in Laurel Canyon in "one of his suicidal, downer" moods, and Densmore suggested they go to the top of the canyon to watch the sunset which they did. As a dazzling display of sunset colours reflected off the top of the clouds, Krieger said Morrison's mood flipped-flopped and Jim said he realized he felt so depressed because "if you're strange, people are strange". Jim proceeded to write the lyrics right there, and Krieger explained "I came up with the music" (p. 68).

In *Riders On The Storm*, Densmore version of the story is similar, only he recalled he wasn't there and it was Robby who suggested they walk up the hill from Robby and John's house on Lookout Mountain Drive to get a spectacular view of L.A. from Appian Way (pp. 124-25).

There is a transcription of the song done by Patrick Mabry in the March 1994 issue of Guitar World (pp. 135-38).

## MY EYES HAVE SEEN YOU
Densmore, in *Riders On The Storm*, wrote that the group composed this song in the garage of Manzarek's parents before Krieger joined the group (p. 127).

The song was one of the six songs recorded by group (before Robby Krieger joined) on a demo at Aura Records (a subsidiary of World Pacific Studios) in Los Angeles on September 2, 1965.

## WHEN THE MUSIC'S OVER
Lyric as written by Jim Morrison is published in *The American Night* (pp. 105-107).

In the selection entitled, "An American Prayer", is printed the image that music "inflames temperament", which echoes the "dance on fire" image in this song (*The American Night*, p. 5; and p. 7 of booklet in the posthumous album, *An American Prayer*).

After the opening dirge of lyrics about turning out the lights and music being your only friend until the end, there follows a very masked line which Gerstenmeyer transcribes as, "Aah – fuck you in the ass, baby!" (p. 50), which is a bit more discernible on bootleg live recordings.

In Densmore's account of the recording session of "When The Music's Over", he indicates that the lyric about the "scream of the butterfly" is literally an obscure reference to the title of a skin flick "blazing across the marquee" of a porno theatre near Eighth Avenue and 40th Street in New York (*Riders On The Storm*, pp. 134-35).

In the Alan Paul interview printed in *Guitar World* (March 1994), Krieger explained the two guitar solos played simultaneously were improvised on the spot and he has never been to reproduce them again: "That solo was a real challenge because the harmony is static. I had to play 56 bars over the same riff" (p. 66).

WAITING FOR THE SUN [album].
*Elektra Records, EKL-74024 Mono, EKS-74024 Stereo, July 1968.*
Side 1:
Hello, I Love You
Love Street
Not To Touch The Earth
Summer's Almost Gone
Wintertime Love
The Unknown Soldier
Side 2:
Spanish Caravan
My Wild Love
We Could Be So Good Together
Yes, The River Knows
Five To One

Producer, Paul A. Rothchild
Production Supervisor, Jac Holzman
Engineer, Bruce Botnick

Additional Musicians: Doug Lubahn (of Clear Light), fuzz bass
Kerry Magness (of Popcorn), bass ("The Unknown Soldier)
Leroy Vinegar, acoustic bass ("Spanish Caravan")

Waiting For The Sun *[cassette]*, *TC5-4024.*
Waiting For The Sun *[8-track tape]*, *ET8-4024.*
Waiting For The Sun *[cassette]*, *60156-4, August 1982.*
Waiting For The Sun *[CD]*. *Elektra/Asylum Records, 74024-2,*
*August 1985.*
Waiting For The Sun *[24KT Gold Plated CD]*. *DDC Compact*
*Classics, Inc.*
*(Northridge, CA), GZS-1045, October 1993. (Pressed in Japan.)*

January or February-June 1968 – The Doors do recording sessions
for WAITING FOR THE SUN at Sunset Sound Recording Studios, Los
Angeles.

BILLBOARD's TOP LP'S

| | | | |
|---|---|---|---|
| Dec. 2 | # 5 | Dec. 7 | # 68 |
| Aug. 10, 1968 | #110 | Jan. 4, 1969 | # 41 |
| Aug. 17 | # 29 | Jan. 11 | # 43 |
| Aug. 24 | # 4 | Jan. 18 | # 43 |
| Aug. 31 | # 3 | Jan. 25 | # 47 |
| Sept. 7 | # 1 | Feb. 1 | # 64 |
| Sept. 14 | # 1 | Feb. 8 | # 64 |
| Sept. 21 | # 1 | Feb. 15 | # 67 |
| Sept. 28 | # 2 | Feb. 22 | # 87 |
| Oct. 5 | # 1 | Mar. 1 | # 87 |
| Oct. 12 | # 2 | Mar. 8 | #100 |
| Oct. 19 | # 4 | Mar. 15 | #128 |
| Oct. 26 | # 11 | Mar. 22 | #136 |
| Nov. 2 | # 11 | *out of chart* | |
| Nov. 9 | # 15 | Aug. 9 | #173 |
| Nov. 16 | # 23 | Aug. 16 | #177 |
| Nov. 23 | # 43 | Aug. 23 | #182 |
| Nov. 30 | # 49 | Aug. 30 | #181 |
| Dec. 7 | # 42 | Sept. 6 | #189 |

| Dec. 14 | # 42 | | Sept. 13 | #189 |
|---|---|---|---|---|
| Dec. 21 | # 44 | | Sept. 20 | #198 |
| Dec. 28 | # 42 | | | |

## HELLO, I LOVE YOU

'Hello, I Love You'/'Love Street' was released by Elektra as a 45 rpm single (#45635), June 1968.

The song was one of the six songs recorded by group (before Robby Krieger joined) on a demo at Aura Records (a subsidiary of World Pacific Studios) in Los Angeles on September 2, 1965.

### BILLBOARD's HOT 100

| June 29, 1968 | #108 | | Aug. 17 | # 2 |
|---|---|---|---|---|
| July 6 | # 77 | | Aug. 24 | # 3 |
| July 13 | # 22 | | Aug. 3 | # 4 |
| July 20 | # 9 | | Sept. 7 | # 5 |
| July 27 | # 9 | | Sept. 14 | # 9 |
| Aug. 3 | # 1 | | Sept. 21 | # 23 |
| Aug. 10 | # 1 | | | |

In *Riders On The Storm*, Densmore wrote the arranging of 'Hello, I Love You' made the song sound "contrived" because of the "tons" of guitar distortion via the fuzz box (which was the latest electronic toy) and because of Krieger's suggestion of turning the beat around like Cream did in 'Sunshine Of Your Love' (p. 160).

On the radio special, *History of Rock 'n' Roll*, Manzarek describes the song's origins: 'Hello, I Love You' was written for a black girl that Jim and I saw walking down the beach. And she was a black girl, a dusky, dark complexion, dark skin, and she was just a little jewel walking by. And then Jim went home that night and wrote a song about just walking up to a girl that you didn't know or anything, and saying, 'Hello, I love you'.

In *No One Here Gets Out Alive*, Sugerman and Hopkins wrote that Morrison wrote the lyric in 1965 after sitting on the beach at Venice and "watching a young, long thin black girl insinuate her way toward him" (p. 59).

Many accused The Doors of cloning Ray Davies and the Kinks' "All

Day and All of the Night'. In an interview over ten years after the release of the song, Manzarek commented on the alleged Kink-derivative, saying that the group initially thought the song was "a lot like a Kinks song", but added, "It's all rock and roll, we're all family, we're not stealing anything from them, we're sort of...(hums melody)...Yes it is a lot like it, isn't it? Sorry, Ray" (Pete Fornatale, Musician, August 1981, p. 49).

LOVE STREET
'Hello, I Love You' b/w 'Love Street' was released by Elektra as a 45 rpm single (# 45635), June 1968.

In the poem, "DON'T START THAT...", in *The American Night*, appear the images, "Love Street parade" and "Love Street brigade" (p. 147).

In *No One Here Gets Out Alive,* Jerry Hopkins and Danny Sugerman wrote the song was written about where Jim and Pam lived in an apartment on Rothdell Trail in Laurel Canyon; Jim often sat with a beer on the balcony and watched people come and go from the neighbouring small grocery store, called the Country Store (pp. 110, 112). In their book, *Break On Through*, James Riordan and Jerry Prochnicky added that the address was 1812 Rothdell Trail (pp. 123, 247).

NOT TO TOUCH THE EARTH
A song labelled as 'Go Insane' was one of the six songs recorded by group (before Robby Krieger joined) on a demo at Aura Records (a subsidiary of World Pacific Studios) in Los Angeles on September 2, 1965. This demo included part of 'Not To Touch The Earth' along with another segment of 'The Celebration Of The Lizard'.

Lyric is an internal segment in the selection, "The Celebration Of The Lizard", written by Jim Morrison and published on the inner sleeve of this third album and in *The American Night* (pp. 43-44).

Plans for this third album had begun as grandiose with one side devoted to a twenty minute-plus version of a piece by Morrison, 'The Celebration Of The Lizard'. But the studio recording of the piece proved to be too crude, and the only passage produced for this album was the 'Not To Touch The Earth' segment.

According to Hopkins and Sugerman in *No One Here Gets Out*

*Alive*, the first two lines of this song about not touching the earth and not seeing see the sun came from the table of contents of *The Golden Bough* (p. 179). Actually, the two lines were taken from Sir James George Frazer's *Aftermath: A Supplement To The Golden Bough* (New York: Macmillan Company, 1937; included in 1951 multi-volume edition of *The Golden Bough*). Frazer, at the first part of the twentieth century, wrote what became a definitive study and history of magic and religion of the world. The multi-volume work was published in 1921. In the table of contents (p. xviii) of Aftermath are listed the following two chapters: chapter LXV – Not to touch the Earth pp. 443-446; chapter LXVI – Not to see the Sun  pp. 447. Both chapters deal with various culture's taboos of not touching the Earth or not looking into the Sun after certain events or rites.

SUMMER'S ALMOST GONE
The song was one of the six songs recorded by group (before Robby Krieger joined) on a demo at Aura Records (a subsidiary of World Pacific Studios) in Los Angeles on September 2, 1965.

WINTERTIME LOVE
In *The Doors: The Complete Lyrics*, song's by-line is, "Lyrics by Robby Krieger" (p. 89).

The article, "Doors' CD Mystery Baffles Experts" in ICE (March 1992, pp. 1, 10), discusses an unexplained vocal difference in the rendition of 'Wintertime Love' on the CD release of *Waiting For The Sun*. Futhermore, Heinz Gerstenmeyer wrote to ICE to point out a switching of the channels on which the organ and rhythm guitar parts were recorded ("Doors Difference", July 1994, p. 4).

THE UNKNOWN SOLDIER
'The Unknown Soldier' b/w 'We Could Be So Good Together' was released by Elektra as a 45 rpm single (# 45628), March 1968. The song was subsequently banned by several radio chains.

BILLBOARD's HOT 100

| Mar. 30, 1968 | # 79 | Apr. 27 | # 48 |
| Apr. 6 | # 62 | May 4 | # 39 |

| Apr. 13 | # 58 | May 11 | # 39 |
| Apr. 20 | # 48 | May 18 | # 39 |

In a radio special produced by The Source, Manzarek explained the song's origins:

Jim said, "Let's do a war song". I said, "Everybody's doing a Vietnam song". And he said, "Nah, nah, this isn't a Vietnam song. This is just a song about war".

Hopkins and Sugerman recalled the song began in October of 1967 and was developed on the road and over the next couple of months, and "the dirge became a celebration...a rhythm that was both military (metronomic) and carnivalesque" (*No One Here Gets Out Alive*, pp. 149-50).

In his book, *The Lizard King: The Essential Jim Morrison*, Jerry Hopkins wrote that 'Unknown Soldier' was from Morrison's writings when he lived in Venice Beach the summer of 1965, right after graduating from UCLA (pp. 93, 95).

In a 1972 interview by John Tobler with the three surviving Doors, Densmore explained that the group did the gun shot on stage by dropping a reverb unit (*ZigZag*, September 1972, p. 29).

Mitchell Cohen saw the short film which promoted the song at a Doors concert at the Fillmore East in March 1968 and wrote in retrospect for an article in Fusion magazine that the film was a "crude work and filled with Morrison-as-martyr iconography" and simulated "vomiting and political montage...yet it worked" (June 1974, p. 19).

## SPANISH CARAVAN

In *The Doors: The Complete Lyrics*, song's by-line is, "Lyrics by Robby Krieger" (p. 91).

In an interview printed in *Creem Special Edition: The Doors* (Summer 1981), Krieger stated he composed the song, 'Spanish Caravan' (Matheu, p. 59).

'Andalusia' (or Andalucia), the area referred to in the first stanza, is the southernmost part of Spain. The region compromises about 1/6 of Spain, is home to about 1/5 of the country's population, and has a rich history of conquests by Cathaginians, Romans, Vandals, Visgoths, and Moors. Though this region was divided in 1833 into eight provinces, its historical name has remained the most common reference. Andalucia

Baja (Lower Andalusia) consists of a fertile, productive plain; mountains rising to more than 11,000 feet dominate the Andalucia Alta (Upper Andalusia). Rather than gold and silver, wealth from these mountains has come in the form of copper, coal, and lead.

## MY WILD LOVE
The line, 'My Wild Love', is the foundation of a different untitled poem published in *Wilderness* (p. 65).

Heinz Gerstenmeyer wrote to *ICE* magazine and noted that Morrison hums at the end of the song over 6 bars on the LP, but over 12 bars on the CD and that the song is nine seconds longer on the CD ("Doors Difference", July 1994, p. 4).

## WE COULD BE SO GOOD TOGETHER
'The Unknown Soldier' b/w 'We Could Be So Good Together' was released by Elektra as a 45 rpm single (# 45628), March 1968.

A middle stanza is deleted on a [West] German CD pressing, done by Polygram (Elektra/Asylum Records 74024-2, Europe: 042 041, August 1985). Gerstenmeyer informs me that on the second pressing, "the digitally remastered one from 1988, this stanza is not deleted".

In the stanza about angels, Gerstenmeyer only capitalizes the first angel (p. 74). In the Hyperion edition, both times, the word angels is capitalized (p. 98); in the Delta paperback edition, only the first angels is capitalized (p. 94). I believe the lyric suggests the proper nominative of Angels – the human aspirations and values we ascribe to the profound realm rather than to our profane world, those angels we knowingly and unknowingly destroy.

## YES, THE RIVER KNOWS
In *The Doors: The Complete Lyrics*, song's by-line is, "Lyrics by Robby Krieger" (p. 91).

In the Matheu interview that appeared in *Creem Special Edition: The Doors* (Summer 1981), Krieger stated that he composed the song, 'Yes, The River Knows' and that it was one of his favourites (p. 59).

## FIVE TO ONE
Densmore wrote in *Riders On The Storm* that Morrison kept bugging him to play a very primitive drumbeat, and when John finally relented

with the "dumbest 4/4 beat" he knew, Jim started singing the opening lyrics 'Five To One', Robby added a guitar riff, and Ray joined with the organ (pp. 160-61).

Morrison offered an explanation of the title to Hank Zevallos in an 1970 interview pubished in *Poppin*. The song, which Morrison said he didn't think of as political, was an idea he got while waiting in the audience before starting a concert at San Jose, California: "It was one of those big ballroom places and the kids were milling around and I just got an idea for a song" ("Jim Morrison" (interview), March 1970, p. 50). On November 19, 1967, The Doors performed at the San Jose Continental Ballroom in San Jose, California.

In *The Doors: The Complete Lyrics*, the spoken passage at the end of the song includes the line about getting "fucked up" (p. 100), which is not on the studio released recording, but is on bootlegs of live recordings. Gerstenmeyer transcribes the line the same (p. 79), but in a personal correspondence, he indicates he had to print the line that way.

THE SOFT PARADE [album].
*Elektra Records, EKS-75005, July 1969.*
Side 1:
Tell All The People
Touch Me
Shaman's Blues
Do It
Easy Ride
Side 2:
Wild Child
Runnin' Blue
Wishful Sinful
The Soft Parade

Producer, Paul A. Rothchild
Production Coordinator, Jac Holzman
Engineer, Bruce Botnick
Additional Musicians: Harvey Brooks (of Electric Flag), bass
Curtis Amy, saxophone

George Bohanan, trombone
Champ Webb, English horn
Jesse McReynolds, mandolin
Jimmy Buchanan, fiddle
Reinol Andino, congas

The Soft Parade *[cassette], TC5-5005.*
The Soft Parade *[8-track tape], ET8-5005.*
The Soft Parade *[CD]. Elektra/Asylum Records, 75005-2, May 1988.*

In an interview printed in the July 1995 issue of *20th Century Guitar*, session player, bassist Harvey Brooks, talked about the recording of the album, *The Soft Parade*, and he immediately mentioned seeing hippie pillows and a lot of other stuff all over the studio. He recalled how he would show up at noon or one o'clock and it would be seven or eight at night before everyone collected themselves and the recording would finally come together. He said he should have been given writer's credit for many of the songs because he did a lot of the arrangements. Brooks also noted that all the horn and strings charts on the album were done by Paul Harris. (Mark Lotito & Don Celenza, "Harvey Brooks", p. 113.)

November 1968-July 1969 – The Doors do recording sessions for THE SOFT PARADE at Elektra Sound Recorders, Los Angeles.

BILLBOARD's TOP LP'S

| Aug. 9, 1969 | # 24 | Nov. 15 | # 26 |
|---|---|---|---|
| Aug. 16 | # 9 | Nov. 22 | # 42 |
| Aug. 23 | # 6 | Nov. 29 | # 52 |
| Aug. 30 | # 6 | Dec. 6 | # 49 |
| Sept. 6 | # 7 | Dec. 13 | # 49 |
| Sept. 13 | # 7 | Dec. 20 | # 79 |
| Sept. 20 | # 9 | Dec. 27 | # 73 |
| Sept. 27 | # 7 | Jan. 3, 1970 | # 91 |
| Oct. 4 | # 9 | Jan. 10 | # 91 |
| Oct. 11 | # 9 | Jan. 17 | #106 |
| Oct. 18 | # 12 | Jan. 24 | #152 |

| Oct. 25 | # 17 | Jan. 31 | #157 |
| Nov. 1 | # 28 | Feb. 7 | #166 |
| Nov. 8 | # 28 | Feb. 14 | #182 |

TELL ALL THE PEOPLE (Krieger)
'Tell All The People' b/w 'Easy Ride' was released by Elektra as a 45 rpm single (# 45663), May 1969.

BILLBOARD's HOT 100

| June 14, 1969 | #100 | July 19 | # 58 |
| June 21 | # 82 | July 26 | # 58 |
| June 28 | # 69 | Aug. 2 | # 57 |
| July 5 | # 62 | Aug. 9 | # 57 |
| July 12 | # 62 | | |

In an interview printed in *Creem Special Edition: The Doors* (Summer 1981), Krieger stated he composed the song, "Tell All The People" (Matheu, p. 59).

In his book, *The Lizard King: The Essential Jim Morrison*, Jerry Hopkins wrote that Morrison didn't want people to think he wanted others to follow him because he neither trusted leaders nor wanted to be a leader (p. 120).

In *Riders On The Storm*, Densmore retold a similar story that Krieger had thought the song was perfect for Morrison, but Jim, after months of silence, finally said he didn't want people to think they should get guns and follow HIM (p. 187).

TOUCH ME (Krieger)
'Touch Me' b/w 'Wild Child' was released by Elektra as a 45 rpm single (# 45646), December 1968.

BILLBOARD's HOT 100

| Dec. 28, 1968 | # 72 | Feb. 15 | # 3 |
| Jan. 4, 1969 | # 37 | Feb. 22 | # 4 |
| Jan. 11 | # 18 | Mar. 1 | # 4 |
| Jan. 18 | # 8 | Mar. 8 | # 9 |

| Jan. 25 | # 7 | Mar. 15 | # 16 |
| Feb. 1 | # 4 | Mar. 22 | # 31 |
| Feb. 8 | # 4 | | |

In the Robert Matheu interview in *Creem Special Edition: The Doors* (Summer 1981), Krieger said that he composed the song and that originally the song was 'Hit Me', not 'Touch Me', but Jim said he wouldn't sing that lyric (p. 59). Densmore expounded on this, writing that Robby had written, "Come on, come on, come on, now, HIT me, babe!", from one of the many rumoured intense domestic squabbles between him and his girlfriend, but had offered no resistance when Jim suggested the change to "touch me" (*Riders On The Storm*, p. 190).

In some earlier live recordings of "When The Music's Over", Morrison interjected a section which included the lines,

> Something wrong, something not quite right
> Touch me baby
> All through the night, yeah.

At the end of the song, the boys in the band chant, "Stronger than dirt!" At the time, Ajax detergent was running an often viewed commercial with a white knight galloping across the television screen and zapping things clean; the slogan for the commercial was, "Stronger than dirt!" Session player, bassist Harvey Brooks, recalls in an interview printed in the July 1995 issue of *20th Century Guitar* that The Doors "had to pay tribute to where it [this last line] came from. It was such an embarrassing lick (laughs)". (Mark Lotito & Don Celenza, "Harvey Brooks", p. 113.)

SHAMAN'S BLUES (Morrison)
On the vinyl album, the line, "And your mind", is repeated four times; on the CD, six times.

According to Densmore, the spoken coda which ends the song was created by "schizophrenic multi-tracking" – sliding in and out ad-lib bits from various vocal takes of Morrison's (*Riders On The Storm*, p. 205).

269

---

---

## DO IT (Morrison/Krieger)

'Runnin' Blue' b/w 'Do It' was released by Elektra as a 45 rpm single (# 45675, August 1969.

In *The Doors: The Complete Lyrics*, song's lyrics are credited to Jim Morrison (p. 109).

## EASY RIDE (Morrison)

'Tell All The People' b/w 'Easy Ride' was released by Elektra as a 45 rpm single (# 45663), May 1969.

## WILD CHILD (Morrison)

'Touch Me' b/w 'Wild Child' was released by Elektra as a 45 rpm single (# 45646), December 1968.

## RUNNIN' BLUE (Krieger)

'Runnin' Blue' b/w 'Do It' was a released by Elektra as a 45 rpm single (#45675), August 1969.

### BILLBOARD's HOT 100

| | |
|---|---|
| Sept. 6 | # 89 |
| Sept. 13 | # 85 |
| Sept. 20 | # 76 |
| Sept. 27 | # 71 |
| Oct. 4 | # 64 |
| Oct. 1 | # 75 |

On the singles, albums (except *Weird Scenes Inside The Gold Mine*), and CDs released by Elektra, the song is titled, 'Runnin' Blue'. In the book, *The Doors: The Complete Lyrics*, the song is titled, 'Runnin' Blues' (p. 120). On *Weird Scenes Inside The Gold Mine*, the song is titled, 'Running Blue'.

In a personal correspondence, Fred Baggen writes that Morrison used the opening three lines of this song (about "poor Otis" being dead and gone and the "pretty little girl" wearing a red dress) during two live performances recorded on bootlegs: during 'When The Music's Over' at one of the performances during their three-day engagement at Winterland in San Francisco on December 26, 27, 28,

1967 (Morrison sang these lyrics just before the final refrain of "When the music's over"), and during 'Soul Kitchen' at a concert in the Chicago Coliseum on May 10, 1968. 'Runnin' Blue' is a tribute to Otis Redding who died in a plane crash on December 10, 1967; Redding had been scheduled to play with The Doors at Winterland.

WISHFUL, SINFUL (Krieger)
'Wishful, Sinful' b/w 'Who Scared You' was released by Elektra as a 45 rpm single (# 45656), February 1969.

BILLBOARD's HOT 100

| Mar. 29, 1969 | # 79 |
| Apr. 5 | # 60 |
| Apr. 12 | # 45 |
| Apr. 19 | # 44 |
| Apr. 26 | # 44 |
| May 5 | # 48 |

In an interview printed in *Creem Special Edition: The Doors* (Summer 1981), Krieger said he composed the song, 'Wishful, Sinful' (Matheu, p. 59).

THE SOFT PARADE (Morrison)
In a 1981 interview with *BAM*, producer Paul Rothchild stated that a lot of the song was composed with bits of poetry out of Jim's notebooks that he and Jim thought fit rhythmically and conceptually (3 July 1981, p. 19). In his book, *The Lizard King: The Essential Jim Morrison*, Jerry Hopkins wrote that the song was Morrison's images of "people walking along Sunset Boulevard" (p. 121).

Lyric as written by Jim Morrison is published in *The American Night* (pp. 49-52). The image, "soft parade", also appears as a line in these selections written by Morrison as: "The Soft Parade" in an untitled selection in *Wilderness* (p. 19); as "Soft parade" in the poem, "DON'T START THAT...", in *The American Night* (p. 147).

In *The Lords And The New Creatures*, a poem opens with a line about the "soft parade" having begun "on Sunset" and includes a line about "the soft parade" soon beginning (p. 130). For a more poetically rendered version of what Jim called our "universe of organic gears", see the selection titled, "DRY WATER", in Wilderness (p. 157-58) and also in *Jim Morrison: An Hour For Magic* (p. 111).

In an untitled selection in *Wilderness* are printed lines, which are also used in this song, about "calling to the dogs" and a radio "moaning softly" while some animals are still "left in the yard" (p. 110).

In *Wilderness*, the poem entitled, "Horse Latitudes", includes lines, which are also used in this song, about people having difficulty "describing sailors" to what Morrison called the "undernourished" (p. 94).

In the printed versions in *The Doors: The Complete Lyrics* (p. 123) and in *The American Night* (p. 52), the confusing passage at the end about meeting at the crossroads is very close to the lyrics Morrison vocalized for the recording of "The Soft Parade" taped for the NET television special, *Critique* (13 May 1969).

Morrison repeatedly uses the "crossroads" imagery in several poems in his two books, *Wilderness* and *The American Night*. Two notable usages offer an extensive description of the "crossroads": on page 46 in *Wilderness* and the poem entitled, "THE CROSSROADS" on page 64 in *The American Night*.

In *Wilderness*, a poem entitled, "Horse Latitudes" (p. 95), includes many of the lines sung and spoken at the end of the song, 'Soft Parade'.

WHO SCARED YOU? (Morrison/Krieger)
'Wishful Sinful' b/w 'Who Scared You' was released by Elektra as a 45 rpm single (# 45656), February 1969. 'Who Scared You' was not included on the album, *The Soft Parade*.

In a personal correspondence, Fred Baggen writes that Morrison used the opening lyrics to this song within a rendition of 'When The Music's Over' during The Doors' Matrix Club show on March 7, 1967. Baggen also writes that Morrison used a variation of the lyrics about a rider carrying a sack of gold in a rendition of 'The End' during a concert at Danbury High School Auditorium, October 17, 1967:

I see a rider coming down the road
He had a burden carrying a heavy sack of gold
One bag of silver and one sack of gold.

Morrison uses these lines just before the Oedipal section of 'The End'.


MORRISON HOTEL [album].
*Elektra Records, EKS-75007, February 1970.*
Side 1:
Roadhouse Blues
Waiting For The Sun
You Make Me Real
Peace Frog
Blue Sunday
Ship of Fools
Side 2:
Land Ho!
The Spy
Queen of the Highway
Indian Summer
Maggie M'Gill

Producer, Paul A. Rothchild
Engineer, Bruce Botnick
Additional Musicians: Ray Neapolitan, bass
Lonnie Mack, bass
Giovanni Puglese (John Sebastian of Lovin' Spoonful),
harmonica ("Roadhouse Blues")

Morrison Hotel *[cassette], TC5-5007.*
Morrison Hotel *[8-track tape], ET8-5007.*
Morrison Hotel *[CD]. Elektra/Asylum Records, 75007-2,*
*May 1985.*

November 1969-January 1970 – The Doors do recording sessions
for MORRISON HOTEL at Sunset Sound Recording Studios in Los
Angeles.

BILLBOARD's TOP LP'S

| Mar. 7, 1970 | # 51 | June 13 | # 56 |
|---|---|---|---|
| Mar. 14 | # 12 | June 20 | # 63 |
| Mar. 21 | # 4 | June 27 | # 68 |
| Mar. 28 | # 4 | July 4 | # 61 |
| Apr. 4 | # 4 | July 11 | # 95 |
| Apr. 11 | # 4 | July 18 | #117 |
| Apr. 18 | # 7 | July 25 | #119 |
| Apr. 25 | # 7 | Aug. 1 | #124 |
| May 2 | # 12 | Aug. 8 | #129 |
| May 9 | # 13 | Aug. 15 | #131 |
| May 16 | # 18 | Aug. 22 | #146 |
| May 23 | # 22 | Aug. 29 | #156 |
| May 30 | # 26 | Sept. 5 | #182 |
| June 6 | # 44 | | |

ROADHOUSE BLUES (Morrison/The Doors)
'You Make Me Real' b/w 'Roadhouse Blues' was released by Elektra as a
45 rpm single (# 45685), March 1970.

A live version of 'Roadhouse Blues' is part of the opening of side 2
of the posthumous album, *An American Prayer*.

In *The Doors: The Complete Lyrics*, the opening lyrics are
transcribed to keep your "hands" on the wheel (p. 129). Gerstenmeyer
transcribes the line with hand, rather than hands (p. 111). Live
recordings suggest that Morrison is indeed singing, hand, and is not
dropping the "s" of hands. According to Sugerman and Hopkins in *No
One Here Gets Out Alive*, these opening lines about keeping your eyes
on the road and hand(s) on the steering wheel Jim said to his
perpetually on-and-off again girlfriend, Pamela, as she drove to a
cottage Jim had bought behind a country bar and club in Topanga
Canyon, located just northwest of L.A. (p. 271; see also Hopkins, *The
Lizard King: The Essential Jim Morrison*, p. 129). So logically, you
better keep your eyes on the road and hands on the wheel after you
leave the free-wheeling interstates of L.A. and drive the tightly curved
Topanga Canyon road winding through the mountains north of Malibu.
But either hand or hands would fit within the context of the lyrics,
though hand leaves unaccountable what the other hand is doing...

In *Riders On The Storm*, Densmore recalls how Lonnie Mack on bass (p. 235) and John Sebastian on harmonica (p. 236) contributed to the song.

WAITING FOR THE SUN (Morrison)
In an untitled selection in *Wilderness*, Morrison sketches out similar imagery of a naked couple racing down by the quiet side of a beach that is "vast" and "radiant" under a moon that is "cool" and "jewelled" where they revelled with laughter of "soft mad children" (p. 136). An almost identical version is part of the selection titled, "Ghost Song", on the posthumous album, *An American Prayer* (p. 1 of booklet).

YOU MAKE ME REAL (Morrison)
'You Make Me Real' b/w 'Roadhouse Blues' was released by Elektra as a 45 rpm single (# 45685), March 1970.

BILLBOARD's HOT 100

| | |
|---|---|
| Apr. 11, 1970 | # 97 |
| Apr. 18 | # 75 |
| Apr. 25 | # 55 |
| May 2 | # 50 |
| May 9 | # 56 |
| May 16 | # 67 |

PEACE FROG (Morrison/Krieger)
Parts of this lyric are published in *The American Night* (pp. 109-110).

According to Densmore, Krieger had "this great rhythm guitar lick", but Morrison didn't have any lyrics to go with it; eventually though, Rothchild had Jim record two poems on top of each other – one poem as a metaphor of Jim's life, the other of Pam (*Riders On The Storm*, pp. 244-45).

In his book, *The Lizard King: The Essential Jim Morrison*, Jerry Hopkins wrote that, in one of Morrison's notebooks, Manzarek found "Abortion Stories", which included the litany of blood sung in 'Peace Frog' (p. 129).

The lyric about ghosts of dead Indians crowding a youngster's "fragile egg-shell mind" alludes to an early childhood memory of an accident Morrison's family came upon on a highway. This image shaped the opening images for Oliver Stone's film, *The Doors*. In the posthumous album, *An American Prayer*, a narrative of this event in the selection, "Dawn's Highway", is printed on page 2 of the lyric booklet inside the album. These two lines lead into the narrative, and a recorded portion of "Peace Frog" follows the narrative.

In an untitled selection in *Wilderness*, the imagery about ghosts of dead Indians crowding a youngster's "fragile egg-shell mind" is printed (p. 139). The lines appear in another untitled selection in *Wilderness* (p. 180).

For a more detailed account of the making and recording of 'Peace Frog', see pp. 270-71 in Hopkins and Sugerman's *No One Here Gets Out Alive*.

SHIP OF FOOLS (Morrison/Krieger)
In *The Doors: The Complete Lyrics*, song's lyrics are credited to Jim Morrison (p. 128).

In 1962, Katherine Anne Porter (1890-1980), best known for her short storys, published her first novel, *Ship Of Fools* (Boston: Little, Brown and Company). The story is about the voyage of a German passenger ship from Mexico to Germany in 1931 just before the rise to power of Hitler and the Nazis. Porter weaves together a rich tapestry of threads that detail and intertwine the fascinating and the mundane of the novel's spectrum of characters in this drifting micro-world of humanity. The novel took her twenty years to write, from August 1941 to August 1961 (p. 497). The movie version of Porter's story was a box office hit in 1965. Porter noted in the paragraph that prefaces her novel that the title of her book was a "translation from the German of *Das Narrenschiff*, a moral allegory by Sebastian Brant (1458-1521) first published in Latin as *Stultifera Navis* in 1494". She added that earth as a ship on its voyage to eternity is a simple, universal image that transcends the ages, and she concluded her preface paragraph: "I am a passenger on that ship".

After photographs from the Apollo moon flights came back, especially the earth rise photos, many readily perceived the image that Earth was just an shimmering island, a vibrant spaceship in the vast sea of the universe. Whether or not inspired by the title of Katherine Anne Porter's novel, the "ship of fools" image has been rendered in many different shades by many different artists, and in this song the image of a ship is cast into drug imagery, just as in the debut album's song, "Crystal Ship".

LAND HO! (Morrison/Krieger)

In *The Doors: The Complete Lyrics*, song's lyrics are credited to Jim Morrison (p. 128).

In *Riders On The Storm*, Densmore wrote that he "worked up a complicated skiffle beat to 'Land Ho!'" (p. 234). Skiffle was the sound that inspired John Lennon to form a band with Paul McCartney.

In the Hyperion edition, the lyric is transcribed that grandpa "walked our country miles" (p. 137). The our may be simply a topo, but Morrison clearly sings, "for"...or is it "four"? Gerstenmeyer in a personal correspondence argues that this line could be transcribed with four. In the Delta paperback edition, our has been revised to for (p. 137). There is no really clear distinction between for or four, in context or in enunciation.

THE SPY (Morrison)

The imagery of this lyric may well have been borrowed from the 1954 novel, *A Spy In The House Of Love*, by Anais Nin (1903-1977). In the Doors song, the spy in Morrison's house of love knows the secrets, the deepest fears and dreams, and intonates a sense of control. In Nin's novel, the main character, Sabina, is completely insecure with her behaviour, constantly fears she will expose herself with careless behaviour, and needs to continuously pretend and improvise. Whether or not Morrison actually read this novel, he certainly shared Nin's artistic perspective. From interviews with and articles by Nin printed in *A Woman Speaks: The Lectures, Seminars, And Interviews Of Anais Nin* (1975), Nin uses language quite kindred to ideas Morrison expressed, especially in his interview with Lizze James. Both talk about how the individual inherits his or hers cultural concept of morality; how guilt is induced by your religion, family, and whoever has had prestige over you; and how each individual needs to rid himself or herself of things that are not genuine to him or her. (For Lizze James interviews, see either her article, "Jim Morrison: Ten Years Gone", in *Creem Special Edition: The Doors* [Summer 1981, pp. 16-23] or the entries included by Danny Sugerman and Benjamin Edmonds in *The*

*DOORS: The Illustrated History* [1983] – "Part I: Lizze James Interview with Jim Morrison" [pp. 64-67] and "Part II: Lizze James Interview with Jim Morrison" [pp. 122-24].)

QUEEN OF THE HIGHWAY (Morrison/Krieger)
In *The Doors: The Complete Lyrics*, song's lyrics are credited to Jim Morrison (p. 128).

INDIAN SUMMER (Morrison/Krieger)
In *The Doors: The Complete Lyrics*, song's lyrics are credited to Jim Morrison (p. 128).

In an interview with Alan Paul that was printed in *Guitar World*, March 1994, Krieger states that 'Indian Summer', not 'Moonlight Drive', was The Doors' first song (p. 68). *In Riders In The Storm*, Densmore also wrote that 'Indian Summer' was the group's first song, having stayed "in the can" because of a couple of bad notes from Krieger and Morrison (p. 244).

MAGGIE M'GILL (Morrison/The Doors)
In *The Doors: The Complete Lyrics*, song's lyrics are credited to Jim Morrison (p. 128).

In *Riders On The Storm*, Densmore recounts how the group initially began working out this song after a disastrous concert at the University of Michigan at Ann Arbor (p. 201, 237-39). The Doors performed at the University of Michigan's Homecoming Concert on October 28, 1967.

ABSOLUTELY LIVE [double album – live performances]
*Elektra Records, EKS-9002, July 1970.*
> Side 1:
> Who Do Love
> Medley – Alabama Song/Back Door Man/Love Hides/Five To One
> Side 2:
> Build Me A Woman
> When The Music's Over
> Side 3:
> Close To You
> Universal Mind

Break On Thru #2
Side 4:
The Celebration of the Lizard
Soul Kitchen

Producer, Paul A. Rothchild
Production Supervisor, Jac Holzman
Engineer, Bruce Botnick

Absolutely Live *[cassette]*, *C2-9002.*
Absolutely Live *[8-track tape]*, *T8-9002.*

BILLBOARD's TOP LP'S

| Aug. 8, 1970 | # 69 |
|---|---|
| Aug. 15 | # 17 |
| Aug. 22 | # 12 |
| Aug. 29 | # 9 |
| Sept. 5 | # 8 |
| Sept. 12 | # 11 |
| Sept. 19 | # 16 |
| Sept. 26 | # 16 |
| Oct. 3 | # 27 |
| Oct. 10 | # 27 |
| Oct. 17 | # 27 |
| Oct. 24 | # 40 |
| Oct. 31 | # 40 |
| Nov. 7 | # 46 |
| Nov. 14 | # 48 |
| Nov. 21 | # 56 |
| Nov. 28 | # 87 |
| Dec. 5 | #119 |
| Dec. 12 | #169 |
| Dec. 19 | #169 |

13 [album – compilation]
*Elektra Records, EKS-74079, November 1970.*

Side 1:
Light My Fire
People Are Strange
Back Door Man
Moonlight Drive
The Crystal Ship
Roadhouse Blues
Side 2:
Touch Me
Love Me Two Times
You're Lost Little Girl
Hello, I Love You
Land Ho
Wild Child
The Unknown Soldier

Producer, Paul A. Rothchild
Production Supervisor, Jac Holzman
Engineer, Bruce Botnick

13 *[cassette], TC5-4079.*
13 *[8-track tape], ET8-4079.*

BILLBOARD's TOP LP'S

| Dec. 19, 1970 | # 75 |
| Dec. 26 | # 29 |
| Jan. 2, 1971 | # 27 |
| Jan. 9 | # 27 |
| Jan. 16 | # 25 |
| Jan. 23 | # 40 |
| Jan. 30 | # 40 |
| Feb. 6 | # 40 |
| Feb. 13 | # 51 |
| Feb. 20 | # 59 |
| Feb. 27 | # 59 |
| Mar. 6 | # 77 |
| Mar. 13 | #101 |

Mar. 20    # 97
Mar. 27    # 93
Apr. 3    #103
Apr. 10    #129
Apr. 17    #160
Apr. 24    #158
May 1    #164
May 8    #161


L.A. WOMAN [album].
*Elektra Records, EKS-75011, April 1971.*
    Side 1:
    The Changeling
    Love Her Madly
    Been Down So Long
    Cars Hiss By My Window
    L.A. Woman
    Side 2:
    L'America
    Hyacinth House
    Crawling King Snake
    The WASP (Texas Radio and the Big Beat)
    Riders On The Storm

Produced by Bruce Botnick and The Doors
Additional Musicians: Marc Benno, rhythm guitar
Jerry Scheff, bass

L.A. Woman *[cassette], TC5-5011.*
L.A. Woman *[8-track tape], ET8-5011.*
L.A. Woman *[CD]. Elektra/Asylum Records, 75011-2,*
*March 1985.*
L.A. Woman *[CD]. HMV Classic Collection (London), C88 1-6.*
*Includes a 12-page booklet with text by Max Bell and reprints of*
*three reviews of album. 2500 pressed.*
L.A. Woman *[24KT Gold Plated CD]. DDC Compact Classics, Inc.*
*(Northridge, CA), GZS-1034, March 1993. (Pressed in Japan.)*

In *No One Here Gets Out Alive*, Hopkins and Sugerman wrote that after hearing the first work tape of L.A. Woman, Jac Holzman, Elektra's president, thought, "I'm listening to Jim's final album as a vocalist" (p. 341).

November-December – The Doors do recording sessions for L.A. WOMAN at The Doors Workshop (office for The Doors), Los Angeles.

BILLBOARD's TOP LP'S

| | | | |
|---|---|---|---|
| May 8, 1971 | # 56 | Sept. 4 | # 14 |
| May 15 | # 21 | Sept. 11 | # 18 |
| May 22 | # 10 | Sept. 18 | # 23 |
| May 29 | # 10 | Sept. 25 | # 29 |
| June 5 | # 9 | Oct. 2 | # 35 |
| June 12 | # 11 | Oct. 9 | # 37 |
| June 19 | # 12 | Oct. 16 | # 61 |
| June 26 | # 18 | Oct. 23 | # 61 |
| July 3 | # 17 | Oct. 30 | # 59 |
| July 10 | # 22 | Nov. 6 | # 70 |
| July 17 | # 36 | Nov. 13 | #101 |
| July 24 | # 33 | Nov. 20 | #114 |
| July 31 | # 32 | Nov. 27 | #118 |
| Aug. 7 | # 14 | Dec. 4 | #116 |
| Aug. 14 | # 14 | Dec. 11 | #151 |
| Aug. 21 | # 13 | Dec. 18 | #152 |
| Aug. 28 | # 15 | Dec. 25 | #164 |

THE CHANGELING
'Riders On The Storm' b/w 'The Changeling' was released by Elektra as a 45 rpm single (# 45738), June 1971.

According to Hopkins and Sugerman, the lyrics for 'The Changeling' were written in 1968 (*No One Here Gets Out Alive*, p. 320).

Among the student films that were shown in 1968 at the University of Southern California was one titled, Changeling.

In looking up meanings of the word, changeling, I found several: one apt to change; a disloyal person; a child (usually an infant) secretly substituted for another; (Archaic meaning) a simpleton, idiot, or imbecile. From various dictionaries and encyclopedias about the world of fairy mythology came the following accounts about changelings. A changeling is a fairy substituted for a stolen human baby; the substituted fairy could have been a fairy baby or an elder fairy who was no longer useful to the fairy tribe. Though these tales of changelings were evident in Northern European legends about fairies or dwarfs, the predominant references came from Ireland – the artistic heritage for the drunken Irish poet, Jim Morrison. Usually, according to the accounts, the birth of a handicapped or other exceptionally abnormal child was explained away with the story of a changeling. Kind of appropriate for Morrison's ostracized relationship with his parents...

In her novel, *Ship Of Fools*, Katherine Ann Porter includes a passage about changelings, as one of the main female characters compares her current boyfriend to her childhood memory of what her old Scottish nurse told about changelings (p. 400).

The "swarming street(s)" image of this song appears in several writings by Morrison: in an untitled selection, Morrison writes of being free of the "swarming streets" while in a womb or tomb (*Wilderness*, p. 9); in an untitled selection, Morrison writes about his ears assembling music out of the "swarming streets" (*Wilderness*, p. 79); in the selection entitled, "An American Prayer", Morrison writes about fleeing the streets' "swarming wisdom" (*The American Night*, p. 5; and p. 7 of booklet in the posthumous album, *An American Prayer*).

In an interview with Bob Chorush, Morrison stated he didn't think there had ever been a real riot at any of The Doors' concerts but the commotion had emanated from a "swarming theory" about animal and insect species that swarm together when they start out stripping the food supply: "It's a way of communicating. Working out a solution or signalling an awareness to each other. Signalling that there is a danger..". Jim then extends the idea to discuss people in many big cities feeling crowded: "People are getting very erotic and paranoid and I guess things like rock concerts are a form of human swarming to communicate this uneasiness about overpopulation. I haven't really got it all worked out yet..". ("An Interview With Jim Morrison: The Lizard King Reforms: Taking The Snake And Wearing It", *Los Angeles Free Press*, 15 January 1971, p. 24).

## LOVE HER MADLY

'Love Her Madly' b/w 'Don't Go No Further' (cover of a Willie Dixon song) was released by Elektra as a 45 rpm single (# 45726), March 1971.

### BILLBOARD's HOT 100

| Apr. 3, 1971 | #103 | May 15 | # 11 |
|---|---|---|---|
| Apr. 10 | # 74 | May 22 | # 11 |
| Apr. 17 | # 45 | May 29 | # 12 |
| Apr. 24 | # 37 | June 5 | # 19 |
| May 1 | # 19 | June 12 | # 21 |
| May 8 | # 12 | June 19 | # 25 |

In *The Doors: The Complete Lyrics*, the song's by-line is, "Lyrics by Robby Krieger" (p. 146). In an interview with Robert Matheu, Krieger said he composed the song, "Love Her Madly" (*Creem Special Edition: The Doors*, Summer 1981, p. 59).

## BEEN DOWN SO LONG

The inspiration for the title and refrain of this song was Richard Farina's book, *Been Down So Long It Looks Like Up To Me*, published in 1966 two days before Farina's death in a motorcycle accident. The book catalogs the events of college student (at the time, "campus hippie"), Gnossos Pappadopoulis. The book's cataloguing of the American culture's banality, as Maybelle Lacey wrote in the review of the book in *Library Journal*, "rolls with its own momentum", but "coarse language and the last possible word in sex and physiological descriptions does exceed all limits of good taste" (April 1, 1966, p. 1924). At that time. Basically a culturally saturated cynic whose actions reflect his lingering adolescent perspective of the world, Gnossos probably provided a kindred spirit with whom Morrison identified.

## CARS HISS BY MY WINDOW

This song has an uncanny similarity to John Lee Hooker's 'Nightmare', as released on *John Lee Hooker, The Hook: 20 Years Of Hits & Hot Boogie* [CD] (Chameleon Records, D2-74794, 1989; VeeJay Hall of Fame Series).

According to Hopkins and Sugerman, the lyrics were taken from one of Jim's Venice Beach notebooks (*No One Here Gets Out Alive*, p. 320).

In the final lyrical stanza, I transcribe Morrison singing, "A cold girl'll kill you", as it is in *The Doors: The Complete Lyrics*. Gerstenmeyer transcribes it as, "Ah, cold girl I'll kill you" (p. 140). In a personal correspondence, Gerstenmeyer discusses the possibility of either line and states the Krieger said the "cold girl I'll kill you" is correct. In a later correspondence, Gerstenmeyer writes "cold girl I'll kill" fits better into the context. He lies in the room with a girl who is absolutely passive, and he's active. I'm pretty sure it has to be [this] and that [Morrison] is intentionally mumbling a little bit, so that it does not sound so cruel. And of course he does not mean 'kill' literally... He lies there with a "cold" girl and at the end he decides to "kill" her.

But if this song is viewed in the larger landscape of a maturing artistic vision of The Doors (and hence, Jim Morrison), Morrison may be expressing his own passivity to forces he can't control. Images of being the "Lizard King" who can do anything have faded since that third album. This song laments a far deeper rift between two people that transcends any superficial sarcasm about a plastic twentieth century fox living on Love Street or being a prisoner of her own device. This relationship isn't superficial; it has the power to explode more forcefully and cause more devastation than previous portrayed relationships because there is a chilling reality of expected anticipation from repeated experience, like the waves and cars in this song. Though more subtle, these images are more powerful than the blatant sarcasm in earlier songs because you don't know when or how the scene will explode. The suddenness of a "sonic boom" punctuates the growing possibility that a cold girl will kill him "in a darkened room". Not only emotionally, but very possibly physically. Though Morrison doesn't admit his control has been upset by unexpected forces, there is the undercurrent reality that it has been. No longer condescending toward lovers as in previous songs, Morrison may be realizing others have the power to destroy him – or at least may be recognizing his personal vulnerability. The song wouldn't fit in the context of the previous albums, but fits the landscape rendered in this last album.

Either line certainly adds a sinister twist to the meaning of the lyric. But such altering between what may have been written and what was sung would not have beyond Morrison's artistic liberty – or intent. Listener discretion is advised.

## L.A. WOMAN

Lyric as written by Jim Morrison is published in *The American Night* (pp. 114-15). Compare imagery of this song with imagery in poem about the city in *The Lords And The New Creatures* (p. 12). Also compare Morrison's lyrical portrait of Los Angeles with Arthur Rimbaud's poetic portrait of Paris in Wallace Fowlie's translation of "Parisian Orgy or Paris is Repopulated" ["L'Orgie parisienne, ou Paris se repeuple"] (*Rimbaud: Complete Works, Selected Letters*, pp. 82-87).

Morrison uses the phrase, "city of night", from John Rechy's book, *City Of Night*. Published in 1963, the novel portrays a world of "sexual perversion and homosexuality", a – as Lloyd W. Griffin wrote in his book review in the Library Journal – "cool, level, extremely graphic account of a piece of sub-cultural America as true, unfortunately, as the facets of America revealed by Tom Wolfe or Robert Frost", and follows an unnamed narrator who "has seen it all and has struggled unsuccessfully to break away from a life of loneliness and loss, terror and the search for reality in a hostile (indifferent) and unreal world" (July 1963, pp. 2228-29). Certainly what must have appealed to Morrison was the vividly descriptive physical and psychological tour from Times Square in New York City to Pershing Park in Los Angeles to the Navy docks of San Diego to San Francisco to the grandest parade of masks, the Mardi Gras in New Orleans that Rechy provides of this frenzied, wanton sub-culture which Morrison no doubt had journeyed, if but casually, through in the mid-1960s. Like Rechy's unnamed narrator who perpetually seeks solitude from the city of night only to return, evoking the same feeling most people experience when trying to find self-meaning and security, so Morrison continually returns to his city of night, L.A. Woman.

In *The Doors: The Complete Lyrics*, the lyric, "Mr. Mojo risin'", is printed as "Mister Mojo risin'" (pp. 150-151). In *No One Here Gets Out Alive*, Hopkins and Sugerman transcribe the lyric as "Mr. Mojo Risin'" (p. 320). In *Riders On The Storm*, Densmore details how Morrison showed the group how he could derive "MR MOJO RISIN" from "JIM MORRISON" (p. 259). Sugerman and Hopkins noted in a tone of jest they believed Jim used when he said "Mr. Mojo" was not only part of an anagram for his name, but also the name he would use "when contacting the office after he'd split to Africa" (*No One Here Gets Out Alive*, p. 343). If we accept that, then I agree with Gerstenmeyer who wrote that "if you write 'Mister Mojo' instead of 'Mr. Mojo'...the anagram is lost". Hence, it is "Mr. Mojo", not "Mister Mojo".

Since "mojo" was a black slang word for sexual prowess (Jimmy Smith's blues song, 'Got My Mojo Working'), Densmore wrote that he would "steadily increase the tempo back up to the original speed, a la orgasm" (*Riders On The Storm*, p. 259). Or was "mojo" inspired by the greasy and diminutive character, Oswald Mojo who married Pamela, a British girl who turned out to be an oil heiress, in Farina's *Been Down So Long It Looks Like Up To Me*?

The only recorded live performance of "L.A. Woman" is on the bootleg recording, *If It Ain't One Thing, It's Another* (Live at the Felt Forum N.Y. and Dallas, Texas 1970) [triple album; Felt Forum 17 & 18 January 1970 – sides 1, 2, 3, and 4; Dallas 11 December 1970 – sides 5 and 6]. In this version, Morrison varies the studio recorded lyric, "Never saw a lady". He sings, "Never saw a lady / look so down and so alone", and "Never saw a lady / look so down and all alone." Soon after, Morrison croons variations around the lyric, "never saw someone look so down and all alone". And he alters the second singing of the line about L.A. being "just another lost angel, City of Night" to "just another dark witness in the city of night".

There is a transcription of the song included in an article by Robert L. Doerschuk, "Ray Manzarek of the doors: WAITING FOR THE NUBIANS", printed in the February 1991 issue of *Keyboard* (p. 87).

## L'AMERICA

The word, L'America, appears as Lamerica, LAmerica, L'america, and lamerica in some of Morrison's poetic tidbits: in an untitled poem, Lamerica appears in the first three lines and then lamerica appears in the rest of the poem (*Wilderness*; pp. 7-8); in two other poems, the titles were, "LAMERICA" (*Wilderness*; pp. 26, 45); in another poem, the title was, "LAmerica" (*Wilderness*; p. 87); in another poem entitled, "L'AMERICA", L'america appears in the first line and then Lamerica appears in the rest of the poem (*The American Night*; p. 140); in a handwritten copy of the lyrics, the title is spelt "Lamerica" with the lighter corrections of "A" written over the original spelling (*The Doors*

*Quarterly Magazine*, Issue 25, 1992, p. 28).

Morrison's enunciation is, la-mer-e–ca. Therefore, should it be, La'merica? Morrison's intent is to shift our perception of America – and hence all the typical implied images and meanings with that word – to a different viewpoint with the exotic and strange sounding L'America.

Written and recorded months previous to the rest of the songs for this album, the song was intended for Michelango Antonioni's Zabriskie Point, but it was rejected by Antonioni. Though spared from being part of what critics almost universally had panned as a bomb by the Italian film director, The Doors' artistic vision seemed quite similar in focus to Antonioni's; however, the images and impulses of America that Antonioni clumsily pieced together, The Doors draw into a more fluid impression. After Densmore had explained how Morrison tried telling Antonioni the apostrophe after the "L" was short for Latin America or anywhere south of the border, John described the recording session with Antonioni, surmising that the song was too much for the director since he wouldn't understand the "cryptic references to money (beads) and grass (gold – as in Acapulco)" and the song, with its "dark, dissonant chords" of Robby's guitar resonating like cold steel overshadowing Jim's strong singing, summarized the movie (*Riders On The Storm*, p. 254-55).

Although the rhyme scheme in stanza two suggests the word fuck, neither *The Doors: The Complete Lyrics* or Gerstenmeyer note the very faded shriek of 'uck to close this line. In a personal correspondence, Gerstenmeyer writes, "Ray Manzarek screams 'Uh!' in the background".

In *The Lords And The New Creatures*, Morrison writes that in ancient communities, the "stranger" was perceived as the "greatest menace" (p. 12), a contrast to the friendly strangers in this song.

In the piece titled, "The Celebration of the Lizard", appears a line about rain falling "gently on the town", echoing the image of the strangers in the song coming to town like a "gentle rain" (*The American Night*, p. 41; and on the inside sleeve of the album, *Waiting For The Sun*).

HYACINTH HOUSE
In his book, *Riders On The Storm*, Densmore suggests a connection with the Greek Hyacinth myth (pp. 257-58), but somehow the

disjointed images of Jim's lyric are too mundane or neutral to invoke any sense of despair and tragedy as in the myth. The 'Hyacinth House' seems another version of the house on 'Love Street'; it doesn't offer sanctuary or imprisonment – just something to pass through like a museum.

In *No One Here Gets Out Alive*, Jerry Hopkins and Danny Sugerman wrote that after Morrison sang the line about seeing that the "bathroom is clear", Manzarek played a melody line from Chopin's 'Til The End Of Time' (p. 342).

The lyric about throwing away the jack of hearts may be an allusion to the "jack o' diamonds is a hard card to play" line in a Richard Farina poem (*Long Time Coming*, opening page).

CRAWLING KING SNAKE
by John Lee Hooker and Bernard Besman
(C) 1968 LaCienega Music Company (BMI)
All Rights Reserved  Used by Permission

> Bernard Besman provided the following information:
> Recorded by Bernard Besman
> United Sound Studios, Detroit, Michigan
> 18 February 1949
> Master #B7012
> Leased to Modern Records; released on Modern Records, 1949
> Record #20-714
> Copyright 21 May 1968

The following two versions of the song are printed:
(1) as sung by Jim Morrison;
(2) as sung by John Lee Hooker on his 1949 recording of 'Crawling King Snake'.

CRAWLING KING SNAKE
(John Lee Hooker and Bernard Besman)
(C) 1968 LaCienega Music Company (BMI)
(altered lyrics, Jim Morrison)

Well, I'm the crawling king snake
And I rule my den
I'm the crawling king snake
And I rule my den
Yeah, don't mess 'round with my mate
Gonna use her for myself

Caught me crawling, baby
When the grass is very high
I keep on crawling till the day I die
Crawling king snake
And I rule my den
You better give me what I want
Gonna crawl no more

Caught me crawling, baby
Crawling 'round your door
See anything I want
I'm gonna crawl on your floor
Let's crawl
And I rule my den
Come on, give me what I want
Ain't gonna crawl no more
Ah, let's crawl a while

Come on, crawl
Come on, crawl
Get on out there on your hands and knees, baby
Crawl all over me
Just like the spider on the wall
Oo-oo, we goin' crawl
One more

Well, I'm the crawling king snake
And I rule my den
Call me the crawling king snake
And I rule my den
Yeah, don't mess 'round with my mate
Gonna use her for myself

CRAWLING KING SNAKE
(John Lee Hooker and Bernard Besman)
(C) 1968 LaCienega Music Company (BMI)

Following lyrics were transcribed from the 1949 recording of
'Crawling King Snake' released by Modern Records and transferred to
John Lee Hooker: The Legendary MODERN Recordings 1948-1954
[CD] (Virgin Records America [Flair], 7243 8 39658 2 3, 1993).


Well, I'm a crawling king snake
And I rule my den
Well, I'm a crawling king snake
And I rule my den
I don't want you 'round my mate
Wanna use her for myself

You know you caught me crawling, now baby, when the...
When the grass was very high
I'm just gonna keep on crawling now, baby
Until the day I die
Because I'm a crawling king snake
And I rule my den
Come on and give me what I want, baby
And I won't crawl no more

You know, I'm going away now, baby
But I'll be back before long
When I come to town, now baby
I'll be the same ol' slick again
Now, 'cause I'm a crawling king snake, yes, yeah
And I rule my den
Come on and give me what I want, baby
And I won't crawl no more

Well, I'm crawling, yes, I'm crawling, now baby
I'm, ah, crawling in front of your door
You got anything I want, now baby

I'll crawl upon your floor
Because I'm a crawling king snake
And I rule my den

Morrison's version of the song is closer to a later recording of the
song done by Hooker, a recording reproduced on *The Hook: 20 Years
Of Hits & Hot Boogie* [CD] (Chameleon Records, D2-74794, 1989;
VeeJay Hall of Fame Series). Hooker recorded for VeeJay Records in the
1950s.

## THE WASP (TEXAS RADIO AND THE BIG BEAT)

The lyrics were published in an 1968 Doors' souvenir book. Another
version of this song was part of The Doors' Denmark television
appearance in 1968, which was included in the video, *The Doors: Live
In Europe 1968* (New York: HBO Video, 1988). A variation of the lyric
also was reinterpreted in the selection entitled, 'Stoned Immaculate',
on the posthumous album, *An American Prayer*. Parts of this song are
published under the two selections, 'I Want To Tell You' and 'Now
Listen To This' in *The American Night* (pp. 125-26, 127).

In an untitled selection in *Wilderness* Morrison sketches out a
different portrait of the 'Texas Radio & The Big Beat' image (p. 147).

## RIDERS ON THE STORM

'Riders On The Storm' b/w 'The Changeling' was released by Elektra as
a 45 rpm single (# 45738), June 1971.

### BILLBOARD's HOT 100

| | | | |
|---|---|---|---|
| July 3, 1971 | # 74 | Aug. 14 | # 20 |
| July 10 | # 64 | Aug. 21 | # 16 |
| July 17 | # 50 | Aug. 28 | # 15 |
| July 24 | # 39 | Sept. 4 | # 14 |
| July 31 | # 36 | Sept. 11 | # 25 |
| Aug. 7 | # 23 | Sept. 18 | # 28 |

The last Doors' song on this album was, as Manzarek said in the
radio program, *History Of Rock 'N' Roll*, the last one Morrison ever
sang, the last one The Doors recorded, and the last one for the album.

Segments of the song were used as background for a narrative entitled, 'The Hitchhiker', on the posthumous album, *An American Prayer*.

In the Alan Paul interview printed in *Guitar World* (March 1994), Krieger said the group was "fooling around with 'Ghost Riders In the Sky' one day and somehow it turned into 'Riders On The Storm'" (p. 189).

A variation of the lyric about the killer's brain squirming "like a toad" appears in Morrison's roughed out screen play entitled, *The Hitchhiker (An American Pastoral)*. Jim describes Billy, the murderous hitchhiker, in a car, and he is singing along with "wild abandon" with The Rolling Stones' 'I Can't Get No Satisfaction' while he "squirms in his seat like a toad" (*The American Night*, p. 78).

There is a transcription of the music and lyrics in the December issue (Vol. 1, No. 1) of *Words And Music* (pp. 14-18).

There is a transcription of the song included in an article by Robert L. Doerschuk, "Ray Manzarek of the doors: WAITING FOR THE NUBIANS", printed in the February 1991 issue of *Keyboard* (pp. 84-85).

## POPULAR SONGS
## SEPTEMBER 1966 – MARCH 1967

✓ 'The Beat Goes On' Sonny & Cher
'Black Is Black' Los Bravos
'Bus Stop' The Hollies
'Cherish' The Association
'Cherry, Cherry' Neil Diamond
'Devil With A Blue Dress On & Good Golly Miss Molly'
    Mitch Ryder & The Detroit Wheels
'Eleanor Rigby' The Beatles
'Georgy Girl' Seekers
'Gimme Some Lovin'' Spencer Davis Group
✓ 'Good Vibrations' Beach Boys
'I Had Too Much To Dream (Last Night)' Electric Prunes
✓ 'I'm A Believer' The Monkees
'Kind Of A Drag' Buckinghams
✓ 'Last Train To Clarksville' The Monkees
'Mellow Yellow' Donovan
'Nashville Cats' The Lovin' Spoonful
'96 Tears' The Mysterious
'98.6' Keith
'Poor Side Of Town' Johnny Rivers
'Reach Out I'll Be There' Four Tops
✓ 'Ruby Tuesday' The Rolling Stones
'See You In September' The Happenings
'Snoopy vs. The Red Baron' Royal Guardsmen
'Sugar Town' Nancy Sinatra
✓ 'Summer In The City' The Lovin' Spoonful
'Sunshine Superman' Donovan
'(We Ain't Got) Nothin' Yet' Blue Magoos
'Winchester Cathedral' New Vaudeville Band

'Wipe Out' The Surfaris
'Wouldn't It Be Nice' Beach Boys
'Yellow Submarine' The Beatles
'You Can't Hurry Love' The Supremes
'You Keep Me Hangin' On' The Supremes

## POPULAR & RELEASED ALBUMS
## SEPTEMBER 1966 – MARCH 1967

*Aftermath* The Rolling Stones
*And Then...Along Comes The Association* The Association
*Best Of The Animals* The Animals
*Best Of The Beach Boys* – Vol. 1 Beach Boys
*Best Of Herman Hermits* – Vol. 2 Herman Hermits
*Blonde On Blonde* Bob Dylan
*Dr. Zhivago* (soundtrack to movie)
*Golden Greats* Garry Lewis & The Playboys
*Got Live If You Want It* The Rolling Stones
*Jefferson Airplane Takes Off* Jefferson Airplane
*Je M'Appele Barbara* Barbara Streisand
*The Kinks* Greatest Hits Kinks
*Lou Rawls Soulin'* Lou Rawls
*The Mamas and The Papas* The Mamas and The Papas
*The Monkees* The Monkees
*More Of The Monkees* The Monkees
*Parsley, Sage, Rosemary & Thyme* Simon & Garfunkel
*Pet Sounds* Beach Boys
*Revolver* The Beatles
*Sergio Mendes & Brasil '66* Sergio Mendes & Brasil '66
*Sinatra At The Sands* Frank Sinatra
*The Sound Of Music* (soundtrack to movie)
*S.R.O.* Herb Albert & The Tijuana Brass

*Sunshine Superman* Donovan
*Supremes A' Go-Go* The Supremes
*The Temptations Greatest Hits* Temptations
*That's Life* Frank Sinatra
*What Now My Love* Herb Albert & The Tijuana Brass
*Yesterday...And Today* The Beatles


# POPULAR SONGS
# APRIL – SEPTEMBER 1967

'All You Need Is Love' The Beatles
'Bernadette' Four Tops
'Brown-Eyed Girl' Van Morrison
'Can't Take My Eyes Off Of You' Frankie Valli
'Carrie Ann' The Hollies
'Cold Sweat' James Brown & The Famous Flames
'Come On Down To My Boat' Every Mother's Son
'Creeque Alley' The Mamas and The Papas
'Dedicated To The One I Love' The Mamas and The Papas
'Ding Dong The Witch Is Dead' Fifth Estate
'Don't Sleep In The Subway' Petula Clark
'Don't You Care' Buckinghams
'For What It's Worth' Buffalo Springfield
'Girl, You'll Be A Woman Soon' Neil Diamond
'Groovin'' The Young Rascals
'The Happening' The Supremes
'Happy Together' Turtles
'I Dig Rock and Roll Music' Peter, Paul & Mary
'I Got Rhythm' Happenings
'I Think We're Alone Now' Tommy James and The Shondells
'I Was Made To Love Her' Stevie Wonder

'Let's Live For Today' Grass Roots
'The Letter' Box Tops
'Little Bit O' Soul' Music Explosion
'A Little Bit You, A Little Bit Me' The Monkees
'Mirage' Tommy James and The Shondells
'My Cup Runneath Over' Ed Ames
'Never My Love' The Association
'Ode To Billie Joe' Bobbie Gentry
'On A Carousel' The Hollies
'Penny Lane' The Beatles
'Pleasant Valley Sunday' The Monkees
'Reflections' Diana Ross & The Supremes
'Release Me (And Let Me Love Again)' Engelbert Humperdinck
'Respect' Aretha Franklin
'Return Of The Red Baron' Royal Guardsmen
'San Francisco Wear Some Flowers In Your Hair' Scott McKenzie
'She'd Rather Be With Me' Turtles
'Society's Child' Janis Ian
'Somebody To Love' Jefferson Airplane
'Somethin' Stupid' Nancy Sinatra and Frank Sinatra
'Strawberry Fields Forever' The Beatles
'Sunday Will Never Be The Same' Spank and The Gang
'Thank The Lord For The Night Time' Neil Diamond
'There's A Kind Of Hush' Herman Hermits
'Up – Up and Away' The Fifth Dimension
'Western Union' Five Americans
'White Rabbit' Jefferson Airplane
'A Whiter Shade Of Pale' Procol Harum
'Windy' The Association

# POPULAR & RELEASED ALBUMS
## APRIL – SEPTEMBER 1967

*Absolutely Free* Frank Zappa & Mothers Of Invention
*Are You Experienced* Jimi Hendrix Experience
*Aretha Arrives* Aretha Franklin
*The Best Of The Lovin' Spoonful* The Lovin' Spoonful
*The Best Of Sonny and Cher* Sonny & Cher
*Between The Buttons* The Rolling Stones
*Born Free* Andy Williams
*Da Capo* Love
*Flowers* The Rolling Stones
*Greatest Hits* Bob Dylan
*Greatest Hits* The Hollies
*Groovin'* The Young Rascals
*Headquarters* The Monkees
*I Never Loved A Man The Way I Love You* Aretha Franklin
*Insight Out* The Association
*Janis Ian* Janis Ian
*The Mamas and The Papas Deliver* The Mamas and The Papas
*Mellow Yellow* Donovan
*Moby Grape* Moby Grape
*Mr. Fantasy* Traffic
*Paul Revere & The Raiders Greatest Hits* Paul Revere & The Raiders
*Reach Out* Four Tops
*Release Me* Engelbert Humperdinck
*Revenge* Bill Cosby
*Rewind* Johnny Rivers
*Sounds Like Herb Albert & The Tijuana Brass*
*Sergeant Pepper's Lonely Hearts Club Band* The Beatles
*Surrealistic Pillow* Jefferson Airplane
*There's A Kind Of Hush All over The World* Herman Hermits

*Up, Up and Away* The Fifth Dimension
*The Velvet Underground & Nico* The Velvet Underground

## POPULAR SONGS
## NOVEMBER 1967 – FEBRUARY 1968

'Bend Me, Shape Me' American Breed
'By The Time I Get To Phoenix' Glen Campbell
'Chain Of Fools' Aretha Franklin
'Daydream Believer' The Monkees
'Different Drum' Stone Poneys
'Goin' Out Of My Head / Can't Take My Eyes Off Of You' Lettermen
'Green Tambourine' Lemon Pipers
'Hello Goodbye' The Beatles
'Hey Baby (They're Playing Our Song)' The Buckinghams
'I Can See For Miles' The Who
'I Heard It Through The Grapevine' Gladys Knight & The Pips
'I Say A Little Prayer Dionne Warwick
'I Second That Emotion' Smokey Robinson & The Miracles
'I Wonder What She's Doing Tonight' Tommy Boyce & Bobby Hart
'Incense and Peppermints' Strawberry Alarm Clock
'It Must Be Him' Vikki Carr
'Itchycoo Park' Small Faces
'Judy In Disguise (With Glasses)' John Fred & The Playboy Band
'Kentucky Woman' Neil Diamond
'The Last Waltz' Engelbert Humperdinck
'Little Ole Man (Uptight–Everything's Alright)' Bill Cosby
'The Look Of Love' Dusty Springfield
'Love Is Blue' Paul Mauriat & His Orchestra
'A Natural Woman' Aretha Franklin
'An Open Letter To My Teenage Son' Victor Lundberg

'Please Love Me Forever' Bobby Vinton
'The Rain, The Park & Other Things' Cowsills
'Soul Man' Sam & Dave
'Spooky' Classics IV
'Summer Rain' Johnny Rivers
'To Sir, With Love' Lulu
'Woman, Woman' Gary Puckett & The Union Gap
'Your Precious Love' Marvin Gaye & Tammi Terrell

# POPULAR & RELEASED ALBUMS
# NOVEMBER 1967 – FEBRUARY 1968

*After Bathing At Baxters* Jefferson Airplane
*Bee Gees First* Bee Gees
*Camelot* (soundtrack to movie)
*Days Of Future Passed* Moody Blues
*Diana Ross & The Supremes Greatest Hits*
        Diana Ross & The Supremes
*Disraeli Gears* Cream
*Farewell To The First Golden Era* The Mamas and The Papas
*Forever Changes* Love
*Four Tops Greatest Hits* Four Tops
*Golden Hits* Turtles
*Greatest Hits* The Byrds
*History Of Otis Redding* Otis Redding
*Incense & Peppermints* Strawberry Alarm Clock
*It Must Be Him* Vikki Carr
*The Last Waltz* Engelbert Humperdinck
*Love, Andy* Andy Williams
*Lumpy Gravy* Frank Zappa
*Magical Mystery Tour* The Beatles

*Ninth Herb Albert & The Tijuana Brass*
*Ode To Billie Joe* Bobbie Gentry
*Paul Mauriat & His Orchestra* Paul Mauriat & His Orchestra
*Pisces, Aquarius, Capricorn & Jones, Ltd.* The Monkees
*Simply Streisand* Barbara Streisand
*Their Satanic Majesties Request* The Rolling Stones
*Vanilla Fudge* Vanilla Fudge
*White Light / White Heat* The Velvet Underground

# POPULAR SONGS
## MARCH – NOVEMBER 1968

'Ain't Nothing like The Real Thing' Marvin Gaye & Tammi Terrell
'Born To Be Wild' Steppenwolf
'Classical Gas' Mason Williams
'Cry Like A Baby' Box Tops
'Dance To The Music' Sly & The Family Stone
'Do You Know The Way To San Jose' Dionne Warwick
'Fire' Crazy World Of Arthur Brown
'For Once In My Life' Stevie Wonder
'The Good, The Bad and The Ugly'
        Hugo Montenegro Orchestra & Chorus
'Journey To The Center Of Your Mind' Amboy Dukes
'Harper Valley P.T.A.' Jeannie C. Riley
'Hey Jude' The Beatles
'Honey' Bobby Goldsboro
'Hurdy Gurdy Man' Donovan
'Hush' Deep Purple
'In-a-Gadda-Da-Vida' Iron Butterfly
'Indian Lake' Cowsills
'I've Got To Get A Message To You' Bee Gees

'Jennifer Juniper' Donovan

'Jumpin' Jack Flash' The Rolling Stones

'Just Dropped In (To See What Condition My Condition Was In)' Kenny Rogers & The First Edition

'Lady Madonna' The Beatles

'Lady Willpower' Gary Puckett & The Union Gap

'Light My Fire' Jose Feliciano

'Love Child' Diana Ross & The Supremes

'MacArthur Park' Richard Harris

'Magic Bus' The Who

'Magic Carpet Ride' Steppenwolf

'Midnight Confessions' Grass Roots

'The Mighty Quinn' Manfred Mann

'Mony Mony' Tommy James and The Shondells

'Mrs. Robinson' Simon & Garfunkel

'People Got To Be Free' The Rascals (formerly Young Rascals)

'Revolution' The Beatles

'Scarborough Fair / Canticle' Simon & Garfunkel

'Simon Says' 1910 Fruitgum Company

'(Sittin' On) The Dock Of The Bay' Otis Redding

'Stoned Soul Picnic' The Fifth Dimension

'Sunshine Of Your Love' Cream

'Suzie Q' Creedence Clearwater Revival

'Those Were The Days' Mary Hopkins

'Time Has Come Today' Chamber Brothers

'Tuesday Afternoon' Moody Blues

'This Guy's In Love With You' Herb Albert

'Valleri' The Monkees

'Walk Away Renee' Four Tops

'White Room' Cream

'Young Girl' Gary Puckett & The Union Gap

'Yummy, Yummy, Yummy' Ohio Express

# POPULAR & RELEASED ALBUMS
# MARCH – NOVEMBER 1968

*Anthem Of The Sun* The Grateful Dead
*Aretha Now* Aretha Franklin
*At Folsom Prison* Johnny Cash
*Axis: Bold As Love* Jimi Hendrix Experience
*The Best Of The Brass* Herb Albert & The Tijuana Brass
*The Birds The Bees and The Monkees* The Monkees
*Bookends* Simon & Garfunkel
*By The Time I Get To Phoenix* Glenn Campbell
*Cheap Thrills*
        Big Brother & The Holding Company (w/ Janis Joplin)
*Child Is Father To The Man* Blood, Sweet & Tears
*Crazy World Of Arthur Brown* Crazy World Of Arthur Brown
*Creedence Clearwater Revival* Creedence Clearwater Revival
*Crown Of Creation* Jefferson Airplane
*The Dock Of The Bay* Otis Redding
*Donovan In Concert* Donovan
*Electric Ladyland* Jimi Hendrix Experience
*Feliciano!* Jose Feliciano
*Funny Girl* (soundtrack to movie)
*Gentle On My Mind* Glen Campbell
*God Bless* Tiny Tim
*Goin' Out Of My Head* Lettermen
*The Good, The Bad and The Ugly* (soundtrack to movie)
*The Graduate* (soundtrack to movie) Simon & Garfunkel
*Honey* Bobby Goldsboro
*In Search Of The Lost Chord* Moody Blues
*In-a-Gadda-Da-Vida* Iron Butterfly
*John Wesley Harding* Bob Dylan
*Lady Soul* Aretha Franklin

*A Long Time Comin' Electric Flag* (w/ Mike Bloomfield)
*Look Around* Sergio Mendes & Brasil '66
*Magic Bus* The Who
*Once Upon A Dream* The Rascals (formerly Young Rascals)
*The Papas and The Mamas* The Mamas and The Papas
*Quick Silver Messenger Service* Quick Silver Messenger Service
*Realization* Johnny Rivers
*Reflections* Diana Ross & The Supremes
*Steppenwolf The Second* Steppenwolf
*Shades Of Deep Purple* Deep Purple
*Steppenwolf* Steppenwolf
*Super Sessions* Mike Bloomfield, Al Kooper, Steve Stills
*Time Has Come* Chamber Brothers
*Time Peace: Greatest Hits* The Rascals (formerly Young Rascals)
*To Russell, My Brother, Whom I Slept With* Bill Cosby
*Together* Country Joe & The Fish
*Truth* Jeff Beck
*Unicorn* Irish Rovers
*We're Only In It For The Money*
        Frank Zappa & Mothers Of Invention
*Wheels Of Fire* Cream
*Wildflowers* Judy Collins
*Woman, Woman* Gary Puckett & The Union Gap
*Wow* Moby Grape
*Young Girl* Gary Puckett & The Union Gap

## POPULAR SONGS
## DECEMBER 1968 – NOVEMBER 1969

'Abraham, Martin and John' Dion
'And When I Die' Blood, Sweat & Tears

'Aquarius/Let The Sunshine In' The Fifth Dimension
'Atlantis' Donovan
'Bad Moon Rising' Creedence Clearwater Revival
'The Ballad Of John and Yoko' The Beatles
'Both Sides Now' Judy Collins
'The Boxer' Simon & Garfunkel
'A Boy Named Sue' Johnny Cash
'Build Me Up Buttercup' The Foundations
'Cherry Hill Park' Billy Joe Royal
'Cloud Nine' Temptations
'Come Together' The Beatles
'Crimson & Clover' Tommy James & The Shondells
'Crossroads' Cream
'Crystal Blue Persuasion' Tommy James & The Shondells
'Dizzy' Tommy Roe
'Easy To Be Hard' Three Dog Night
'Eli's Coming' Three Dog Night
'Everybody's Talking' Nilsson
'Everyday People' Sly & The Family Stone
'Galveston' Glen Campbell
'Get Back' The Beatles
'Good Morning Starshine' Oliver
'Hair' Cowsills
'Hang 'Em High' Booker T. & The M.G.'s
'Hawaii Five-O' Ventures
'Hello, It's Me' Nazz
'Holly Holy' Neil Diamond
'Honky Tonk Woman' The Rolling Stones
'Hooked On A Feeling' B.J. Thomas
'Hot Fun In The Summer Time' Sly & The Family Stone
'I Heard It Through The Grape' Marvin Gaye
'I'm Gonna Make You Love Me' Diana Ross & The Supremes

'In The Ghetto' Elvis Presley

'In The Year 2525 (Exordium & Termins)' Zager & Evans

'Indian Giver' 1910 Fruitgum Company

'It's Your Thing' Isley Brothers

'I've Gotta Be Me' Sammie Davis Jr.

'Jean' Oliver

'Lay Lady Lay' Bob Dylan

'Love Child' Diana Ross & The Supremes

'Love Theme from Romeo & Juliet' Henry Mancini & Orchestra

'My Cherie Amour' Stevie Wonder

'Na Na Hey Hey Kiss Him Goodbye' Steam

'One' Three Dog Night

'One Tin Soldier' The Original Caste

'Pinball Wizard' The Who

'Proud Mary' Creedence Clearwater Revival

'Ramblin' Gamblin' Man' Bob Seger

'Ruby, Don't Take Your Love To Town'
Kenny Rogers & The First Edition

'Something' The Beatles

'Son-of-a Preacher Man' Dusty Springfield

'Spinning Wheel' Blood, Sweat & Tears

'Stormy' Classics IV

'Sugar, Sugar' Archies

'Suite: Judy Blue Eyes' Crosby Still & Nash

'Suspicious Minds' Elvis Presley

'Sweet Caroline' Neil Diamond

'Take A Letter Maria' R.B. Greaves

'These Eyes' The Guess Who

'Time Of The Seasons' Zombies

'Traces' Classics IV

'Undun' The Guess Who

'Wedding Bell Blues' The Fifth Dimension

'Wichita Lineman' Glen Campbell
'You've Made Me So Very Happy' Blood, Sweat & Tears

## POPULAR & RELEASED ALBUMS
## DECEMBER 1968 – NOVEMBER 1969

*Abbey Road* The Beatles
*Age Of Aquarius* The Fifth Dimension
*Alice's Restaurant* Arlo Guthrie
*Aretha's Gold* Aretha Franklin
*The Association, Greatest Hits, Vol. 1* The Association
*At San Quentin* Johnny Cash
*Axomoxoa* The Grateful Dead
*The Band* The Band
*Bayou Country* Creedence Clearwater Revival
*The Beatles (White Album)* The Beatles
*Beck-Ola* Jeff Beck
*Beggar's Banquet* Rolling Stone
*Best Of Cream* Cream
*The Best Of Bee Gees* Bee Gees
*Bless Its Pointed Little Head* Jefferson Airplane
*Blind Faith* Blind Faith
*Blood, Sweat & Tears* Blood, Sweat & Tears
*Brave New World* Steve Miller Band
*Chicago Transit Authority* (double LP) Chicago
*Clouds* Joni Mitchell
*Crimson & Clover* Tommy James & The Shondells
*Crosby Stills and Nash* Crosby Stills & Nash
*Cruising With Ruben and The Jets*
*Frank Zappa & Mothers of Invention*
*Diana Ross & The Supremes Join The Temptations*

Diana Ross & The Supremes and The Temptations

*Elvis* Elvis Presley

*Feliciano / 10 To 23* Jose Feliciano

*Fool On The Hill* Sergio Mendes & Brasil '66

*From Elvis In Memphis* Elvis Presley

*Galveston* Glen Campbell

*Goodbye* Cream

*Greatest Hits* Donovan

*Green River* Creedence Clearwater Revival

*Hair* (soundtrack to movie)

*Happy Heart* Andy Williams

*Happy Trails* Quicksilver Messenger Service

*Help Yourself* Tom Jones

*Hot Buttered Soul* Isaac Hayes

*It's A Beautiful Day* It's A Beautiful Day

*I've Got Dem Ol' Kozmic Blues Again Mama!* Janis Joplin

*Kickin' Out The Jams* MC5

*Last Exit* Traffic

*Led Zeppelin* Led Zeppelin

*Livin' The Blues* Canned Heat

*Love Child* Diana Ross & The Supremes

*Nashville Skyline* Bob Dylan

*Nazz, Nazz* Nazz

*On The Threshold Of A Dream* Moody Blues

*On Time* Grand Funk Railroad

*Portrait Of Petula* Petula Clark

*Puzzle People* Temptations

*Romeo & Juliet* (soundtrack to movie)

*Santana* Santana

*Smash Hits* Jimi Hendrix Experience

*Songs from A Room* Leonard Cohen

*Ssshh* Ten Years After

*Stand!* Sly & The Family Stone
*Stand Up* Jethro Tull
*Stonedhenge* Ten Years After
*Suitable For Framing* Three Dog Night
*T.C.B.* Diana Ross & The Supremes with The Temptations
*The Velvet Underground* The Velvet Underground
*Three Dog Night* Three Dog Night
*Through The Past Darkly (Big Hits Vol. II)*
The Rolling Stones
*Tommy* The Who
*Traffic* Traffic
*Uncle Meat* Frank Zappa & Mothers Of Invention
*Wheatfield Soul* The Guess Who
*Wichita Lineman* Glen Campbell
*Yellow Submarine* The Beatles

# POPULAR SONGS
# DECEMBER 1969 – NOVEMBER 1970

'ABC' The Jackson 5
'After Midnight' Eric Clapton
'American Woman / No Sugar Tonight' The Guess Who
'Ain't No Mountain High Enough' Diana Ross
'Band Of Gold' Freda Payne
'Big Yellow Taxi' Joni Mitchell
'Bridge Over Troubled Water' Simon & Garfunkel
'Candida' Dawn
'Cecilia' Simon & Garfunkel
'Celebrate' Three Dog Night
'Close To You' The Carpenters
'Come and Get It' Badfinger

'Cracklin' Rose' Neil Diamond
'Does Anybody Really Know What Time It Is?' Chicago
'Down On The Corner' Creedence Clearwater Revival
'El Condor Pasa' Simon & Garfunkel
'Everything Is Beautiful' Ray Stevens
'Evil Ways' Santana
'Fire and Rain' James Taylor
'Green-Eyed Lady' Sugerloaf
'Gypsy Woman' Brian Hyland
'Hand Me Down World' The Guess Who
'Hi-De-Ho' Blood, Sweat & Tears
'Hitchin' A Ride' Vanity Fare
'(I Know) I'm Losing You' Rare Earth
'I Think I Love You' The Partridge Family
'I'll Be There' The Jackson 5
'I'll Never Fall In Love Again' Dionne Warwick
'In The Summertime' Mungo Jerry
'Indiana Wants Me' R. Dean Taylor
'Instant Karma (We All Shine On)' John Lennon
'It Don't Matter To Me' Bread
'Julie, Do Ya Love Me' Bobby Sherman
'Kentucky Rain' Elvis Presley
'Leaving On A Jet Plane' Peter, Paul & Mary
'Let It Be' The Beatles
'The Letter' Joe Cocker
'The Long and Winding Road' The Beatles
'Look What They've Done To My Song Ma' New Seekers
'Love Grows (Where My Rosemary Goes)' Edison Lighthouse
'Make It With You' Bread
'Make Me Smile' Chicago
'Mama Told Me (Not To Come)' Three Dog Night
'Mississippi Queen' Mountain

'Montego Bay' Bobby Bloom
'No Matter What' Badfinger
'No Time' The Guess Who
'Ohio' Crosby Stills Nash & Young
'Our House' Crosby Stills Nash & Young
'Patches' Clarence Carter
'Psychedelic Shack' Temptations
'Question' Moody Blues
'Rain Drops Keep Fallin' On My Head' B.J. Thomas
'The Rapper' Jaggers
'Ride Captain Ride' Blues Image
'Rubber Duckie' Ernie (Jim Henson/'Sesame Street')
'Shilo' Neil Diamond
'Signed Sealed Delivered (I'm Yours)' Stevie Wonder
'Solitary Man' Neil Diamond
'Someday We'll Be Together' Diana Ross & The Supremes
'Spill The Wine' Eric Burdon & War
'Spirit In The Sky' Norman Greenbaum
'Teach Your Children' Crosby Stills Nash & Young
'Tears Of A Clown' Smokey Robinson & The Miracles
'Thank You (Falettin Me Be Mice Elf Agin)'
Sly & The Family Stone
'Time Waits For No One' Friends Of Distinction
'Travelin' Band / Who'll Stop The Rain'
Creedence Clearwater Revival
'25 or 6 To 4' Chicago
'Up Around The Bend' Creedence Clearwater Revival
'Vehicle' Ides Of March
'Venus' Shocking Blue
'War' Edwin Starr
'We've Only Just Begun' The Carpenters
'Whole Lotta Love' Led Zeppelin

'Woodstock' Crosby Stills Nash & Young
'Yester-me, Yester-you, Yesterday' Stevie Wonder

# POPULAR & RELEASED ALBUMS
# DECEMBER 1969 – NOVEMBER 1970

*ABC* The Jackson 5
*Abraxas* Santana
*After The Goldrush* Neil Young
*Alone Together* Dave Mason
*American Woman* The Guess Who
*Beaucoups Of Blues* Ringo Starr
*Benefit* Jethro Tull
*Black Sabbath* Black Sabbath
*Blood, Sweat & Tears 3* Blood, Sweat & Tears
*Bridge Over Troubled Water* Simon & Garfunkel
*Butch Cassidy & The Sundance Kid* (soundtrack to movie)
Burt Bacharach
*Captured Live At The Forum* Three Dog Night
*Chicago* Chicago
*Close To You* The Carpenters
*Closer To Home* Grand Funk Railroad
*Cosmo's Factory* Creedence Clearwater Revival
*Curtis* Curtis Mayfield
*Deja Vu* Crosby Stills Nash & Young
*The Devil Made Me Buy This Dress* Flip Wilson
*Diana Ross* Diana Ross
*Easy Rider* (soundtrack to movie)
*Ecology* Rare Earth
*Elton John* Elton John
*Empty Rooms* John Mayall

*Engelbert Humperdinck* Engelbert Humperdinck
*Eric Burdon Declares War* Eric Burdon & War
*Eric Clapton* Eric Clapton
*Everybody Knows This Is Nowhere* Neil Young & Crazy Horse
*Frijid Pink* Frijid Pink
*Gasoline Alley* Rod Stewart
*Get Ready* Rare Earth
*Get Yer Ya-Ya's Out* The Rolling Stones
*Gold* Neil Diamond
*Grand Funk* Grand Funk Railroad
*Greatest Hits* The Fifth Dimension
*Greatest Hits* Gary Puckett & The Union Gap
*Greatest Hits* Sly & The Family Stone
*Band Of Gypsys* Jimi Hendrix w/ Buddy Miles & Billy Cox
*Here Comes Bobby* Bobby Sherman
*Hey Jude* The Beatles
*Hot Buttered Soul* Issac Hayes
*I Am The President* David Frye
*Idlewild South* Allman Brothers Band
*In The Court Of The Crimson King: An Observation by King Crimson* King Crimson
*Iron Butterfly Live* Iron Butterfly
*The Isaac Hayes Movement* Isaac Hayes
*It Ain't Easy* Three Dog Night
*James Gang Rides Again* James Gang
*Joe Cocker!* Joe Cocker
*John Barleycorn Must Die* Traffic
*Led Zeppelin II* Led Zeppelin
*Led Zeppelin III* Led Zeppelin
*Let It Be* The Beatles
*Let It Bleed* The Rolling Stones
*Live Steppenwolf* Steppenwolf

313

*Live At Leeds* The Who
*Live / Dead* The Grateful Dead
*Live Cream* Cream
*Live In Las Vegas* Tom Jones
*Plastic Ono Band – Live Peace In Toronto* Plastic Ono Band
*Mad Dogs & Englishmen* Joe Cocker
*Marrying Maiden* It's A Beautiful Day
*McCartney* Paul McCartney
*Metamorphosis* Iron Butterfly
*Monster* Steppenwolf
*Moondance* Van Morrison
*Mountain Climbing* Mountain
*New Morning* Bob Dylan
*Number 5* Steve Miller Band
*On Stage: February 1970* Elvis Presley
*On The Waters* Bread
*Monterey – Otis Redding and The Jimi Hendrix Experience*
(soundtrack) Otis Redding & Jimi Hendrix Experience
*The Partridge Family Album* The Partridge Family
*Psychedelic Shack* Temptations
*A Question Of Balance* Moody Blues
*Rain Drops Keep Fallin' On My Head* B.J. Thomas
*Self Portrait* Bob Dylan
*Sentimental Journey* Ringo Starr
*Sex Machine* James Brown
*Signed Sealed Delivered* Stevie Wonder
*Stage Fright* The Band
*Sweet Baby James* James Taylor
*10 Years Together* Peter, Paul & Mary
*Third Album* The Jackson 5
*To Bonnie From Delaney* Delaney & Bonnie
*To Our Children's Children's Children* Moody Blues

*Tom* Tom Jones
*Tom Rush* Tom Rush
*Ummagumma* Pink Floyd
*USA Union* John Mayall
*Volunteers* Jefferson Airplane
*Willie and The Poor Boys* Creedence Clearwater Revival
*Woodstock* (soundtrack to movie)
*Workingman's Dead* The Grateful Dead

## POPULAR SONGS
## DECEMBER 1970 – SEPTEMBER 1971

'Ain't No Sunshine' Bill Withers
'Amos Moses' Jerry Reed
'Another Day' Paul McCartney
'Bangla Desh' George Harrison
'Beginnings / Colour My World' Chicago
'Black Magic Woman' Santana
'Bridge Over Troubled Water' Aretha Franklin
'Brown Sugar' The Rolling Stones
'Chick-a-Boom' Daddy Dewdrop
'Don't Pull Your Love' Hamilton, Joe Frank & Reynolds
'Draggin' The Line' Tommy James
'For All We Know' The Carpenters
'Get It On' Chase
'Go Away Little Girl' Donny Osmond
'Have You Ever Seen The Rain' Creedence Clearwater Revival
'Hot Pants Pt. 1 (She Got To Use What She Got To Get What She Wants)' James Brown
'How Can You Mend A Broken Heart?' Bee Gees
'I Am...I Said' Neil Diamond

'I Just Want To Celebrate' Rare Earth
'If' Bread
'If I Were Your Woman' Gladys Knight & The Pips
'If Not For You' Olivia Newton John
'If You Could Read My Mind' Gordon Lightfoot
'I'll Meet You Halfway' The Partridge Family
'I'm 18' Alice Cooper
'Immigrant Song' Led Zeppelin
'Indian Reservation' Paul Revere & The Raiders
'It Don't Come Easy' Ringo Starr
'It's Too Late/I Feel The Earth Move' Carol King
'Joy To The World' Three Dog Night
'Just My Imagination (Running Away With Me)' Temptations
'Knock Three Times' Dawn
'Layla' Derek & The Dominos
'Liar' Three Dog Night
'Lonely Days' Bee Gees
'Love Story (Where Do I Begin)' Andy Williams
'Love The One You're With' Stephen Stills
'Lucky Man' Emerson, Lake & Palmer
'Maggie May' Rod Stewart
'Me and Bobby McGee' Janis Joplin
'Me and My Arrow' Nilsson
'Me and You and A Dog Named Boo' Lobo
'Mercy Mercy Me (The Ecology)' Marvin Gaye
'Moon Shadow' Cat Stevens
'Mr. Big Stuff' Jean Knight
'Mr. Bojangles' Nitty Gritty Dirt Band
'My Sweet Lord / Isn't It A Pity' George Harrison
'Never Can Say Goodbye' The Jackson 5
'Never Ending Song Of Love' Delaney & Bonnie & Friends
'The Night They Drove Old Dixie Down' Joan Baez

'One Bad Apple' Osmonds
'One Less Bell To Answer' The Fifth Dimension
'One Toke Over The Line' Brewer & Shipley
'Power To The People' John Lennon & Plastic Ono Band
'Proud Mary' Ike & Tina Turner
'Put Your Hand In The Hand' Ocean
'Rainy Days and Mondays' The Carpenters
'Reason To Believe' Rod Stewart
'Resurrection Shuffle' Ashton, Gardner & Dyke
'She's A Lady' Tom Jones
'Signs' Five Man Electric Band
'Smiling Faces Sometimes' Undisputed Truth
'Sooner or Later' Grass Roots
'Spanish Harlem' Aretha Franklin
'Stoney End' Barbara Streisand
'The Story In Your Eyes' Moody Blues
'Superstar' The Carpenters
'Superstar (Jesus Christ Superstar)'
Murray Head with The Trinidad Singers
'Sweet and Innocent' Donny Osmond
'Take Me Home, Country Roads' John Denver
'Temptation Eyes' Grass Roots
'That's The Way I've Always Heard It Should Be' Carly Simon
'Theme from Love Story' Henry Mancini & His Orchestra
'Timothy' Buoys
'Treat Her Like A Lady' Cornelius Brothers & Sister Rose
'Uncle Albert / Admiral Halsey' Paul & Linda McCartney
'Want Ads' Honey Cone
'We Gotta Get You A Woman' Todd Rundgren
'Wedding Song (There Is Love)' Paul Stookey
'What Is Life' George Harrison
'What's Going On' Marvin Gaye

'What The World Needs Now Is Love / Abraham, Martin & John'
    Tom Clay
'When You're Hot, You're Hot' Jerry Reed
'Wild World' Cat Stevens
'Won't Get Fooled Again' The Who
'Your Song' Elton John
'You've Got A Friend' James Taylor


## POPULAR & RELEASED ALBUMS
## DECEMBER 1970 – SEPTEMBER 1971

*All Things Must Pass* George Harrison
*Aqualung* Jethro Tull
*Aretha Live At Fillmore West* Aretha Franklin
*At Fillmore East* Allman Brothers Band
*B S & T 4* Blood, Sweat & Tears
*Best Of The Guess Who* The Guess Who
*Blows Against The Empire* Paul Kantner & The Jefferson Starship
*Blue* Joni Mitchell
*Carly Simon* Carly Simon
*Carpenters* The Carpenters
*Chase* Chase
*Chicago III* Chicago
*Cry Of Love* Jimi Hendrix
*Elvis Country* Elvis Presley
*Emerson Lake and Palmer* Emerson, Lake & Palmer
*Every Good Boy Deserves Favour* Moody Blues
*Every Picture Tells A Story* Rod Stewart
*Four Way Street* Crosby Stills Nash & Young
*Golden Biscuits* Three Dog Night
*Homemade* Osmonds

*If I Could Only Remember My Name* David Crosby

*If You Could Read My Mind* Gordon Lightfoot

*James Taylor and The Original Flying Machine* James Taylor

*Jesus Christ Superstar Various Artists*

*John Lennon / Plastic Ono Band* John Lennon & Plastic Ono Band

*Ladies Of The Canyon* Joni Mitchell

*Layla & Other Assorted Love Songs* Derek & The Dominos

*Live Album* Grand Funk Railroad

*Lola vs. Powerman & the Moneygoround* Kinks

*Love It To Death* Alice Cooper

*Love Story* (soundtrack to movie)

*Love Story* Andy Williams

*Manna* Bread

*Maybe Tomorrow* The Jackson 5

*Mud Slide Slim and The Blue Horizon* James Taylor

*Nantucket Sleighride* Mountain

*Naturally* Three Dog Night

*Osmonds* Osmonds

*Paranoid* Black Sabbath

*Pearl* Janis Joplin

*Pendulum* Creedence Clearwater Revival

*Poems, Prayers & Promises* John Denver

*The Point!* Nilsson

*Ram* Paul & Linda McCartney

*Rose Garden* Lynn Anderson

*Runt* Todd Rundgren

*17-11-70 (European dating: day-month-year)* Elton John

*Shaft* (soundtrack to movie) Isaac Hayes

*Songs For Beginners* Graham Nash

*Stephen Stills* Stephen Stills

*Sticky Fingers* The Rolling Stones

*Stoney End* Barbara Streisand

*Super Bad* James Brown
*Survival* Grand Funk Railroad
*Tapestry* Carole King
*Tarkus* Emerson, Lake & Palmer
*Tea For The Tillerman* Cat Stevens
*Thirds* James Gang
*This Is A Recording* Lily Tomlin
*To Be Continued* Isaac Hayes
*Tumbleweed Connection* Elton John
*Up To Date* The Partridge Family
*Whales & Nightingales* Judy Collins
*What's Going On* Marvin Gaye
*Who's Next* The Who
*Worst Of Jefferson Airplane* Jefferson Airplane

# AMERICAN TELEVISION
## 1966 FALL PRIME TIME SCHEDULE

| | 7:30 | 8:00 | 8:30 | 9:00 | 9:30 | 10:00 | 10:30 |
|---|---|---|---|---|---|---|---|
| ABC | Voyage to Bottom of Sea(7-8) | The FBI | The ABC Sunday Night Movie | | | | |
| SUN CBS | It's About Time | Ed Sullivan Show | Garry Moore Show | Line? | Candid Camera | What's My | |
| SUN NBC | Walt Disney's Wonderful World of Colour | | Hey Landlord! | Bonanza | | Andy Williams Show | |
| SUN ABC | Iron Horse Squad | he Rat Patrol | The Felony | Peyton Place | | The Big Valley | |
| MON CBS | Gilligan's Island | Run, Buddy, Run | The Lucy Show | Andy Griffith | Family Affair Show | Jean Arthur | I've Got a Secret |
| MON NBC | The Monkees | I Dream of Jeannie | Roger Miller Show | The Road West | | Run For Your Life | |
| MON ABC | Combat! | The Rounders Southampton | The Pruitts of Rooftop | Love on a | The Fugitive | | |
| TUE CBS | Daktar | Red Skelton Hour Junction | | Petticoat | | CBS News Hour | |
| TUE NBC | The Girl From U.N.C.L.E. Wife | | Occasional | NBC Tuesday Night at the Movies | | | |
| TUE ABC | Batman | The Monroes | The Man Who Never Was | Peyton Place | ABC Stage '67 | | |
| WED CBS | Lost in Space | The Beverly Hillbillies | Green Acres | Gomer Pyle, USMC | Danny Kaye Show | | |
| WED NBC | The Virginian | Bob Hope Show and Specials | | | I Spy | | |
| WED ABC | Batman | F Troop | Tammy Grimes Show | Bewitched | That Girl | Hawk | |
| THU CBS | Jericho | My Three Sons | The CBS Thursday Night Movies | | | | |
| THU NBC | Daniel Boone | Star Trek | The Hero | | Dean Martin Show | | |
| THU ABC | The Green Hornet | The Time Tunnel | | Milton Berle Show | | 12 O'Clock High | |
| FRI CBS | The Wild, Wild West | | Hogan's Heroes | | The CBS Friday Night Movies | | |
| FRI NBC | Tarzan | The Man From U.N.C.L.E. | | T.H.E. Cat | Laredo | | |
| FRI ABC | Shane | Lawrence Welk Show | | The Hollywood Palace | | ABC Scope | |
| SAT CBS | Jackie Gleason Show | | Pistols 'N' Petticoats | Mission: Impossible | | Gunsmoke | |
| SAT NBC | Flipper Eat the Daisies | Please Don't | Get Smart | Saturday Night at the Movies | | | |

321

## AMERICAN TELEVISION
## 1966-67 SEASON

SOME OF THE SATURDAY MORNING CARTOONS
'Atom Ant'
'The Beatles'
'Bugs Bunny Show'
'Bullwinkle Show' (Sunday mornings)
'Cool McCool'
'The Flintstones'
'The Jetsons'
'Magilla Gorilla'
'Mighty Mouse'
'Road Runner Show'
'Space Ghost'
'Tom and Jerry'
'Underdog'

SOME OF THE DAYTIME SOAPS
'Another World'
'As The World Turns'
'Dark Shadows'
'Days Of Our Lives'
'The Doctors'
'Edge Of Night'
'General Hospital'
'Secret Storm'

NIGHTLY NEWS
'ABC Evening News with Peter Jennings'
'CBS Evening News with Walter Cronkite'
'Huntley-Brinkley Report' (NBC)

# AMERICAN TELEVISION
# 1967 FALL PRIME TIME SCHEDULE

|          | 7:30 | 8:00 | 8:30 | 9:00 | 9:30 | 10:00 | 10:30 |
|----------|------|------|------|------|------|-------|-------|
| ABC      | Voyage to Bottom (7-8) | The FBI | The ABC Sunday Night Movie and Specials | | | | |
| SUN CBS  | Gentle Ben | Ed Sullivan Show | Smothers Brothers Comedy Hour | | Mission: Impossible | | |
| SUN NBC  | Walt Disney's Wonderful World of Colour | | Mothers-in-Law | Bonanza | The High Chaparral | | |
| SUN ABC  | Cowboy in Africa | The Rat Patrol Squad | The Felony | Peyton Place | The Big Valley | | |
| MON CBS  | Gunsmoke | The Lucy Show | Andy Griffith Show | Family Affair | Carol Burnett Show | | |
| MON NBC  | The Monkees | The Man from U.N.C.L.E. | | Danny Thomas Hour | | I Spy | |
| MON ABC  | Garrison's Gorillas | | The Invaders | N.Y.P.D. | The Hollywood Palace | | |
| TUE CBS  | Daktari | Red Skelton Hour World | Good Morning CBS News Hour | | | | |
| TUES NBC | I Dream of Jeannie | Jerry Lewis Show | | NBC Tuesday Night at the Movies | | | |
| TUES ABC | Custer Years | Second Hundred | | The ABC Wednesday Night Movie and Specials | | | |
| WED CBS  | Lost in Space Hillbillies | The Beverly | Green Acres | He & She | Dundee and The Culhane | | |
| WED NBC  | The Virginian | | The Kraft Music Hall | | Run For Your Life | | |
| WED ABC  | Batman | The Flying Nun | Bewitched | That Girl | Peyton Place | Good Company Local | |
| THU CBS  | Cimarron Strip | | The CBS Thursday Night Movies | | | | |
| THU NBC  | Daniel Boone | Ironside | Dragnet 1968 | Dean Martin Show | | | |
| THU ABC  | Off to See the Wizard Will Sonnett | | Hondo | The Guns of | Judd, For the Defense | | |
| FRI CBS  | The Wild, Wild West | | Gomer Pyle, USMC | The CBS Friday Night Movies | | | |
| FRI NBC  | Tarzan | Star Trek | Accidental Family | NBC News Specials / Bell Telephone Hour | | | |
| FRI ABC  | The Datinge Game Game | The Newlywed | Lawrence Welk Show | | Iron Horse | ABC Scope | |
| SAT CBS  | Jackie Gleason Show | My Three Sons | Hogan's Heroes Junction | Petticoat | Mannix | | |
| SAT NBC  | Maya | Get Smart | Saturday Night at the Movies | | | | |

## AMERICAN TELEVISION
## 1967-68 SEASON


SOME OF THE SATURDAY MORNING CARTOONS
'Atom Ant'
'The New Beatles'
'Bugs Bunny Show' (Sunday mornings)
'Bullwinkle Show' (Sunday mornings)
'Cool McCool'
'The Flintstones'
'George Of The Jungle'
'Johnny Quest'
'Shazzan!'
'Space Ghost'
'Spiderman'
'Tom and Jerry' (Sunday mornings)
'Underdog' (Sunday mornings)

SOME OF THE DAYTIME SOAPS
'Another World'
'As The World Turns'
'Dark Shadows'
'Days Of Our Lives'
'The Doctors'
'Edge Of Night'
'General Hospital'
'One Life To Live'
'Secret Storm'

NIGHTLY NEWS
'ABC Evening News with Peter Jennings'
'CBS Evening News with Walter Cronkite'
'Huntley-Brinkley Report' (NBC)

# AMERICAN TELEVISION
## 1968 FALL PRIME TIME SCHEDULE

| | 7:30 | 8:00 | 8:30 | 9:00 | 9:30 | 10:00 | 10:30 |
|---|---|---|---|---|---|---|---|
| ABC | Land of the Giants (7-8) | The FBI | The ABC Sunday Night Movie | | | | |
| SUN CBS | Gentle Ben | Ed Sullivan Show | Smothers Brothers Comedy Hour | | Mission: Impossible | | |
| SUB NBC | Walt Disney's Wonderful World of Colour | | Mothers-in-Law | Bonanza | | Beautiful Phyllis Diller Show | |
| SUN ABC | The Avengers | | Peyton Place | The Outcasts | | The Big Valley | |
| MON CBS | Gunsmoke | Here's Lucy | Mayberry R.F.D. | Family Affair | Carol Burnett Show | | |
| MON NBC | I Dream of Jeannie | Rowan and Martin's Laugh-In | | NBC Monday Night at the Movies | | | |
| MON ABC | Mod Squad | It Takes A Thief | | N.Y.P.D. | | That's Life | |
| TUE CBS | Lancer | Red Skelton Hour | | Doris Day Show | | CBS News Hour / 60 Minutes | |
| TUE NBC | Jerry Lewis Show | | Julia | NBC Tuesday Night at the Movies / News Special (once a month) | | | |
| TUE ABC | Here Come the Brides | | Peyton Place | The ABC Wednesday Night Movie | | | |
| WED CBS | Daktari | The Good Guys | The Beverly Hillbillies | Green Acres | Jonathan Winters Show | | |
| WED NBC | The Virginian | | The Kraft Music Hall | | The Outsider | | |
| WED ABC | The Ugliest Girl in Town | The Flying Nun | Bewitched | That Girl | Journey to the Unknown | | Local |
| THU CBS | Blondie | Hawaii Five-O | | The CBS Thursday Night Movies | | | |
| THU NBC | Daniel Boone | Ironside | | Dragnet 1969 | Dean Martin Show | | |
| THU ABC | Operation: Entertainment Squad | | The Felony Show | Don Rickles | The Guns of Will Sonnett | Judd, For the Defense | |
| FRI CBS | The Wild, Wild West | USMC | Gomer Pyle, | The CBS Friday Night Movies | | | |
| FRI NBC | The High Chaparral | | The Name of the Game | | | Star Trek | |
| FRI ABC | The Dating Game | Game | The Newlywed Show | Lawrence Welk | The Hollywood Palace | Local | |
| SAT CBS | Jackie Gleason Show | My Three Sons | Hogan's Heroes Junction | Petticoat | Mannix | | |
| SAT NBC | Adam-12 | Get Smart | The Ghost and Mrs. Muir | NBC Saturday Night at the Movies | | | |

# AMERICAN TELEVISION
# 1968-69 SEASON

## SOME OF THE SATURDAY MORNING CARTOONS
'Archie Show'
'Banana Splits Adventure Hour'
'The New Beatles' (Sunday mornings)
'Bugs Bunny / Road Runner Hour'
'Bullwinkle Show' (Sunday mornings)
'The Flintstones'
'George Of The Jungle'
'Johnny Quest'
'Shazzan!'
'Spiderman'
'Tom and Jerry' (Sunday mornings)
'Underdog'

## SOME OF THE DAYTIME SOAPS
'Another World'
'As The World Turns'
'Dark Shadows'
'Days Of Our Lives'
'The Doctors'
'Edge Of Night'
'General Hospital'
'Guiding Light'
'One Life To Live'
'Secret Storm'

## NIGHTLY NEWS
'ABC Evening News with Frank Reynolds'
'CBS Evening News with Walter Cronkite'
'Huntley-Brinkley Report' (NBC)

# AMERICAN TELEVISION
# 1969 FALL PRIME TIME SCHEDULE

|         | 7:30 | 8:00 | 8:30 | 9:00 | 9:30 | 10:00 | 10:30 |
|---------|------|------|------|------|------|-------|-------|
| ABC     | Land of the Giants (7-8) | | The FBI | The ABC Sunday Night Movie | | | |
| SUN CBS | To Rome with Love | Ed Sullivan Show | | Leslie Uggams Show | | Mission: Impossible | |
| SUN NBC | Walt Disney's Wonderful World of Colour | | Bill Cosby Show | Bonanza | | The Bold Ones | |
| SUN ABC | The Music Scene | | The New People | The Survivors | Love, American Style | | |
| MON CBS | Gunsmoke | Here's Lucy | Mayberry R.F.D. | Doris Day Show | | Carol Burnett Show | |
| MON NBC | My World and Welcome to It | Rowan and Martin's Laugh-In | | NBC Monday Night at the Movies / News Specials | | / Bob Hope Specials | |
| MON ABC | Mod Squad | | Movie of the Week | | | Marcus Welby, M.D. | |
| TUE CBS | Lancer | Red Skelton Hour | | The Governor | | CBS News Hour / 60 Minutes and J.J. | |
| TUE NBC | I Dream of Jeannie | Debbie Reynolds Show | Julia | NBC Tuesday Night at the Movies / First Tuesday (once a month) | | | |
| TUE ABC | The Flying Nun | Courtship of Eddies' Father | Room 222 | The ABC Wednesday Night Movies | | | |
| WED CBS | Glen Campbell Goodtime Hour | | The Beverly Hillbillies | Medical Center | | Hawaii Five-O | |
| WED NBC | The Virginian | | The Kraft Music Hal | | Then Came Bronson | | |
| WED ABC | The Ghost and Mrs. Muir | That Girl | Bewitched | This is Tom Jones | | It Takes a Thief | |
| THU CBS | Family Affair | Jim Nabors Hour | | The CBS Thursday Night Movies | | | |
| THU NBC | Daniel Boone | Ironside | | Dragnet 1970 | | Dean Martin Show | |
| THU ABC | Let's Make A Deal | The Brady Bunch | Mr. Deeds Goes to Town | Here Come the Brides | | Jimmy Durante Presents the Lennon Sisters Hour | |
| FRI CBS | Get Smart | The Good Guys | Hogan's Heroes | The CBS Friday Night Movies | | | |
| FRI NBC | The High Chaparral | | The Name of the Game | | | Bracken's World | |
| FRI ABC | The Dating Game | The Newlywed Game | Lawrence Welk Show | The Hollywood Palace | | | Local |
| SAT CBS | Jackie Gleason Show | | My Three Sons | Green Acres | Petticoat Junction | | Mannix |
| SAT NBC | Andy Williams Show | | Adam-12 | NBC Saturday Night at the Movies | | | |

# AMERICAN TELEVISION
# 1969-70 SEASON

SOME OF THE SATURDAY MORNING CARTOONS
'Archie Comedy Hour'
'Banana Splits Adventure Hour'
'Bugs Bunny / Road Runner Hour'
'Bullwinkle Show' (Sunday mornings)
'The Flintstones'
'Hot Wheels'
'The Jetsons'
'Pink Panther Show'
'Scooby-Doo, Where Are You?'
'Spiderman' (Sunday mornings)
'Tom and Jerry' (Sunday mornings)
'Underdog'

SOME OF THE DAYTIME SOAPS
'Another World'
'As The World Turns'
'Dark Shadows'
'Days Of Our Lives'
'The Doctors'
'Edge Of Night'
'General Hospital'
'Guiding Light'
'One Life To Live'
'Secret Storm'

NIGHTLY NEWS
'ABC Evening News' (w/ Frank Reynolds and Howard K. Smith)
'CBS Evening News with Walter Cronkite'
'Huntley-Brinkley Report' (NBC)

# AMERICAN TELEVISION
## 1970 FALL PRIME TIME SCHEDULE

| | 7:30 | 8:00 | 8:30 | 9:00 | 9:30 | 10:00 | 10:30 |
|---|---|---|---|---|---|---|---|
| ABC | The Young Rebels (6-7) | The FBI | The ABC Sunday Night Movie | | | | |
| SUN CBS | Hogan's Heroes | Ed Sullivan Show | | Glen Campbell Goodtime Hour | | Tim Conway Comedy Hour | |
| SUN NBC | Walt Disney's Wonderful World of Colour | | Bill Cosby Show | Bonanza | | The Bold Ones | |
| SUN ABC | The Young Lawyers | | The Silent Force | NFL Monday Night Football (replaced after Dec. 14 w/ movies) | | | |
| MON CBS | Gunsmoke | Here's Lucy | Mayberry R.F.D. | Doris Day Show | | Carol Burnett Show | |
| MON NBC | Red Skelton Show | Rowan and Martin's Laugh-In | | NBC Monday Night at the Movies / Bob Hope Specials / News Specials | | | |
| MON ABC | Mod Squad | Movie of the Week | | | | Marcus Welby, M.D. | |
| TUE CBS | The Beverly Hillbillies | Green Acres | Hee Haw | To Rome with Love | CBS News Hour / 60 Minutes | | |
| TUE NBC | Don Knotts Show | | Julia | NBC Tuesday Night at the Movies / First Tuesday (once a month) | | | |
| TUE ABC | Courtship of Eddies' Fathe | Make Room for Granddaddy | Room 222 | Johnny Cash Show | | Dan August | |
| WED CBS | The Storefront Lawyers | | The Governor and J.J. | Medical Center | | Hawaii Five-O | |
| WED NBC | The Men from Shiloh | | The Kraft Music Hall | | Four-In-One | | |
| WED ABC | Matt Lincoln | Bewitched | Barefoot in the Park | The Odd Couple | | The Immortal | |
| THU CBS | Family Affair | Jim Nabors Hour | The CBS Thursday Night Movies | | | | |
| THU NBC | Flip Wilson Show | | Ironside | Nancy | Dean Martin Show | | |
| THU ABC | The Brady Bunch | Nanny and the Professor | The Partridge Family | That Girl | Love, American Style | This is Tom Jones | |
| FRI CBS | The Interns | The Headmaster | The CBS Friday Night Movies | | | | |
| FRI NBC | The High Chaparral | | The Name of the Game | | Bracken's World | | |
| FRI ABC | Let's Make A Deal | The Newlywed Game | Lawrence Welk Show | | The Most Deadly Game | | Local |
| SAT CBS | Mission: Impossible | | My Three Sons | Arnie | Mary Tyler | Mannix | |
| SAT NBC | Andy Williams Show | | Adam-12 | NBC Saturday Night at the Movies | | | |

## AMERICAN TELEVISION
## 1970-71 SEASON

SOME OF THE SATURDAY MORNING CARTOONS
'Archie's Funhouse'
'Bugs Bunny / Road Runner Hour'
'Bullwinkle Show' (Sunday mornings)
'Heckle and Jeckle Show'
'Hot Wheels'
'The Jetsons' (Saturday afternoons)
'Johnny Quest' (Sunday mornings)
'Josie and the Pussycats'
'Pink Panther Show'
'Scooby-Doo, Where Are You?'
'Tom and Jerry' (Sunday mornings)
'Woody Woodpecker Show'

SOME OF THE DAYTIME SOAPS
'Another World'
'As The World Turns'
'Dark Shadows'
'Days Of Our Lives'
'The Doctors'
'Edge Of Night'
'General Hospital'
'Guiding Light'
'One Life To Live'
'Secret Storm'

NIGHTLY NEWS
'ABC Evening News' (w/ Harry Reasoner and Howard K. Smith)
'CBS Evening News with Walter Cronkite'
'NBC Nightly News' (w/ David Brinkley, John Chancellor, and Frank McGee)

# SOME OF THE MOVIES THAT PLAYED OR PREMIERED DURING 1966

Alfie
An American Dream
Agent 38-24-36
Ambush Bay
The Appaloosa
Arabesque
Batman
The Bible
Blow-Up [Italian]
The Blue Max
Born Free
The Chase
Dear John
Fantastic Voyage
Fahrenheit 451
Fireball 500
The Fortune Cookie
A Funny Thing Happened on the Way to the Forum
Gambit
Georgy Girl
The Ghost and Mr. Chicken
Glass Bottom Boat
Grand Prix
Harper
Hawaii
Hotel Paradiso
Inside Daisy Clover
It Happened Here
Judith
Lady L
Lt. Robin Crusoe, U.S.N.
The Liquidator
Love, the Italian Way
A Man and a Woman

A Man for All Seasons
Morgan!
The Naked Prey
Nevada Smith
Operation Bikini
Our Man Flint
The Professionals
Return of the Seven
The Russians Are Coming!
The Russians Are Coming!
The Sand Pebbles
The Shop on Main Street
The Singing Nun
Stop the World – I Want to Get Off
3 on a Couch
Time Lost and Time Remembered
Torn Curtain
The Trouble with Angels
What's Up Tiger Lily?
Who's Afraid of Virginia Woolf?
You're a Big Boy Now


# SOME OF THE MOVIES THAT PLAYED OR PREMIERED DURING 1967

Barefoot in the Park
The Battle of Algiers [Italian]
The Big Mouth
Bonnie and Clyde
Camelot
Casino Royale
The Comedians
Cool Hand Luke
The Dirty Dozen
Divorce American Style
Doctor Doolittle
Easy Come, Easy Go

El Dorado
Far from the Madding Crowd
Falstaff
A Fistful of Dollars
For a Few Dollars More
The Graduate
Guess Who's Coming to Dinner
A Guide for the Married Man
The Happening
The Happiest Millionaire
Hombre
Hotel
How I Won the War
How to Stuff a Wild Bikini
Hurry Sundown
In Cold Blood
In the Heat of the Night
The Jokers
Jungle Book
King of Hearts
The Love-Ins
The Man Called Flintstone
Point Blank
The President's Analyst
St. Valentine's Day Massacre
The Taming of the Shrew
Thoroughly Modern Millie
To Sir, With Love
The Trip
Two for the Road
Ulysses
Up the Down Staircase
Valley of the Dolls
Wait until Dark
The Way West
The Whisperers
You Only Live Twice
You're a Big Boy Now

# SOME OF THE MOVIES THAT PLAYED OR PREMIERED DURING 1968

Barbarella
The Boston Strangler
Bullit
Candy
Charly
Chitty Chitty Bang Bang
Cogan's Bluff
The Detective
Faces
Finan's Rainbow
The Fixer
Funny Girl
The Good, the Bad and the Ugly
The Green Berets
Hang 'Em High
Head
The Heart is a Lonely Hunter
Here We Go Round the Mulberry Bush
The Horse in the Gray Flannel
Hot Millions
How Sweet It Is!
How to Save a Marriage – and Ruin Your Life
Ice Station Zebra
The Impossible Years
The Lion in Winter
No Way to Treat a Lady
The Odd Couple
Oliver!
Paper Lion
The Party
Petulia
Planet of the Apes
The Producers
Rachel, Rachel

Rosemary's Baby
Salt and Pepper
The Secret Life of an American Wife
The Secret War of Harry Frigg
The Sergeant
The Shakiest Gun in the West
Star!
The Subject Was Roses
The Thomas Crown Affair
2001: A Space Odyssey
War and Peace [Russian]
Where Were You When the Lights Went Out
Wild in the Streets
With Six You Get Eggroll
Yellow Submarine
Yours, Mine and Ours

# SOME OF THE MOVIES THAT PLAYED OR PREMIERED DURING 1969

Alice's Restaurant
A Boy Named Charlie Brown
Bob & Carol & Ted & Alice
The Brotherhood
Butch Cassidy and the Sundance Kid
Cactus Flower
Che!
The Comic
The Damned
Death of a Gunfighter
Easy Rider
Fanny Hill [Swedish]
Gaily, Gaily
Goodbye, Columbus
Goodbye, Mr. Chips
The Great Bank Robbery
Guns of the Magnificent Seven

335

The Happy Ending
Hard Contract
Hell in the Pacific
Hellfighters
Hello, Dolly!
Hell's Angels
Hook, Line & Sinker
I Am Curious (Yellow) [Swedish]
If...
The Illustrated Man
The Love Bug
The Loves of Isadora
The Maltese Bippy
Marooned
Midnight Cowboy
On Her Majesty's Secret Service
Once Upon a Time in the West
Paint Your Wagon
Popi
The Prime of Miss Jean Brodie
The Rain People
Staircase
The Sterile Cuckoo
Support Your Local Sheriff
Sweet Charity
Take the Money and Run
Tell Them Willie Boy is Here
They Shoot Horses, Don't They
Those Daring Young Men in Their Jaunty Jalopies
Three in the Attic
Topaz
True Girt
The Wedding Party
Where Eagles Dare
The Wild Bunch
Winning
Z [French]

# SOME OF THE MOVIES THAT PLAYED OR PREMIERED DURING 1970

Airport
Anne of the Thousand Days
The Baby Maker
The Ballad of Cable Hogue
Beneath the Planet of the Apes
Bloody Mama
A Boy Named Charlie Brown
The Boys in the Band
Catch-22
The Cheyenne Social Club
Chisum
The Computer Wore Tennis Shoes
Cotton Comes to Harlem
Diary of a Mad Housewife
Fellini Satyricon [Italian]
Five Easy Pieces
The Forbin Project
Gimme Shelter
How to Succeed with Sex
I Never Sang for My Father
In Search of Gregory
Kelly's Heroes
King of the Grizzlies
The Landlord
Let It Be
Little Big Man
Love Story
Lover's and Other Strangers
Loving
The Magic Christian
A Man Called Horse
M*A*S*H
My Lover, My Son
My Night at Maud's
My Sweet Charlie
Myra Breckenridge

On a Clear Day You Can See Forever
The Owl and the Pussycat
The Passion of Anna
Patton
Rider on the Rain
Ryan's Daughter
Scrooge
Shark!
Soldier Blue
Start the Revolution without Me
The Strawberry Statement
Sympathy for the Devil
There's a Girl in My Soup
Tora! Tora! Tora!
Two Mules for Sister Sara
Which Way to the Front?
Women in Love
Woodstock
Zabriskie Point.pa

# SOME OF THE MOVIES THAT PLAYED OR PREMIERED DURING 1971

The Abominable Dr. Phibes
The Andromeda Strain
Bananas
Bedknobs and Broomsticks
Big Jake
Billy Jack
Black Jesus
Bless the Beasts and Children
Carnal Knowledge
A Clockwork Orange
The Conformist [Italian]
Daughters of Darkness
Death in Venice
Diamonds Are Forever
Dirty Harry
Escape from the Planet of the Apes

Fiddler on the Roof
The French Connection
Get Carter
The Go-Between
The Great Chicago Conspiracy Case
The Great White Hope
A Gunfight
Hoa Binh
The Hospital
Investigation of a Citizen above Suspicion
Is There Sex After Death?
Klute
Kotch
The Last Movie
The Last Picture Show
Little Murders
McCabe and Mrs. Miller
Minnie and Muskowitz
Murphy's War
Play Misty for Me
Rio Lobo
Shaft
Skin Game
Summer of '42
Sunday Bloody Sunday
Sweet Sweetback's Baadasssss Song
They Might Be Giants
200 Motels
Vanishing Point
The Villain
When Dinosaurs Ruled the Earth
Who is Harry Kellerman, and Why Is He
 Saying Those Terrible Things about Me?
The Wild Country
Wild Rovers
Willard
Willie Wonka and the Chocolate Factory